Cultures of Curriculum

Using "cultures of curriculum" as a lens, this clear, compelling text reveals and critically examines the belief systems and classroom practices of curricular orientations in contemporary American society. It is designed to foster awareness, examination, and deliberation about the curricula planned for and carried out in classrooms and schools; to inspire conversations about theory and practice as well as political, social, and moral issues; and to expand critical consciousness about approaches to curriculum and practice. Readers are encouraged to give serious attention to the issues this book raises for them, and to join with their colleagues, students, and communities in considering how to create curricula with purpose and congruent practices and to reculture classrooms and schools. A framework of inquiry is presented to facilitate such reflection and to accomplish these goals.

Changes in the second edition:
- Four new chapters:
  - "Narrowing the Curriculum" (current trends of standardization and high-stakes testing)
  - "Educating Through Occupations" (Deweyan progressive and career/technical education)
  - "Sustaining Indigenous Traditions" (Native American/indigenous education)
  - "Envisioning Peace" (peace, global, human rights, and environmental education)
- Updates and pertinent scholarship in all chapters reflecting recent events and discourses
- Curricular cultures all are examples of progressive alternatives to traditional education
- New two-part structure: Curriculum Studies and Curricular Cultures

Pamela Bolotin Joseph is a senior lecturer in the Education Program, University of Washington Bothell.

STUDIES IN CURRICULUM THEORY
William F. Pinar, Series Editor

For additional information on titles in the Studies in Curriculum Theory series visit
www.routledge.com/education

Cultures of Curriculum

Second Edition

Edited by
Pamela Bolotin Joseph
University of Washington Bothell

Routledge
Taylor & Francis Group

NEW YORK AND LONDON

First published 2000
by Lawrence Erlbaum Associates, Inc.
10 Industrial Avenue, Mahwah, NJ 07430

This edition published 2011
by Routledge
711 Third Avenue, New York, NY 10017

Simultaneously published in the UK
by Routledge
2 Park Square, Milton Park, Abingdon, Oxon OX14 4RN

Routledge is an imprint of the Taylor & Francis Group, an informa business

© 2000 Lawrence Erlbaum Associates, Inc.
© 2011 Taylor & Francis

The right of Pamela Bolotin Joseph to be identified as the author of the editorial material, and of the authors for their individual chapters, has been asserted by them in accordance with sections 77 and 78 of the Copyright, Designs and Patents Act 1988.

Typeset in Minion and Gill Sans by EvS Communication Networx, Inc

Library of Congress Cataloging in Publication Data
Cultures of curriculum / edited by Pamela Bolotin Joseph. — 2nd ed.
p. cm. — (Studies in curriculum theory)
Includes index.
1. Curriculum planning—United States. 2. Education—Curricula—Social aspects—United States. I. Joseph, Pamela Bolotin.
LB2806.15.C73 2011
375'.001—dc22
2010022045

ISBN 13: 978-0-415-99186-5 (hbk)
ISBN 13: 978-0-415-99187-2 (pbk)
ISBN 13: 978-0-203-83727-6 (ebk)

In honor of our parents

Claire and Jack Bolotin
Dorothy and Mort Luster
Margaret and Meryle Mikel
Laura Payton Stewart and Blair Stewart
Valerie and Clete Windschitl
Albert and Bessi Yazzie

The first antinomy is this: on the one hand, it is unquestionably the function of education to enable people, individual human beings, to operate at their fullest potential, to equip them with the tools and the sense of opportunity to use their wits, skills and passions to the fullest. The antinomic counterpart to this is that the function of education is to reproduce the culture that supports it—not only reproduce it, but further its economic, political, and cultural ends.

Jerome Bruner, 1996, *The Culture of Education*, p. 67

Contents

Preface

We originally wrote *Cultures of Curriculum* to conceptualize curriculum as culture by taking into account the histories, norms, beliefs, values, roles, patterns of behavior, and environments of educational practice. We affirmed Maxine Greene's (1973) proposition that studying curriculum as culture makes it possible for educators to view curriculum holistically, to contemplate the totality of the educational experience, and to interrogate the commonplace. Moreover, we wished to portray curricular orientations which, unlike conventional curricula, demonstrate congruent philosophy-centered practices; these archetypes—replete with examples of practice—depict models for educators who want to profoundly change curriculum in their classrooms and schools. We described each of the curricular cultures by consistently using a heuristic: visions, assumptions about learners, teachers, content, milieu, planning, assessment, curriculum evaluation, dilemmas of practice, and critique of the orientation and its aims.

As we wrote about curricular cultures, we drew from powerful ideas within the field of curriculum theory. In developing the book, it became clear to us that we could not present our models without first explaining the concepts that extend and deepen our understanding of curriculum, pedagogy, and schooling. Therefore we began our text with explanations of theories for interpreting and analyzing curriculum. We believe that with such knowledge curriculum workers can to go beyond discussions of specific programs, outcomes, and effectiveness so to engage in curriculum inquiry—to interrogate the purposes of education and their roles as educators by "investigating everyday phenomena, problematizing and questioning the commonplace" (Joseph, 2007, p. 283).

As before, our purpose in the second edition is to expand critical consciousness about approaches to curriculum and practice. Using "cultures of curriculum" as a platform for inquiry, we encourage readers to consider if their curriculum work reflects a mélange of unarticulated methods and purposes, a struggle to maintain a coherent vision amidst many competing pressures, or an overarching aim enacted daily and embodied within a congruous set of practices.

We have developed a framework of inquiry that accomplishes these specific goals to:

- Acquaint our readers with patterns of curricular thinking that have influenced the development of the concept of cultures of curriculum.
- Elucidate the concept of curriculum as culture—a revealing system of implicit and explicit beliefs, values, behaviors, and customs in classrooms and schools which are deliberated within communities and other public spheres.
- Give historical insight about shifting educational and social priorities that have influenced the course of curriculum in United States schooling.
- Integrate moral and political discourse into recognition and discussion of curriculum.
- Encourage metaphoric thinking that enables new ways to perceive commonplace assumptions and embedded belief systems.
- Deepen awareness of dilemmas of practice inherent in curriculum work.
- Hold each culture of curriculum up to critical inquiry of its assumptions, purposes and claims.

It has been more than a decade since the publication of the first edition of *Cultures of Curriculum*. Over time it has become a resource for teachers and administrators—including some engaged in school reform efforts—and, although our examples predominantly focus on K–12 curriculum, adult educators have employed the concept of curricular culture and its heuristic to analyze higher education curriculum. Also, despite its focus on education in the United States, our book has been adopted for curriculum studies classes in Canada and Europe. References to curricular cultures have appeared in international scholarship and an edition of *Cultures of Curriculum* has been published in China.

We have learned that readers appreciate our emphasis on visions to guide curriculum work and some have shared with us how this text helped them to conceive or re-imagine themselves teaching with purpose and integrity. This sense of transformation is conveyed in a published case study of middle school teachers whose use of the construct of curricular cultures guided their curriculum development work and led to "a different way of thinking about curriculum":

> This way of thinking reshapes both the "what" and the "how" of curriculum. Using the curriculum-as-culture model, teachers involved in this curricular project felt the freedom to have students create rather than merely display knowledge. They found ways to satisfy state curricular objectives as minimal accomplishment, with student-created understandings far surpassing that level as the norm. (Schnuit, 2006, p. 5)

Eventually, it became apparent that we needed to update and expand *Cultures of Curriculum* in view of developments in the United States educational scene—the pervasive high-stakes testing and standardized curriculum milieu influenced by the No Child Left Behind legislation. Regardless of our grave concerns about the direction of curriculum based on Goals 2000 and the influence of business on education expressed in the first edition, we needed to attend to the state of curriculum in following years in a time that William Pinar (2004) characterizes as the "nightmare" of "miseducation" (p. 5). Teaching children to be successful test-takers has increasingly become a dominant goal in public schools—far superseding aspirations for students to become creative life-long learners or educated citizens who can participate in a democracy. So, too, in this test-frenzied climate, it has become even harder for teachers to create curricula that encourage students to question and work against the societal norms of competition, warfare, and environmental degradation.

Correspondingly, schools of education are under pressure from state and national directives to focus exclusively on the attainment of standards—to the neglect of curriculum studies courses. New and experienced teachers learn about instruction to increase student achievement but are less likely to be encouraged to reflect critically on the political and ethical purposes of schooling, to enact culturally relevant curriculum that deals with diversity in significant ways, or to become activists concerned with ingrained practice and systems. Therefore, in response to the ubiquity of the "standardized management paradigm" (Henderson & Gornik, 2006) with its limited, top-down view of curriculum, it has become even more imperative for curriculum workers to learn about alternatives that confront dominant worldviews and traditional curricula.

For the above reasons, the second edition of *Cultures of Curriculum* contains a number of new and revised chapters now organized into two parts. As before, we begin by introducing readers new to curriculum studies with two chapters, "Conceptualizing Curriculum" and "Understanding Curriculum as Culture" that explore the powerful concepts and patterns that help us to imaginatively understand curriculum as a dynamic process. We have made several additions to "Conceptualizing Curriculum" including sections on paradigms, adult education, and African American curricular orientations. The first part, Curriculum Studies, also focuses on curriculum transformation. We have added an additional chapter, "Narrowing the Curriculum," that reviews how curriculum has been shaped by high-stakes testing, standardization, and business influences on schooling—to make the case for why curriculum must be recultured. We also expanded the chapter, "Reculturing Curriculum," to attend more to transformative curriculum and curriculum leadership; the decision to place this chapter in the first part (rather than as the final chapter of the book) was in response to readers' recommendations that we explain more of our ideas about curricular cultures before describing them. The second part, Curricular Cultures, presents eight curricular orientations. However, in the second edition, all of these curricular cultures chapters now consist only of philosophies that are alternatives to mainstream curriculum. It is our hope that these eight orientations will provide inspiration and ideas for curriculum transformation as well as affirming practices of progressive educators.

As the narrow goal of curriculum to create employees is anathema to our beliefs that educators should create meaningful, ethical, and life-affirming curriculum, a new curricular culture chapter based on John Dewey's conception of "Educating Through Occupations" (Dewey, 1899/2008) has replaced "Training for Work and Survival." Its authors write about curriculum that reflects young people's interest in real life occupations integrated with rigorous knowledge of academic disciplines as well as critical exploration of the meaning of work. (Components of Nancy Green's chapter from the first edition on work preparation and life skills are incorporated into this chapter and into descriptions of the dominant order within the chapter "Narrowing Curriculum.")

Another new curricular culture chapter, "Sustaining Indigenous Traditions," by Tarajean Yazzie-Mintz, envisions culturally responsive curriculum by depicting Indigenous education as an integrated holistic curriculum of language, culture, history, sciences and arts. This curricular culture illustrates learning for deep cultural knowledge—a vast contrast to the fragmented curriculum in much of mainstream U.S. curriculum. Yazzie-Mintz shows the way for educators interested in teaching culturally responsive curriculum to mitigate Eurocentric models and for those who want to develop Indigenous curriculum in a variety of classrooms, including public, magnet, and tribal schools.

In the third new curricular culture chapter, "Envisioning Peace," Pamela Joseph writes about the curricula of peace studies, conflict resolution education, global education, human rights education, and environmental education. In totality, these orientations call for educators to have a have deep understanding of education for the wellbeing of humanity and restoration of the Earth. Joseph explains a discourse of nonviolence as a way to envision nurturing, non-competitive classrooms and to imagine a world of peace. This chapter ends the book on a note of hope and provides another curricular alternative for curriculum workers who truly wish to teach against the grain.

Another change in the second edition is the reordering of the curricular culture chapters. These chapters now begin with "Constructing Understanding" as all the curricular cultures that we discuss highlight in some way elements of constructivism: the centrality of the learner, engagement, complex curricular content, and curriculum meaningful to students' experiences. As well, there are some changes to several other original chapters to update them with examples from more recent scholarship.

Finally, as our multiple authorship/editorship became too unwieldy, there is a single editor for the second edition. Still, there is much "we" in this book as contributors continued to make collaborative decisions and responded to each other's ideas and writing. And as before, this edition encompasses numerous examples and stories shared with us by teachers through their accounts of standardized as well as innovative and transformative curriculum.

References

Dewey, J. (1899/2008). *The school and society.* New York: Cosimo Classics.

Greene, M. (1973). *Teacher as stranger: Educational philosophy for the modern age.* Belmont, CA: Wadsworth.

Henderson, J. G., & Gornik, R. (2006). *Transformative curriculum leadership* (3rd ed.). New York: Prentice Hall.

Joseph, P. B. (2007). Seeing as strangers: Teachers' investigations of lived curriculum. *Journal of Curriculum Studies, 39*(3), 283–302

Pinar, W. (2004). *What is curriculum theory?* Mahwah, NJ: Erlbaum.

Schnuit, L. (2006). Using curricular cultures to engage middle school thinkers. *Middle School Journal, 38*(1), 4–12.

Acknowledgments

We once more acknowledge David Purpel's encouragement to write the first edition and appreciate his friendship and confidence in us. David's brilliant scholarship, moral sensitivity, and passion for social justice inspired us and many scholars and practitioners in the curriculum studies field. We will cherish his memory.

We also are grateful for the continued support and patience of our editor Naomi Silverman. We appreciate that Bill Pinar welcomed *Cultures of Curriculum* into the *Studies in Curriculum Theory Series* and are honored by its inclusion. Again, we reaffirm our intellectual debts to Paul Bohannon, Joe Park, Ann Berlak, and Harold Berlak—whose ideas about culture, philosophy, and schooling were so important in our thinking as we originally developed this project.

We acknowledge the teachers and colleagues whose examples and ideas for the first edition appear also in this volume: Robbie Barnes, Jim Beane, Paul Brahce, Doris Brevoort, Barb Brodhagen, Charlie Burleigh, Cindy Catalano, Cecile Eastman, Gary Greene, Mickie Gunderson, Stan Hiserman, Jean Ann Hunt, Tom Ingalls, Sylvie Kashdan, Sue Kawakubo, Tom Kelly, Leigh Knapp, Shelly Lacy, Carol Lieber, Susan Longstreth, Dennis Macmillan, Mike Magrath, Jori Martinez, John Moen, Mathew Page, Sunny Pervil, Connie Saari, Stacy Scoles, Mary Ann Simpson, Dawn Simpson, Mark Smith, Michael Sylvan, and George Wood.

We recognize all who contributed to and influenced our writing in the second edition: Mariella Arredondo, Kimberlee Badal, Cynthia Bennett, Janine Bowen, Kim Bush, Gerald Campano, Gail Davis, Sheila Dearden, Allison Ersfeld, Hai Evans, Mary Fox, Erik Gearhart, Jonathan Knapp, Sarah Heller McFarlane, Mike McGrath, Ron Miller, Walter Parker, Emily Perlatti, Sabrina Porter, Erik Rosenkranz, Ken Rubin, Doug Selwyn, Bridget Shee, Marcia Ventura, Mary Ann Yamaguchi, Ethan Yazzie-Mintz, Breidablik Elementary School, Environmental and Adventure School, and the Native educators and teachers from Seneca Nation, Cherokee Nation, and Navajo Nation. We especially thank Leslie Smith Duss whose research provided numerous examples of peace pedagogy and Jon Garfunkel who contributed examples of school-wide practices of human rights, global, and environmental education as well as his conviction that reculturing must extend beyond the classroom.

Part I

Curriculum Studies

Chapter 1

Conceptualizing Curriculum

Pamela Bolotin Joseph

> A theory that works is altogether a miracle: it idealizes our varying observations of the world in a form so stripped down as to be kept easily in mind, permitting us to see the grubby particulars as exemplars of a general case.
>
> Jerome Bruner, 1996, *The Culture of Education*, pp. 88–89

To apprehend their dynamic roles as curriculum workers, educators must abandon the conviction that curriculum is an object—explicit, proscribed, and given. Regrettably, this way of characterizing curriculum can lead teachers to think of themselves as technicians whose realm only includes lesson plans, curriculum guides, outcomes, and tests but excludes their own artistry and their students' curiosity from curriculum development and enactment. As well, when educators focus on discrete parts of curriculum and do not see the big picture, they may view themselves as employees controlled by educational systems and not as empowered professionals. Or, they may continue to skate on the surface by not seeing the complex sociocultural, political, and ethical layers of meaning in curriculum and pedagogy. Even educators engaged in major curricular reform oftentimes may not deeply understand the significance of their efforts if they work to change structures but do not consider ultimate aims for students and society.

For curriculum to be understood as process for transforming educational aims and practices, it must be conceptualized as an undertaking that encompasses inquiry and introspection. Therefore, the concept of curriculum should include in-depth examination of practices, interactions, values and visions as well as "an inward journey" (see Slattery, 1995, p. 56) of personal reflection. It is "the purpose of curriculum…to engage the imagination" (Doll, 2000, p. xi) so that we can reflect on our beliefs and actions and to engage in a vigorous discourse about moral and social visions for education.

How can educators develop such a perspective so that they understand curriculum as a reflective endeavor as well as a dynamic personal and social process? We believe that that engagement in curriculum theory (curriculum studies) facilitates this transformation because this rich and deep field of scholarship and inquiry offers language and patterns of thought which allow for the naming, questioning, and critique of dominant perspectives and the imagining of alternatives to conventional curriculum. Such knowledge of curriculum helps practitioners to interrogate the purposes of schooling and their own roles by "investigating everyday phenomena, problematizing and questioning the commonplace" (Joseph, 2007, p. 283). In that way, they can become "critically conscious of what is involved in the complex business of teaching and learning" and to "break with fixed, customary modes of seeing" to "remove the blinders of complacency" (Greene, 1973, pp. 8–11).

The study of curriculum is closely connected to qualitative research which seeks meaning rather than control or an ultimate version of truth.

> …the general field of curriculum, the field interested in the relationships among school subjects as well as issues within the individual school subjects themselves and with the relationships between the curriculum and the world, that field is no longer preoccupied with development…the field today is preoccupied with *understanding*…it is necessary to understand the contemporary field as discourse, as text, and most simply but profoundly as words and ideas. (Pinar, Reynolds, Slattery, & Taubman, 1995, pp. 6, 7)

Thus we learn to inquire into the embedded metaphors, assumptions, and visions within curriculum and to comprehensively critique our assumptions, goals, and practices. Also, we can examine and reflect on the norms and values that have direct and unforeseeable influences upon schooling. Accordingly, the study of curriculum becomes a catalyst for moral and political deliberation within "complicated curricular conversations" (see Henderson, 2001) and the desire for curriculum transformation. Certainly, one of the most important ethical obligations of curriculum inquiry is to ask such critical questions as what is our vision of the educated person? How do our curricular decisions affect children? And, how do we create schools as humane environments that nurture the potentials of all students? Curriculum as understanding leads us to become more aware of possibilities for education.

As we work with teachers, adult educators, administrators, community activists, and curriculum specialists, our paramount purpose is realized when these educators expand their consciousness of their ways of viewing and understanding curriculum as well as their own roles as curriculum workers. Theories, frameworks, and images are the means for us to explore curricular meaning and to imagine how we can change curriculum content and classroom and school structures. This chapter portrays the powerful approaches to conceptualizing curriculum in the past and in contemporary times drawn from the field of curriculum theory that have contributed to our construct of cultures of curriculum.

Multiple Curricula

Perhaps no other discussion of curriculum has grounded our idea of curricular cultures as meaningfully as Elliot Eisner's (1985) conception of "three curricula that all schools teach." Eisner's heuristic allows us to examine curriculum that is:

- *Explicit* (obviously stated)
- *Implicit* (not official, often referred to as "hidden")
- *Null* (non-existing—the curriculum that schools do not teach)

The *explicit* curriculum is manifest in publicly stated goals of education, e.g., teaching students American history or health. Explicit curriculum can be found in the school's presentation of itself to the public, in official curriculum guides, and in academic or behavioral outcomes in courses and lessons.

The *implicit* curriculum is the learning and interaction that occurs that is not explicitly announced in school programs. Implicit curriculum may be intentionally taught, e.g., a teacher, fearful of confrontation from the very conservative community in which she works, continually tries to teach critical thinking but never announces these goals to parents or students. Implicit curriculum also may be inadvertent, e.g., we may not have realized how our classrooms or schools teach competition as a social value.

The *null* curriculum deals with what is systematically excluded, neglected, or not considered. Thus, we find null curriculum if we teach history as "the true story" but do not present the perspective of peoples from non-dominant cultures—or we choose as "the greatest literature" only works written by European males. (A caveat to the concept of null curriculum is that not all excluded curricula fall into this category; educators always make choices but what they do not choose is not necessarily null curriculum, e.g., selecting one textbook over another because of preference for an author's writing style.) The concept of null curriculum is compelling—as a reminder of the choices we made or did not even think about—as we examine our own practice as curriculum workers.

Larry Cuban (1993) also proposes a framework of multiple curricula for curriculum investigation. He suggests that we view curricula in four categories:

- *Official* curriculum can be found in curriculum guides and conforms with state-mandated assessment.
- *Taught* curriculum is what individual teachers focus upon and choose to emphasize—often the choices represent teachers' knowledge, beliefs about how subjects should be taught, assumptions about their students' needs, and interests in certain subjects.
- *Learned* curriculum encompasses all that students learn; learned curriculum may be what teachers planned or have not intended, e.g., modeling teachers' behaviors or what students learn from other students.

- *Tested curriculum* means the assessments—whether derived from the teacher, the school district, state, or national testing organizations—that represent only part of what is taught or learned.

As does Eisner (1985), Cuban (1993) warns us not to be captivated by curriculum that is symbolic (how the school or state represents itself) but not necessarily indicative of what takes place in classrooms. Cuban explains that we need to consider these multiple versions of curricula if we really care about educational reform; changes in official and tested curricula may be meaningless unless we attend to the taught and learned curricula. The multiple curricula approach to curriculum inquiry reminds us that whenever we speak of curriculum, we must ask, "which curriculum?" We cannot engage in curriculum deliberation without reflecting upon curriculum as many-sided meanings and experiences.

Curriculum as Text

When we understand curriculum as having diverse meanings, we develop lenses to "see" curriculum as multiple layers of phenomena. We might also imagine curriculum as a multitude of discourses. William Pinar, William Reynolds, Patrick Slattery, and Peter Taubman (1995), writing extensively about the historical and contemporary field of curriculum, teach us how to "hear" various curricular voices or to recognize different "languages."

> To understand the contemporary field it is necessary to understand the curriculum field as discourse, as text, and most simply but profoundly, as words and ideas. By discourse we mean a particular discursive practice, or a form of articulation that follows certain rules and which constructs the very object it studies. Any discipline or field of study can be treated as discourse and analyzed as such. To do so requires studying *the language of the field*. Yes, the curriculum field is about what happens in schools, but in being about schools it employs and is comprised by the language which both reflects and determines what "being about schools" means. (Pinar et al., p. 7)

Conceiving curriculum as text or discourse compels us to listen to and make sense of the words, phrases, and patterns of language that characterize curriculum and to be aware of how this language itself shapes curriculum. We are encouraged to consider not only the ways that people talk about curriculum, but to seek understanding of inherent themes and structures.

These scholars (Pinar et al., 1995) depict curriculum as various discourses or texts:

- *Historical*
- *Political*

- *Racial*
- *Gender*
- *Phenomenological*
- *Poststructuralist, Deconstructed, Postmodern*
- *Autobiographical/Biographical*
- *Aesthetic*
- *Theological*
- *Institutionalized*
- *International*

Each discourse has its own premises and foci; each creates a particular *reality* of phenomena. For instance, aesthetic text represents curriculum as art and artistic experience; it features the teacher (curriculum worker) as artist, the appreciation of curriculum as connoisseurship, and the curriculum as a creative process, e.g., as tempo, dance, or theater. Curriculum as institutionalized text concerns the structure of schools, curricular planning and design, implementation, supervision, evaluation, and technology. We find that each discourse contains particular language, patterns of thoughts, and norms about what is appropriate and valuable. Curriculum as text illustrates the continuing dialogue of culture (Spindler & Spindler, 1987, p. 153)—the conversations and themes that are important to people who "live" in the culture or who portray it.

Curriculum Commonplaces

Another avenue for understanding curriculum is the framework of curriculum commonplaces developed by Joseph Schwab (1973). Schwab discusses "five bodies of experiences" (p. 502) necessary to consider for curriculum revision. When people come together to revise curriculum, they need to be familiar with knowledge about (in Schwab's order):

- *Subject Matter*
- *Learners*
- *Milieus (Context)*
- *Teachers*
- *Curriculum-Making Process (Curriculum Specialist)*

Subject matter refers to knowledge of curriculum materials, the discipline of study, and its underlying system of thought. For instance, Schwab would say that for a science curriculum to be revised, one of the people involved in this curriculum work must have expertise in science—specifically in the area of the curriculum, e.g., biology, and likewise, must know what it is to be a scientist and biologist.

Knowledge of *learners* involves familiarity with the children who will be learning the subject matter. Such knowledge includes awareness of their developmental abilities, "what aspirations and anxieties which may affect learning" (Schwab, 1973, p. 502), the unique qualities of the children, and understanding about their probable "future economic status and function" (p. 503). Certainly, this element of Schwab's framework focuses more on *what is* and far less on the possibilities of education for social mobility and transformation.

The *milieus* refer to the school and classrooms, e.g., the social structure in those environments. Schwab also wants to know what are the influences upon the classroom and school; he asks, "what are the conditions, dominant preoccupations, and cultural climate of the whole polity and its social classes, insofar as they may affect the careers, the probable fate, and ego identity of the children whom we want to teach?" (1973, p. 504). Thus, Schwab asks about a multitude of values and attitudes stemming from the community and culture surrounding the school, e.g., from religions, social classes, and ethnic backgrounds.

Knowledge about *teachers* means what "these teachers are likely to know and how flexible and ready they are likely to be to learn new materials and new ways of teaching" as well as their possible biases, political stances, personalities, and "prevailing moods" (Schwab, 1973, p. 504). Schwab does not assume that those who revise curriculum would automatically have such knowledge of teachers because he does not suggest that teachers themselves are involved in curriculum revision.

The final body of experience is knowledge of the *curriculum-making process*. The person who has this knowledge is the curriculum specialist.

> It is he who reminds all others of the importance of the experience of each representative to the (curriculum-making) enterprise as a whole. It is he, as chairman, who monitors the proceedings, pointing out to the group what has happened in the course of their deliberations, what is currently taking place, what has not yet been considered, what subordinations and super-ordinations may have occurred which affect the process in which all are engaged. (Schwab, 1973, p. 505)

To Schwab it is the curriculum specialist who has the "big picture" and is the person who should guide the process of curriculum revision. It is the specialist who is in charge and has the power to influence curriculum; the voices of teachers, students, parents, or community members for the most part are not personally represented.

Schwab's (1973) scheme of commonplaces denotes a science of curriculum planning that is in opposition to the concept of lived curriculum in which verities of daily life and myriad decisions teachers make to shape curriculum are acknowledged. Notwithstanding, his insistence upon the unique nature of each classroom (which flies in the face of the belief that only standardization can create good curriculum) and his awareness of the numerous influences upon curriculum inside and outside of the classroom is a scaffold for imagining curriculum revealed within classrooms cultures.

Others have utilized Schwab's (1973) commonplaces to ground their thinking about curriculum. Connelly and Clandinin (1988) strongly emphasize the commonplaces for analyzing curriculum, giving it meaning, and understanding one's own stance as a curriculum worker (pp. 84–86). To them, commonplaces serve as a frame of analysis to uncover the "logic" or emphasis in a given rationale for curriculum as expressed by teachers, parents, or in national debate. This framework seeks answers to questions such as: what assumptions are held about learners—how they learn and what they need to learn? what expectations are made about the role of teachers? who should have power over curriculum-making? However, unlike those who advocate scientific curriculum-making controlled by specialists, Connelly and Clandinin understand curriculum planning as fluid narrative, often stemming from the teacher's sense of self and place.

Exploration of the commonplaces also reveals the metaphors that undergird belief systems about education and that help curriculum workers "to attend to the fundamental assumptions expressed about children and schools" (Foshay, 1980, p. 94). What content and methods shall we consider if we believe that the learner is an empty vessel compared with the learner as a dynamic maker of knowledge? How shall we structure the classroom if we conceive of the teacher as a fellow learner rather than as the transmitter of knowledge? Such metaphors indeed are "commonplace" in that they often are not perceived or considered—and yet they function as strong influences upon debate and curriculum decisions.

Bruner (1996) likens such metaphoric thinking to folk pedagogies—deeply embedded cultural knowledge about education.

> Folk pedagogies, for example, reflect a variety of assumptions about children: they may be seen as willful and needing correction; as innocent and to be protected from a vulgar society; as needing skills to be developed only through practice; as empty vessels to be filled with knowledge that only adults can provide; as egocentric and in need of socialization. Folk beliefs of this kind, whether expressed by laypeople or by "experts," badly want some "deconstructing" if their implications are to be appreciated. For whether these views are "right" or not, their impact on teaching activities can be enormous. (p. 49)

We might infer that as people (parents, teachers, politicians, etc.) act upon these folk pedagogies, they accept their reasoning as normal, or true, or the best way of thinking about learners or education.

Commonplaces offer us one set of powerful analytic tools. We gain deeper understanding of what is taking place when we pay attention to the rationale behind curriculum choice, noticing which commonplace receives the greatest emphasis. This framework allows us to scrutinize the assumptions, beliefs, and values we hold and to discern what matters most to other people as we work within educational and political arenas to affect curriculum.

Curriculum as Complex Questions

When we have the means to reflectively examine curriculum, we can get beyond superficial and unexamined meanings and think with complexity about curriculum as aims and experiences. The strength of the commonplaces heuristic is its facility for generating questions for understanding curriculum. The field of curriculum studies seeks to examine and challenge everyday assumptions, including those beliefs that educators and the public implicitly hold. A framework for examination of curriculum is a starting point but not sufficiently complex for curriculum scholars who hold that curriculum deliberation and inquiry should stem from diverse and complex questions.

Beyer and Apple (1988) provide a set of questions that contributes a sophisticated approach to curriculum inquiry. They insist that "no list can ever do justice to the complexity of curriculum deliberations" (p. 5); rather, they utilize this set of questions as a guideline, and we are encouraged to imagine what questions are important for understanding curriculum. Beyer and Apple pose questions in eight categories: epistemological, political, economic, ideological, technical, aesthetic, ethical, and historical:

- *Epistemological:* What should count as knowledge? As knowing? Should knowledge be considered a process or separate divisions of cognitive, affective, and psycho-motor areas?
- *Political:* Who shall control the selection and distribution of knowledge? Through what institutions?
- *Economic:* How is the control of knowledge linked to the existing and unequal distribution of power, goods, and services in society?
- *Ideological:* What knowledge is of most worth? Whose knowledge is it?
- *Technical:* How shall curricular knowledge be made accessible to students?
- *Aesthetic:* How do we link the curriculum knowledge to give personal meaning to students? How do we practice curriculum design and teaching in artful ways?
- *Ethical:* How shall we treat others responsibly and justly within the realm of education? What ideas of moral action and community ground our stance toward student and teachers?
- *Historical:* What traditions help us to understand curriculum and to answer the above questions? (p. 5)

Beyer and Apple (1988) add political, economic, and aesthetic dimensions to our conceptions of curriculum through a critical examination of issues of power and control. Moreover, they explicitly place curriculum inquiry into the realm of moral discourse by recognizing inherent moral visions and the importance of ethical debate. They compel us to not only question if curriculum is effective but to ask, is it moral?

Paradigms

In the field of curriculum studies, paradigms comprise assumptions about learning and teaching, the nature of reality, knowledge, intelligence, inquiry, discourse, the naming of problems and approaches to problem solving, and social and political values. Knowledge of paradigms—encompassing worldviews and curricular orientations—is important to help us to understand why an individual's view of curriculum may be so fundamentally different from someone else's, why it may be so difficult to understand another's perspective, and why serious conversations about curriculum among people whose worldviews are strongly embedded within particular paradigms can be frustrating.

Three major curricular paradigms have been delineated by curriculum scholar William Doll (1993):

- *Pre-Modern*
- *Modern*
- *Postmodern*

Although these paradigms have developed over time, they also exist simultaneously without one completely replacing another (Joseph, 2010, pp. 629–630).

The *Pre-Modern Paradigm* sets forth an ideal of order, symmetry, balance, and harmony. In this paradigm, education consists of striving to learn essential and eternal truths or principles for how one lives in the world. In earlier times, this conservative worldview held that knowledge is unchanging and there is a social order in which individuals must know their place; however, as this paradigm evolved in the 20th century, it contained a more democratic vision. Ideas about content and practice in this paradigm include a course of study that aims to create well-rounded, wise individuals—with educators initiating learners into traditional knowledge, beliefs, and values (Doll, 1993).

The *Modern Paradigm* has been the dominant paradigm of 20th-century European American education. It emphasizes an individualistic, mechanistic, and progress-driven worldview, control and domination of the environment, competition, and directly perceived reality. This paradigm's themes include efficiency, linearity, rationalism, empirical knowledge, scientific method, measured outcomes, and standardization. Descriptions of the modern paradigm focus on an engineered, goal-driven, and segmented disciplinary curriculum—at times portraying students as raw material shaped into products for the benefit of society and industry. In this paradigm, the role of educators is to deliver the curriculum and to provide the right experiences so that the prescribed goals, created by others outside of the classroom, are met (Joseph, 2010).

The third paradigm, *Postmodernism*, holds a complex, multifaceted worldview; its adherents are critical of Modern and Pre-Modern paradigms because they reject both the belief in an empirically known reality and eternal truths. The postmodern outlook suggests the world is not orderly but complicated and unpredictable, that history is not linear and segmented but evolving and contradictory. Postmodernism knowledge consists of multiple truths; as follows, it is important for to interpret individuals' personal experiences as well as a multiplicity of perspectives through the lens of race, ethnicity, social class, gender, and sexual orientation (see Joseph, 2010). This paradigm also highlights the social construction of knowledge and emphasizes integrated curriculum, authentic assessment, education for understanding, dialogue, interaction, perspective taking, creativity, and playfulness (see Clark, 1991).

Curriculum scholar William Schubert (1986) also writes about the importance of paradigms for understanding curriculum. His three paradigmatic categories are:

- *Technical*
- *Practical*
- *Critical*

The *technical paradigm*, reflecting the curriculum development framework created by Ralph Tyler (1949), dominated curriculum theory for a number of decades and still strongly influences curriculum planning in schools. The "Tyler Rationale" focused on four questions:

- What educational purposes should the school seek to attain?
- How can learning experiences be selected which are likely to be useful in attaining these objectives?
- How can learning experiences be organized for effective instruction?
- How can the effectiveness of learning experiences be evaluated?

The *practical paradigm* represents Joseph Schwab's (1973) consideration of curriculum planning as an interaction among various elements (the commonplaces: teachers, learners, subject, and milieu) that "continually influence one another" (Schubert, 1986, p. 176). Schubert explains that Schwab attended to the realities of the classroom for which "we must turn for practical inquiry and for deliberation about the continuously changing dynamics of the commonplaces" (p. 176). The *critical paradigm* relates to the postmodern paradigm and focuses upon critical consciousness of forces that disempower people and the goal of liberation (p. 177).

Another set of paradigms proposed by James Henderson and Rosemary Gornik (2007) refers to curriculum as enacted and developed in contemporary schooling. Their paradigms include:

- *Standardized Managements*
- *Constructivist Best Practices*
- *Curriculum Wisdom*

Each of Henderson and Gornik's (2006) paradigms can be understood by focusing on student performances but also on the discourses by which educators and others consider educational practices and achievement. The *standardized management* paradigm involves the limited and instrumental aim of success on standardized texts—succinctly describing the dominant curriculum of contemporary schooling. In the *constructivist best practices* paradigm, educators' concern is students' understanding of subject matter; acceptance of this paradigm can mean significant change within classrooms and schools immerse in teaching for tests. The third paradigm, *curriculum wisdom*, emphasizes the "enhancement of students' self-knowledge and their self-knowledge and their commitment to, and capacities within, democratic societies" (Heyer & Pifel, 2007, p. 569). It is the paradigm of curriculum wisdom that offers the possibilities for sweeping curriculum transformation (Henderson & Gornik, 2007).

Curricular Orientations

The naming of curricular orientations has a long tradition in curriculum scholarship within the fields of the philosophy of education and curriculum theory. Schemes for conceptualization of curriculum continue to be part of the dialogue about the goals of schooling and practice. This line of inquiry focuses on the ultimate aims of education and the means of reaching those aims.

Curriculum conceptualized as orientations gives theorists and practitioners a meaningful strategy for comprehending the field of curriculum. The naming of curricular orientations provides a platform for awareness, analysis, and critique that allows for interpretation of a broad and perplexing field and for the encouragement of dialogue about curricular intentions and consequences. Recognition of diverse purposes of education and the means of accomplishing them is an important springboard for educational dialogue. We cannot help but make discourse more insightful and vigorous by clarifying our beliefs and experiences around curriculum, finding commonalities with others, and learning about what we truly value.

Educational Philosophies

Emphasizing the contested worth of kinds of knowledge, philosophers of education postulate educational theories or alternatives in education. George Kneller (1971) divides educational philosophy—and corresponding practice such as the teacher's role—into five major categories: *Perennialism, Progressivism, Essentialism, Reconstructionism,* and *Existentialism*:

- *Perennialism*: the belief in unchanging human nature and the need to teach knowledge of eternal truths.
- *Progressivism*: modifying education in the light of new knowledge and social conditions, a focus on the interests of students, and learning in a democratic environment.
- *Essentialism*: focuses on subject matter; advocates of this orientation do not suggest teaching eternal truths, but they believe that there is a variable body of knowledge or expertise that learners must obtain.
- *Reconstructionism*: teaching about serious social and economic problems and to work toward developing a new social order of political and economic democracy.
- *Existentialism*: reflects a worldview emphasizing the choices individuals make and individual responsibility; by connecting existentialism and education, the teachers must respect their students' freedom and urge their students to recognize their freedom—to become actors in the drama of learning, not spectators. (pp. 42–84)

John Goodlad, a curriculum scholar and reformer in teacher education, also highlights the aims of education, seeking to understand "what schools are for." Goodlad (1979/1994) explains that "goals for schooling emerge through a sociopolitical process in which certain sets of interests prevail over others for a period of time" (p. 43). He generates 12 goals that can be placed within four categories:

- *Academic*: emphasis on sufficient schooling to learn the principles of religion and the laws of the land (functional literacy)
- *Vocational*: readiness for productive work and economic responsibility
- *Social and Civic*: socialization for participation in a complex society
- *Personal*: the goal of personal fulfillment (pp. 43–44)

Goodlad (1979/1994) views the goals not only as reflections of what researchers have seen in schools, but also as ideals (p. 45). He believes that listing goals serves as "a beginning point in a dialogue about education" and a way for communities to evaluate what is going on in schools (p. 45).

Conflicting Conceptions of Curriculum

A classic work in the curriculum field by Elliot Eisner and Elizabeth Vallance, *Conflicting Conceptions of Curriculum* (1974), also points to the existence of five different curricular orientations "in terms of the goals and assumptions embedded within them" (p. 2). Eisner and Vallance see these orientations not just as ultimate aims but as systems of thought, values, and actions around curriculum, e.g., the nature of learning. These orientations are:

- *Development of Cognitive Processes*: Refining intellectual operations, sharpening of intellectual processes, and developing a set of cognitive skills that can be applied to learning virtually anything.
- *Curriculum as Technology*: Finding efficient means to a set of predefined, nonproblematic ends to facilitate learning.
- *Self-Actualization—Curriculum as Consummatory Experience*: Seeking personal purpose with education seen as an enabling process that would provide the means to personal liberation and development.
- *Social Reconstruction-Relevance*: Emphasizing the role of education and curriculum content within the larger social context; stressing of societal needs over individual needs, social reform, and responsibility to the future of society.
- *Academic Rationalism*: Enabling the young to acquire the tools to participate in the Western cultural tradition and providing access to the greatest ideas and objects that humans have created. (pp. 5–12)

Eisner and Vallance (1974) declare the need for professional educators and lay people to understand that:

> Controversy in educational discourse most often reflects a basic conflict in priorities concerning the form and content of curriculum and the goals toward which schools should strive; the intensity of the conflict and the apparent difficulty in resolving it can most often be traded to a failure to recognize conflicting conceptions of curriculum. Public educational discourse frequently does not bother to examine its conceptual underpinnings. (pp. 1–2)

Vallance (1986), taking a second look at "conflicting conceptions" a decade later, considers which orientations held steady or declined and raises questions about whether the scheme could "adequately describe curriculum discourse today" (p. 26). She also reflects upon the nature of these orientations, remarking that four orientations concern the goals of education and one (the technological conception) is an anomaly in that it does not deal with purposes but with means (p. 25). Vallance then describes two new orientations:

- *Personal Success*: Including the study of business, computer science, and engineering—with the discouragement of courses in humanities and social sciences.
- *Personal Commitment to Learning*: Supporting "an underlying passion for the hard work and joys of intellectual exploration." (pp. 27–29)

Adult Education Philosophical Orientations

Philosophical alternatives in adult education oftentimes parallel goals of education promulgated for elementary and secondary schools. Lorraine Zinn (1990) offers five orientations for adults who study in colleges, universities, and informal learning settings:

- *Liberal (Classical)*: To develop intellectual powers of the mind; to make a person literate in the broadest sense—intellectually, morally, and spiritually.
- *Behaviorist*: To bring about behavior that will ensure survival of human species, societies, and individuals; to promote behavioral change
- *Progressive*: To transmit culture and societal structure to promote social change; to give learner practical knowledge and problem-solving skills, to reform society
- *Humanistic*: To develop people open to change and continued learning; to enhance personal growth and development; to facilitate self-actualization, to reform society.
- *Radical*: To bring about fundamental, social, political, economic changes in society through education; to change culture and its structure.

Another lens for depicting philosophical perspectives on adult education more broadly categorizes curricular aims. Elizabeth Tisdell and Edward W. Taylor (2000) conceptualize two major themes: autonomy-driven and relationally-driven philosophies. In their construction, the philosophical perspectives and goals of adult education focused on autonomy include:

- *Humanist*: for personal fulfillment and growth as a self-directed learning
- *Critical-Humanist*: for developing as an autonomous, critical, and socially responsible thinking through emphasis on rationality
- *Critical-Emancipatory*: for becoming an autonomous critical thinking for the purpose of promoting collective social change

The adult educational philosophies that emphasize relationship are:

- *Feminist-Humanist*: for personal development and the development of voice in a relational community of support

- *Feminist-Emancipatory*: for social transformation through examination of the intersections of race, gender, and class as multiple systems of privilege and oppression. (pp. 6–11)

Thus Tisdell and Taylor (2000) holistically consider worldviews, goals of education, views of difference, teachers' roles, and students' roles in delineating the different philosophies within adult education (p. 7).

African American Curriculum Orientations

William Watkins (1993) applies the construct of curriculum orientations to African American education for children and adults, describing six Black Curriculum Orientations and their historical contexts:

Functionalism: Education for functional literacy, basic mathematics, and skills for trade and community life. In slavery, this education was reserved for a small minority who would be allowed to engage in household management and some commercial activities. Although some basic literacy was taught to allow religious reading, most efforts for literacy were forbidden and therefore kept "underground."

Accommodationism: Focus on vocational training, physical and manual labor, and character building through glorification of hard work. This education emphasized subservience and postponement of equality for African Americans and Native Americans. This orientation was publicized by Booker T. Washington's writings in the late nineteent and early twentieth centuries and the education taught at the Tuskegee Institute.

Liberal education: The philosophy of teaching wisdom, academic excellence, and leadership from the traditions of humanism and liberal democratic culture; its emphasis on critical thinking and social participation expanded the classical notion of liberal education. This became the curriculum for African Americans in the nineteenth century in the North and for Black colleges in the South following the civil war. In the early twentieth century, W.E.B. Dubois was a proponent of liberal education to create a core of African American leaders.

Black Nationalist: Emphasis on African cultural values, Black Studies curriculum, Pan-Africanism, and separatism. This orientation started in the early nineteenth century out of concern for international slavery, colonization, the debasement of Africa and African people. Its twentieth-century proponents, including Marcus Garvey, Elijah Muhammad, and Malcolm X, responded to the vicious forces of racism in American society and focused on the importance of learning cultural history and traditions for social cohesion, rejection of assimilation, and economic self-sufficiency.

Afrocentric: Curriculum based on rejection of Western social theories as only mode of inquiry, reclaiming of traditional African culture, and historical interpretation with an African core. Although the Black Nationalist orientation was its forerunner, the Afrocentric curriculum orientation began in the 1960s. Advocates, such as Molefi K. Asante and Asa Hilliard, are critical of standard curriculum in United States schools that fails to provide significant teaching about African history, cultural differences among Africans, as well as resistance to slavery and oppression.

Social Reconstructionism: Education to challenge unjust economic, political, and social arrangements focusing on democratic socialist reform, leadership, and improved race relations. Paralleling and very connected to the Social Reconstructionism orientation originating in the 1930s, the Black version emphasized in particular how the capitalist economic system was racist and destructive to African Americans. W.E.B. Dubois, who earlier argued for a liberal education, expressed the need for education not just for leadership but to change society. (pp. 321–338)

Watkins (1993) explains that these approaches do not just conflict but "are the result of complex overlapping historical forces" (p. 323). He makes the case that philosophical orientations are not chosen freely but are "tied to the history of the Black experience in the United States" (p. 322).

Black social, political, and intellectual development in all cases evolved under socially oppressive and politically repressive circumstances involving physical and intellectual duress and tyranny….Thus, the way African Americans have developed their views on education, and especially the curriculum, is connected to their socio-historical realities. (p. 322)

Although Watkins focused on African American educational philosophies and experiences, his point that curricular choices reflect historical circumstances has great relevancy for all other curricular orientations, especially when we consider the history of education for working class, immigrant, and female students. That school systems and educators felt that a particular curricular orientation was "appropriate" for certain children based on their family backgrounds or anticipated abilities illustrates that curricular orientations must be understood historically and not solely as choices made freely by students and their families.

Cultures of Curriculum

We enter this conversation on curricular orientations by offering the construct of *cultures of curriculum*. Informed by previous delineations, we generated a classification of curricular orientations influenced especially by "conflicting conceptions of curriculum" (Eisner & Vallance, 1974) as well as other previous categorizations. We affirm the relevance of curriculum orientations as an effective way to classify curriculum, especially because of their possibilities as a springboard for dialogue so that we may better understand how our assumptions and values about curriculum may be conflict with those held by others. But we increasingly began to understand that different curriculum orientations share assumptions about learners, instructional practices, and certain curriculum, for example, disparate curricular cultures contain interdisciplinary content. Such overlaps suggest that we also need to think about curriculum as overlapping systems that may share significant commonalities. Furthermore, as Watkins (1993) clearly demonstrates, the historical circumstances and social contexts in which curricular orientations are developed, chosen, or required cannot be discounted and must be a crucial component of the study curricular.

In this book, we articulate curricular cultures that consist of humanistic, progressive philosophies and pedagogies. And although the dominant practices in U.S. classrooms and schools in contemporary times often reflect a consistent culture—the standardized management paradigm (Henderson & Gornik, 2007)—we view that orientation as visionless. Aiming to have students achieve adequate scores for literacy and mathematics on standardized tests with the utilitarian rationale of national economic competitiveness is not what we consider to transformative for individuals or society.

The following are the names we have chosen for these eight curricular cultures and brief descriptions of their ultimate goals:

- *Constructing Understanding*: To develop fluid, active, autonomous thinkers who know that they themselves can construct knowledge through their study of the environment and collaborative learning with others.
- *Developing Self and Spirit*: To learn according to self-directed interests in order to nurture individual potential, creativity, and knowledge of the emotional and spiritual self.
- *Educating through Occupations*: To understand connections between academic subjects and real world endeavors so to explore the meaning of work through rigorous knowledge of academic disciplines integrated with the study of occupations.
- *Connecting to the Canon*: To acquire core cultural knowledge, traditions, and values from the dominant culture's exemplary moral, intellectual, spiritual, and artistic resources as guidelines for living.

- *Sustaining Indigenous Traditions*: To develop deep cultural understanding of Indigenous traditions through a place-based, integrated, holistic curriculum of language, culture, history, sciences, and arts.
- *Deliberating Democracy*: To learn and to experience the deliberative skills, knowledge, beliefs, and values necessary for participating in and sustaining a democratic society.
- *Confronting the Dominant Order*: To examine and challenge oppressive social, political, and economic structures that limit self and others and to develop beliefs and skills that support activism for the reconstruction of society.
- *Envisioning Peace*: To develop a deep understanding of peace and non-violence in relationships with others and the Earth through the study of peace education, global education, human rights education, environmental education, and conflict resolution.

We named these orientations "cultures" because of our understanding of how they are revealed in belief systems, everyday behaviors and interactions, the artifacts that participants create, the use that people make of time and space, and the allocation of decision-making power. These curricular orientations comprise visions and practice—including assumptions about the needs and nature of learners, the role of teachers and instruction, norms about subject matter, learning environments, curriculum planning, and evaluation; in addition, we consider dilemmas of practice and critique of the inherent visions within these curricula.

Also, in our depiction of cultures of curriculum, a key feature is coherency. This means that all of the curricular commonplaces, including the teachers' role, practices, content, milieu, are consistent to the greatest extent possible with the vision or aims of the curricular culture. Moreover, we expect that when a curricular culture that is chosen and enacted, all of the stakeholders involved—learners, educators, and families—would be able to articulate or, at the very least, understand the curricular culture's key goals and features.

Thus in our approach to conceptualizing curriculum, it is our hope to inspire educators—to help them to imagine what their classrooms and schools might be like if all (or most of) the curriculum work taking place had congruence. We see the development of a curricular culture as a deliberate pattern of planning, practices, and evaluation that would support visions and aims. That is why in a culture of curriculum, all participants or stakeholders could say, "This is what education is about and how it is experienced here."

References

Beyer, L. E., & Apple., M. W. (1988). *The curriculum: Problems, politics, and possibilities*. Albany: State University of New York Press.

Bruner, J. (1996). *The culture of education*. Cambridge, MA: Harvard University Press.

Clark, E. T. (1991). The search for a new educational paradigm: The implications of new assumptions about thinking and learning. In R. Miller (Ed.), *New directions in education: Selections from holistic education review* (pp. 16–37). Brandon, VT: Holistic Education Press.

Connelly, F. M., & Clandinin, D. J. (1988). *Teachers as curriculum planners: Narratives of experience*. New York: Teachers College Press.

Cuban, L. (1993). The lure of curricular reform and its pitiful history. *Phi Delta Kappan, 75*(2), 182–185.

Doll, M. A. (2000). *Like letters in running water: A Mythopoetics of curriculum*. New York: Routledge.

Doll, W. E. (1993). *A post-modern perspective on curriculum*. New York: Teachers College Press.

Eisner, E. W. (1985). *The educational imagination: On the design and evaluation of school programs*. New York: Macmillan.

Eisner, E. W., & Vallance, E. (1974). *Conflicting conceptions of curriculum*. Berkeley, CA: McCutchan.

Foshay, A. W. (1980). Curriculum talk. In A. W. Foshay (Ed.), *Considered action for curriculum improvement* (pp. 82–94). Alexandria, VA: Association for Supervision and Curriculum Development.

Goodlad, J. I. (1979/1994). *What schools are for* (2nd ed.). Bloomington, IN: Phi Delta Kappa Educational Foundation.

Greene, M. (1973) *Teacher as stranger: Educational philosophy for the modern age*. Belmont, CA: Wadsworth.

Henderson, J. G. (2001). Deepening democratic curriculum work. *Educational Researcher, 30*(9), 18–21.

Henderson, J. G., & Gornik, R. (2007). *Transformative curriculum leadership* (3rd ed.). New York: Prentice Hall.

Heyer, K. D., & Pifel, A. (2007). Extending the responsibilities for schools beyond the school door. *Policy Futures in Education, 5*(4), 567–580.

Joseph, P. B. (2007). Seeing as strangers: Teachers' investigations of lived curriculum. *Journal of Curriculum Studies, 39*(3), 283–302.

Joseph, P. B. (2010). Paradigms. In C. Kridel (Ed.), *Encyclopedia of curriculum studies* (pp. 629–630). Thousand Oaks, CA: Sage.

Kneller, G. F. (1971). *Introduction to the philosophy of* education (2nd ed.). New York: Wiley.

Pinar, W. F., Reynolds, W. M., Slattery, P., & Taubman, P. M. (1995). *Understanding curriculum: An introduction to the study of historical and contemporary curriculum discourses*. New York: Peter Lang.

Schubert, W. H. (1986). *Curriculum: Perspective, paradigm, and possibility*. New York: Macmillan.

Schwab, J. J. (1973). The practical 3: Translation into curriculum. *School Review, 79*, 501–522.

Slattery, P. (1995). *Curriculum development in the postmodern era*. New York: Garland.

Spindler, G., & Spindler, L. (1987). Ethnography: An anthropological view. In G. D.

Spindler (Ed.), *Education and cultural process: Anthropological approaches* (2nd ed., pp. 151–156). Prospect Heights, IL: Waveland Press.

Tisdell, E. J., & Taylor, E. W. (2000). Adult education philosophy informs practice. *Adult Learning, 11*(2), 6–11.

Tyler, R. W. (1949) *Basic principles of curriculum and instruction.* Chicago: The University of Chicago Press.

Vallance, E. (1986). A second look at conflicting conceptions of curriculum. *Theory Into Practice, 25*(1), 24–30.

Watkins, W. H. (1993). Black curriculum orientations: A preliminary inquiry. *Harvard Educational Review, 63*(3), 321–338.

Zinn, L. M. (1990). Identifying your philosophical orientation. In M. W. Galbraith (Ed.), *Adult learning methods* (pp. 39–56). Malabar, FL: Krieger.

Chapter 2

Understanding Curriculum as Culture

Pamela Bolotin Joseph

> [Culture] is in fact a prison unless one knows that there is a key to unlock it. While it is true that culture binds human beings in many unknown ways, the restraint it exercises is the groove of habit and nothing more. [Humans] did not evolve culture as a means of smothering [themselves] but as medium in which to move, live, breathe, and develop…
>
> Edward T. Hall, 1959/1981, *The Silent Language*, p. 187

Although there are a numerous ways to engage in curriculum inquiry, we have found that considering curriculum as culture is a way to attain a holistic understanding of education, not only as planned curricular content, but as experienced or lived "in the presence of people and their meanings" (Aoki, 1991, p. 14). We also have learned that this line of inquiry helps educators to go beyond awareness of explicit curriculum as a set of guidelines or objectives (Westbury, 2000), to "'make the commonplace problematic" (Pink 1990, p. 139) by challenging the idea of curriculum as a singular reality. Instead we consider curriculum as deeply influenced by culture and thus to do curriculum inquiry is "to become aware of belief systems that influence what is considered normal, or alternative, or simply unthinkable" (Joseph, 2007, p. 286).

Curriculum theorist Maxine Greene (1973) eloquently makes the case that teachers must see through an anthropological lens when they do curriculum inquiry, to "become aware of the structure and patterns of the cultures in which they teach," of "orthodoxies and sacred writs," and their roles in the "sense-making process" (p. 10). She introduces the compelling metaphor, "teacher as stranger," to explain how teachers can use curriculum inquiry to become "critically conscious" (p. 7), to "break with fixed, customary modes of seeing." Greene believes that in this way, teachers can "remove the blinders of complacency" to understand the norms and meanings that exist in classrooms and schools (p. 8); when teachers learn to see their cultures and "may liberate [themselves] for understanding and for choosing"; they may liberate themselves for "reflective action" (p. 7). However, when "teachers do *not* see their classrooms and schools as cultures and become enmeshed within the structures of schooling, they may accept the prevailing culture as normal or unalterable" (Joseph, 2007, p. 284).

The Nature of Culture

To perceive curriculum as culture, we must start with an essential grasp of the nature of culture. Anthropologists describe culture as "that complex whole which includes knowledge, belief, art, morals, law, custom, and any other capabilities and habits acquired by [a human] as a member of society" (Tylor in Herskovits, 1967, p. 3). Within this complex whole are shared ways in which people perceive, learn, categorize, prize, employ language, think about reality or common sense, show emotion, utilize time and space, work, play, and deal with each other (Geertz, 1983; Hall, 1959/1981; Hall, 1977). Accordingly, culture influences epistemological beliefs; do people consider knowledge as authoritative, unchanging, or sacred? or fluid, personal, or open to question?

Culture essentially means sense-making. It becomes the system in which people organize their perceptions of their environment and their lives. Culture is "the meaning which people create, and which creates people, as members of societies" (Hannerz, 1992, p. 3).

> *Homo Sapiens* is the creature who "makes sense." She literally produces sense through her experience, interpretation, contemplation, and imagination, and she cannot live in a world without it. The importance of this sense-making in human life is reflected in a crowded conceptual field: ideas, meaning, information, wisdom, understanding, intelligence, sensibility, learning, fantasy, opinion, knowledge, belief, myth, tradition. (p. 3)

Although individuals will not have identical understandings, the existence of a culture suggests that there are shared systems of meanings as revealed in ideas and public and aesthetic expression.

Culture also can be interpreted as symbols and rituals. Symbols represent cultural values and have mutual meanings to individuals and may even provoke similar responses such as awe or devotion. Symbols are woven into activities that have significance to members of the culture; these rituals (as opposed to mere habits) "form the warp on which the tapestry of culture is woven" (McLaren, 1986, p. 36). Symbols and rituals socialize individuals and help them to articulate their understandings of their lives and values.

Individuals learn their culture and internalize its complex system of values and behaviors throughout infancy, childhood, and adolescence. Child-rearing embodies a multitude of messages about what it means to become an adult—from appropriate nonverbal communication, to the specific rules and beliefs that should be transmitted to the next generation, to the ways in which a culture defines itself or what it strongly emphasizes, e.g., whether it values individuals, the tribe, or the nation, the young or elders, artistic expression or economic output. Complex patterns of knowledge and interaction are learned through formal and informal means of cultural transmission, e.g., parenting, role-modeling, religion, story and myths, art, media, and schooling.

These patterns include "action chains" (Hall, 1977; Bohannon, 1995) in which a fairly predictable series of actions—one followed by another—take place and thus "common understandings emerge" (Bohannon, 1995). We see culture as action chains of daily behaviors, e.g., get up, get dressed, go to work, etc., or how people within a culture commonly respond to a problem, e.g., you call your family to help you, you call representatives of government, you work out collaborative situations, or you respond with aggressive behavior. When people are involved in acting out these cultural action chains, their behavior seems completely ordinary to them; only alternative patterns would seem odd or jarring.

In addition, we can understand culture is as "a continuing dialogue that revolves around pivotal areas of concern in a given community" (Spindler & Spindler, 1987, p. 153). For instance, in the dominant European American culture in the United States, this dialogue often has focused on the theme of individuality; it is a motif in history, arts, in the selection of cultural heroes and heroines, in advertising, in political and everyday conversation, and in the way schools customarily assess the behaviors and work of students. Continuing dialogue could also center on a problem, e.g., declining standards of morality in popular culture or public life.

Becoming Aware of Culture

Anthropologists caution that we usually are unaware of the culture that surrounds us because culture appears as usual life, what seems normal or natural. "If a fish were to become an anthropologist, the last thing it would discover would be water" (in Spindler, 1982, p. 24). This saying, attributed to anthropologist Margaret Mead, warns us that familiarity with the surrounding environment makes it terribly difficult to perceive the medium in which we live. In the normal, undisturbed course of living, we seldom recognize that it is our culture that influences what we take in and pay attention to, what choices we consider to be normal, and what we intend to do about those choices (Hall, 1977). Likewise, it is not obvious how cultural knowledge becomes communicated or internalized; directives about how to live one's life often remain unconscious or, at the very least, unexamined.

Why do we have such a problem perceiving and examining our culture? We are hampered because culture is our lens, our way of seeing and reasoning. "[We] cannot even think about culture except through the categories of thought that we have learned from the culture we grew up in and the one in which we have been trained." In order to see differently so that we can understand our own culture, we must "step outside our culture-laden views" and "must struggle to examine our own culture in the same framework as every other culture" (Bohannon, 1995, p. 4).

How, then, can we see our culture? One way to perceive the culture in which we live is to experience disequilibrium or culture shock by living in another culture. Only after extensive travel or staying for years in another culture do individuals come back to their native culture, recognize behaviors or customs, and properly attribute these familiar patterns as belonging to the culture. Previously, before experiencing another culture, what seemed natural, ordinary "normal" or was indistinguishable.

Another way to see our culture is to discipline ourselves to use a systematic means of analysis. An insightful approach to understanding culture is to study the "primary message systems" within any given culture, "a complex series of activities interrelated in many ways" (Hall, 1959/1981, p. 58). We thus can pose a series of questions such as, how is society organized and structured? how do people think about and deal with the environment? what activities are considered work and which are considered play? Thus, we can learn about a culture's implicit and explicit rules for appropriate behavior in such realms as social interactions, use of space, the rhythm of life and activities, gender, and humor (Hall, 1959/1981). An analytic classification helps us to understand how a culture has its unique characteristics and how its organization reflects a pattern of innumerable complex interactions that, in totality, make it unlike others.

Still, the task of perceiving a distinct culture is made more complicated because human cultures do not exist in isolation; cultures influence other cultures and share some attributes. Furthermore, within a culture, a small (micro) culture may exist that possesses unique qualities but shares many features with the larger (macro) culture and, in fact, it may influence the larger culture. As people interact with others from different cultural groups, their cultures do not remain singular or static. Recognizing a singular culture is no simple task.

There are hindrances to our ability to perceive and understand culture, and yet recognition of the existence of culture and the spheres in which cultural teaching take place gives us insight about powerful influences upon our perceptions, behaviors, and values. If we remain clueless, unable to see or understand the predominant patterns and forces that affect our lives, we are without the ability to make substantial changes in the way we conduct our personal lives, live in our society, and—as we hope to explain—educate our young.

Seeing Curriculum as Culture

In recent years, we have come to realize that classrooms and schools (as well as universities and other educational settings) have their own cultures. However, scrutiny of such cultures brings forth many of the same difficulties that we have when we study any culture: There rarely are "pure" cultures that develop without influences from others; we may be unaware of how we learn our culture, and we may find it hard to discern patterns of beliefs and behaviors that seem normal to us. More importantly, although people may share similar understandings of their societies and everyday life and hold shared values, nevertheless, individuals construe their own personal interpretations of events, practices, and symbols; they are not merely docile actors in a scripted cultural play but dynamic creators of meaning.

Thus, when we think about a school or classroom culture we must simultaneously imagine not a static entity but a assemblage of individuals who have different family cultures, different understandings and values influenced by race or ethnicity, gender, sexual orientation, social class, and religion as well as their own creativity and imagination; that in the classroom or school they participate in common activities, understand these activities somewhat similarly, and affirm certain values about knowledge, learning, and conduct—we can suggest the existence of a culture, albeit not in a monolithic sense.

We learn to see classrooms and schools as cultures by seeking answers to key questions: In what activities do people participate? What are everyday practices? What rules and laws influence these practices? What behaviors and attitudes are encouraged or discouraged? How are social groups organized? What are the relationships between students and instructors? Who has power to make decisions and who does not? And how are these power relationships maintained? How does the surrounding community and other outside stakeholders historically and currently influence the school? What has symbolic meaning in the environment and in what ways are these symbols communicated? What systems of thought are valued and modeled? What is the nature of the course of study? Whose history or literature is considered important or universal? What undertakings and talents are prized and rewarded? What do people believe to be appropriate goals of education? Clearly, all aspects of curriculum reflect culture.

In *The Culture of Education* (1996), Bruner provides many examples of culture as a mirror to describe and interpret curriculum:

> Schools have always been highly selective with respect to the uses of mind they cultivate—which uses are to be considered "basic," which "frills," which the school's responsibility and which the responsibility of others, which for girls and which for boys, which for working-class children and which for "swells." Some of this selectivity was doubtless based on considered notions about what the society required or what the individual needed to get along. Much of it was a spillover of folk or social class tradition. Even the more recent and seemingly obvious objective of equipping all with "basic literacy" is premised on moral-political grounds, however pragmatically those grounds may be justified. School curricula and classroom "climates" always reflect inarticulate cultural values as well as explicit plans; and these values are never far removed from considerations of social class, gender, and the prerogatives of social power. (p. 27)

Bruner illustrates how curriculum reflects cultural beliefs—folk traditions—as well as social and political values and organization. Using a cultural lens, we begin to regard curriculum not just as an object (content), but as a series of interwoven dynamics. Curriculum conceptualized as culture educates us to pay attention to belief systems, values, behaviors, language, artistic expression, the environment in which education takes place, power relationships, and most importantly, the norms that affect our sense about what is right or appropriate. For example, a deep-seated norm about curriculum is that it is linear—taught sequentially—and divided into separate disciplines (see Doll, 2008); likewise school structures reflect the norm of discontinuity:

> Modern American culture reveals an aesthetic preference for efficient production, which is manifested in schedules, refined tasks, and interchangeable designs. Simply put, we are used to engaging in one activity, stopping it, and beginning another. In school, students are used to going from class to class, which may be unrelated in content or method—e.g., going from an art class to math. In the workplace, one may be used to working on one project, stopping it for a meeting on a topic of a different nature, and then returning to the earlier project. Even on the assembly line, where one repeats a series of tasks, one's job is to return to an earlier motion rather than follow the sequence of activities to build the item. Thus, the job has a start-and-stop quality to it. (Uhrmacher, 1997, pp. 75–76)

Through the discipline of anthropology or ethnographic inquiry, we can better understand curriculum by evoking authentic representation of schooling, looking for patterns of belief and behavior within classrooms and educational systems. Ethnography allows us to study curriculum not just as explicit aims or plans, but as experiences encountered by teachers and students, the values inherent in the environment of the classroom and school, and connections to the encompassing culture surrounding the school. Ethnography enables us look systematically at the cultures of classrooms and schools—to look beyond planned outcomes, purposes, or instructional strategies to see how curriculum is manifest as culture through rituals, customs, values, and the implicit beliefs of folk pedagogies.

The ethnographic approach to studying curriculum suggests some ways of overcoming the roadblocks to understanding culture. To begin, ethnographers suggest that those who study classrooms, schools, and communities must temporarily imagine themselves as strangers to get through the roadblocks to perception created by familiarity (Spindler, 1982). Thus to help see the culture of our own schools, we should first observe educational systems that are unfamiliar. We might, for example, discern the beliefs held by other cultures about the benefits of knowledge and who should be educated to come to terms with our often unstated or taken-for-granted assumptions about schooling; or, we would identify dominant patterns of instruction and how, in other cultures, students and teachers interact—to spur us into paying attention to our own methods and behaviors.

Even without leaving our homes, we can still gain insight about our own system of education by studying aspects of schooling in different cultures, e.g., through research, journals, or artifacts. For instance, by reading the history texts of other cultures, we may be better able to see how our own textbooks sanction values, such as nationalism. Exposure to the unfamiliar through primary sources helps us to better perceive the familiar.

Experiencing disequilibrium also can occur within one's own neighborhood. A visit to an alternative school in which students choose their own course of study seems fairly "foreign" when one's classroom has a mandated course of study that everyone must teach or learn (and the other way around). We are called upon to examine our own assumptions and structures when we see a classroom or lecture hall with its orderly rows compared to a community-based school or class in which the neighborhood and the resources of the city comprise the learning environment. What we experience as routine is called into question when educators have opportunities to see others' situations or hear their stories.

But, without experiencing disequilibrium, how shall we understand the goals and lived experiences of curriculum within more familiar settings, e.g., classrooms in our own workplace or schools similar to ours? How can we make the "familiar" strange enough for us to be insightful about our own classroom cultures?

One possibility for learning about our own practice is to create inquiry along the lines of a qualitative research study. First, we collect data about what we see and hear. We need to capture impressions, engaging in a pilot study, beginning with several snapshots or tape-recordings of conversations.

Then, we analyze the record we make of ordinary activities and conversations. What visual and linguistic patterns signal us that a culture of curriculum might exist, e.g., what images and metaphors permeate speech, art, mission statements, and public relations materials? Would similar actions and dialogue reappear each time we observed? How do people utilize time and space and create ceremonies? How do they apportion power and authority among people? What seems "normal" to people within that culture and what seems unusual or even taboo? Eventually, we notice patterns of participants' behaviors and the meanings they give to their experiences. We also must study the less overt expectations and behaviors that undergird curricular cultures— the hidden curriculum of unquestioned assumptions and actions.

By looking for prominent aspects—the themes or continuing dialogue that point out what members of the culture hold as concerns or aspirations—we start to imagine the existence of a curricular culture. We can pay attention to a core notion or theme that permeates the school and classroom culture tacitly and overtly. What seems to matter most to people? Is there a theme that continues to appear and influence curricular decisions? What commonly

held assumptions or beliefs are routinely expressed? When content and practice become recast, what events, ideas, or forces influence change? We need to
understand curriculum—in any given place at any given time—as a conflu-
ence of environment, events and interactions.

We also learn by reading documents, the literature of the theory and practice. We develop an understanding of the belief system that is held by those
(academics, practitioners, or both) who write similarly about curriculum along
with those people we observe or talk with in our ethnographic studies. These
studies help us to develop language to articulate the culture of curriculum.

In addition, we need to learn if people who teach or learn in the culture (or
advocate for it) identify with ideas expressed decades or centuries ago. Is there
a "folk pedagogy"—that is, a collection of deeply imbedded notions of learning, schooling, and teaching passed along from generation to generation? By
historical investigation we can discover if a culture of curriculum accurately
may be linked to long-term commitment to beliefs, actions, or norms. Or, do
the issues raised and educational activities noticed seem more a response to a
recent discovery in psychology, an educational innovation, or a unique social
or technological problem reflecting contemporary concerns and aspirations?

Interpretation of our initial observations of classrooms and conversations
through recognition of themes (the continuing dialogue) leads us toward
identifying the belief systems (premises and aims) underpinning a curricular
culture. As we talk with students, teachers, administrators, and the community, we begin to understand that aims for students (implicitly understood or
explicitly set forth) illustrate beliefs about what schools can do for individuals
and society.

A Framework for Studying Curriculum as Culture

We approach the study of curriculum through the development of a systematic
framework of analysis (see Table 2.1) that gives us a structure used in the following chapters to describe cultures of curriculum. This heuristic provides the
means for us both to see and to question explicit practice, underlying beliefs
about teaching and learning, implications of curriculum work, and implicit
social and political visions.

We begin our depiction of curriculum as culture with a brief crystalliza-
tion of the curricular culture by presenting a telling quote from an advocate.
From the start, we wish to make evident a major idea that distills the essence
of the curricular culture, helping us to focus on the cogent elements of visions
and practice. We then consider a description of the everyday life in the classroom and/or school to provide a "snapshot" or impression of the culture. This
scenario should introduce the themes, beliefs, and practices that we would
find if we observed this culture over time. The next part of the heuristic is a
summary of major themes—the continuing dialogue manifest in each curric-

Table 2.1 A Framework for Understanding a Culture of Curriculum

Focus	Question
Quote	• What statement(s) synthesizes major beliefs within this culture of curriculum?
Impressions	• What depiction of education within this culture of curriculum captures many of its important themes and assumptions?
Visions	• What are the goals of education or schooling for the individual? • What is the ultimate benefit for society if all individuals were educated in this culture of curriculum? (may be implicitly stated)
History	• How has this culture of curriculum been present in schooling? • What are the forces, events, and ideas that influenced this culture of curriculum?
Students	• What are the beliefs about students' needs, development, competencies, motives, and interests? • How have these beliefs influenced practice?
Teachers	• What are the beliefs about the role of teachers? • How should they facilitate learning?
Content	• What constitutes the subject matter? • How is the subject matter organized?
Context	• What is the environment of the classroom? of the school? • How is instruction organized?
Planning	• What are the models of curriculum development? • Who plans the curriculum? Who has the power to make decisions?
Evaluation	• How should students be assessed? • How is the worth or success of the curriculum determined?
Dilemmas of Practice	• What problems or challenges do teachers face when they work in or try to implement this culture of curriculum?
Critique	• What problems are inherent in the vision of this curriculum for individuals and society? • What are the blind spots not perceived by advocates of this culture of curriculum?

ular culture. This is followed by explanation of visions, the aims or purposes for each curricular culture. Further, we depict the historical background of this curriculum in U.S. schooling, including the influencing societal events and forces.

We then turn to analyses of the belief systems of the culture, utilizing the concept of "commonplaces of curriculum" (Connelly & Clandinin, 1988) to understand assumptions about students and teachers, content and context, planning and evaluation. We explore explicit beliefs as well as the images and metaphors that implicitly demonstrate them.

We begin examination of the belief system by exploring assumptions about learners held by those who create curriculum. We question, how do those who plan or influence curriculum perceive learners? Expectations of learners and learning (at the crux of folk pedagogy) have dynamic consequences for the development and implementation of curriculum. In this curricular culture, do educators believe that students *need* basic skills? enrichment? world-class standards? discipline? self-esteem? Are students unique learners with their own interests and styles, at-risk, or gifted? Do students learn best by hands-on experiments, drills and repetition, or stories? Answers to such questions have a tremendous impact upon curriculum.

The questions we pose about learners correlate with conceptualizations of the role of teachers. Within the curricular culture, what does it mean to be a teacher? Is the teacher's fundamental task to create democratic learning communities, to stimulate questioning, to teach language and culture, or to learn about student's passions for learning and to facilitate their attainment of personal goals?

We then turn to descriptions of content that characterize a curricular culture. Are there particular books that exemplify learning in this culture? Do required subjects represent traditional academic disciplines or interdisciplinary topics or fields of study? Is the major emphasis on instruction or is curricular content particularly important? What content is taught and what is ignored (null curriculum)? And what criteria make the difference between content taught and content excluded? Furthermore, do students' interests have any role in content selection?

Also, what educational environment do adherents recommend and create? Do they imagine a class with students responding to the active questioning of the teacher? students engaged in projects at work stations? learners interviewing elders within the community? What is the relationship between students and teachers in the learning process and in what ways do teachers interact with colleagues and parents? Is the school day broken into segments according to subjects? Do students study within the classroom walls or make their own choices about utilizing the resources of the entire school?

We also investigate curriculum planning to make sense of the culture. Do teachers employ particular curriculum content stemming from previously developed models? Is the planning based upon requirements set by the nation, state, district, or school? Do teachers develop curriculum based on their own professional understanding of students' needs or according to their own expertise and interests? Do students, parents, or the community have voice or power in determining curriculum?

Finally, how does assessment and evaluation of the curriculum occur? Do standardized tests form the basis for continuation or change? Do learners have opportunities for a multiple demonstration of their learning accomplishments? Who evaluates the teachers and upon what bases does evaluation occur? What do people deem important for making decisions about resources to support curriculum? Who decides the success of curriculum and upon what grounds? And, is there opportunity to consider or reconsider the aims or worth of the curriculum, e.g., do we ask not only if the curriculum is successful but is it really worth teaching and learning?

This heuristic for understanding cultures of curriculum culminates with two pathways for further examination and reflection. First, we consider dilemmas of practice and secondly, critique of the culture—its essential assumptions, emphases, and visions. Inquiry into dilemmas of practice enables us to consider what practitioners confront when they teach within the culture. Dilemmas include choices in selecting content, the challenges in preparing to teach within this orientation, and the political issues that bring into question community reaction or the education of parents. Investigation of assumptions and convictions of advocates of each curricular orientation, the critique, leads us to probe advocates' social visions and whether or not there are connections between beliefs and actions. Also, we question the pedagogical, social, and political consequences of practice and revisit the idea of the null curriculum by contemplating what is not taught as well as the consequences of inattention or disregard. Finally, we interrogate aims and visions in light of moral or social concerns.

Cultures of Curriculum

We recognize that it is tremendously difficult to imagine a teacher working only within one curricular culture or to find a separate, isolated culture of curriculum. Exceptions can be found in some alternative schools that consciously adhere to a particular philosophy and sustain a distinct culture of curriculum. But even in many alternative schools and certainly in most public school classrooms, a multitude of instructional aims and goals for students and society exist side-by-side. Even those teachers who have a clear vision of their curriculum work, a solid philosophical core understanding, may not consistently teach according to their own ideals because of a variety of factors. Teachers face pressures to meet the demands of numerous constituencies: individual learners, parents, and administrators as well as community, state, and national influences. Ethnography often shows us that the "real" world is messy; a myriad of experiences, beliefs, and aims—often inconsistent and contradictory—co-exist in that world.

Nonetheless, in this book we intend to illustrate archetypes of cultures of curriculum that are distillates of most real classroom cultures. Although we believe it is crucial to see the implicit curriculum of schools and classrooms by learning how to observe the practice, interactions, taboos, values, and beliefs held about learning and bringing children to adulthood, our purpose is not to disclose a "slice of life"—despite the intellectual debt we owe to ethnography in making known patterns of meaning. Rather, our intention is to name, articulate, and reveal curricula as visions and belief systems. We analyze these curricular worlds through philosophical inquiry informed by our understanding of various cultural components.

Philosophical inquiry is a powerful means for understanding not only "what's going on here?" but what is the worth of this activity (Scriven, 1988). Conceptual analysis enables us to examine the inter-relatedness among various elements of curriculum and to envision ultimate aims of education and the moral visions of education. Such inquiry encourages us to ask—what is the purpose of curriculum? And, how does our curriculum work contribute to the education of the individual and to a good society? Through conceptual analysis we are able to clarify our beliefs and behaviors, to scrutinize the inconsistencies in our thoughts and actions—to consider when our practices conflict with our goals—and to ethically consider the consequences of our actions and aims.

Philosophy, however, does not attend to the disordered nature of individuals teaching and learning in actual schools and classrooms in real communities. Holding a particular philosophical aim of education does not necessarily result in a clearly defined guide for putting ideals into practice; a unified philosophical aim for education may not provide much insight about how to create an environment for day-to-day curriculum-making and practice. Our approach to curriculum inquiry, accordingly, is a hybrid of the disciplines of anthropology and philosophy. We ground our understanding of curricular cultures within the context of norms and practices and provide a framework for reflection by drawing upon philosophical and ethical inquiry to name, question, and critique visions and practices. In explaining how educators try to put visions into practice, we attempt to balance the ideal and the real by not losing sight of how curriculum workers must grapple with dilemmas about planning, teaching, and evaluating curriculum.

In conclusion, for educators who do curriculum inquiry through an anthropological lens, it becomes possible to discern if there is an overarching vision for education and if a coherent curriculum exists. Such inquiry also makes known if an ad hoc curriculum—featuring a multitude of sometimes contradictory of purposes and activities—characterizes the experiences of schooling for learners and teachers. To grasp a holistic understanding of lived curriculum and to do the serious work of transforming schooling and pedagogy, educators need to understand curriculum as culture. Further, we believe that by comparing personal practices to coherent models, educators gain a deeper understanding of their own curriculum work. A curricular culture framework is a starting point for comparison and contrast, for contemplating the goals and practices within educators' classrooms, schools, and communities—for asking if practices are congruent with our visions. It is our hope that knowledge of curricular cultures leads to awareness that there are ethical and progressive alternatives to visionless curriculum.

References

Aoki, T. T. (1991). *Inspiriting curriculum and pedagogy: Talks to teachers.* Faculty of Education, Department of Secondary Education, University of Alberta.

Bohannon, P. (1995). *How culture works.* New York: The Free Press.

Bruner, J. (1996). *The culture of education.* Cambridge, MA: Harvard University Press.

Connelly, F. M., & Clandinin, D. J. (1988). *Teachers as curriculum planners: Narratives of experience.* New York: Teachers College Press.

Doll, W. E. (2008). Complexity and the cultures of curriculum. *Educational Philosophy and Theory, 40*(1), 190–212.

Foshay, A. W. (1980). Curriculum talk. In A. W. Foshay (Ed.), *Considered action for curriculum improvement* (pp. 82–94). Alexandria, VA: ASCD.

Geertz, C. (1983). *Local knowledge: Further essays in interpretative anthropology.* New York: Basic Books.

Greene, M. (1973). *Teacher as stranger: Educational philosophy for the modern age.* Belmont, CA: Wadsworth.

Hall, E. T. (1959/1981). *The silent language.* New York: Anchor Books/Doubleday.

Hall, E. T. (1977). *Beyond culture.* Garden City, NY: Anchor Press/Doubleday.

Hannerz, U. (1992). *Cultural complexity: Studies in the social organization of meaning.* New York: Columbia University Press.

Herskovits, M. J. (1967). *Cultural dynamics,* New York: Alfred A. Knopf.

Joseph, P. B. (2007). Seeing as strangers: Teachers' investigations of lived curriculum. *Journal of Curriculum Studies, 39*(3), 283–302.

McLaren, P. (1986). *Schooling as a ritual performance: Towards a political economy of educational symbols and gestures.* London: Routledge & Kegan Paul.

Pink, W. T. (1990). Implementing curriculum inquiry: Theoretical and practical implications. In J. T. Sears & J. D. Marshall (Eds.), *Teaching and thinking about curriculum* (pp. 138–153). New York: Teachers College Press.

Scriven, M. (1988). Philosophical inquiry methods in education. In R. M. Jaeger (Ed.), *Complementary methods for research in education* (pp. 131–148). Washington, DC: American Educational Research Association.

Spindler, G. D. (Ed.). (1982). *Doing the ethnography of schooling: Educational anthropology in action.* New York: Holt, Rinehart & Winston.

Spindler, G., & Spindler, L. (1987). Ethnography: An anthropological view. In G. D. Spindler (Ed.), *Education and cultural process: Anthropological approaches* (2nd ed., pp. 151–156). Prospect Heights, IL: Waveland Press.

Uhrmacher, P. B. (1997). Evaluating change: Strategies for borrowing from alternative education. *Theory into Practice, 36*(2), 71–78.

Westbury, I. (2000). Teaching as reflective practice: What might Didaktik teach curriculum? In I. Westbury, S. Hopmann, & K. Riquarts (Eds.), *Teaching as a reflective practice: The German Didaktik tradition* (pp. 15–40). Mahwah, NJ: Erlbaum.

Chapter 3

Narrowing the Curriculum

Pamela Bolotin Joseph, Nancy Stewart Green,
Edward R. Mikel, and Mark A. Windschitl

> The first step we can take toward changing reality—waking up from the night-
> mare that is the present state of pubic miseducation—is acknowledging that we
> are indeed living a nightmare.
>
> William F. Pinar, 2004, *What is Curriculum Theory?*, p. 5

The notion of curriculum seems particularly lacking in recent times, as the word itself has nearly disappeared from public discourse and has been replaced instead by the terms standards and outcomes. Curriculum—as an imaginative concept that attends to learners' experiences as well as the enduring consequences of education for individuals or society—does not enter contemporary political discussions focused on "accountability," "competition," and "achieving excellence." Completely lost within this climate is the ethical question: What should the educated person become?

Within schools, curriculum may still be part of the vocabulary, but it usually pertains to planning for specific programs and effective procedures to attain educational outcomes embodying a narrowly specialized set of skills with the emphasis upon "technique" over "substance" (Beyer & Apple, 1988, p. 3).

> We are referring here to the transformation of curriculum theory and
> practice from a concern about *what* should be taught and *why* we should
> teach it to those problems associated with *how to* organize, build, and
> above all now, evaluate curriculum and teaching. The difficult ethical and
> political questions of content, of what knowledge is of most worth, have
> been pushed to the background in our attempts to define technically ori
> ented methods that will "solve" our problems once and for all. (p. 3)

As a result, there is little interest in how to create curriculum for students to study meaningful questions based on their curiosity about the world; nor do schools help learners to imagine how they could change the world. We rarely know of debate within conventional schooling about the possibilities of education as a catalyst for the transformation of individuals or for social reform.

Similarly, seldom do educators deliberate about the purposes of education or reflect upon, question, and challenge curricular aims and actions. Instead we hear teachers, administrators, and parents speak of curriculum as an object devoid of substantive ethical concerns. We often hear teachers refer to curriculum as a commodity: "At our school we teach [Publishing Company's] math curriculum"; "In my classroom, I have to teach a dozen different [published] curriculums." Or, teachers understand curriculum as explicitly required information and skills: "Curriculum is what I am supposed to cover during the school year as stated in the grade-level guide"; "Curriculum is what the school board tells me to teach." Once more, we listen to teachers say: "We don't really have a curriculum anymore—we just get the children ready to take the standardized tests." Correspondingly, administrators and parents tout curriculum as something instrumental, not worthy in itself, but as the means to get to an explicit end: "Our curriculum prepares students to enter the workforce"; and, "We expect our children to have a rigorous curriculum so they can get into good universities." And, despite the sincerity of many teachers who try each day to do right by their students, educators often are too immersed in their particular circumstances to note, to name, and to question the most dominant structures of school culture and what is taught to young people.

Yet, we know of educators who want to enact rich, creative, multi-disciplinary curriculum so to guide learners toward self-knowledge, caring for others, and deep understanding of the world. Unfortunately, in many schools educators who hold such aims for education encounter so much resistance that their most visionary teaching has become a covert curriculum practiced behind closed doors. That there is opposition to teachers creating meaningful curriculum work is regrettable on ethical grounds but also because a narrow focus on learning outcomes and achievement does not create classrooms that engage students in learning or motivates students to do challenging work.

Educators who understand the moral purposes of their work think about curriculum as dynamic. They do not refer to curriculum as an object or commodity but understand curriculum as a process of creating a rich and meaningful course of study that integrates their knowledge of pedagogy, scholarship in the academic disciplines, educational research, and learners' and families' needs and interests. Educators with such expertise understand that high standards can and should be embedded in rigorous, meaningful study and they do not have to think of curriculum as truncated elements for the sole purpose of passing tests. As well, we know educators who truly are reflective practitioners and contemplate their broader philosophical and ethical aims. Fortunately, some of these teachers work in schools in which administrators, families, and the community support their utmost ethical intentions and visions. It is these curriculum workers who have tried to change the status quo of schooling, have assumed curriculum leadership, and are inspiring role models for those entering the teaching profession or becoming administrators. Despite our grave concerns about the current educational climate with its narrow aims, innovative curriculum exists because of talented, creative, and courageous educators.

We believe that it is possible to reconceive education and to bring about the transformation of classrooms and schools. But for educators to be able to challenge the status quo, they must be able to articulate and understand deeply ingrained patterns the envelop them. We begin therefore with these questions: What have been the prevailing classroom and school cultures in United States education? How has the current "nightmare" of "miseducation" (Pinar, 2004, p. 5) to prepare for the workplace and to support national economic viability come into existence? What are the obstacles to developing transformative curriculum or conceptualizing curriculum as a reflective process rather than a narrow object? Finally, what is lost when the education becomes reduced to standardized and measurable skills needed to succeed in the world of work?

Prevailing Classroom and School Cultures

Although there are teachers who individually work to develop inspired curriculum, with the exception of some alternative schools in public systems and independent schools, the cultures of schools seem bereft of vision and appear to simply perpetuate largely unquestioned norms, habits, values, and goals. Many curricular practices are generated from ad hoc decisions, often in response to competing demands from various constituencies rather than from articulated beliefs. Rather than encouraging thoughtfully coherent missions, schools "have been too open to accommodating all interest groups, all the time" (Nehring, 2007, p. 428). And yet, certain consistent threads permeate school and classroom cultures.

Despite a history of contradictory impulses, e.g., beliefs about the value of standardized curriculum vs. child-centered education (Cuban, 1993), classroom cultures have not been diverse; there has been a typical and deeply entrenched culture of classrooms and schools. In a study of more than 1,000 classrooms, Goodlad (1984) found an "extraordinary sameness" of learning environments featuring "bland, repetitive procedures of lecturing, questioning, monitoring, and quizzing" (p. 249). Other researchers note that in the prevailing conditions of American classrooms—similar to those throughout the 20th century—"[m]ost teachers talk most of the time; students sit, listen, do seatwork, and take tests. This occurs for approximately 85% of the 75% of the class time devoted to instruction" (Heckman, 1987, p. 70). Also, many teachers, administrators, and parents expect an educative classroom to be quiet and orderly with students seated and not talking to each other, assuming that engagement means students being attentive—not speaking, gesturing, building, or moving about—with heterogeneous grouping heavily resisted (Oakes, Quartz, Ryan, & Lipton, 2000).

Furthermore, the de facto curriculum for many teachers has been encyclopedic textbooks which have fueled pressures to cover an ambitiously broad and thin curricular content and not to help students deeply construct knowledge (Windschitl, 2002). In fact, oftentimes the public believes that textbooks equal curriculum—as through no other knowledge sources would or should matter. This sentiment seems to energize public discussion of district textbook adoption but, unfortunately, also creates an agenda that encourages a culture of rote learning and precludes teachers from spending class time on authentic forms of inquiry. In such institutional environments, teaching and learning that is not pre-scripted and geared toward "right answers" is viewed with suspicion (Gabella, 1993). In addition, the compulsion to cover material is antithetical to several aims of progressive reform, e.g., the deep and elaborate understanding of selected core ideas, democratic curriculum planning, and critical examination of social conditions.

The culture in many schools has been one of coping and compliance, where teachers control students' intellectual activity to ensure uniform exposure to the curriculum and maintain discipline, as students play the role of unquestioning, passive learners. This prevailing culture is not necessarily unsystematic. Indeed, many teachers depended upon the regularities of curricula fashioned and organized by external intellectual authorities, inflexible models of instruction, and a narrow definition of learning. These limited vehicles of teaching and learning represent some of the most consistent and persistent phenomena known in the social and behavioral sciences (Sirotnik, 1983).

In the late 20th century, there had been some modification of the teacher-centered landscape (Cuban, 1993). Educators gravitated toward student-centered instruction, adopting partial strategies that included classroom learning centers, cooperative learning, and project or problem-based learning—these activities typically integrated into a core of otherwise teacher-centered practices. Most teachers, however, limited students' participation in curriculum, denying them full partnership in planning of content and choice of learning activities.

However, classrooms with more student-centered activities do not necessarily signify coherent progressive visions and practices. But such classrooms do suggest the emergence of modifications of the historically monolithic culture of schooling. Still, deviations from the traditional structure must be recognized as special events, experiments that are exceptions to the day-to-day business of schooling; these events—such as empowering students to make meaningful curricular choices, developing poignant humanistic themes, or integrating class work with other subject areas—challenge ingrained practices. Generally, however, conversations about significant curricular reform are not heard in the dominant discourse; institutional text (Pinar, Reynolds, Slattery, & Taubman, 1995)—testing, procedures, and classroom management—has characterized most conversations around curriculum.

The existence of this entrenched culture is particularly noticeable in large studies that overlook individual educators and the worlds that they make. We realize, however, that teachers have never functioned as automatons;

they weave their own expertise, interests, cultural knowledge, values, and responsiveness to individual students into the structures and routines of the prevailing culture of schools. Classrooms and schools were—and still are— combinations of default and desire. There may be more richness of experience in them than is revealed in the distillate of wide-scaled studies, but their sum and substance have not been visionary. Certainly, these efforts in nontraditional curriculum did not reach the extent of a paradigm change and were not able to withstand the threat to progressive philosophies and practices into the following years of the 21st century.

The Business of Schooling: History

The idea that schooling should emphasize only fundamental academic skills and exist only to serve the national economic interest is a modern occurrence in U.S. education. Albeit with a narrow and inequitable view of who can qualify for full citizenship, the educational vision of the new nation began with the premise that children should be taught values, history, and basic literacy skills for democratic participation, and for some, academic study to prepare for leadership. Furthermore, it was hoped that study of similar curricula for all children "might mitigate the advantages enjoyed by the fortunate" (Deschenes, Cuban, & Tyack, 2001, p. 529). Although there were a myriad of informal and formal apprenticeships arranged for young people to learn a trade or craft prior to the industrial age, the conception of an educated person did not mean someone educated for the workplace. The pragmatic rationale to teach "what is useful" that appeared in a variety of sources, including Benjamin Franklin's writing on education, did not represent the majority of proposed goals or practices.

Yet, as at the dawn of the industrial age—as the self-image of America no longer was an agrarian ideal, craftsmen and their apprentices were replaced by factories and family farms declined in importance while cities grew (see Wiebe, 1967)—educators claimed a place for schools in the production of employees. Training for work became part of the rationale for educating children, especially children of immigrants and the working class. In the 1840s, Horace Mann appealed to employers to support public schools on the basis that educated students (by which he meant students who had completed from 3 to 6 years of elementary schooling) would make better workers—more prompt, more responsible, and less likely to be led astray by "firebrands." The 19th-century kindergarten established in urban school systems emphasized teaching "moral habits, cleanliness, politeness, obedience, regularity, and self-control" (Spring, 1997, p. 201). Authors of teacher-training textbooks in the first several decades of the 20th century equated classroom management with the building of "good industrial habits of the type needed on the assembly line" (Spring, 1997, p. 216) and in "training childhood for the highest possible degree of efficiency" (Joseph, 2001, p. 149). Inevitably, schooling for work, especially for the children of the poor and working classes, became an established norm in American culture.

But the phenomenon of linking all of schooling—rather than just vocational preparation for some students—to the success of the economic and military success of the United States made its foremost appearance in the mid-20th century. In the 1950s those who criticized alleged sub-standard curricular content did so by complaining that "Johnny could not read and asking why we could not hold a candle to the Russians" (Sobol, 1997, p. 630)—despite the public's earlier pride in the accomplishments of the American schools system with its public support for free education through high school (see Goldin & Katz 1997/2008). But even during a time of experimentation and innovation in curricular content in the 1960s and 1970s, "the business of schooling" began to influence cultural norms through assumptions that there were "ready-made technocratic solutions to educational problems" that brought business-oriented management techniques to school systems and also to curriculum (Tyack & Cuban, 1995, p. 114):

> ...to treat public schools as a marketplace of instructional services in which corporations could compete in teaching children by using the latest technologies of instruction and behavioral engineers, such as teaching machines and extrinsic rewards for learning. Business methods of planning and budgeting, competition, and incentives, aided by new technologies—these could transform antiquated public schools into centers of efficient learning. (p. 114)

Moreover, considering schooling as a business increasingly meant an acceptance of an agenda to encourage privatization of schools (see Sleeter, 2008; Symcox, 2009).

The next round of criticism of schooling came from the 1983 report, *A Nation At Risk* (National Commission on Excellence in Education), commissioned 2 years earlier by the United States Secretary of Education. And although contradictory evidence was suppressed, and the report was based on unsubstantiated statistics and faulty assumptions about the connection between high test scores and economic competitiveness (see Bracey, 2003), it dared to suggest that "If an unfriendly foreign power had attempted to impose on America the mediocre educational performance that exists today, we might well have viewed it as an act of war" (National Commission on Excellence in Education, 1983, p. 1)—implying again that if the cold war was lost, it would be the fault of schools. *A Nation At Risk* recommended changes to make curriculum more strenuous, e.g., increased course credits, but did not impose requirements for implementation and sanctions on school districts for noncompliance.

Again in the mid-1990s—even in times of economic prosperity—concern was raised about lack of global competitiveness because of mediocre schools and this focus became the dominant conversation about schooling:

> In recent years, however, discourse about the purposes of education has been impoverished by linking it insistently to the wealth of nations. The underlying rationale of most recent reforms —to use schooling as an instrument of international economic competitiveness—is not new, but its dominance in policy talk is unprecedented. (Tyack & Cuban, 1995, p. 136)

Prompted by such rhetoric, governors and business leaders came together to compel school reform through Goals 2000, a program that emphasized academic standards, in particular, skills needed for industry but also preparation for responsible citizenship. Goals 2000: Educate American Act (1994) was a significant departure in the history of U.S. schooling, representing "one of the greatest intrusions of the federal government into education policy" and was a revolutionary attempt to promote education reform on a national scale (Superfine, 2005, p. 10). During this time, conservatives expressed fears about federal involvement in education, eventually eliminating the law when they returned to power. However, Goals 2000 was well received by schools and states because it was "flexible" and had "so few constraints on the expenditure of its funds" (Schwartz & Robinson, 2000, p. 204).

Nevertheless, this national school reform failed to accomplish its major goals of all children would start school ready to learn, the high school graduation rate would be at least 90%, all adults would be literate, and all schools would be free of drugs and violence—all by the year 2000. This failure is not particularly surprising in that the legislation omitted any concern for social realities facing schools, inequality of resources among school districts, or cultural diversity. Although "a number of states made a great deal of progress in creating standards, assessments, and accountability systems," another of the aims of Goals 2000—students leaving grades 4, 8, and 12 needed to demonstrate competency over subject matter in a wide-range of curricular content—also fell short as the law did not have strong provisions for accountability (Superfine, 2005, pp. 25–26).

Yet just several years later, legislation that would become the leading influence on United States schooling did include enforceable measures for standardized testing and accountability. The No Child Left Behind Act (2001) tremendously extended the power of the federal government to influence public schools across all the states and gained support across the political spectrum, despite conservatives' earlier objections to federal intrusion in education. NCLB's stated aim was to help poor and minority children achieve academic success but its primary instrument was the institution of yearly standardized tests as chosen by the states but with approval of the U.S. Department of

Education. Rather than infusing vast resources into schools for lowering class sizes, tutoring, and professional development, schools were held accountable for children's lack of achievement as published in yearly "report cards" and could eventually be threatened with probation and closure—a system based upon competitive elimination.

> The basic essence of NCLB is this: some schools are identified as failing schools, based solely on standardized test scores. Parents then have the option of moving their students to successful schools, based solely on test scores. This is it. This is the great NCLB innovation built on a business paradigm by business-thinking people. The untested hypothesis is that all the happy successful schools will grew and prosper, all the "bad" failing schools will disappear someplace. The reasoning behind this, if you want to call it that, is that this system seems to work well with Wal-Mart stores, McDonald's restaurants, and Kwik-E Mart convenience stores, so it must therefore work similarly well with schools. (Johnson, 2006, p. 36)

Regardless of the government's argument that such testing brought about higher standards, the system of measurement and insistence on constant improvement insured that by its the target date 2014 the majority of schools would fail (FairTest, 2008). A case in point, in "Minnesota, where eighth graders are first in the nation in mathematics and on a par with the top countries in the world, had 80 percent of schools on track to be labeled failing according to the federal rules" (Darling-Hammond, 2007, p. 14). Such results reinforce the unexamined belief that schools are failing and are used as fuel for critics' advocacy of the privatization of schooling within a "larger corporatocratic project of privatizing public services" (Sleeter, 2008, p. 148). Moreover, NCLB has had enthusiastic support from the business community who continued to believe in the competitive nature of standardized testing to create better workers (Hoff, 2006). Undoubtedly, those companies that provided standardized tests to states also had interest in the continuation of NCLB as schools as billions of dollars of states' scarce revenues have been spent to pay for these assessments (see Arce, Luna, Borjian, & Conrad, 2005; Miner, 2004/2005).

It appears that some of the more critical problems of NCLB will be addressed in future years. Growing concerns about its punitive measures have led to reconsideration of NCLB's requirements and calls for developing a national curriculum to ensure a richer, more balanced education for all students—ironically perhaps, to use national standards to combat the excesses of standardized testing. Nonetheless, NCLB and its provisions have left behind a legacy of test-oriented classroom and school cultures that do not honor children's or teachers' interests, creativity, or intellectual development. NCLB itself may be measured some day for its effect upon a generation of children and a decade of teaching.

The Business of Schooling: Norms

It is not surprising that curriculum mirrors public values as the connection between school and society is persistent and strong; local control not only affects curriculum but state and national mandates increasingly influence the goals and substance of schooling in the United States. But the foremost barriers to progressive curriculum lie not just in the forces for and dominance of conventional curriculum but in the embedded assumptions that support it. In particular, a great hindrance to curriculum transformation is unquestioned acceptance of certainties about schooling and learners—even when these convictions cannot be supported by substantive educational research or may contradict each other.

In contemporary American society, the paramount supposition is the relationship between schools and industry—that education should serve the needs of commerce and schools should imitate business models. This dominant viewpoint and its associate beliefs shape the fabric of schooling and obstruct transformative curriculum in a multitude of ways. In the main, schools reflect these basic premises: (a) Success, whether personal or societal, manifests itself in material well-being; (b) work has moral significance and attributes of "good work" such as thoroughness, promptness, neatness, reliability and punctuality are to be valued; (c) the free-market system is the most efficient and beneficent economic system; and, (d) economic and technological trends are immutable and essentially uncontrollable.

In addition to the above assumptions, there exist widespread beliefs that specifically connect economic values to schooling: First, schools have a vital role in the country's economic future. Therefore, when elected officials meet to address the problem of American education, the issue is framed in economic terms, prompting such questions as: What will happen to America's economic status in the world if our students cannot perform well in comparison to those of other countries? Or, how can we compete if students can graduate from high school without knowing how to read and write? Second, since the most important goal of schooling is to promote the economic well-being of the country and its citizens, business leaders can assist schools by telling them what future employees will need to know. And third, schools can ameliorate the effects of social and economic inequality created by the free-market system and uncontrollable economic trends; for instance, education is the crucial means by which disadvantaged students can become productive members of society no matter the extent to which poverty affects their lives.

This economic or business orientation of schooling as preparation for the workplace is such a strong cultural norm that it becomes manifest in the classroom. Critics see how when elementary teachers say, "You must be in your seat with your pencil sharpened by the time the bell rings," or, "You must finish your work before you can play in the toy corner," their rationale indeed may be to prepare their students for jobs as surely as when teachers of older children say, "You must learn to work in teams because that's what you'll have to do on the job." Even in kindergarten, children learn that their purpose is to work—and play is the reward of work—rather than thinking about learning as a pleasurable activity in itself (Apple & King, 1983, p. 89). Further, young children become "prepared for not only participation in the bureaucratic organization of large modern school systems, but also for the large-scale occupational bureaucracies of modern society" (Gracey, 1975/2004, p. 148).

Most of all, the belief in the worth of competition influences and sustains the dominant curriculum. The competitive tenet is undergirded by the supposition that through winning good grades and achieving high test scores, students will grow up ready to compete against each other or allow the nation to be competitive in the global economy. It is accepted as proper and normal for schools to train individuals for competition and to foster their sense of worth within a system of rewards. As a result, students continually compete for grades, placement in enrichment classes, academic honors, and social recognition. This belief also supports the assumptions that fear of failure will convince students to learn more and teachers to work harder—and when schools and/or states battle against each other for funding, competition will somehow improve education.

Learning, therefore, is for the purpose of getting ahead—or not falling behind—and young people are trained to play the game of life; they are educated to know the world as it is, not to improve it or even to deeply understand it. Hence the economic leitmotif of schooling contains a conservative social vision holding "the development of individual talent" as "the most desirable trait of good education (Kaplan, 1997, p. 427). Thus "conventional education in the United States has been dominated by an ethos of individualism" (Goodman & Kuzmic, 1997, p. 80) and although schools may promote collaborative projects and cooperation toward accomplishing a specific academic goal, there is no vision of working to create a community in which individuals feel obligation for each other and for the greater society. The business of schooling mindset suggests that the major worth of an individual lies in economic success (and related power) and has little vision of individual transformation or ethical development.

The Business of Schooling: Consequences

Schooling to serve and emulate industry has led to a contraction of the curriculum so that the underlying mission of schooling has become the passing standardized tests and not the development of well-rounded individuals. Such limited aims have had devastating consequences affecting children's educational experiences, creating inequality of school resources and opportunities, and devaluing teachers as professionals. These aims are manifest in the ubiquitous "standardized management paradigm" (Henderson & Gornik, 2007) that offers a top-down view of curriculum focusing on "how best to improve student performance in standardized tests" and "methods such as memorization, drill, test preparation, and other related types of learning activities that it is believed help students perform well on standardized tests" (Heyer & Pifel, 2007, p. 569).

The narrowing of curriculum springs from a circular logic beginning with the association of high standards with standardized curriculum, thus leading to standardized tests as the prime means of measuring student achievement of standards. Acceptance of this logic has led to a number of outcomes including teaching to the test, curriculum fragmentation, scripted curriculum, disregard of content or goals deemed untestable, and diminishment of high-quality instruction. Critics note that "No Child Left Behind has actually made it harder for states to improve the quality of teaching" as tests are influenced by "a narrow view of what constitutes learning" (Darling-Hammond, 2007, p. 14) and do not test for "higher-order thinking" (Neill, 2003, p. 225). "The mandated testing regimen require[es] teachers to reconfigure nearly every teaching or planning moment into a form of test preparation" (Symcox, 2009, p. 59) as "teaching to the test substitutes for deeper intellectual inquiry" (Sleeter, 2008, p. 148).

Moreover, schools drain their resources on testing preparation and implementation of testing (Symcox, 2009, p. 59) as NCLB did not adequately fund its provisions (Neill, 2003).

> A growing number of studies conclude that enabling all children to attain proficiency will require perhaps doubling the per-capita spending for low-income students...One theory behind NCLB was that the law would push states to provide adequate resources to all schools. Yet most states are cutting their education budgets in the face of lingering budget shortfalls. States are also having to spend more than [provided]...to meet the new federal requirements. (Neill 2003, p. 226)

The ironic end result of the narrowed curriculum is that limited funds for education support expensive standardized testing rather than improving the quality of education, e.g., class size, school climate, school environments, or professional development (Portelli, & Vilbert, 2002/2003). Kozol (1997) exposes this absurdity by noting that people "think that tests teach reading. I say, Tests don't teach reading. Only well-paid teachers teach reading." Likewise, he comments, "...the lamb farmers say, you don't fatten your lambs by weighing them. But there's an awful lot of weighing of the lambs nowadays, while the lambs are getting thinner and thinner" (p. 2).

Once more, testing mandates explicitly and implicitly label some subject matter and instruction as inferior—including attainment of collaborative, creative, and critical thinking—despite the fact that "high-achieving nations focus their curriculums on critical thinking and problem solving, using exams that require students to conduct research and scientific investigations, solve complex real-world problems and defend their ideas orally and in writing" (Darling-Hammond, 2007, p. 14). In particular, the emphasis on math and reading has "widen[ed] the gap in other curricular areas" (Rothstein & Jacobsen, 2006, p. 265), reducing instruction in "science, social studies, and the arts" (Ravitch, 2010, p. 108). The narrowing of the curriculum affects the experiences of all learners, even very young children as "kindergartens have become test-prep centers" and "[p]aints, easels, and Froebel blocks have vanished...[c]reativity has been pushed out of the curriculum, along with play and recreation activities...." (Symcox, 2009, p. 60). Moreover, instead of supporting literacy with a rich curriculum in the arts, sciences, and social sciences that could engage learners, the curriculum in low-performing schools increasingly eliminate such untested subjects (Neill, 2003).

And what are the effects of such testing environments on learners? Indeed, some students have improved their testable math and literacy skills but critics also question the quality of instruction and if students can develop deep comprehension of these basic curricular areas or in others when "[b]road, scattered coverage replaces comprehension" and "there is no time to find out if students have mastered a skill before moving on to then next one (Symcox, 2009, p. 60). Another very serious issue is student engagement—when children come to "hate school for all the reasons anybody would hate institutions that tend to be boring, unengaging, regimented, and run by adults saturated with the fear engendered by accountability politics" (Sacks, 1999, p. 256). In test-driven environments students may not have the motivation or interest to succeed and stay in school (Herman & Gomez, 2009, p. 65) as the curricula fostered in such a milieu "run completely counter to higher-end learning or research-based knowledge about what stimulates students at all levels of ability to want to work hard" (Lewis, 2007, p. 483).

A further issue about the narrowed curriculum is that it "[undermines] education for the most vulnerable students" (Darling-Hammond, 2009/2010, p. 9)—often poor children of color and ethnic minorities – who attend schools with the fewest resources. As those schools generally have lower test scores, pressure mounts to reduce offerings in untested subjects including social studies, science, and the arts and even to take recess away from children (Neill, 2003; Hargreaves & Shirley, 2009) and "the higher the stakes, the more teaching to the test" (Neill, 2003, p. 225). But when schools only emphasize test preparation with drills and memorization, "students' intellectual growth and ownership over the learning process is stunted" (Sleeter, 2008, p. 148). Again, Kozol's writing about the test-focused climate, even before NCLB, highlights how poor children get less opportunity to take stimulating courses than their wealthier counterparts.

> Increasingly they take moronic courses in job readiness and leave the treasures of the earth, from Milton to Molière to Toni Morrison, leave all that to the children in the suburbs. This is the way you make two social castes that will never know each other. (1997, p. 2)

Consequently, the achievement gap that proponents of NCLB sought to close still exists (Lewis, 2007) and an authentic achievement gap—not only measured by test scores—actually may be widening as "student drop-out rates are escalating" (Sleeter, 2008, p. 148). These current school environments may drive out students because of their lack of interest in the test-focused curriculum (see Herman & Gomez, 2009, p. 65) and schools' crassly calculated strategies "to exclude low-achieving students in order to boost scores" (Darling-Hammond, 2009/2010, p. 9). Although high-stakes testing affects the curriculum and experiences of students in more advantaged schools, those children "have a bigger chance of surviving the system" (Portelli, & Vilbert, 2002/2003, p. 11) as their opportunities for educational enrichment may be more available through their families and communities.

Because the conversation has changed from how to help children and improve schools to a simplistic litany of test scores and outcomes, little attention is paid to assuring that there are equitable opportunities for children—including rich curricula, teachers with expertise, and welcoming school environments.

> But in the No Child Left Behind era, the words equal educational opportunity have largely faded from the public discourse. In their place, there is talk of eliminating the "achievement gaps" between various groups of students.... Achievement gap is all about measurable "outputs"—standardized-test scores—and not about equalizing resources, addressing poverty, combating segregation, or guaranteeing children an opportunity to learn. The No Child Left Behind Act is silent on such matters. Dropping equal educational opportunity, which highlights the role of inputs, has a subtle but powerful effect on how we think about accountability. It shifts the entire burden of reform from legislators and policymakers to teachers and kids and schools. (Crawford, 2007, p. 31)

Thus the standardized management paradigm promotes a "continuing comfort with profound inequality" (Darling-Hammond, 2009, p. 8).

The standardized management paradigm also has serious ramifications for educators: narrowing of professional roles, demoralizing working conditions, and teachers' lack of authority for curriculum development. To begin, administrators have felt pressure to evaluate performance solely on test scores and to devalue teachers' nurturing of children and planning of innovative curriculum; thus the "standardized examination system becomes a powerful evaluative device in confining teachers' professional autonomy in teaching" (Wong, 2006, p. 29). Within such milieus, teachers "mourn the loss of their own and their students' creativity (Hargreaves & Shirley, 2009, p. 2510) as the narrowed curriculum takes "the soul out of teachers and the joy out of teaching" (Kozol, 1997, p. 2). Ultimately, such an environment devalues teachers' academic expertise and dismisses the moral dimensions of teaching that encompass caring, nurturing, and attention to children's developmental or emotional needs.

Hence, administrators and politicians may appreciate teachers only for their ability to increase test scores and not for the other important features of their work, including creative curriculum making. Such circumstances increasingly pressure teachers to think about themselves as technicians rather than educators.

> Stripped of autonomy and intentionality, emptied of inner life, reduced to conglomerations of skills that are employed in environments in order to stimulate predetermined responses, teachers can easily be replaced by bureaucrats, mechanics, or machines. Reduced to information and metacognitive skills, the curriculum lends itself to teacher-proof scripts. (Taubman, 2009, p. 194)

This current state of affairs refers to the "deskilling" of teachers (see Apple, 1986) in which "educators lose their dynamic roles as curriculum workers when they no longer are allowed to create or modify curriculum" (Joseph, 2010, p. 283). Deskilling means that

> as teachers deliver curriculum rather than use their academic and pedagogical expertise, they will in fact lose some skills. Or, teachers may be hired because they do not have strong knowledge and skills because they can be paid low salaries and will be compliant—readily following scripted curriculum and feeling dependent on the state or administration to give them curriculum. Moreover, teachers may accept their deskilled roles as the discourse of corporatism and managerialism becomes legitimized. (Joseph, 2010, pp. 283–285)

Critics of schooling note that as teachers become "more and more viewed as technicians called upon to implement classroom objectives that are tightly controlled and defined by others higher upon the administrative chain of command" (Purpel & Shapiro, 1995, p. 109), they continue to lose their authority as professionals.

> Such a role increasingly precludes the involvement of teachers from any real authority for decision making in the school. It robs them of the opportunity to think creatively about how they teach or what it is that should be taught. And it denies them the moral and political significance of what they do....The 'deskilled' teacher is required to teach with little consciousness or conscience about the fundamental values that he or she is trying to initiate in the classroom. (Purpel & Shapiro, 1995, p. 109)

Again, there is a particular logic at work here. As there is increased emphasis on teaching to the test or reliance on "teacher-proof" programs or curriculum packages in which teachers become the "delivery system" by following scripts or recipes and providing copies of prepared handouts to their students, it is assumed that teachers cannot be trusted to develop curriculum (or to co-create it with their students) and it is not necessary to give them time to reflect upon, deliberate, or create curriculum. In addition, in the wake of attacks on schools and the demands for accountability to uniform educational goals, the teaching profession holds decreasing power to control curricular decisions. Accordingly, there is less of a chance that anyone will challenge the narrowing curriculum.

Curriculum Abandoned

As this standardized management paradigm is such a pervasive force in current curriculum, we need to consider what we abandon when the essential vision of education offers little beyond schooling for success, excellence, and "racing to the top" by concentrating almost exclusively on the economy, global competition, and teaching for specific workplace and basic literacy skills. One way of critically viewing the systemic test-focused education that so highly emphasizes competition and individual achievement is to contemplate its null curriculum—what is omitted. Ultimately, the narrowing of curriculum has meant the neglect of the full range of historic and contemporary aims of education such as democratic participation, personal fulfillment, intellectual autonomy, attainment of deep cultural learning, and development of critical thinking and skills for social action. In this thin view of curriculum,

> [L]aughter wouldn't achieve any outcome, would it? Beauty really wouldn't achieve any measurable outcome, either. Neither would a moment that's spiritually intense. Tears, love wouldn't achieve any outcome that would get you any points on [an]…exam. (Kozol, 1997, p. 2)

An outcomes-based curriculum obliterates the notion of the teacher as a creative force and teaching "as existential encounter, as an endeavor whose results are impossible to predict" (Taubman, 2009, p. 124). The fear-driven climate of education leads to the creation of automatons and not to a community of learners. Does that truly improve education? Does this make for a better future?

> Do we really need more kids who know how to play the grading and testing games that schools now encourage? Do we really doubt that what we need instead are human beings who have the capacity to meet the extraordinary challenges and demands that are before us as a civilization? (Shapiro, 2009)

As well, we must question if lively classrooms in which spontaneity, joy, and creativity which animate the learning process truly stands in the way of a quality education with high standards?

Technocratic education—now and in previous eras—promotes extrinsic motivation for learning, competition, and individualism and "sacrifices both moral and intellectual growth [and]...the inherently social spirit that otherwise moves the child through education...." (Kaplan, 1997, p. 427). Advocates for progressive curriculum transformation note:

> One recurrent theme is that something must be wrong with an education that substitutes knowledge of technology for the understanding of human beings; substitutes inquiry into fragments for the study of nature in its complexity; substitutes efficiency in producing things for caring about living beings; and stresses the importance of competition instead of encouraging cooperation between human beings. (Nordland, 1994, p. 10)

> One looks in vain in the discourse of teaching "excellence" for a concern with education as a potentially powerful vehicle for the renewal of a culture of active and meaningful citizenship; one in which education has a principal role in nurturing the skills, values, and commitments necessary to a culture in which individuals care about, and participate in, the making of a society that is just, compassionate, and free. (Shapiro, 1998, p. 54)

It is this kind of utilitarian education to which Montessori (1949/1972) blamed for causing "the individual to dry up and his spiritual values to wither away. He becomes a cipher, a cog in the blind machine that his environment represents" (p. xiv). Certainly, this orientation creates a bound world in which the status quo is accepted as critical thinking, caring, and interdependence are of no importance. Whether purposefully chosen or unintended consequences of the standardized management paradigm, these distressing outcomes must be understood and challenged.

References

Apple, M. W. (1986). *Teachers and texts*. New York: Routledge.

Apple, M., & King, N. (1983). What do schools teach? In H. Giroux & D. Purpel (Eds.), *The hidden curriculum and moral education* (pp. 82–99). Berkeley, CA: McCutchan.

Arce, J., Luna, D., Borjian, A., & Conrad, M. (2005). No Child Left Behind: Who wins? Who loses? *Social Justice, 32*(3), 56–71.

Beyer, L. E., & Apple., M. W. (1988). *The curriculum: Problems, politics, and possibilities*. Albany: State University of New York Press.

Bracey, G. W. (2003). April foolishness: The 20th anniversary of a Nation at Risk. *Phi Delta Kappan, 84*(8), 616–621.

Crawford, J. (2007). A diminished vision of civil rights: No Child Left Behind and the growing divide in how educational equity is understood. *Education Week, 26*(39), 31–40.

Cuban, L. (1993). *How teachers taught: Constancy and change in American classrooms 1890–1990* (2nd ed.). New York: Teachers College Press.

Darling-Hammond, L. (2007). Evaluating No Child Left Behind. *The Nation, 284*(20), 11–28.

Darling-Hammond, L. (2009). *The flat world and education: How America's commitment to equity will determine our future.* New York: Teachers College Press.

Darling-Hammond, L. (2009/2010). America's commitment to equity will determine our future. *Phi Delta Kappan, 91*(4), 8–14.

Deschenes, S., Cuban, L., & Tyack, D. (2001). Mismatch: Historical perspectives on schools and students who don't fit them. *Teachers College Record, 103*(4), 525–547.

Elementary and Secondary Education Act of 2001 [No Child Left Behind Act], Public Law 107-110. *U.S. Statutes at Large.*

FairTest (2008). Confronting the myths of No Child Left Behind. Retrieved January 15, 2010, from http://www.fairtest.org/confronting-myths-no-child-left-behind

Gabella, M. S. (1993, April). *The unsure thing: Ambiguity and uncertainty as a context for inquiry.* Paper presented at the Annual Meeting of the American Educational Research Association, Atlanta, GA.

Goals 2000: Educate America Act of 1994, Pub. L. No. 103-227, 1-3, 108 Stat. 125 (1994).

Goldin, C., & Katz, L. (1997/2008). Why the United States led on education: Lessons from secondary school expansion, 1910 to 1940, *NBER Working Paper 6144.* Retrieved January 11, 2010, from http://ws1.ad.economics.harvard.edu/faculty/goldin/files/whyusa.pdf

Goodlad, J. (1984). *A place called school.* New York: McGraw-Hill.

Goodman, J., & Kuzmic, J. (1997). Bringing a progressive pedagogy to conventional schools: Theoretical and practical implications from Harmony. *Theory into Practice, 36*(2), 79–86.

Gracey, H. (1975/2004). Learning the student role: Kindergarten as academic boot camp. In J. H. Ballantine & J. Z. Spade (Eds.), *Schools and society: A sociological approach to education* (2nd ed., pp. 144–148). New York: Thomson Wadsworth.

Hargreaves, A., & Shirley, D. (2009). The persistence of presentism. *Teachers College Record, 111*(11), 2505–2534.

Heckman, P. E. (1987). Understanding school culture. In J. Goodlad (Ed.), *The ecology of school renewal: Eighty-sixth yearbook of the National Society for the Study of Education, Part I* (pp. 63–78). Chicago: University of Chicago Press.

Henderson, J. G., & Gornik, R. (2007). *Transformative curriculum leadership* (3rd ed.). Upper Saddle River, NJ: Merrill/Prentice Hall.

Herman, P., & Gomez, L. M. (2009). Taking guided learning theory to school: Reconciling the cognitive, motivational, and social contexts of instruction. In S. Tobias & T. M. Duffy (Eds.), *Constructivist instruction* (pp. 62–81). New York: Routledge.

Heyer, K. D., & Pifel, A. (2007). Extending the responsibilities for schools beyond the school door. *Policy Futures in Education, 5*(4), 567–580.

Hoff, D. J. (2006). Big business going to bat for NCLB. *Education Week, 26*(8), 1, 24.

Johnson, A. P. (2006). No child left behind: Factory models and business paradigms. *Clearing House: A Journal of Educational Strategies, Issues and Ideas, 80*(1), 34–36.

Joseph, P. B. (2001). The ideal teacher: Images in early 20th-century teacher education textbooks. In P. B. Joseph & G. E. Burnaford (Eds.), *Images of schoolteachers in America* (pp. 135–158). Mahwah, NJ: Erlbaum.

Joseph, P. B. (2010). Deskilling. In C. Kridel (Ed.), *Encyclopedia of curriculum studies* (pp. 283–285). Thousand Oaks, CA: Sage.

Kaplan, A. (1997). Work, leisure, and the tasks of schooling. *Curriculum Inquiry, 27,* 423–451.

Kliebard, H. M. (1995). *The struggle for the American curriculum 1893–1958.* New York: Routledge.

Kozol, J. (1997, October 17). Race and class in public education. Address presented at the State University of New York at Albany Transcript available from http://www.alternativeradio.org/programs/KOZJ002.shtml

Lewis, A. C. (2007). Washington commentary: Looking beyond NCLB. *Phi Delta Kappan, 88*(7), 483–484.

Miner, B. (2004/2005). Keeping public schools public: Testing companies mine for gold. *Rethinking Schools, 19*(2). Retrieved January 15, 2010, from http://www.rethinkingschools.org/special_reports/bushplan/test192.shtml

Montessori, M. (1949/1972). *Education and peace.* Chicago: Henry Regenery Company.

National Commission on Excellence in Education. (1983). *A Nation at risk: The imperative for educational reform.* Washington, DC: U. S. Department of Education.

Nehring, J. H. (2007). Conspiracy theory: Lessons for leaders from two centuries of school reform. *Phi Delta Kappan, 88*(6), 424–432.

Neill, M. (2003). Leaving children behind: How No Child Left Behind will fail our children. *Phi Delta Kappan, 85*(3), 225–228.

Nordland, E. (1994). New world-new thinking-new education. In B. Reardon & E. Nordland (Eds.), *Learning peace: The promise of ecological and cooperative education* (pp. 1–20). Albany: State University of New York Press.

Oakes, J., Quartz, K., Ryan, S., & Lipton, M. (2000). *Becoming good American schools: The struggle for civic virtue in educational reform.* San Francisco: Jossey-Bass.

Pinar, W. F. (2004). *What is curriculum theory?* New York: Routledge.

Pinar, W. F., Reynolds, W. M., Slattery, P., & Taubman, P. M. (1995). *Understanding curriculum: An introduction to the study of historical and contemporary curriculum discourses.* New York: Peter Lang.

Portelli, J., & Vilbert, A. (2002/2003). Standards, equity, and the curriculum of life. *Analytic Teaching, 22*(1), 4–19.

Purpel, D. E., & Shapiro, S. (1995). *Beyond liberation and excellence: Reconstructing the public discourse on education.* Westport, CT: Bergin & Garvey.

Ravitch, D. (2010). *The death and life of the great American school system: How testing and choice are undermining education.* New York: Basic Books.

Rothstein, R., & Jacobsen, R. (2006). The goals of education. *Phi Delta Kappan, 88*(4), 264–272.

Sacks, P. (1999). *Standardized minds: The high price of America's testing culture and what we can do to change it.* Cambridge, MA: Perseus Books.

Schwartz, R. B., & Robinson, M. A. (2000). Goals 2000 and the standards movement. In D. Ravitch (Ed.), *Brookings papers on education policy, 2000* (pp. 173–206). Washington, DC: Brookings Institution.

Shapiro, S. (1998). Public school reform: The mismeasure of education. *Tikkun, 13,* 51–55.

Shapiro, S. (2009). A new bottom line in education. *Tikkun.* Retrieved December 30, 2009, from http://www.tikkun.org/article.php/Shapiro-ANewBottomLine

Sirotnik, K. (1983). What you see is what you get: Consistency, persistency, and mediocrity in the classroom. *Harvard Educational Review, 53,* 16–31.

Sleeter, C. E. (2008). Teaching for democracy in an age of corporatocracy. *Teachers College Record, 110*(1), 139–159.

Sobol, T. (1997). Beyond standards: The rest of the agenda. *Teachers College Record, 98*(4), 629–636.

Spring, J. (1997). *The American school 1642–1996* (4th ed.). New York: McGraw-Hill.

Superfine, B. M. (2005). The politics of accountability: The rise and fall of Goals 2000. *American Journal of Education, 112*(1), 10–43.

Symcox, L. (2009). From "A Nation at Risk" to "No Child Left Behind": 25 years of neoliberal reform in education. In J. Andrzejewski, M. Baltodano, & L. Symcox (Eds.), *Social justice, peace, and environmental education: Transformative standards* (pp. 53–65). New York: Routledge.

Taubman, P. (2009). *Teaching by numbers: Deconstructing the discourse of standards and accountability in education.* New York: Routledge.

Tyack, D., & Cuban, L. (1995). *Tinkering toward utopia: A century of public school reform.* Cambridge, MA: Harvard University Press.

Wiebe, R. H. (1967). *The search for order, 1877–1920.* New York: Hill and Wang.

Windschitl, M. (2002). Framing constructivism in practice as the negotiation of dilemmas: An analysis of the conceptual, pedagogical, cultural, and political challenges facing teachers. *Review of Educational Research, 72*(2), 131–175.

Wong, J. L. N. (2006). Control and professional development: Are teachers being deskilled or reskilled within the context of decentralization? *Educational Studies, 32*(1), 17–37.

Chapter 4

Reculturing Curriculum

Pamela Bolotin Joseph, Edward R. Mikel, and Mark A. Windschitl

---

> To restructure is not to reculture.... Changing formal structures is not the same as changing norms, habits, skills, and beliefs.
>
> Michael Fullan, 1993, *Change Forces,* p. 49

In a time of broad cultural and political acceptance of utilitarian goals of education, curriculum transformation cannot come about from superficial and piecemeal changes. To the contrary, it will take shared visions, coherent practices, and commitment to profoundly change the cultures of classrooms and schools. Challenges to the dominant "standardized management paradigm" (Henderson & Gornik, 2007) need to be initiated by educators, families, and communities who understand what is at stake, both educationally and politically, and are ready to engage in serious discourse about revisioning curriculum. In addition to participation in platforms for inquiry, dialogue, and reflection, educators have to be willing to create and enact transformative curriculum in classrooms and schools and work for institutional infrastructures of appropriate resources and support.

Reculturing

To change the prevailing culture of schooling—to reculture curriculum—educators must recognize, challenge, and then profoundly change commonly held assumptions, values, norms, and practices. Reculturing demands more than just partial modifications. Changing school structures, adopting incremental standards, or trying new instructional methods cannot by themselves significantly alter core assumptions about learning and teaching or beliefs about the ultimate aims of schooling. For instance, when a district adopts new textbooks, schools create flexible scheduling, and teachers introduce group work or allow students limited choices of learning activities, these occurrences may change traditional routines leading to substantially different experiences for students, but these events may not bring about significant curriculum transformation. Instead, these efforts may just be "bricolage" or "tinkering" (Huberman, 1995) in which new practices do not disrupt the cultural norms.

To make specific changes in structures of classrooms and schools, even when they enhance learning, is not the same as reculturing curriculum.

The differences between restructuring and reculturing schools are illuminated through the concepts of first and second order change (see Table 4.1; Watzlawick, Weakland, & Fisch, 1974). First order change, often instituted with top-down measures, exists when the norms of the system remain the same. In school reform, first order changes improve the efficiency and effectiveness of what is being done already "without disturbing the basic organizational features, without substantially altering the way that children and adults perform their roles" (Cuban, 1988, p. 342). In second order change—that typically begins when a number of stakeholders feel "dissatisfaction with present arrangements" (Cuban, 1988, p. 342)—norms are challenged and changed. Further, second order change transforms fundamental properties of the system. In school reform, [s]econd-order changes "alter the fundamental ways in which organizations are put together, including new goals, structures, and roles" (Fullan, 1991, p. 29). This comes about as stakeholders "collectively... "shape those ideas into a set of community beliefs" (Suiter, 2009).

In this way, reculturing as second order change transforms fundamental beliefs about all aspects of curriculum and pedagogy by profoundly altering persistent regularities of school practice. Fullan (1993), a leading analyst of educational change, claims that even the best-intentioned, well-resourced, and most highly concentrated efforts cannot succeed in bringing about meaningful change without transforming the culture of schooling. It is the culture of schooling that casts light on the distinctive nature of practices (p. 49). He reminds us: "To restructure is not to reculture...changing formal structures is not the same as changing norms, habits, skills, and beliefs" (p. 49).

Table 4.1   First-Order and Second-Order Change

Characteristics of First-Order Change	*Characteristics of Second-Order Change*
Adjustments within the existing structure	New way of seeing things
Doing more or less of something	Shifting gears
Incremental	Complex
Restoration of balance (homeostasis)	Transformation to something quite different
New learning is not required	Requires new learning
An extension of the past	A break with the past
Within existing paradigms	Challenges prevailing values and norms
Implemented by experts	Implemented by stakeholders

See Bergquist, 1993; Cuban, 1988; Fullan, 1991; Waters, Marzano, & McNulty, 2003; Watzlawick, Weakland, & Fisch, 1974.

Prerequisites for Reculturing

Cycles of school reform have called into question traditional curricula even though these movements seldom have transformed dominant practices (see Tyack & Cuban, 1995). More publicized reform movements such as *A Nation at Risk* or No Child Left Behind have not provided models of curriculum transformation as have grassroots efforts to create inspirational, humane, and progressive classrooms and schools (see Cremin, 1961; Dewey & Dewey, 1915; Goodman & Kuzmic, 1997; Semel & Sadovnik, 1999). We learn far less about reculturing from top-down, one-view reforms than from local experiences of visioning, experimentation, and reflection that reveal reculturing as a complex process involving interrelated elements of reflection, vision, communication, learning communities, systems thinking, and shared leadership.

Historical and contemporary research documents that recultured schools come about through the efforts of people who share similar goals and values and clearly articulate their visions. This process often begins through recognition of common problems (Grant & Murray, 1999, p. 191)—an awareness of the need for change (Heckman, 1993).

> A catalyst is needed to start and sustain school culture change. For significant change—sometimes referred to as "second-order change"...to occur, fundamental questions would be asked regularly about the practices and structures of schools and the beliefs and theories of teachers about these enactments. (Heckman, 1993, p. 266)

Then occurs a cycle of scrutiny and reflection to assess not only the outcomes but the worth of chosen goals in light of new knowledge, research, or changing social conditions. Such reflection may begin in small groups (Giles & Hargreaves, 2006) as well as in more public forums with questioners and dialogue facilitators (Heckman, 1993). Reflection and deliberation are crucial because those who desire change must understand the significance of their actions; therefore, they need "to reflect on, and understand, the broader human and social purposes of what they do and to make decisions about what and how they teach in the light of their commitments to attain these purposes" (Purpel & Shapiro, 1995, p. 110).

Research on reculturing also emphasizes the power of shared visions or beliefs held by teachers, parents, and community members (Giles & Hargreaves, 2006; Selby, 2000; Suiter, 2009; Tyack & Tobin, 1994). A vision cannot be given, transposed, or imposed upon a school (Uhrmacher, 1997) but must be built over time though an ongoing process of conversations, study, and reflection (Wood, 1990). Schools that sustain reculturing "renew their teacher cultures" (Giles & Hargreaves, 2006, p. 152) so that their visions stay fresh, compelling, and continue to be shared. To hold on to their visions, it behooves recultured schools to recruit and hire new teachers and administrators who share their philosophies (Wasserman, 2007). And, when new hires join vision-centered schools, existing staff need to share goals, practices, and institutional memory (Semel & Sadovnik, 2008).

Because of the importance of sharing beliefs and information within schools and with the community, communication is an important element in reculturing. Educators involved in successful reculturing work know the importance of networking—within the school and the larger educational community (Meier, 2009)—and often use technology to provide information about meetings and developments and to engage in discussions (Giles & Hargreaves, 2006, p. 141). But communication can also be quite "low-tech" with small face-to-face meetings, such as lunch roundtables, in which people can share ideas and mobilize for action (Selby, 2000, p. 94). Conversations should take place not only within the school but with the public (Giles & Hargreaves, 2006, p. 141; Tyack & Tobin, 1994, p. 478) particularly about "relationship to the school's efforts and the broader reform vision" (Bezzina, 2006, p. 162).

> Teachers and others are more likely to change existing school regularities when they are encouraged to be mindful, to make explicit the meanings that are the basis for their enactment of particular events and actions in schools and classrooms…. Both understanding one's meaning and making it *public* are critical to significant change, thoughtful action, and efficacy and motivation to act in an environment as complex as a school. (Heckman, 1993, p. 267)

Teachers and administrators together should be prepared to go on record with the school community about why the beliefs and practices associated with progressive curriculum reforms are congruent with the community's vision of education. They also need to explain their vision with a well-founded and coherent rationale that links their understanding of classroom learning to the larger goals of education, especially when it is contrary to historical and cultural norms.

Another commonality in examples of curricular reform is that stakeholders believe that "the school is the center of change" (Bezzina, 2006, p. 160). As such, they are comfortable with the idea that a school can become a place of experimentation and even uncertainty (Gabella, 1995; Giles & Hargreaves, 2006; Grant & Murray, 1999). Schools that reculture develop collaborative learning communities focused on professional development, teaching, learning, and assessment of progress (Bezzina, 2006; Peterson, 2009); such communities develop the capacity to be creative, solve problems, make decisions, and are able to sustain their reform work as well as their professional communities over time (Bezzina, 2006; Giles & Hargreaves, 2006, Semel & Sadovnik, 2008; Wasserman, 2007). Interactions within professional learning communities "are characterized by mutual respect, a sense of fairness and democratic decision-making...." (Grant & Murray, 1999, p. 192) and are models for schools themselves that sustain visionary curriculum and are caring communities (Selby, 2000; Semel & Sadovnik, 2008, Wasserman, 2007). Furthermore, schools support learning communities by providing adequate resources and time for collaboration (Giles & Hargreaves, 2006; Meier, 2009; Selby, 2000).

Moreover, participants in reculturing resist an either/or mentality or believing in hasty fixes—such as published curriculum packages—and instead engage in systems thinking:

> Through "systems thinking," their members would be able to see the "big picture" of their organizations and understand how parts and whole were interrelated and how actions in one domain create consequences in another. They would see the connections between people's personal and interpersonal learning, and how the organization learned collectively, as the key to change and success. (Giles & Hargreaves, 2006, p. 126)

By understanding a systems approach, participants consider the culture of the school and of its teachers (Apple & Beane, 2007, p. 37; Giles & Hargreaves, 2006, p. 141) and appreciate complexity and ambiguity (Apple & Beane, 2007, p. 37; Gabella, 1995, p. 238). With a systems view, they are likely to have a "long view, patience, and persistence" (Apple & Beane, 2007, p. 37) because they know that change is a long and complicated process.

Shared leadership—a principle of systems thinking—also is an important feature within recultured schools. In the fullest sense, shared leadership includes participation by parents, community members, and students (Selby, 2000; Peterson, 2009). In that way "decision making is moved as close as possible to the people responsible for implementation" (Giles & Hargreaves, 2006, p. 141). Principals or heads of schools must foster shared decision making and recognize the importance of teachers' autonomy and their critical leadership role in reculturing (Meier, 2009; Peterson, 2009; Wasserman, 2007). Notwithstanding, administrators are called upon to have a variety of leadership roles, especially as facilitators for and negotiators of shared visions and stewards of these visions (Bezzina, 2006, p. 162). Strong leadership is necessary to "maintain a school's philosophy" and to "forge alliances within and outside their school to help institute change or resist external demands" (Semel & Sadovnik, 2008, p. 1764). Further, administrators need to be involved with planning leadership succession to ensure that school's vision stays alive (Giles & Hargreaves, 2006, p. 152).

Obstacles to Reculturing

Research on school reform points to numerous obstacles that must be overcome to make profound changes to schooling. These hurdles include endorsement of ad hoc curriculum planning, entrenched norms of schooling antagonistic to reculturing, traditional organization of curriculum and school structures that work against creation of learning communities, and difficulties in sustaining curricular transformation.

First, a commonly enacted assumption about schooling is that curriculum need not be based on an overarching vision but can be modified haphazardly in response to a multitude of presumed needs of the community and society. Various other propositions, such as creating benchmarks or curriculum alignment, also shape discussions about school reform, but these initiatives do not communicate clear visions, lead teachers toward their own understanding of congruent practices and aims, or invite critique. Such mandates often create compliance pressures on teachers who feel dominated from above (Hill, 1995). As such, the "teachers' natural response... will be to avoid taking initiative and to concentrate on ways to protect themselves in the fact of bureaucratic scrutiny" (Knapp, 1997, p. 231).

As well, participants in existing school cultures may be fixated on short-term goals such as getting through a unit of instruction, preventing disarray in the classroom, perhaps even "getting more kids involved in learning," but these are not premised on deeper ideals. Even when schools' mission statements appear to be visionary, these ideals may in fact mask real practices that respond primarily to immediate necessities or are driven by a body of incentives and disincentives. It is a cruel irony when schools, in single-minded pursuit of higher test scores, proclaim a mission to prepare students to become citizens and life-long learners but neither provide education for civic engagement nor curriculum based upon learners' curiosity. Current critics describe contemporary traditional schooling as "regimes of accountability, a standardized and packaged curriculum, and a lock-step pedagogy that are combined with a focus on privatization and regulations that hold teachers' and administrators' feet to the fire of competition" (Apple & Beane, 2007, p. 36).

Entrenched patterns of schooling also can be barriers. Research on schooling in the recent past suggests that in school cultures most formative beliefs remain unstated (Heckman, 1987, p. 67) and curriculum is influenced by "folk pedagogies" (Bruner, 1996) that are composed of incoherent, deeply embedded beliefs about what is normal. Therefore, beliefs systems in most schools are difficult to articulate, interrogate, and change and it is difficult to take the first steps toward reculturing because educational practices are rarely subject to critical internal and public reflection beyond those related to efficiency in maintaining the status quo.

As well, when new teachers enter the profession, they deal with an almost unmanageable array of responsibilities and thus tend to rely on a combination of available past images and specific survival techniques to guide their thinking. Cuban (1993) describes this initiation:

> The complicated practices of establishing routines that will induce a group of students to behave in an orderly way while learning subject matter that the teacher is still unfamiliar with, the teacher is driven to use practices that he or she remembers seeing used or that veterans advise using. By taking such advice, entrants absorb through a subtle osmosis, the school's norms and expectations about what it takes to survive as a teacher. The folklore, occupational gimmicks, norms, and daily teaching reinforce existing approaches rather than nourish skepticism. (p. 254)

Furthermore, even experienced teachers may depend upon their memory of their own days as students, putting into action the conservative, familiar images of what is proper, possible, and efficient in a classroom setting (Russell, 1993).

Obstacles to innovation also are found in the norms surrounding the traditional organization of the curriculum. Walled classrooms, set class periods, and discrete academic departments persist because they seem *normal* (part of the folk pedagogy of education) or because they are convenient.

> The basic "grammar" of schooling, like the shape of classrooms, has remained remarkably stable over the decades. By the "grammar" of schooling we mean the regular structures and rules that organize the work of instruction. Here we have in mind, for example, standardized organizational practices in dividing time and space, classifying students and allocating them to classrooms, and splintering knowledge into "subjects." (Tyack & Tobin, 1994, p. 454)

For example, the deeply ingrained norm that schools should be orderly and predictable and that "ambiguity and uncertainty...are rarely welcome" (Gabella, 1995, p. 238) discourages reculturing. The idea of schools as environments of experimentation, as Dewey and others envisioned when they created laboratory schools, goes against the grain of traditional schooling. The prevailing culture of schools also perpetuates itself is through the tendency of conventional educators as well as the public to disdain any kind of curriculum work not part of the status-quo, that seems "abnormal." Even when teachers work together to try innovative curriculum, they may be viewed with suspicion from other colleagues (Giles & Hargreaves, 2006). Moreover, caricatures abound when other alternatives are mentioned (no doubt, reinforced by popular culture): curriculum calling attention to power relationships branded as radical and dangerous; child-centered learning as non-academic, sentimental or indulgent; alternative schools as undisciplined and out of control;

and a vigorous liberal education as elitist. Such caricatures are overly simplistic and certainly not useful in curricular discourse leading to imagining alternatives.

A further way to view the ingrained patterns is to again consider the influence of business that permeates the culture of schooling as "an aesthetic preference for efficient production, which is manifested in schedules, refined tasks, and interchangeable designs...[with] students are used to going from class to class, which may be unrelated in content or method" (Uhrmacher, 1997, p. 75). The segregation of subjects has made genuine curriculum integration rare. Likewise, beliefs about the nature of subject matter or learners discourage curriculum transformation. Examples of curriculum norms include the idea that young children cannot investigate social injustice or that human rights education has no place in mathematics classes; another assumption is that that study of occupations belongs only within vocational classes rather than integrated across the curriculum.

Research on school reform also suggests that challenges to reculturing emanate from persistent institutional conditions that thwart efforts for innovation and limit the possibility for real change. Above all, schools have cultural regularities that inhibit teachers' interactions with peers and other professionals thus limiting reflection about teaching practices and exposure to new ideas (Russell, 1993). Once more, "[w]hen working alone, teachers get used to certain patterns of learning, teaching, assimilating, changing, or retaining the status quo" (Bezzina, p. 164).

> [S]chools are typically characterized by norms of primacy... and isolation.... Teachers participate alone in the structures, activities, events, and materials of classroom enactments and infrequently discus among themselves what they do in their classrooms.... The privacy norm and the structural isolation of teachers prevent the kind of social interaction that can serve as a catalyst for cultural change. (Heckman, 1993, p. 267)

The privacy norm and the structural isolation of teachers prevent the kind of social interaction that can serve as a catalyst for cultural change (Heckman, 1993, p. 267). Especially in times of financial hardship, resources and time for planning may be especially scarce. In the prevailing culture of schooling, teachers have little time and support for taking the first important steps for reculturing— deliberation and reflection.

Political forces outside and within schools also thwart teachers' involvement in curricular transformation. Historically, policy makers have sought to control curriculum and standardize teaching rather than to educate teachers to be sophisticated curriculum planners (Apple, 1982; Rogers, 1999). Granting teachers the authority to create curriculum is often greeted with resistance from political conservatives who fear not only the teacher's autonomy in choosing content but also children's learning of critical thinking skills

(Elliott, 1994). Such conservatives view teachers as technicians—called upon to implement classroom objectives that are tightly controlled and defined by others higher up on the administrative chain of command (Joseph, Mikel, & Windschitl, 2002). Moreover, top-down imposition of curriculum impedes curriculum reform because it excludes teachers and the community from the change process (Peterson, 2009) and is the antithesis to the prerequisites for reculturing:

> Successful and sustainable school change, Fullan (1997) suggests, requires coherence, integration, diversity, continuous skills development, the creation of collaborative work cultures, multiple foci of change with multi-directional communication flows across the school and community, and a broadening of the leadership net to include as many teachers, parents, and students as possible. The role of external change agents is not to represent "one more project" but to interrelate with "the total reform agenda of the school." (Selby, 2000, p. 91)

Researchers also "have noted the tendency for large-scale reform to displace locally initiated innovation" (Giles & Hargreaves, 2006, p. 125) with the standardized testing movement being particularly deadly to recultured schools (Giles & Hargreaves, 2006; Semel & Sadovnik, 2008).

Especially sobering to those of us who hope for curricular transformation is the challenge of sustaining it. Historian David Tyack writes, "The notion that reforms in instruction should be or can be permanent ignores historical experience...." (1990, p. 187).

> No magic wand of restructuring can set things permanently straight. We will always have waves of education reform that seek to alter the substantial structures we have built, for values differ, interests conflict, generational perspectives change. For the last century Americans have been constantly tinkering toward utopia in school reform. It has been our way of creating the future that we want. (Tyack, 1990, p. 188)

This "weak record of sustainability of innovative schools over time"—"a well-documented tendency to fade after an initial 'golden age'" and "to rejoin the mainstream and soon look like any other school or to vanish altogether" (Giles & Hargreaves, 2006, p. 125)—stems from a variety of reasons that cast light on the complexity of reculturing and the frailty of human efforts.

Curriculum transformation often begins with a catalyst—one or more inspirational leaders who facilitate the inquiry, deliberation, and reflection needed for reculturing. Yet, when such leaders are charismatic, people may seem to support them, but may not really be on board and committed to the vision of change (Semel & Sadovnik, 2008). It can also be the case that leaders may not adequately bring in the community to support the vision and/or become "embroiled in community controversy and strife" (Giles & Hargreaves, 2006, p. 125) especially when fundamental reforms "violated the public's notions of a 'real school'" (Tyack & Tobin, p. 477). Innovators have failed to get genuine acceptance of visions from their colleagues in schools or, afterwards, did not take the time to orient new teachers into the school's values "to attempt to transfer the culture of the school [and] to re-establish the commitment to each other as a community with shared values" (Suiter, 2009). In short, sometimes innovators "lack of political savvy" (Tyack & Tobin, 1994, p. 477) and knowledge of systematic change. And, perhaps despite their utmost efforts, innovators may not be able to overcome the enormity of the political issues involved in reculturing, for example, lack of support and even "animosity" from colleagues who did not share the vision or who resented innovations for fear of displacement of existing resources (Giles & Hargreaves, 2006, p. 125).

But even when reculturing truly engages stakeholders and curricular transformation takes place, the issue of leadership still can be a problematic. When strong leaders move on, reculturing work can dwindle or collapse— unless tremendous care has been expended to find successors with strong leadership skills and commitment to the vision agreed upon by the school and community (Apple & Beane, 2007, p. 38; Grant & Murray, 1999; Giles & Hargreaves, 2006).

A final obstacle to sustaining transformation relates to the sheer effort it requires from participants. Above and beyond the work of teaching, educators who become immersed in reculturing must take the time for deliberation and conversations, become educated in best practices to support visions, share ideas with colleagues and the community, network with other educators and organizations, and continually reflect on aims and practices. Knowledge of the process of reculturing means working against becoming "insulated from alternative ideas" by fostering self-inquiry and professional knowledge (Giles & Hargreaves, 2006, p. 127). And too often all these activities must be undertaken within a context generally unsupportive of curricular transformation and teacher leadership. Therefore one crucial factor has been "turnover and burnout" as altering "basic organizational patterns created considerable cognitive and emotional strain" (Tyack & Tobin, 1994, p. 478).

Nevertheless, as it is idealistic to expect reculturing to be an easy and everlasting process or naive to underestimate the power of the status-quo order to maintain itself, it also is unrealistic to believe that curriculum transformation is impossible. Research on school reform suggests that "innovative schools seem to possess a predictable, evolutionary life span of creativity and experimentation, overreaching and entropy, and survival and continuity" (Giles & Hargreaves, 2006, p. 125). That is why it is necessary for reformers to have a "patience, persistence, and a long view" (Apple & Beane, 2007, p. 38) and reject the notion of quick fixes. Reculturing is not doomed to fail, especially when former habits change, new norms take hold (Grant & Murray, 1999), and new identities are formed (Joseph et al., 2002).

Curriculum Leadership and Reculturing

To bring about curriculum transformation, educators must become curriculum leaders. Teachers and administrators need to envision progressive, humane, and ethical curriculum and imagine themselves in new identities as powerful and dedicated creators of it. Within a clear vision of recultured curriculum, educators thus articulate the framing ideals, standards, and organizing categories, bring together ideas and desires, and catalyze various initiatives to attain their vision. As educators attempt to cross the long terrain, their leadership continuously emerges in response to the challenges they encounter and the struggles they undertake to reconstitute curriculum and renew themselves as practitioners. The outcome, therefore, is that educators will possess new identities in their characteristic roles, and hold a dramatically changed orientation to study, understanding, development, interaction and regard for one another and their students.

The first step toward curriculum leadership is engaging in curriculum inquiry to gain deep understanding of the norms, patterns, structures that obstruct as well make curriculum transformation possible. Essentially, this means making known familiar discourses, forces, structures, and hierarchies that remain unquestioned (Bowers, 2010; Greene, 1978):

> Change in the culture of school requires examination and alteration of both thought and action in the context of the school.... All of the teachers, principal, and other staff members—examine what already exists and explore alternative explanations, meanings, and actions.... By promoting reflection in action—questioning everything and trying out many ideas in thought and action—culture is less likely to invisibly determine what goes on in school. (Heckman, 1993, p. 270)

Naming of structures and forces must lead to problem posing to understand the agendas for schools held by outside forces and to "transcend a belief that the system of schooling is neutral" and gain "a historic sense of the roots of antidemocratic trends in curriculum" (Wood, 1990, pp. 101–102, 107). It is such scrutiny and attention that Maxine Greene (1978) encouraged when she implored educators to shake off "indifference, a lack of care, an absence of concern" (p. 43) and "to make sense of what is happening…to be autonomous (p. 44). It is by becoming "wide awake" can educators "develop the sense of agency required for living a moral life" (p. 44).

The practice and habit of inquiry is part of the identity of educators as "transformative intellectuals" (Giroux, 1985/2010). For some educators, this becomes an essential change of self-understanding, moving away from conceiving solely as oneself as a technician, skills-developer, or knowledge imparter.

> If we believe that the role of teaching cannot be reduced to merely train-
> ing in the practical skills, but involves instead, the education of a class of
> intellectuals vital to the development of a free society, then the category
> of intellectual becomes a way of linking the purpose of teacher education,
> public schooling and inservice training to the very principles necessary
> for developing a democratic order and society.
>
> I have argued that by viewing teachers as intellectuals those persons
> concerned with education can begin to rethink and reform the traditions
> and conditions that have prevented schools and teachers from assuming
> their full potential as active, reflective scholars and practitioners. (Gir-
> oux, 1985/2010, p. 202)

Others have characterized identities of such educators as "curriculum workers" who are "public moral intellectuals who work within an embryonic
democracy unafraid of stirring controversy, stimulating critical analysis,
challenging orthodoxy, pursuing collaboration, and searching for consensus"
(Sears, 2004, p. 8). These identities include both intellect and agency for progressive educational reform.

Becoming a curriculum leader itself calls for a significant leap of faith to a
recast identity and professional orientation—and thus emergent curriculum
leadership has its existential side. When educators seek to institute the new
meaning systems of recultured curriculum, they must embrace the new identities and orientations—always coming to moments in which personal histories and professional careers are in existential balance. As such, curriculum
workers face moments when the risk and unfamiliarity and exhilaration of
reaching for possibilities of profound change—interim steps toward their ultimate vision—hover around the decision to engage lightly, heavily, or not at all
in curriculum transformation.

Moreover, as curriculum workers acquire a new vision of curriculum and
bring themselves to reach for the uncertain, they must continue to develop a
practical capability to enact suitably recultured curriculum in their own classrooms both to develop expertise and to provide models of transformation.
These efforts would necessarily entail at least some significant connections
to the world beyond the classroom, drawing upon informational and classroom-based resources, people and contacts, collaboration with parents and
the community, professional networks and programs, colleagues within the
school, support from administrators, and advice from specialists. We cannot
underestimate or undervalue teachers having recultured curricular content
and best practices in hand—and this can only come from carefully directed
professional learning grounded closely in a plan for changing curriculum. Nor
can we underestimate the importance of working strategically and politically
to change the larger school context—the infrastructure of the institutional
school—as the vehicle toward establishing the larger conditions for a recultured classroom curriculum.

In their continually emerging leadership, curriculum workers give themselves over to a steadily deepening commitment to what a good education and worthy curriculum would mean in the lives of students now and in the future—to moral concerns for the lives of their own students. A later and broader focus of this concern for human well-being is turned to the lives of students more generally, a more ethical sociopolitical focus that expands outward from the classroom to more distant school locales. The evolving commitment of emerging teacher leadership for recultured curriculum and schooling provides the fire for engagement that sustains teachers and renews them along the way (Joseph et al., 2002)—allowing for professional careers of integrity rather than cynicism and regret (Huberman, 1993).

Curricular Cultures

We propose that the concept of curricular cultures can be useful to understanding the process of reculturing and to help curriculum workers to change their own practices and curriculum in their schools. We previously defined a culture of curriculum as a coherent set of aims and practices that can be articulated by all stakeholders including learners, educators, and families. Curricular cultures should not be perceived as static, but as dynamic or evolving because belief systems are acted upon by historical events, societal change, scholarly discoveries, and transformative moral discourse. We do not suggest that the cultures of curriculum we describe are infinite or universal but rather are representatives of curricular orientations present in particular times and places.

When a culture of curriculum exists, the learning experience reflects a rationale with intention and purpose. A thoughtful body of beliefs, then, serves to cohere what would otherwise be a succession of classroom activities with little integrity. In ordinary cultures of classrooms and schools, a distinct and meaningful vision is not required. All classrooms and schools reveal cultures in the sense of having norms, values, beliefs, practices, stories, and power relationships. In contrast, ordinary classroom and school cultures lack unifying visions that characterize what we call curricular cultures. Once more, a culture of curriculum is different from a real culture in that it makes its beliefs and aims explicit, open to scrutiny and evaluation.

Curricular Cultures for Inquiry

We believe that using a framework for naming a curricular culture provides a lens for self-scrutiny and for systematic inquiry to change consciousness about the curriculum field and the curriculum manifest in classrooms (see Table 4.2). Studying the curriculum in one's classroom and school allows for questioning: Is there is a vision or visions that guide curriculum work? Are there shared beliefs about how children learn and what are learners' needs?

Table 4.2 Investigating Curriculum

Focus	Explanation	What are the existing beliefs and norms in classrooms and schools?
Visions	Ultimate purposes of education	
Students	Students' needs and how they learn	
Teachers	Role of teachers	
Context	Subject matter and its organization	
Context	Environment of the classroom and school	
Planning	How curriculum should be planned and who should be involved	
Evaluation	How students should be assessed and curriculum evaluated	

And, what should be the role of teachers? Such investigation also highlights contradictory beliefs as well as mismatches of visions and practices such as disparities between school mission and practices, or conversely, practices that support goals. Educators may believe that they hold similar values about what they want students to learn, yet they may hold very different visions—even when supposedly teaching similar curricula.

This heuristic also allows educators and the community to scrutinize purposes and practices around specific curricula. As an illustration, multicultural curriculum represents a cacophony of content, practices, and goals depending upon its enactment within a curricular culture; it prepares students for a workplace that includes colleagues of other ethnic backgrounds and prepares for competition in a global market or it encourages learning from others' perspectives, appreciation for one's own cultural identity, preservation of cultural traditions, as well as the development of critical perspectives to understand and confront racism. So, too, cooperative learning can be identified with several curricular orientations; it has been adopted in some classrooms because it encourages cooperation for the workplace, in other classrooms because it facilitates the construction of knowledge, and in others because it fosters democratic decision-making or draws out students' voices to create dialogue with others. Another example is the use of technology in classrooms as it can be a tool for business, provide access to cultural knowledge, enable self-directed learning, facilitate communication with others, and be a powerful medium for social action. These examples show the need for curriculum inquiry to explore what are teachers' purposes and what meanings have students constructed. In this way, the curricular cultures framework permits a deeper understanding of lived curriculum (Aoki, 1991).

We also suggest that a framework for curricular cultures can guide individuals and groups when they contemplate their aims and means of accomplishing them. We believe that individuals need to name their visions and assumptions, look for irreconcilable conflicts that would make it impossible for them to "do it all," and eventually to characterize the culture of curriculum that best describes their beliefs and values.

We encourage reflection about visions and practices to begin in teacher education and to be revisited by individuals throughout their careers. Inquiry and reflection about curriculum work should become habitual, so individuals stay attuned to their moral purposes for becoming teachers by continually asking themselves if they are working to realize their ideals. Further, such inquiry in collaboration with families and communities can be very powerful, especially as an impetus for reculturing.

We are not suggesting, however, that naming one's culture of curriculum should be the only goal. A chosen curricular culture must be held up to scrutiny. Individuals must recurrently engage in critique, questioning if their visions, assumptions, and practices reflect naiveté or conclusions based on research and evaluation. Have they, for example, learned from students what curriculum has meaning, or, have they questioned if the environment of the classroom and school as well as instructional practices support their goals? Scrutiny means a constant examination of visions and practice and the articulation of the relationship between them. Accordingly, all cultures of curriculum need to be revisiting periodically to assess their timeliness and vitality.

The framework of curricular cultures can be starting point for dialogue with colleagues and community members for eliciting visions and beliefs as they initiate curriculum changes or develop alternative schools (see Table 4.3). We can imagine a forum in which people sit in a circle and share their visions for the purposes of education or their beliefs about how students learn best. Or, a facilitator could start with a beliefs or visions, asking participants to (literally) take a stand of support or opposition along a line—illustrating a continuum—drawn on the floor.

The discussion would continue so that people could further understand the nature of their beliefs about curriculum and articulate their values. The participants who focus only on the short-term goals of instruction would be urged to imagine the political, social, and moral consequences of education; those who think broadly of education leading to changing or sustaining a particular social vision must be encouraged to deal with pedagogy. Through a more articulated framework, participants then could work to understand not only what culture best describes their understanding of curriculum, but how their positions are similar and different from others. Because curricular cultures are not isolates, participants may discover shared social visions but see

Table 4.3 Beginning a Curricular Conversation

Focus	Explanation	What are your beliefs?	How should these beliefs be reflected in practice?
Visions	Ultimate purposes of education		
Students	Students' needs and how they learn		
Teachers	Role of teachers		
Context	Subject matter and its organization		
Context	Environment of the classroom and school		
Planning	How curriculum should be planned and who should be involved		
Evaluation	How students should be assessed and curriculum evaluated		

different pedagogical means for attaining their visions. Or, they may agree about instruction, but assume very different social and political ends.

We anticipate several possible outcomes of such dialogue. Articulation of beliefs may inspire conversations about pedagogical goals and practices as well as political, moral, and social issues. Those of like mind may begin planning how they can create an environment to support their goals. It may be possible, too, that people who have not talked to each other before, or who have assumed that there are substantial differences among them, could discover what assumptions and visions they might hold in common—a good starting point for further conversations and collaboration. We imagine that even dissonance would produce insight as people learn from each other, are challenged, and develop clearer and perhaps modified articulations of their beliefs.

The danger, of course, is that these conversations may produce disturbing discord in which participants find that they have drastically different goals; lines may be drawn in which people learn that some of their positions cannot be compromised and a community or school would be faced with the dilemmas of how to accommodate conflicting visions. But, in the long run, vigorous public discourse about meaningful pedagogical, social, and moral issues would challenge the prevailing culture of "business as usual" in which beliefs and practices go unexamined. Further, such conversations around school reform "is also a prime arena for debating the shape of the future of society. Such debate is a broad civil and moral enterprise in which all citizens are stake-holders" (Tyack & Cuban, 1995, p. 136).

Curricular Cultures in Classrooms and Schools

We believe that it is a mistake to try to create a hasty amalgam of curricular cultures. If educators try to be all things to all learners, promising a potpourri of outcomes from all classroom cultures, the effort is likely to result in a morass of incongruous educational practices. When content and learning activities are used for a multiple but unrelated purposes, they contribute to an ad hoc curriculum that has little significance to learners or teachers.

We see advantages in having the same classroom culture consistently present across the classes of a learner's school day. A culture of curriculum would have a great impact on the lives of students if its beliefs and practices were consistently present across the range of school subjects and sustained throughout the educational career of the learner. For students trying to participate functionally in several different cultures in a single school day, there is little continuity across subjects, and, over years of schooling, they cannot clearly envision the goals of learning. Undoubtedly, a school community devoted to the same vision and working to create and maintain congruent practices would produce far less dissonance for learners and teachers. Additionally, community members and parents could clearly understand the school's educational mission.

If this culture continues over a student's school career, its subtle but powerful belief system will exert its distinctive influence. Learners then will come to have certain expectations of themselves and their teachers and shared understanding of the nature of knowledge, schooling, and the community. Only after students experience prolonged engagements in these curricular cultures will they internalize notions of what learning is good for, who has authoritative knowledge, or what the relationship should be between students and teacher. Clearly, many of the same issues about the benefits of a single coherent culture in the classroom pertain to the question about a unified, schoolwide approach to curriculum.

We realize that some practices fundamental to one curricular culture may hardly seem feasible to incorporate into another. For instance, a teacher in a child-centered classroom would not create a critical pedagogy culture unless students chose to shape their education toward social action. Students learning in an indigenous language and culture program would not be likely to make sense out of curriculum intended to focus on occupational study linked to academic disciplines—unless such study focused on the history and culture of their people. Similarly, a constructivist approach to learning traditional wisdom may result in a group of students who have such different constructions of the canon that any sense of a common body of knowledge is lost amidst a sea of personal interpretations.

Notwithstanding, we have seen how educators create hybrids because they believe that commingling elements of different curricular cultures meet a community's needs. A historical example is New York City's Central Park East

High School that developed thematic curriculum relating to critical inquiry in a core humanities curriculum and also fostered emergent curriculum stemming from students' interests (see Meier, 1991, Wood, 1992/1993). In Washington State, the Tulalip Indian Tribal School had developed a curriculum incorporating native language and Montessori constructivist methods. Currently, educators at the Native American Community Academy in Albuquerque, New Mexico, teach from a hybrid curriculum model based on holistic education emphasizing wellness as well as knowledge of indigenous language and culture. In fact, Montessori education exemplifies a hybrid of three curricular orientations described in this book: constructivist, child-centered, and peace education.

The above examples prompt questions: When we integrate two or more curricular cultures, which elements of one culture can be meaningfully transposed into the other? As long as beliefs from two curricular cultures are neither contradictory nor preemptive, it seems reasonable that they are, to a degree, transposable from one culture to another. A good deal of reflection and planning would be necessary to understand which components would be in harmony, which would be incompatible, and overall, what would be lost by attempting a hybridization. Or, we can create composites knowing that we will have to work with inherent tensions, for example, investigating themes about power relationships when studying the canon or negotiating a democratic as well as child-centered curriculum.

Whether or not it is desirable for a student to experience total immersion in only one curricular culture is open to debate. We can conceive of some scenarios for several curricular cultures coexisting within a school, but these would arise from *deliberated* design, not because of short-term goals or ad hoc-ness. For instance, a school community may be concerned that a singular vision held by all would not generate healthy challenges to beliefs and practices. The school staff could create a laboratory setting by trying out several curricular cultures in different classrooms—creating an intellectual climate of inquiry for research and evaluation. In such a situation, visions and practices would have to be made explicit; students and teachers would study their experiences of living with several curricular cultures. A school might also create a sequential plan, based upon perceived needs of children and adolescents, to expose learners developmentally to different cultures for several years at a time, perhaps a child-centered primary education, a democratic middle school, and a critical culture for high school.

Ultimately, as an expression of reculturing, no curricular culture can exist where the institutional structure of a school is incongruent with its vision, beliefs, practices, activities, and values. Coherent, articulated curriculum cannot arise without some measure of deliberate change from the current culture of schooling. Thus, curriculum that challenges the status quo obligates its adherents to strive through coalitions, platforms, and policy against the givens of the school as a non-visionary set of short-term goals and institutional practices.

The Nature of Vision

The benefit of creating a curricular culture lies in the power of a clear, publicly conscious, and unifying vision that guides the articulation of goals, brings together ideas and desires, and becomes the catalyst for change. It is vision that propels successful curricular change and separates schools with transformative curriculum from schools with status-quo cultures (Grant & Murray, 1999; Henderson & Gornik, 2007; Semel & Sadovnik, 2008). For instance, researchers depict vision as a core component of school culture, as a "goal-consensus" grounded in the daily interactions of school participants (Staessens & Vandenberghe, 1994). Individual classrooms, likewise, can assume a distinctive culture with a vision conveying the overarching general sense of what sets this culture apart. Its participants would hold an associated stock of images of exemplary practices underpinned by their defining beliefs and values. Such goal consensus has a cognitive dimension, representing a rationality of articulated aims and conscious consensus. But, vision also "creates coherence" and has a "cathectic" dimension; the school culture becomes invested with emotional and intellectual energy (Staessens & Vandenberghe, 1994, pp. 192, 188).

But having a vision and shared beliefs about the purpose of education certainly is not the whole story. Westheimer (1998) writes that "many researchers and reformers maintain that what is important [for transforming schooling] is that beliefs are shared" yet he doubts that analysts of restructuring care "whether the beliefs that are shared are worth sharing." He asks us to consider "what kind of world should we strive for?"—insisting that we must look hard at school cultures to see if "marginalized voices are heard" and if they "reflect ideals of participatory and egalitarian communities" (pp. 139, 142). Similarly, Wood (1990) cautions that "talk about empowering teachers as curriculum workers needs to be rethought. To empower teachers is not enough. We must ask to what end, to what shared agenda?" (p. 107). We also believe that purposes and beliefs do matter and that curriculum transformation is not a value-free phenomenon. Another way to think about the value basis of education is to consider Eli Weisel's comments about the education of the Holocaust perpetrators that apparently omitted consideration of "understanding of human beings, the study of nature, caring about living beings, and cooperation among human beings" (Nordland, 1994, p. 10).

There are many paths possible for the reculturing of curriculum such as helping students to see themselves as intelligent change-makers (Christiensen, 2009), participants in democratic society (Parker, 2005), and activists who know how to resist environmental degradation and violence to cultures

(Bowers, 2004). These visions for students parallel what we believe must be a crucial aim of reculturing: to foster classroom and school cultures in which overarching ethical questions are asked and their answers pondered. "At it's core, morality concerns the questions: How should we live?" (Snauwaert, 2008, p. 68).

> To educate a human being is not merely to make one a knowledgeable, productive members of society (transmission) or an active, engaged citizen (transaction), but also to help each person discover the deeper meaning of his or her life. Who are we? Why are we on earth? What is our relationship to other living beings, and to the evolution of the cosmos itself?... Education should be practiced in such a way as to encourage young people to pursue this understanding; essentially, this starts with teaching a reverence for life. (Miller, 2000, pp. 4–5)

Consequently, how do we educate children to become ethical and caring human beings? Reculturing curriculum means to create environments for helping students to develop as human beings and not just as workers, test-takers, or technicians; all conceptualizations of reculturing involve meaning making so that children and adolescents make sense of their world, respect all of life, and develop their moral selves. The view that a child has the right to an education that will develop a sense of moral and social responsibility has been a long-standing principle, articulated by Dewey (1897) at the end of the 19th century and proclaimed in the United Nation's *Declaration of the Rights of the Child* (UNICEF, 1959). Such understanding of curriculum may be transformative but it is hardly revolutionary.

As follows, it is crucial to name an ethical vision for curriculum, to use it as a guide and as a beacon for new attainments. Vision is far-reaching in nature, emanating from the heart of the culture, giving significance to everything it encompasses. Vision is shared with passion by all participants, taking its shape and central place by being forged in a myriad of efforts over a long period of time. Finally, vision forces us to scrutinize the culture of curriculum, the culture of the school and classroom that we create—continually moving us to work toward its actualization, constantly reminding us to compare the real with the ideal.

References

Aoki, T. T. (1991). *Inspiriting curriculum and pedagogy: Talks to teachers*. Edmonton, AB: Faculty of Education, Department of Secondary Education, University of Alberta.

Apple, M. (1982). *Education and power*. London: Routledge & Kegan Paul.

Apple, M. W., & Beane, J. A. (2007). Schooling for democracy. *Principal Leadership*, 8(2), 34–38.

Bergquist, W. (1993). *The modern organization: Mastering the art of irreversible change.* San Francisco: Jossey-Bass.

Bezzina, C. (2006). "The Road Less Traveled": Professional communities in secondary schools. *Theory Into Practice, 45*(2), 159–167.

Bowers, C. A. (2004). Revitalizing the commons or an individualized approach to planetary citizenship: The choice before us. *Educational Studies, 36,* 45–58.

Bowers, C. A. (2010). Understanding the connections between double bind thinking and the ecological crises: Implications for educational reform. *Journal of the American Association for the Advancement of Curriculum Studies, 6.* Retrieved March 10, 2010, from http://www.uwstout.edu/soe/jaaacs/vol6/Bowers.htm

Bruner, J. (1996). *The culture of education.* Cambridge MA: Harvard University Press.

Christiensen, L. (2009). Teaching for joy and justice. *Rethinking Schools, 23*(4). Retrieved March 26, 2010, from http://www.rethinkingschools.org/archive/23_04/joy234.shtml

Cremin, L. A. (1961). *The transformation of the school: Progressivism in American education, 1876-1957.* New York: Knopf.

Cuban, L. (1988). A fundamental puzzle of school reform. *Phi Delta Kappan, 69*(5), 340–344.

Cuban, L. (1993). *How teachers taught: Constancy and change in American classrooms 1890-1990* (2nd ed.). New York: Teachers College Press.

Dewey, J. (1897). My pedagogic creed. *School Journal, 54,* 77–80.

Dewey, J., & Dewey, E. (1915). *Schools of tomorrow.* New York: E. P. Dutton.

Elliott, B. (1994). Education, modernity and neo-conservative school reform in Canada, Britain, and the US. *British Journal of Sociology of Education, 15,* 165–185.

Fullan, M. (1991). *The meaning of educational change* (2nd ed.). New York: Teachers College Press.

Fullan, M. (1993). *Change forces: Probing the depths of educational reform.* New York: Falmer.

Gabella, M. S. (1995). Unlearning certainty: Toward a culture of student inquiry. *Theory Into Practice, 34*(4), 236–242.

Giles, C., & Hargreaves, A. (2006). The sustainability of innovative schools as learning organizations and professional learning communities during standardized reform. *Educational Administration Quarterly, 42*(1), 124–156.

Giroux, H. (1985/2010). Teacher as transformative intellectuals. In A. Canestrari & B. Marlow (Eds.), *Education foundations: An anthology of critical readings* (pp. 197–204). Thousand Oaks, CA: Sage.

Goodman, J., & Kuzmic, J. (1997). Bringing a progressive pedagogy to conventional schools: Theoretical and practical implications from Harmony. *Theory into Practice, 36*(2), 79–86.

Grant, G., & Murray, C. E. (1999). *Teaching in America: The slow revolution.* Cambridge, MA: Harvard University Press.

Greene, M. (1978). *Landscapes of learning.* New York: Teachers College Press.

Heckman, P. E. (1987). Understanding school culture. In J. Goodlad (Ed.), *The ecology of school renewal: Eighty-sixth yearbook of the National Society for the Study of Education, Part* I (pp. 63–78). Chicago: University of Chicago Press.

Heckman, P. E. (1993). School restructuring in practice: Reckoning with the culture of school. *International Journal of Educational Reform, 2*(3), 263–272.

Henderson, J. G., & Gornik, R. (2007). *Transformative curriculum leadership* (3rd ed.). New York: Prentice Hall.

Hill, P. T. (1995). *Reinventing public education*. Santa Monica, CA: RAND Corporation, Institute on Education and Training.

Huberman, M. (1993). The model of an independent artisan in teachers' professional relations. In J. Little & M. McLaughlin (Eds.), *Teachers' work* (pp. 11–50). New York: Teachers College Press.

Huberman, M. (1995). Networks that alter teaching: Conceptualizations, exchanges and experiments. *Teachers and Teaching: Theory and Practice, 1*(2), 193–211.

Joseph, P. B., Mikel, E., & Windschitl, M. (2002, April 2). *Reculturing curriculum: The struggle for curriculum leadership*. Paper presented at the annual meeting of the American Educational Research Association. New Orleans, LA.

Knapp, M. (1997). Between systemic reforms and the mathematics and science classroom: The dynamics of innovation, implementation, and professional learning. *Review of Educational Research, 67,* 227–266.

Meier, D. (1991). The kindergarten tradition in the high school. In K. Jervis & C. Montag (Eds.), *Progressive education for the 1990s: Transforming practice* (pp. 135–148). New York: Teachers College Press.

Meier, D. (2009). Reinventing schools that keep teachers in teaching. *Rethinking Schools, 23*(3). Retrieved March 26, 2010, from http://www.rethinkingschools.org/archive/23_03/rein233.shtml

Miller, R. (2000). Philosophies of learning communities. In *A coalition for self learning, creating learning communities*. Retrieved January 24, 2010, from http://www.creatinglearningcommunities.org/book/roots/miller4.htm

Nordland, E. (1994). New world-new thinking — New education. In B. Reardon & E. Nordland (Eds.), *Learning peace: The promise of ecological and cooperative education* (pp. 1–20). Albany: State University of New York Press.

Parker, W. C. (2005), Teaching against idiocy. *Phi Delta Kappan, 86*(5), 344–351.

Peterson, B. (2009). Big city superintendents: Dictatorship or democracy? Lessons from Paulo Freire. *Rethinking Schools, 24*(1), 20–25.

Purpel, D. E., & Shapiro, S. (1995). *Beyond liberation and excellence: Reconstructing the public discourse on education*. Westport, CT: Bergin & Garvey.

Rogers, B. (1999). Conflicting approaches to curriculum: Recognizing how fundamental beliefs can sustain or sabotage school reform. *Peabody Journal of Education, 74*(1), 29–67.

Russell, T. (1993). Learning to teach science: Constructivism, reflection, and learning from experience. In K. Tobin (Ed.), *The practice of constructivism in science education* (pp. 247–258). Hillsdale, NJ: Erlbaum.

Sears, J. T. (2004). The curriculum worker as a public moral intellectual. In R. A. Gaztambide-Fernandez & J. T. Sears (Eds.), *Curriculum work as a public moral enterprise* (pp. 1–13). Lanham, MD: Rowman & Littlefield.

Selby, D. (2000). A darker shade of green: The importance of ecological thinking in global education and school reform. *Theory into Practice, 39*(2), 88–96.

Semel, S. F., & Sadovnik, A. R. (1999). *"Schools of tomorrow," schools of today:* What happened to progressive education. New York: Peter Lang.

Semel, S. F., & Sadovnik, A. R. (2008) The contemporary small school movement: Lessons from the history of progressive education. *Teachers College Record, 110*(9), 1774–1771.

Snauwaert, D. (2008). The moral and spiritual foundations of peace education. In M. Bajaj (Ed.), *Encyclopedia of peace education* (pp. 67–73). Charlotte, NC: Information Age.

Staessens, K., & Vandenberghe, R. (1994). Vision as a core component in school culture. *Journal of Curriculum Studies, 26*(2), 187–200.

Suiter, D. (2009). Sustaining change: The struggle to maintain identity at Central Park East Secondary School. *Horace, 25* (2 & 3). Retrieved March 22, 2010, from http://www.essentialschools.org/cs/resources/view/ces_res/636

Tyack, D. (1990). "Restructuring" in historical perspective: Tinkering toward utopia. *Teachers College Record, 92*(2), 170–191.

Tyack, D., & Cuban, L. (1995). *Tinkering toward utopia.* Cambridge, MA: Harvard University Press.

Tyack, D., & Tobin, W. (1994). The "grammar" of schooling: Why has it been so hard to change? *American Educational Research Journal, 31*(3), 453–479.

Uhrmacher, P. B. (1997). Evaluating change: Strategies for borrowing from alternative education. *Theory into Practice, 36*(2), 71–78.

UNICEF. (1959). Convention on the Rights of the Child. Retrieved April 9, 2010, from http://www.unicef.org/crc/

Wasserman, S. (2007). Dare to be different, *Phi Delta Kappan, 88*(5), 384–390.

Waters, T., Marzano, R. J., & McNulty, B. (2003). *Balanced Leadership: What 30 years of research tells us about the effect of leadership on student achievement.* Aurora: CO: Mid-Continent Research for Education and Learning.

Watzlawick, P. Weakland, J. H., & Fisch, R. (1974). *Change: Principles of problem formation and problem resolution.* New York: Norton.

Westheimer, J. (1998). *Among schoolteachers: Community, autonomy, and ideology in teachers' work.* New York: Teachers College Press.

Wood, G. H. (1990). Teachers as curriculum workers. In J. T. Sears & J. D. Marshall (Eds.), *Teaching and thinking about curriculum: Critical inquiries* (pp. 97–109). New York Teachers College Press.

Wood, G. H. (1992/1993). *Schools that work: America's most innovative public education programs.* New York: Dutton.

Part II

Curricular Cultures

Chapter 5

Constructing Understanding

Mark A. Windschitl

> If we cannot make these new connections for ourselves, we do not really grasp
> what we have been told...
>
> Eleanor Duckworth, 1996, *The Having of Wonderful Ideas,* p. 18

Ms. Garcia's sixth-grade classroom is a noisy place, and if you come to visit, she is often hard to find. Today, students are clustered in small groups, bent over note cards and diagrams they have assembled in order to determine whether Australian dingoes can co-habitate with marmosets—and just how much it will cost to feature Australian mammals rather than North American mammals. Ms. Garcia conferences with a group of student in a corner of the room, encouraging them to consider what would happen if they include carnivores in their plans.

It is mid-year and the students have just participated in 3 days of discussion and readings about interrelationships among mammals. Ms. Garcia has negotiated with each of four student groups (as she has done several times earlier in the year) about their work with a complex problem reflecting the students' interests and abilities. One group chose a design problem: create a habitat for a local zoo that will support at least three kinds of mammals naturally found in the same geographic area. After the students decided on this problem, Ms. Garcia led the group in two brief brainstorming sessions. The first session concerned the possibilities and constraints of building such habitats and the second session was to come to consensus on what the criteria should be for a successfully designed habitat. Among other conditions, students decided that the habitats should be economical to maintain, should not be cruel to animals, and should be as self-sustaining as possible.

The students are now engaged for the next 2 weeks on this project. They find and share dozens of resources, many of which are spread out on tables and on the floor around the room. Allen brings to class a video he shot at the zoo last week so everyone can see what different habitats look like. Michelle loads up a CD ROM on mammals that she brought from home, and James donates one of his mother's landscape architecture books for ideas on how to diagram spaces and buildings.

Watching the students work, it seems that solving small problems generates new insights, and the insights provide opportunities to pose new problems:

Allan: We can have coyote, deer, and opossum together because the opossum can just climb a tree to get away from the coyote, and the deer can just run away.

Michelle: Trees? How big do trees have to be to hold a opossum?

James: We can't have any trees 'cause deer come into our back yard at home and eat the bark off the trees and kill them.

Allan: That's just because in the winter they don't have enough food, and we are going to supply their food so they won't eat the tree bark.

James: We still can't have deer because the coyote will eat their young unless we can find a way to separate them.

Michelle: We can build a wall!

James: No, we can do it naturally. We'll make a low spot in the habitat and flood it during the season when the deer are young. That will work if the coyotes can't swim.

Ms. Garcia has been listening to this dialogue and senses that good ideas are developing, but worries about her students' assumptions.

I guess if I were solving these kinds of problems I'd try to find out more information first. You may be basing some of your decisions on an idea that isn't accurate. Are you sure that coyotes prey on young deer? Is there a way to divide up some of this work and check these kinds of facts?

During the next 2 weeks, these students will develop an understanding of how animals interact with one another, how they exhibit purposeful behavior, possess evolved form and function to aid survival, and are subject to the natural cycles of reproduction, the seasons, feast and famine, etc. These complex ideas begin with kernels of the students' own personal experiences and mature with guided exposure to resource materials and with goal-oriented collaboration with others. Concepts such as "competition for resources" and "reproductive capacity"—whose definitions could have been memorized—are instead, made sense of within a problem-solving context. These concepts are built upon the experiences of the students, and are essential, interconnected considerations in the success of these students' habitat design. In the end, the students have created a physical model for the habitat which embodies their collective understanding of these ideas and represents their ability to work together.

In the final presentation of their model to the class, the students describe the rationale for its design, offering statements about what they have learned from this project. Michelle concludes with a surprising remark:

When we were almost finished with our habitat, we thought, "Isn't this pretty artificial?" I mean, we were making this plan work for us, *for our benefit*, but animals don't really live like this. They eat each other, they migrate, they go off by themselves if they want to, they do all kinds of behaviors they can't do in a zoo. So…maybe that's the best thing that we learned.

This is one of many faces of the constructivist classroom.

§

The culture of curriculum, "Constructing Understanding," is characterized by three themes. Although there are wide variations as to how this curricular culture manifests itself, these themes permeate the goals and activities of all constructivist classrooms. The first theme is the *centrality of the learner.* The students' lived experience acts as a powerful referencing framework that allows them to compare new concepts with what they already know and to give these concepts meaning within the students' world. Also, learners are recognized as capable agents of knowledge production, rather than passive consumers of information; as such, they have the periodic freedom to identify intellectual problems and approaches to tasks that are relevant to their own lives as well as to curricular content.

The second theme is *complexity.* Teachers employ problem-based learning as a way for students to participate in the kind of complex inquiry that characterizes most human endeavors outside the classroom. Students also investigate ideas from various perspectives including the practical, aesthetic, historical, and scientific dimensions. In doing so, they strive for a richer, more integrated view of the world. Complexity also refers to the ways in which teachers incorporate diverse learner abilities such as musical, physical, interpersonal, linguistic, and mathematical, into the life of the classroom. The unique distribution of such abilities in individuals mediates how they make sense of their world and how they are empowered to express their understandings to others.

The final theme is *engagement.* Students begin units of study by experiencing the content they are studying, rather than having abstract explanations provided to them ahead of time. For example, students manipulate computer-generated graphs in math class before they discuss what "slope" is, they breed fruit flies in science class and analyze the results before formulas for inheritance are suggested by teachers, and, in social studies, they contemplate Martin Luther King's *Letter From Birmingham Jail* before explanations of non-violent protest are introduced.

Also, learners are engaged in class projects because they work closely with the teacher to negotiate the specifics of problems that they will address, as well as the kinds of evidence of learning they will provide. Students select problems that are important to them and these problems stimulate an authentic curiosity that connects experiences in their own lives with the themes under study. In addition to being engaged with their own projects and interacting with teachers, students collaborate with each other on tasks of inquiry and design, sharing dialogue, and challenging each other's ideas.

These themes suggest that students learn best by first interacting with phenomena and ideas, and by having opportunities to reorganize their view of the world. This curricular culture encourages learners to utilize their lived experiences, intellectual strengths, and interactions with others to bridge the domains of formal knowledge with the rich, continually evolving world of the individual mind.

Visions

Constructivism, as a theory and philosophy about the nature of knowledge and how learners come to know their world, underpins this curricular culture. Constructivism is appreciated more fully when it is framed against the antithetical but historically dominant position of objectivism and its influence on education. Objectivism suggests that there is an external world, independent of human consciousness, which serves as a foundation for claims of truth (Willis, 1995). Related to this view is the belief that language can be used as a precise, neutral tool to describe the real world and to effectively map knowledge from the minds of instructors to the minds of learners. These two philosophical views have supported the persistent presence of transmission models of instruction (also known as direct instruction, didacticism) in which lecture and demonstration are the preferred modes of "delivering knowledge" to learners. Psychological theories, most notably behaviorism, have been consistent with objectivist philosophies and have attempted to make learning processes more efficient (with success in many contexts). Behaviorist instructional principles suggest, in part, that knowledge and skills may be decomposed, the components removed from context, acquired separately by learners through systematic reinforcement of incremental target learning behaviors, and then concatenated by the learner to form a coherent whole (Reynolds, Sinatra, & Jetton, 1996).

In contrast to objectivism, constructivism is premised on the belief that learners actively create and restructure knowledge, constantly comparing ideas introduced in formal instruction to their existing knowledge which has been assembled from personal experiences, the intellectual, cultural, and social contexts in which these ideas occur, and a host of other influences that serve to mediate understanding.

When learners make sense of the world, they are in fact, creating knowledge. A central aim of the constructivist culture is cultivating learners who believe that they can create knowledge themselves and that knowledge does not exist outside them as some objective, universal entity. All students hold epistemological beliefs about whether they can learn how to learn, whether or not there are alternatives to knowledge being accepted from unquestioned "authoritative" sources, and whether or not knowledge has contextual limitations (Schommer, 1993). Children who are immersed in the constructivist culture tend not only to have a greater capacity for generating their own knowledge through problem solving but also for identifying problems, and perhaps most importantly, for persisting in problem-solving efforts (Duckworth, 1978). Constructivist teachers believe that students, when provided with intellectual opportunities, can be motivated to explore subject matter, create understandings at various levels of sophistication, and effectively solve problems.

Constructivists believe that one of traditional education's hallmarks is the monolithic presence of an external, authoritarian body of knowledge immediately represented in the teacher and the textbook. Learning, in that tradition, is roughly equivalent to accepting a set of irrevocable truths which older and more able others have acquired through processes that are inaccessible to students. To discover something significant for oneself, to come to a unique understanding or to have your own way of knowing, is not a norm of traditional education.

By contrast, in a constructivist culture, a premium is placed on creating unique rather than uniform understandings and developing a powerful sense of agency in learners. This sense of agency relates directly to psychologist Jean Piaget's larger view of the purpose of education: to develop intellectual and even moral autonomy in learners. Kamii (1984) has elaborated on this aspect of Piagetian constructivism:

> The idea that children acquire moral values and knowledge by construction from within—by putting things into relationships—still stands, as does the idea that social interactions are essential for this construction to take place. Moreover, according to Piaget, honest exchanges of points of view are bound to lead, in the long run, to autonomy. (p. 415)

Piaget (1963) argued that children refine their existing notions of personal ethics as well as their use of logic when, during social interaction, they view the ideas of others in critical comparison with their own. It is clear that developing autonomy, both intellectual and moral, involves more than the common-sense view of internalizing the observed behaviors of others—it involves exchanging viewpoints with others, to immerse oneself in intersubjectivity.

Beyond autonomy, however, constructivism does not offer a coherent vision of a society that transcends the notion of a collective of capable, independent thinkers. From the roots of constructivism—learning psychology, anthropology, and linguistics—come a system of values that have been difficult to locate within the sphere of human concern. Some scholars, however, have described a type of critical constructivism (Loving, 1997) that endorses "questioning the value of individualism, objectivity, rationality and efficiency as well as the resulting forms of pedagogy and curriculum" (Matthews, 1994, p. 145). This version of constructivism suggests that teachers should convey to learners that all knowledge is provisional and makes explicit the political and social context of this knowledge. Knowledge itself, then, becomes an object of study.

In addition to fostering a critical attitude toward knowledge, constructivist cultures also encourage learners to expand on the ideas of others, to explore the possibilities not only of how to solve authentic problems, but to consider alternative ways of seeing what problems exist in a given situation. These are the ways of thinking that are so valuable to many disciplines and to the 21st-century image of the capable worker. Even outside the work environment, as citizens who shape the social and political landscape, individuals who have participated in the constructivist culture should be able to stimulate dialogue in fellow community members by asking questions that probe, prompt reflection, and organize thought: "What is the purpose for...? " "Can we reframe the problem by...?" or, "How can we work together to...?"

What then, is the larger vision of a society of individuals educated within the constructivist culture? Citizens are able to collaborate effectively with one another in addressing challenges facing the community. They have the ability to understand and appreciate the points of view of others as well as incorporate diverse ideas into problem solutions. Negotiations are tempered by open-mindedness with regard to intellectual and moral differences. These citizens are also life-long learners who understand the value and limitations of knowledge; they appreciate the different forms that "knowing" can take and accept that knowledge is only one dimension of human experience. Furthermore, there is a prevailing respect for children's ways of seeing the world which avoids patronization and embraces the complexity of the young intellect.

History

Historically, elements of constructivist thought have appeared in the philosophical framework of several educational institutions. Notable schools founded over the past 100 years have based their curriculum on the intellectual curiosity and social experiences of the learner rather than on the development of prescribed skills or the transmission of subject matter. Although institutions such as the University of Chicago's Laboratory School, the Montessori schools, or the Reggio Emilia schools of Italy were not founded explicitly on constructivist philosophy, they serve as models for reframing the design of formal schooling around the experiential, culturally mediated world of the child.

The image of modern constructivist instruction has been shaped in no small way by Dewey and the historical record of his progressive school. John and Alice Dewey opened the Laboratory School in Chicago in 1896, and with it set out to "test, verify, and criticize" educational theory as well as to contribute new ideas to education (Dewey, 1972). The success of the Laboratory School led Dewey to argue eloquently that (a) the curriculum should spring from the "genuine" experiences of children, (b) authentic problems should be identified within these experiences to serve as stimuli for thought, (c) students should be allowed the freedom to gather the information necessary to deal with these problems, (d) students should accept responsibility to develop solutions in an orderly way, and, (e) students should be given opportunities to test these ideas through application to make their meaning clear and test their validity (Dewey, 1916).

Dewey effectively took a stand against the inculcation of learners into a culture of compliance and rote learning in which subject matter had little connection with the life of the child. He suggested that the child, if presented with situations of interest and relevance, would be capable of independent exploration, experimentation, and reflection. Dewey did not, however, advocate an extreme version of child-centered education. He contended that education was a process of the continuous reconstruction of a child's present experience by means of adult experiences that were organized into "bodies of truth we call studies" (Hendley, 1986, p. 23). These bodies of truth contained a valuable intellectual and cultural heritage and represented a set of pre-configured knowledge bases. Although Dewey could not be identified as a practitioner of the more radical forms of constructivist instruction—which do not recognize the existence of objective "truths" nor advocate instructional convergence upon prescribed concepts (Von Glaserfeld, 1993)—his focus on children's experiences and respect for their ways of knowing did foreshadow the extensive documentation during the latter 20th century that children strive to construct meaning from social and scientific phenomena, and that their mental models of these phenomena do indeed serve to organize and explain the world around them (Driver, 1981).

Other schools have emerged in this century to emphasize the natural powers of children to fashion elaborate understandings of the world around them, with little influence from direct instruction. Montessori schools, particularly popular for early childhood education, utilize highly trained teachers who act as facilitators for children who are free to pursue learning experiences out of innate interest and curiosity, albeit within a controlled setting of materials supplied by the teacher. The children are envisioned as busily re-constructing themselves as adults as they try to understand the world around them. The curriculum accommodates rather than dictates a developmental path for children to become a participants in society, as well as to gain the basic knowledge and skills necessary to deal with the world (Montessori, 1967). The teacher acts as the architect of the environment, the resource person who plans the array of materials and activities from which the child ultimately chooses. A fundamental belief of Montessori advocates is that children are natural learners and are in a better position to make appropriate learning choices than their adult mentors. Other than periodic didactic presentations to the children, the adults play a supportive rather than a directive role in the learners' environment (Loeffler, 1992).

Also, schools that exemplify the constructivist philosophy are those of Reggio Emilia, founded originally in northern Italy in 1946. The primary educational activities in these schools are long-term, intrinsically interesting projects carried out in a rich variety of physical settings both in the school and throughout the community. The activities include not only teachers, but family and community members as participants. Proponents assert that the objective of the schools is to increase the possibilities for the child to invent and discover, and furthermore, that schemes or structures should not be presented directly to children nor should words should be used as shortcuts to knowledge. Children are viewed as capable of making meaning from their daily life experiences through mental acts involving planning, coordination of ideas, and abstraction (Edwards, Gandini, & Forman, 1996).

In one Reggio Emilia project, four young children were asked to design the school's upcoming long-jump competition (Forman, 1996). They were asked not only to conduct the event, but to construct the long-jump area, decide on a method for measuring the jumps, and devise a set of rules for competition. With minimal adult help the students engaged in repeated cycles of dialogue with each other, analyzing photographs of Olympic jumpers, modeling the jumping motion using wooden dolls and drawings, and developing a system of measuring distance that involved transforming marks on a measuring tape to tally marks and finally to a number system with place values. In short, the students learned how to use models and symbol systems in a meaningful context, employing a persistent attitude toward invention in order to successfully complete a complex task. (Perhaps the most amazing aspect of the activity was that each of the children was only five and a half years old.)

The history of constructivism is not restricted to its various incarnations in school settings. The metaphor of "construction" is perhaps most closely associated with the work of 20th-century psychologist Jean Piaget. Piaget viewed learning as a way of constantly reorganizing one's world, reconciling new information with past experience. Knowledge, according to Piaget, is not an internalized representation of the real world, but rather a collection of conceptual structures that are sensible only within the knowing subject's range of experience (Von Glaserfeld, 1989). To know something, said Piaget, is to act upon it, and transform it. The work of Piaget has been foundational to theories associated with *cognitive constructivism*, that is, the system of explanations for how learners, as individuals, impose structure on their worlds. Some of the major ideas connected with cognitive constructivism are: that meaning is rooted in and indexed by personal experiences (Brown, Collins, & Duguid, 1989), that young learners possess complex but inaccurate conceptions of how the world works, and, that these conceptions influence how they respond to formal instruction (Driver & Easley, 1978).

Related to cognitive constructivism are the theories of *social constructivism* and *socio-cultural learning* that describe how knowledge has social and cultural as well as individual components, and how these components cannot be viewed as separate in any meaningful way (Cobb, 1994; Rogoff, 1990). More specifically, individuals construct knowledge in the presence of others who both constrain and enrich the environment through the use of tools such as language, conventions such as pre-established concepts, accepted practices for creating and judging knowledge (Vygotsky, 1979). An illustration of how accepted classroom practices can mediate learning is found in a study by Cobb and Yackel (1996). They observed a group of first graders who took it for granted that, when conversing with the teacher during mathematics class, they were to infer the answer that the teacher had in mind rather than articulate their own understandings. The teacher found that she had to renegotiate classroom social norms with students in order to liberate them from previous expectations, to allow them to relate to her as young inquirers, and to encourage them to interact in a more exploratory way with the subject matter.

Both the classroom culture and the larger culture in which we live influence how we interpret the world; without acknowledging this basis for "common understanding," an individual's personal constructions would be meaningless. Indeed, "It is the cultural situatedness of meanings that assures their negotiability and their communicability" (Bruner, 1996, p. 3). Within the socio-cultural perspective, knowledge is not an individual possession, but is socially shared and emerges from participation in cultural activities (Cole, 1991). Scholars have synthesized the cognitive and socio-cultural constructivist perspectives, claiming that knowledge is personally constructed and socially mediated (Tobin & Tippins, 1993).

Beliefs and Practices: Learners and Teachers

One of this curricular culture's central tenets is that learners are continually involved in reorganizing their world, actively imposing order and meaning on their experiences and "creating" the world in which they live. The ideas in their world are linked to a constellation of life episodes, images, models, and metaphors which give shape to their conceptions and provide references against which they interpret new ideas. Students' personal knowledge about the world is often elaborate although lacking in depth and consistency. Students' ways of explaining phenomena can be quite satisfactory to them, even though these explanations may contain inconsistencies and may not be applicable across different contexts. Their perceptions are not dismissed as flawed or insignificant, but used as an intellectual and motivational standpoint from which they will build more coherent ideas. As learners are confronted with new information they often can organize and integrate it unproblematically into their existing understanding of the world.

There are, however, some confounding aspects to the learners' world of experiences, such as the influence of alternative conceptions. Students develop naive or alternative conceptions about such ideas as how electricity flows through circuits, how a polygon's perimeter is related to its area, or how the branches of the U.S. government operate. These can be more than simply mistaken ideas or lack of knowledge. Many alternative conceptions, particularly about topics central to a discipline (e.g., photosynthesis, supply and demand, ratios) are remarkably persistent, even in the face of well-sequenced, logical instruction.

A central belief in this culture of curriculum is that students' extant ideas about the world are not always remediated in some straightforward fashion by direct instruction, but that these alternative conceptions form the foundation upon which more intellectually persuasive approaches to the curriculum must be built. Activities such as independent student experimentation in science class or extended research using a variety of original sources in social studies class often serve to confront students with evidence that runs counter to their alternative conceptions. Students, with teacher guidance, experience first-hand the processes as well as the products of knowledge-building, and these situations provide opportunities for students to carefully reconsider the way in which they explain key aspects of the world.

In concert with this view of learning, teaching becomes less the sequencing of events and more the application of principles responding to the needs of a situation (Lebow, 1993). Teachers put learners in direct contact with the phenomena being studied and then ask students to explain the sense they are making. So, instead of explaining things to students, the teacher joins with the student in making sense out of their developing conceptions (Duckworth, 1986).

To complement the active role of the learner, this curricular culture redefines the teacher as a learning facilitator and a co-developer of understanding with the student rather than a dispenser of knowledge. The teacher often begins instruction by eliciting student ideas about a topic so learning experiences can be fashioned from learners' current understandings. Special techniques such as probing discussions, interviews, having students draw concept maps or other representations of ideas are some of the ways teachers put themselves in touch with where the learner is coming from. Teachers may then engage in judicious direct instruction (presentations, demonstrations), but they also design semi-structured activities that allow students flexibility in incorporating their own experiences and background knowledge. Teachers periodically negotiate with students the inquiry questions, activities, and methods that will stimulate knowledge-building and promote students' regulation of their own learning. When students are engaged in learning activities, teachers select from a range of strategies that guide students and prevent them from encountering frustrating dead-ends (even though mistakes are generally treated as learning opportunities). These strategies include: scaffolding, in which teachers reduce the difficulty of learning tasks by helping students with the most complex aspects of it and gradually give more responsibility to the learner as time passes; modeling, in which teachers either think aloud or act out how they would approach a problem; or, providing hints to learners by asking probing questions or redirecting their attention.

There is an additional demand on the teacher beyond that of developing facilitative skills. Constructivist instruction based on design tasks or problem-solving requires that the teacher have a substantial understanding of the subject matter. The teacher must not only be familiar with the topic of study, but must also be prepared for the variety of ways in which the topic may be addressed by students. For example, if students in science class are studying density, the teacher may need to support the understanding of students who want to approach it from a purely abstract, mathematical perspective as they construct tables, equations, and graphs. In this case, the teacher must understand how tabular data, equations, and graphs are translatable from one to another, interpret how student understandings are developing, and select appropriate interventions if students encounter difficulty. Another group of students may recount the story of the *Titanic*, emphasizing how density played a role in the visibility of the iceberg, the ballast of the ship, and the sinking itself. In this case the teacher must be able to apply his/her "clean," abstract mathematical understanding of density to a real-life, inevitably more complex situation.

Beliefs and Practices: Content and Context

There is no consistent pattern of content selection that effectively characterizes the constructivist culture, however, several norms about content are apparent: the way in which learners approach the subject matter is as important as the topics themselves; the long, critical engagements with the subject matter favored in the constructivist culture suggest that less is more, that is, understanding is fostered by prolonged engagements with a few key topics and encyclopedic coverage of content is avoided; and, the organization of content lends itself to the integrated curriculum (studying, for example, the historical perspectives of art, the mathematics of geography, literature in science).

Certainly the ways in which content is approached has some bearing on what is studied. *Big ideas* such as symmetry in mathematics, voice in language arts, laws and justice in social studies, or conservation of energy in science, which can be investigated in various ways, may be identified as required central themes by the teacher. Students may then elect to study a topic like symmetry by comparing examples of symmetry in nature, by examining the relationship between temporal symmetry in music and spatial symmetry in other art forms, or, by identifying ratios in symmetrical patterns. In this way, students have content structured only to a moderate degree and they are allowed to contextualize that content in a way that stimulates them, thereby creating the powerful "collateral" or incidental learning that often serves to give personal meaning to the original theme selected by the teacher.

Concerning the context of instruction, the focus is the learner rather than the subject matter. The classroom, however, may occasionally appear like the traditional classroom, with the teacher offering structured, didactic lessons. During these didactic lessons, teachers adhere to familiar tenets of good instruction (beginning with engaging questions, starting with references to concrete experiences and moving to the abstract, offering analogies and examples to bolster ideas), but even within this didactic framework the teacher uses techniques informed by constructivism such as situating examples and analogies within contexts meaningful to students, eliciting alternative conceptions that students hold, and confronting existing ideas through classroom dialogue. Teachers are careful, however, not to introduce students to topics by providing exhaustive detail, authoritative explanations, or descriptions of the topic which would leave the students in the position of engaging in their own activities simply to verify canonical knowledge.

Following an orientation to the subject matter area or theme of study, students then engage in those activities most closely associated with the constructivist culture. Teachers provide opportunities for students to witness and participate in each other's thinking by assigning work in small groups. Learners in this environment are exposed to examples of the clear, cogent thinking of some peers as well as the meandering, unreflective thought of others. They express to one another not only opinions but how they see loosely associated bits of information coalescing into an idea, interpretation, or explanation.

In addition to working in groups, students learn to collect evidence and generate interpretations consistent with such evidence. A group of students in a social studies class, for example, might investigate the Civil War by examining its effects on several families living on the Mason-Dixon Line. Students would have access to copies of letters, diaries, newspapers, and other relevant primary documents. Their understanding would not be circumscribed by the previous historical interpretations of others. Students, together with teachers, also examine questions about this learning process. What is problematic about interpreting history this way? How will this help us understand the Civil War in a novel way? How will we be able to synthesize our ideas and demonstrate what we know? These types of questions foster a "thinking about thinking" environment in which students become critically conscious of their own intellectual activity.

Constructivist learning involves long-term engagements with projects and problems. The 50-minute class period is ill-suited for these purposes; block scheduling and interdisciplinary curricula then, are natural outgrowths of this culture's approach to learning. Teachers team with partners in other subject areas and capitalize on the longer class periods by developing more integrated themes for study that bridge the world of science, social studies, math and the arts. These themes are big ideas that span disciplines such as:

the responsibility that humans have for the environment, or, the influence of art on scientific discovery.

Although there are endless possibilities for how curriculum can be shaped in this culture, there are some common characteristics included in the design of most learning experiences:

- Teachers find out where students are intellectually before instruction and then monitor how students gradually make sense of the subject matter;
- Teachers provide students with early investigative experiences relevant to the subject matter rather than start with explanations;
- Students should be given frequent opportunities to engage in problem or inquiry-based activities;
- Such problems are meaningful to the student and not oversimplified or decontextualized;
- Students work collaboratively and are encouraged to engage in dialogue;
- Students have various avenues to express what they know to their peers and to the teacher;
- Teachers encourage students' reflective and autonomous thinking in conjunction with the conditions listed above.

Beliefs and Practices: Curriculum Planning and Evaluation

In "Constructing Understanding" it is considered normal and proper for teachers to shape day-to-day curricular experiences. Although educators may be influenced by the demands of the community and state to set standards for curricular goals, only teachers could have enough knowledge of learners' interests and abilities to be the actual curriculum planners. Teachers shape the curricular process, determine standards for the students' work, and create the structure of classroom activity. Students can, however, have some latitude in choosing problems or designing projects that relate to curricular themes. Students negotiate with the teacher what the criteria are for selecting problems to study and what kinds of evidence must be provided to demonstrate their learning.

Criteria for curricular planning become articulated in the classroom with teachers and students referring to a framework of questions (although not standardized) which embody constructivist principles for learning: Is the chosen problem meaningful, important to the discipline and complex enough? Does it deal with the theme of the unit under study? Does it require original thinking and interpretation or is it simply fact-finding? Can this problem help lead to thinking about related problems? and, Will engaging with this problem result in the acquisition of contextualized facts, concepts, and principles that are fundamental to the theme under study?

Evaluation is based on the processes as well as the products of intellectual activity. Teachers note features of students' learning processes for the purposes of providing feedback, but not necessarily for assignment of grades. Teachers also pay attention to how students regulate their own learning, the quality of collaboration with peers, and how well learners use available resources. This curricular culture does not dismiss the learning of certain relatively unambiguous facts, concepts, and skills that may be taught and assessed objectively, nor does constructivist philosophy preclude objective testing as one source of evidence of understanding. If used exclusively, however, objective testing provides only a limited picture of the scope of learner's knowledge.

Evaluation in the constructivist culture is based primarily on student performances or artifacts generated as a result of substantial effort. These performances or artifacts are rigorously judged against criteria that the students jointly develop with the teacher. The works are publicly displayed/performed so that all class members see a range of both quality and creativity in the projects. Students not only explain but also defend their work; they connect their presentations with the agreed-upon criteria for excellence and describe how their work reflects these criteria.

Over the course of the school year, students maintain portfolios that contain both typical and exemplary works. These works may be videotapes of performances, physical models, research reports, artistic renderings, or any other type of evidentiary "text." The portfolio can also contain objective tests, reflections by the students on their own progress, teacher observations, and completed rubrics. Evaluation in the constructivist culture is rigorous and multidimensional. It is focused on the quality of the learner's understanding— its depth and its flexible application to other relevant contexts. In short, it is congruent with other aspects of the culture such as the kinds of learning objectives promoted, the nature of the learning activities, the role of the student as autonomous learner, and role of the teacher as a facilitator of learning.

Dilemmas of Practice

One of the most difficult challenges in maintaining a culture of constructivism is the need for many teachers to reconceptualize their view of instruction. Models of how teachers were taught shape their behavior in powerful ways. Just as they use images and metaphors to make sense of concepts associated with subject matter and pedagogy, teachers use images to envision lessons in their classrooms, develop innovations, and plan for learning (Kennison, 1990). Even though teacher educators expose novices to instructional theory, when new teachers finally enter the classroom they are more likely to be guided not by theory, but by the familiar images of what is "proper and possible" in this setting (Russell, 1993).

Teachers who choose to create a constructivist classroom culture reject many of the images linked to traditional education. However, they can be seduced by an oversimplified version of constructivism if they consider only the reactionary admonitions against the imagined evils of traditional instruction: "Don't tell students *anything*—let them construct their own knowledge!" Attached to this simplistic view is an attraction to an idealistic approach to teaching which, on the surface, counters traditional authoritarian methods but nevertheless fails to translate into systematic, effective practice (Airasian & Walsh, 1997). If attempts at constructivism remain at such an uncritical level and are left unelaborated, resultant instruction can be chaotic as well as indefensible to peers, parents, and administrators. Constructivist instruction then is reduced to "anything goes." In its most sophisticated and effective forms, constructivism actually integrates both teacher-centered and student-centered models of instruction, has systematic and purposeful structure, and values rigorous evaluations of learning progress.

Constructivism does indeed redefine the roles of learners and teachers. It offers a new look at how educators gather evidence of understanding and what it means to understand. Much of the responsibility for this framework of instruction resides with teachers, and unfortunately, the constructivist culture requires that they have an almost unrealistic degree of subject matter knowledge and pedagogical skill. Cremin (1961) suggested that progressive pedagogies required "infinitely skilled teachers" who, historically, had never been prepared in sufficient numbers to effect instructional change nationwide. Today's constructivist models of instruction appear to require just such high levels of skills in teachers. These skills include negotiating subject matter and evaluation criteria with students, maintaining a pro-social atmosphere in student groups, and coordinating the timetables of the various student projects. When we view the constructivist curricular culture not as an idealized setting but with people with real limitations trying to work together, we see these demands placed on teachers as more than dilemmas; many teachers face practical impossibilities.

Providing a constructivist learning environment taxes the intellectual resources of even the most experienced teachers. They continually investigate the types of instructional approaches, problems, and problem-solving environments that will lead to a deep, albeit highly individualized understanding of the subject matter. Teachers must also understand what a "problem" is, and how to help students select non-trivial problems that have some promise of guiding them to an understanding of the subject matter. And, if autonomy and personal relevance are important, they must question how far to go in letting students select their own problems?

Also, if students are to work collaboratively, teachers must have some understanding of cooperative learning theory and how productive, pro-social interactions can be fostered. Constructivism places great emphasis on students taking advantage of each other's knowledge and constructing shared meaning in collaboration with peers. The tentative nature of collaborative work among schoolchildren is a grave concern in this regard. Group work, collaborative or cooperative, is no instructional panacea. Students require training to function effectively in these groups. Even with training, many of the more capable students may be patently disinterested in helping their peers and unintended consequences of group work such as bickering, exclusion, and academic freeloading frequently affect learning (Slavin, 1995).

Features that make constructivist instruction effective also serve to unnerve teachers, especially new teachers who are concerned about their ability to manage the classroom. There is a common perception that the more quiet and orderly classrooms are, the more likely it is that learning is taking place. Constructivist classrooms, by contrast, are busy places—students generally work in groups and are engaged in activities of their own design. Students may need to move in and out of the classroom to access different resources. Teachers are often uncomfortable with their apparent lack of control over students and they may be quite unwilling to allow these learning activities when guests, who may or may not be supporters of the constructivist culture, plan to visit the classroom.

Another dilemma is addressed by the simple question: What exactly do we want students to construct? In the world of ideas there are facts, concepts, principles, and the like. There are also skills ranging from single-digit multiplication to building consensus among peers or conducting inquiry. Further, there are habits of mind such as inquisitiveness and persistence in the face of adversity.

The issues around construction are the stuff from which critics of constructivism set up the straw man: "We don't want our children to construct that two plus two equals five" or, "We don't want a poem or work of literature to mean just anything!" Admittedly, ideas fall along a continuum of openness or restriction with regard to "re-construction" by learners. However, in the constructivist culture, if a student asserts that the shortest distance between two points is not a straight line, it is an opportunity for the teacher to listen rather than to offer a knee-jerk response: For example, does the student have a rationale for this? Perhaps the student is referring to two points that lie on a sphere rather than in two-dimensional space—in which case, the student is correct. Would students who believe that water freezes at 5 degrees Fahrenheit have some experiences that would lead them to believe this? Are they right under certain circumstances? If a student suggests that dictatorships are beneficent forms of governance, they must provide evidence and a framework of interpretation that supports these views; this testimony then would be held up to group scrutiny, allowing the teachers and other students to generate challenging evidence and arguments.

Finally, ideas in the academic disciplines will differ in the extent to which they can be taught through constructivist instruction. Mathematics has rule-based propositions that may be open to discovery via many experiential pathways (Lehrer, Jaslow, & Curtis, 2003). And, it is equally important that the student engage in sense-making experiences about why $3 \times 2 = 6$ as well as engage in rote learning so that they can master the skills of speedy, accurate single digit multiplication. Science and social studies learning also have characteristic skills, some of which are axiomatic, and others that are open to more degrees of discovery and interpretation. Dealing with the "correctness" of constructions is an ongoing concern, and the arguments have barely been introduced here, but reflection upon these epistemological and curricular issues helps educators develop a critical awareness of the relationships between disciplinary "truths" and learning, between knowledge and ways of knowing.

As we begin the second decade of the 21st century, public discourse around classroom instruction remains polarized into two sets of voices, predictably those favoring traditional forms of instruction and those advocating constructivist, inquiry-based approaches. The "Math Wars" in the United States are the most recent examples of an acrimonious and unhelpful clash of ideologies among teachers, parents, and school administrators (see Marshall, 2006). When people have discussed these issues (e.g., which textbooks will be adopted, how standards will be implemented in their school, or whether to use curriculum kits), they feel as compelled to marginalize the views of those different from themselves as they do to explain why their visions of teaching should dictate new directions (or preserve the old). Traditional talk, then, casts reform classrooms as experimental, child-indulgent free-for-alls, while reform voices criticize traditionalist approaches as rigid, authoritarian, and outmoded.

Reformers and traditionalists tend to use two major strategies to make their points. The first strategy is the use of imagery as the primary tool of persuasion. Traditional talk stirs up images we share from our past, such as the teacher lecturing energetically from the front of the room, the students bent dutifully over worksheets, or groups of learners working to find the one correct answer for the distillation exercise. In short, it seeks to convince through the appeal of the orderly classroom. In contrast, reform talk about active learning describes students in small groups arguing about how to pose questions for a lab experiment, teachers sharing with students the leading of classroom discussions, and learners engaged in projects that demonstrate what they know about a particular idea. While these images reflect potentially powerful learning experiences, they also arouse two deep-seated concerns for teachers: how to control the classroom and how to cover the curriculum (Windschitl, 2006).

We are learning more about the conditions under which young people learn, but the same conceptual schisms that divide practitioners also separate researchers. A recent volume, *Constructivist Instruction: Success or Failure* (Tobias & Duffy, 2009), airs out the current controversy about constructivist versus explicit instruction using empirical studies to shore up the respective arguments. Perhaps the most thoughtful product of the book, however, is its simple summary question: When and under what conditions should teachers use various strategies and tools to help young learners?

Critique

This curricular culture offers a view of learners as capable agents of knowl-edge construction and emphasizes individual as well as socially constructed understandings of subject matter. These perspectives provide a set of values that shape decisions about the roles of teachers and learners. These values are derived, in part, from constructivist theories about learning, and elements of these learning theories are used as references for designing instruction. Curi-ously, these descriptive constructivist ideas about how students learn have not translated well into complementary designs for instruction. Although con-structivism can be viewed as a philosophy that provides guidelines for learn-ing such as promoting student autonomy, collaboration, and sense making, it remains difficult to represent constructivism as a single, coherent set of peda-gogical methods. There is little consensus about whether any of the classroom conditions cited in this chapter are necessary or sufficient to help learners construct meaningful understandings, and critics may (fairly) characterize constructivism as little more than thematic, project-based learning.

Additionally, we must be concerned that the goals of education, articu-lated in national, state, and local standards, do not always seem compatible with the rich and diverse understandings of individual students. Students engaged in projects on photosynthesis, for example, may take radically dif-ferent approaches to developing their knowledge of this phenomenon. One group of students may choose to focus on chemical reactions at the molecular level, while another group may examine how oxygen and carbon dioxide are exchanged between animals and plants on a global scale. These two groups will take disconcertingly divergent paths to understanding but the skilled teacher will ensure that each of the groups approach their problems from multiple perspectives: The group examining chemical reactions should be prompted to consider the effects of photosynthesis on the larger environment; the students examining the implications of the global effects should be familiar with the biochemical bases for these macro-phenomena. But artful guidance by the teacher notwithstanding, it can be unsettling to attempt to reconcile the lan-guage of "standards, benchmarks, and objectives" with the diversity of under-standings that develop in a constructivist classroom.

The strongest criticism that could be leveled at constructivism as a culture is the assertion that it represents merely a set of guidelines for instruction and does not have import with regard to the larger issues of curriculum. There is, for example, no social vision promoted by this culture—therefore there is no concern for caring about others or for the environment, for combating oppression, or for making the world a better place. There are no incentives for learners in this culture to participate in the community or in the larger cul-ture outside of school. Learners are given the intellectual tools to think effec-tively and autonomously, but there are no sustaining moral or social visions that members carry with them from this classroom culture. Constructivism also pays little attention to how politics and privilege affect meaning-making by learners; its pedagogy would clearly be richer and more transformative if students were compelled to consider the influences of race, class, and gender as they "construct" their own images of history, science, and literature (Rivera & Poplin, 1995).

Developing autonomous learners—who believe in their own powers as creators of knowledge—is a start for creating a society in which authority is never blindly followed and individuals' worldviews are not controlled by miseducative influences of peers and popular culture. Autonomy, however, does not automatically translate into community or shared vision of a better society. In truth, the constructivist culture may be a means, but not an end.

References

Airasian, P., & Walsh, M. (1997). Constructivist cautions. *Phi Delta Kappan, 78*(6), 444–449.

Brown, J. S., Collins, A., & Duguid, P. (1989). Situated cognition and the culture of learning. *Educational Researcher, 18*, 32–42.

Bruner, J. (1996). *The culture of education.* Cambridge MA: Harvard University Press.

Cobb, P. (1994). Where is the mind? Constructivist and sociocultural perspectives on mathematical development. *Educational Researcher, 23*(7), 13–20.

Cobb, P., & Yackel, E. (1996). Constructivist, emergent, and sociocultural perspectives in the context of developmental research. *Educational Psychologist, 31*(3&4), 175–190.

Cole, M. (1991). Conclusion. In L. B. Resnick, J. M. Levine, & S. D. Teasley (Eds.), *Perspectives on socially shared cognition* (pp. 398–417). Washington DC: American Psychological Association.

Cremin, L. A. (1961). *The transformation of the school: Progressivism in American education 1876–1957.* New York: Vintage.

Dewey, J. (1916). *Democracy and education.* New York: Macmillan.

Dewey, J. (1972). The university school. In J. A. Boydston (Ed.), *The early works of John Dewey* (p. 437) Carbondale: Southern Illinois University Press.

Driver, R. (1981). Pupils' alternative frameworks in science. *European Journal of Science Education, 3*(1) 93–101.

Driver, R., & Easley, J. (1978). Pupils and paradigms: A review of literature related to concept development in adolescent science students. *Studies in Science Education, 5*, 61–84.

Duckworth, E. (1978). *The African primary science program: An evaluation and extended thoughts.* Grand Forks: North Dakota Study Group on Evaluation.

Duckworth, E. (1986). *Inventing density.* Grand Forks: North Dakota Study Group on Evaluation.

Duckworth, E. (1996). *The having of wonderful Ideas and other essays on teaching and learning.* New York: Teachers College Press.

Edwards, C., Gandini, L., & Forman, G. (1996). Introduction, In C. Edwards, L. Gandini, & G. Forman (Eds.), *The hundred languages of children: The Reggio Emilia approach to early childhood education* (pp. 3–18). Norwood NJ: Ablex.

Forman, G. (1996). Multiple symbolization in the long jump project. In C. Edwards, L. Gandini, & G. Forman (Eds.). *The hundred languages of children: The Reggio Emilia approach to early childhood education* (pp. 171–188). Norwood NJ: Ablex.

Hendley, B. (1986). *Dewey, Russell, Whitehead: Philosophers as educators.* Carbondale: Southern Illinois University Press.

Kamii, C. (1984). Autonomy: The aim of education envisioned by Piaget. *Phi Delta Kappan, 65*(6) 410–415.

Kennison, C. (1990). *Enhancing teachers' professional learning: Relationships between school culture and elementary school teachers' beliefs, images and ways of knowing.* Unpublished specialist thesis, Florida State University, Gainesville.

Lebow, D. (1993). Constructivist values for instructional systems design: Five principles toward a new mindset. *Educational Research, Technology, and Development, 41*(3), 4–16.

Lehrer, R., Jaslow, L., & Curtis, C. (2003). Developing an understanding of measurement in the elementary grades. In D. H. Clements & G. Bright (Eds.), *Learning and teaching measurement. 2003 yearbook* (pp. 100–121). Reston VA: National Council of Teachers of Mathematics.

Loeffler, M. H. (1992). *Montessori and constructivism.* In M. H. Loeffler (Ed.), *Montessori in contemporary culture* (pp. 101–113). Portsmouth, NH: Heinemann.

Loving, C. (1997). From the summit of truth to its slippery slopes: Science education's journey through positivist-postmodern territory. *American Educational Research Journal, 34*(3), 421–452.

Marshall, J. (2006). Math wars 2: It's the teaching stupid! *Phi Delta Kappan, 87*(5), 356–363.

Matthews, M. R. (1994). *Science teaching: The role of history and philosophy of science.* London: Routledge.

Montessori, M. (1967). *The absorbent mind.* New York: Holt, Rinehart and Winston.

Piaget, J. (1963). Cognitive development in children: Piaget. *Journal of Research in Science Teaching, 2*, 176–186.

Reynolds, R. E., Sinatra, G. M., & Jetton, T. L. (1996). Views of knowledge acquisition and representation: A continuum from experience centered to mind centered. *Educational Psychologist, 31*(2), 93–104.

Rivera, J., & Poplin, M. (1995). Multicultural, critical, feminine and constructive pedagogies seen through the lives of youth: A call for the revisioning of these and beyond: Toward a pedagogy for the next century. In C. E. Sleeter & P. L. McLaren (Eds.), *Multicultural education, critical pedagogy, and the politics of difference* (pp. 221–244). Albany: State University of New York Press.

Rogoff, B. (1990). *Apprenticeship in thinking.* New York: Oxford University Press.

Russell, T. (1993). Learning to teach science: Constructivism, reflection, and learning from experience. In K. Tobin (Ed.), *The practice of constructivism* (pp. 247–258). Hillsdale, NJ: Erlbaum.

Schommer, M. (1993). Comparisons of beliefs about the nature of knowledge and learning among postsecondary students. *Research in Higher Education, 34*(3), 355–369.

Slavin, R. E. (1995). *Cooperative learning.* Boston: Allyn and Bacon.

Tobias, S., & Duffy, T. (2009). *Constructivist instruction: Success or failure?* New York: Routledge.

Tobin, K., & Tippins, D. (1993). Constructivism as a referent for teaching and learning. In K. Tobin (Ed.), *The practice of constructivism in science education* (pp. 3–21). Hillsdale, NJ: Erlbaum.

Von Glaserfeld, E. (1989). Cognition, construction of knowledge and teaching. *Synthese, 80,* 121–140.

Von Glaserfeld, E. (1993). Questions and answers about radical constructivism. In K. Tobin (Ed.), *The practice of constructivism in science education* (pp. 23–38). Hillsdale, NJ: Erlbaum.

Vygotsky, L. S. (1979). Consciousness as a problem in the psychology of behavior. *Soviet Psychology, 17*(4), 3–35.

Willis, J. (1995). A recursive, reflective instructional design model based on constructivist-interpretivist theory. *Educational Technology, 35*(6), 5–23.

Windschitl, M. (2006). Why we can't talk to one another about science education reform. *Phi Delta Kappan, 87*(5), 348–355.

Chapter 6

Developing Self and Spirit

Stephanie Luster Bravmann

[We] do endorse, by common consent, the obvious hypothesis that the child rather than what he studies should be the centre of all educational effort.
Burton Fowler, 1930, *Progressive Education 7*, p. 59

Monday through Thursday at 3:30 P.M., just after classes were dismissed and before leaving for the day, students usually dropped by the 11th-grade classroom where Meyer would have posted a note on the bulletin board right inside the door. Just to check. Scrawled on a bit of yellow paper, usually ripped from someplace else, would be a word or a phrase: "*On Liberty,*" "C_2H_5-O-H; C_2H_5-O-C_2H_5; C_2H_3O-H; C_2H_3O-O-C_2H_3O," "Mondrian," "Ontogeny recapitulates phylogeny," "Simone de Beauvoir," or, "Hunger." This was the subject. In the morning there would be a question that had something to do with the displayed words.

Anyone who was interested could come to school 30 minutes early the following day, perhaps having done some preliminary investigation on the topic, and try to answer the teaser that Meyer had appended on a second piece of yellow paper. "Where might there be a relationship between John Stuart Mill's writing and a school principal?" "What do C_2H_5-O-H, C_2H_5-O-C_2H_5, C_2H_3O-H and C_2H_3O-O-C_2H_3O have to do with modern chemistry?" "What is considered revolutionary about Mondrian's painting?" "How is the theory that ontogeny recapitulates phylogeny reflected in the study of history?" Responses were to be written and handed to Meyer, personally, no later than 10 minutes before class began at 8:00 A.M.

Did everyone take part in this activity? Of course not, it was not required. Did the same students always participate? No, individuals and groups changed daily. Were these questions related to anything in the general science and biology classes which Meyer was hired to teach? Not often; they were chosen by Meyer from a deeply rooted knowledge of his students, their current and past interests, and what might complement them. Were there grades or extra-credit points for getting the correct answer to the questions? Never. Were there correct answers? Rarely.

Very occasionally, a well-considered response produced a pass to leave the school grounds for lunch. Even more occasionally, students who had created particularly thoughtful or intriguing replies were invited to select a subject, devise a question themselves, and post it for whomever might wish to take it on. Was this some kind of strange alternative activity trying to pass for schooling or was it education proceeding from a sound, articulated set of principles? Why did adolescents—so often self-absorbed and blasé—bother?

§

Alfred North Whitehead (1929) speaks often of the "romance" of learning — the fascination that initially wells up when a student is fully engaged, intellectually and emotionally, in the process of learning. To foster such engagement, teachers such as Meyer know their students, their students' interests and directions of thought, and their own subjects to so great an extent that they can create curriculum that emanates from learners themselves.

This short scenario represents an enactment of the curricular culture we refer to as "Developing Self and Spirit," an orientation which holds that if the educational process begins with the student at the center—and engages the intellect, the emotions, the body, and the spirit—then all learners will proceed freely and naturally to greater knowledge of themselves and of their world. Proponents of this culture believe that we must learn according to self-directed interests toward the goal of nurturing each individual's potential, creativity, spirituality, and self-knowledge. The foundational belief proposes that affirmation of self is the basis for greater good, it embodies the conviction that good emerges from each of us as we grow and develop in relation to, and relationship with, ourselves and others.

Visions

The aims of those who advocate for "Developing Self and Spirit" sound remarkably similar in spite of the not infrequent differences in time and attitude between those promoting them. They all speak to the well-rounded development of the heart, the body, the mind, and the spirit to the end of life-long learning—the desire to develop (or retain) the goodness, morality, and ethical foundations for leading a righteous life, and the betterment of the immediate community, society, and the world. Fostering both independence and dependability as full participants in society is an ancillary but not subordinate goal. It is a given that those committed to "Developing Self and Spirit" conceive of such affirmation without regard to gender, ethnicity, ability, or need. Sometimes markedly similar declarations are evident in historical portrayals (from Plato to Pestalozzi, Herbart and Froebel, Parker, Dewey, Montessori, Neill, and Steiner), those that are more contemporary (Samples, Pearce, and Greene), and works decidedly modern and postmodern (Moffett, Noddings, and Martin).

As comparable as the central goals may in fact be, the major ideas embedded in "Developing Self and Spirit" are, by the very nature of their grounding in the uniqueness of each learner, often disparate. They do, however, share some basic tenets, beginning with the contention that there is an inseparable unity of mind, body, and spirit in all humankind. They show agreement, as well, that students who are allowed to learn independently, and at their own pace, willingly channel their energy into learning. Motivation and reward are, to the greatest possible degree, intrinsic.

Another shared idea is that mutual trust and respect form the foundation of a true learning community. It is only in such an atmosphere that students are empowered and encouraged to take risks, to succeed, and even to fail in a setting that honors all of their attempts to learn. Whether under the guise of peer tutoring, cooperative education, or some other rubric, most also believe that students helping one another, in community, facilitates both learning and wholesome social interactions.

Whether stated in terms of spirituality or developmental psychology, the most ancient to the most modern advocates of this curricular culture share two notions: that the human organism seeks continued growth throughout its lifetime and that there is a natural, self-regulating order to human growth and learning that must be observed if we are to honor the needs of each individual. They share, as well, the conviction that nature itself is a powerful educator and must be represented fully in the educational process. The importance of a loving, accepting environment, and of respect for children as human beings are seen as the cornerstones of self, and communal, discipline. Finally, all seem to agree that happiness and joy are critical components of a full and contributing life whether as a child in school or as an adult in the larger society and that helping children to find their passions for learning makes this curricular orientation crucial for engagement in learning and for developing life-long learners (Robinson & Aronica, 2009).

The concept of spirituality, which theorists agree is a common and critical element of humanness, is perhaps the most multifaceted component in this curricular culture (see Moffett, 1994; Roehlkepartain, King, Wagener, & Benson, 2005). Believers in learner-centered education come from every variety of religious and secular background; the schools they support are, variously, parochial, independent, and public. Comenius (a 17th-century Moravian clergyman), Rudolf Steiner (an anthroposophist and founder of Waldorf education), and Felix Adler (the founder of Ethical Culture) combined their religious convictions with educational theories that were concerned with the whole child and natural learning; schools that run on these models do so from a solidly religious base. Theorists such as Edith Cobb (*The Ecology of Imagination in Childhood*, 1977), Bob Samples (*The Metaphoric Mind*), and Joseph Chilton Pearce (*The Magical Child*, 1976), on the other hand, acclaim the fundamental spirituality of nature itself as the basis of their beliefs. Maria Montessori, Francis Parker, John Dewey, and Helen Parkhurst, whatever their personal religious convictions and feelings about the importance of nature, used the secular world as their point of departure.

While every social group seeks to transmit its dominant or most cherished values to succeeding generations, political, economic and social visions change, sometimes radically, with the times in which one is living, working, and theorizing. The distinction between values and visions, therefore, is particularly important in this context. Typically, there is at least some complementarity of values from age to age and culture to culture: humans generally esteem good before evil, plenty before need, fairness before injustice. The visions that are held to attain these values, however, are often discrepant and dependent upon particulars of time, place, political structure, and personal proclivity; in other words, visions are more mutable commodities. "Developing Self and Spirit" as a curricular culture must, by its nature, be open to broad degrees of difference in vision, relying on its belief in human goodness to mediate disparities in individual thought, feeling, and sense. This being said, there is a strong and abiding assumption that this curricular culture is most consistent with the furthering of democratic, non-sexist, and multicultural political, economic, and social institutions.

"Developing Self and Spirit," as a school culture, strives to affect the social vision of our world in a number of ways. It acknowledges and accepts the manifestations of human diversity evident in the larger culture and attempts to achieve equality in terms of the power relationships inherent in any human interactions. Additionally, it promotes individual and social tolerance—not in the sense of forbearance but in the sense of acceptance—of all people without regard to ethnicity, gender, or other so-called defining characteristics. It is an educational culture grounded in the belief that people are fundamentally decent and well-meaning, that education through experience and interaction is liberating, and that schooling is not, as Dewey would have said, preparation for life but life itself. "Developing Self and Spirit" enables us to use the past and the present to both inform and create a morally defensible future.

History

Ideas promoting the importance of "child-centered learning," of educating the "whole child," of "natural learning," of "freedom to learn," of "learning by doing," and of "practical application" are actually as old as Plato. The importance, even the primacy, of the place of the individual in religious, spiritual, social, economic, and political constellations of thought—and thus in the thought of educational theorists—has changed throughout history with the only surety being that whatever theory is currently in ascendance, it will change again.

While child-centered education first became popular in the United States during the late 19th century, its roots were solidly European. Although the ideas brought from overseas were shaped, by time and individual thinkers, to reflect a uniquely American consciousness, it is important to look, at least briefly, at the foundations from which they arose.

The Platonic ideal of education outlined a theory concerned with the well-rounded development of the mental, physical, and spiritual aspects of individuals; it focused on the whole person. While early schooling was based in large part on imitation and memorization, as children grew they were expected to self-teach through activities—training the mind, the body, and the spirit through practical interaction with the society surrounding him. John Amos Comenius (1592–1670) firmly believed that all human development was governed by certain indisputable laws of nature that formed the constituent base for all educational theory and practice. He maintained that it was only possible to learn by doing, "Artisans learn to forge by forging, to carve by carving, to paint by painting...let children learn to write by writing, to sing by singing, and to reason by reasoning" (Comenius, 1907, pp. 100, 152).

Jean Jacques Rousseau (1712–1778), is generally named as the source of the ideas that are the framework of modern child-centered progressive education. Contrary to traditional Calvinist teaching that the individual was pure in nature, Rousseau believed that the only way to rid society of corruption and evil was to return to adults the virtue and innocence of children. Based on his assumptions that every child was born unsullied and with inherent natural powers, Rousseau wrote *Emile* in 1762, a work designed to articulate the components of a "real" education. Leaving behind the notion of children as miniature adults, Rousseau saw childhood as a unique time of life, as an unfolding. Children, he felt, were to be educated in nature until they were at least 5 years old, free to play and explore and learn unencumbered by the artifice of society; sensory experience in concrete situations was the next focus and abstract learning came later, developed naturally, from the ages of 12 to 15. While many of the precepts proffered in *Emile* are today considered impractical, such as the concept of the child being educated for many years in isolation from others, Rousseau's ideas made the child the central figure in the educational process.

Holistic theories of children were the touchstone of many who followed Rousseau. Johann Heinrich Pestalozzi (1746–1827) who, following the devastation of the Napoleanic Wars, established a school at Yverdon, Switzerland, for children whom today we would call disadvantaged or at risk. Pestalozzi believed in the innate powers of children and contended that the only way to improve society was through the development of each individual's moral and intellectual capabilities. As such he prescribed, in addition to students' academic lessons, the tasks of farming, cooking, and sewing and—to help support the school financially—the activities of spinning and weaving. Advocating the need for balanced development of the head, the heart, and the hand, Pestalozzi supported the use of sensory experience to develop powers of perception, a study of science and nature, and discipline based on love and respect for children as human beings.

Friedrich Froebel (1782–1852), who worked for Pestalozzi at Yverdon, was particularly interested in young children, and in the application of his belief that childhood was part of the greater unity of human life, he started the world's first formal kindergarten in Blankenberg, Germany, in 1836. A religious mystic, he believed that children were born free of evil but were tainted by it through "arbitrary and willful interference with the original orderly and logical course of human development" (Froebel, 1887, p. 119). Froebel's aim was to help the child's mind grow naturally and spontaneously but, unlike Rousseau, he felt that social activity and participation were the keys to growth and learning in young children. Additionally, he saw the world of play as the single most important developmental component of childhood, an arena for purposeful and creative activity. This, Froebel felt, provided the ideal setting for uniting the spiritual, intellectual, emotional, and physical aspects of the individual as he grew and matured.

Although some hale John Dewey (1859–1952) as bringing progressive education to American schooling almost single-handedly, he was influenced by others. Chief among U.S. educators who advocated the development of self as an educational doctrine was Colonel Francis Wayland Parker (1837–1902). Parker's philosophy of teaching and learning, singular for his time, was shaped in large part by his travels and studies in Europe after the Civil War. Speaking of his first official words as a Carrollton, Illinois, school principal in 1858, Parker recalled telling the students "that my idea of a good school was to have a first class time, and that in order to have a good time they must all take hold and work together" (Griffin, 1906, p. 121). Later, as superintendent of the Quincy, Massachusetts, public schools, Parker developed a system characterized by its intense concentration on individual students—premised on the belief that the ultimate goal of humankind was freedom and an abiding faith that only under democracy could such freedom be fostered. Moving from the East Coast to the principalship of the Cook County Normal School in Chicago, Parker was able to expand his views on freedom for children to the realm of adult education and teacher training and to include in his growing philosophy the concept of freedom for teachers themselves.

Parker saw public schools as the footing upon which a free nation rested and as the only arena in which prejudice could be erased and various peoples knit into a new and better society.

> Here in America we are bringing together all peoples from all parts of the known world, with all their prejudices born of centuries.... Here they come into our broad continent and we propose to have them live together...he social factor in school is the greatest factor of all; it stands higher than subjects of learning. (Parker, 1894/1937, p. 420)

Parker believed that children working together in the environment of the school "before prejudice has entered their childish souls, before hate has become fixed, before mistrust has become a habit" could "make the public school a tremendous force for the upbuilding of democracy" (p. 420)

John Dewey (whose son and daughter attended Parker's school during the years that the Dewey family lived in Chicago and before the opening of Dewey's Laboratory School) was strongly influenced by Parker's ideas. Dewey, as an intellectual and academic, was able to "translate" and explain the practice-based work of Parker into educational theory. Dewey's work as a philosopher, a psychologist, and an educator enabled him to append the "why" and the "how" to Parker's "what." Thus Dewey could articulate the rationale for the experiences that Parker instinctively felt were best for children.

Although Dewey was opposed to the sentimentality of those who proposed a child-centered philosophy so narrow that it all but denied the teacher any role in helping to guide students' experiences (Dewey, 1938/1963), his work clearly mirrored many of the visions and historical antecedents of this curricular culture. In particular, this connection becomes clear in Dewey's early writing, *My Pedagogic Creed* (1897/1981):

> I believe that this educational process has two sides - one psychological and one sociological; and that neither can be subordinated to the other or neglected without evil results following. Of these two sides, the psychological is the basis. The child's own instincts and powers furnish the material and give the starting point for all education. (pp. 443–444)

There are a number of principles undergirding child-centered schools that come directly from those of the Laboratory School that John and Alice Dewey began at the University of Chicago in 1899: The school itself is seen as a community where all members have responsibilities and obligations to the whole rather than merely a place where lessons are learned. The school also is a place where children's curiosity led to active engagement with learning problems and to the challenge to solve them by themselves. Finally, the teacher needs to believe that the learner, not the subject matter, is the center of all teaching and that the child's total growth is the primary objective of teaching. The teacher's job, therefore, is to select worthy experiences for each child that will be both engaging and challenging. In addition, Dewey contended that while schools were a function of society, so society was a function of education. The school was considered by Dewey, as by Parker before him, to be a micro-society (Dewey, 1897/1981). Despite the fact that more than a century has passed since the creation of the Laboratory School, the Deweyan model still influences contemporary modern-day education (Fishman & McCarthy, 1998).

Numerous and diverse schools have developed over time that reflect the curricular culture "Developing Self and Spirit." These models differ from one another, sometimes radically, depending on the emphasis or structure—but not on the goals that underlie the particular situational reality. There is not one "pure" model, as generally the only truly comparable characteristic of the various iterations of this orientation is that curriculum emanates from the needs of the learners.

Helen Parkhurst (1887–1973) founded The Dalton School and developed the three-part Dalton Plan in 1919 (the House, the Assignment, and the Laboratory) grounded in part on her work with Maria Montessori. The objectives of the Dalton concept were to: adapt the school program to each student's individual needs and interests; encourage independence; build students' social skills, feelings of responsibility for others, and affiliation with the broader community. Private schools established on the Dalton formula exist today in Europe, Asia, and South America. Even public schools have explored the possibilities of regularly and systematically providing students with opportunities to make choices about their own learning, to find meaningful ways to discover their own interests, and to take personal responsibility for pursuing those interests in the educational setting.

The Dalton Plan, The Winnetka (Illinois) Plan, The Morrison Plan (Henry C. Morrison, University of Chicago, School of Education) and related models in the past and present favor the creation of contracts between the student and the teacher which forms the basis of each individual's educational program. The use of contracts yields a double benefit for students: they are allowed to learn in natural progression and are often able to structure their school day in ways that allow for maximum concentration on the topic at hand rather than having the hours broken up into unrelated activities.

Maria Montessori (1870–1952) left a widespread legacy of schools throughout the world that are based, totally or in part, on her model. Her writing of *The Montessori Method* (1909) and other works influenced many teachers and parents in the United States and around the world. Although Montessori advocated activities selected by teachers as well as students, and designed materials intended to further her philosophy of sensory, manipulative based learning, she is still considered part of the group of educators promoting development of the individual. Montessori practice emerges from the interests and desires of the child at any given point in time and education proceeds only from that starting point. Often cited as the creator of developmentally appropriate educational practice, Montessori advocated multi-aged classrooms where children could learn by doing—both individually and with older and younger classmates—in a carefully prepared environment. While Montessori's work focused on schooling 3, 4, and 5-year-old children, modern iterations of her ideas continue through the 12th grade. Besides the numerous Montessori private and parochial schools throughout the United States, the movement for public Montessori schools has grown in the United States as a number of school districts have some form of elementary program that is grounded in Montessori principles, employ teachers trained in the Montessori method, and use materials specifically designed for such settings.

Rudolf Steiner (1861–1926), a German educator who in the early part of the 20th century developed the Waldorf School system of education, is another whose ideas are reproduced, often less in whole than in part, in many schools today. There exists an established and growing worldwide network of Waldorf Schools that aim to "bring up free human beings who know how to direct their own lives" (Steiner, 1973, p. 201). The Waldorf model advocates preparation for the child's future life as a member of the broader society. Among the tenets of Steiner's philosophy is the strongly spiritual base of education and the integration of stories, art, and movement into the curriculum at ages appropriate for students. Another premise is that teachers should remain with their students through a number of years (sometimes for all eight elementary grades), in order to enhance the replication of family and community within the school and create optimal conditions for developing feelings of safety and nurture. Forms of the latter idea are present, in varying degrees, in an expanding number of American public and private schools today. Less likely to be adopted is Steiner's admonition to delay the teaching of reading until the individual child signals developmental readiness by the loss of the first baby tooth.

Another model of schooling, the Summerhill School, was begun in England, but its founder, A. S. Neill (1883–1973), is credited by many as having discovered alternative education and pioneered the concept of the open classroom—both of which were extremely popular in the United States the late 1960s and 1970s. Summerhill is, and was, an international boarding school based on the concept of absolute freedom tempered only by a concern for health and safety; children can do as they wish as long as they do not physically endanger themselves or others. It is a doctrine, in Neill's words, of "freedom not license," with freedom being defined as the right of all, children and adults, to personal choice. The Summerhill School operates on the basis of a one-person, one-vote government that meets on a weekly basis to establish community laws and norms, handle student and staff concerns, and deal with infractions of rules. All classes are optional for students and required for staff. Elements of Summerhill can be seen in the prevalence of class meetings or community meetings of various types found in today's schools and in principles that encourage children's natural cognitive and emotional growth in settings devoid of fear or coercion and where they, not adults, have control over their lives in school.

An important historical influence derived from psychotherapy and humanistic psychology is the humanistic learning theory of Carl Rogers (1902–1987) which continues to influence those writing about holistic education. While his ideas apply primarily to work with adult learners, they must also be contemplated as an extension of earlier theories about children's learning. Rogers believed that meaningful learning must be experience-based and always address the needs and desires of the student; experiential learning, in his framework, is equivalent to personal change and growth. Learning is optimal when the student initiates and has control over the nature and the direction of the process, when it directly confronts practical, social, or personal problems, and when self-evaluation is the primary method of assessment (Rogers, 1969). These principles are applied in numerous high school and adult education settings; Rogers' view complements adult self-directed learning theory, andragony (Knowles, 1984).

In recent times, this curricular orientation often is referred to as holistic education although known also as child-centered education and, as applied to adult education, as self-directed learning. Educators began to refer to the term, "holistic curriculum," in the late 1970s and this designation became established with Ron Miller's publication of the *Holistic Education Review* in 1988 and John P. Miller's book, *The Holistic Curriculum*, published in the same year. Both authors continue to synthesize the theory and curriculum of holistic education in contemporary publications (see Miller, 2007: Miller, 2006).

Most commonly practiced versions encountered in schools of today are those models that explicitly or implicitly enact the developmental unity of "head, heart, and hands." Examples of such models include the ubiquitous country day schools—generally private and nonsectarian—as well as a variety of small, non-traditional parochial schools. There also are other alternative models such as the Piney Woods Country Life School in Piney Woods, Mississippi—a private, mostly scholarship-supported school that has worked for almost a century to enhance the development of at-risk, primarily African American, young people. Regardless of form, all of the schools subscribing to this particular model share a devotion to each child's intellectual, physical, and spiritual development. Many, in addition, have manual work components (maintenance requirements, animal keeping, farming, grounds work, etc.) as an integral part of their programs. In recent times, with the growing popularity of alternative public schools, many are being formed that are based (loosely or strictly), on interpretations of the inherent beliefs of holistic education.

Belief and Practices: Learners and Teachers

"Developing Self and Spirit" as a curricular culture focuses first and most intently on the learners in all of their complexities as physical, intellectual, social, and spiritual beings that naturally seek growth. Perhaps the most basic assumption that sustains this culture is that students need love, safety, freedom, and guidance to be able to learn. In effect, it is presumed that students need all of those things that combine to make anyone an active, participating human being. They need, as would any sentient beings, to find meaning in what they do through purposeful activity and reflection, to feel valued and valuable, and to be provided access to the skills and knowledge with which to fulfill their goals.

When educators who subscribe to this orientation are questioned about how students learn, their responses are remarkably similar. Children are described as learning "through experience," "by engagement," "when material is meaningful," "when they are empowered," "by doing and experiencing," and by "everything is an experience," "actively," "through all of their senses," and "when they love what they're doing—not every minute of the time, but when they basically love to learn." One middle school teacher summarized her assumptions about how students learn in this curricular culture as:

> Proceeding as if they were on a trip, not a vacation but a long, loosely planned journey. On a journey you don't necessarily know what you're going to encounter in your travels, you have a general plan and then you interact with the your physical environment, the people around you, the things you already know, your own assumptions and feelings and all of these things have an effect on what turns you make, where you stop, what you concentrate on. The fact that you're going on the journey is a given; where and how it progresses, what stalls it, when it ends, and if it will ever end, are all unknowns. (Class Journal)

Another teacher concretely developed curriculum influenced by the metaphor of "journey." His combined third and fourth-grade class developed a year-long "Journey Journal" assignment that was written weekly and shared among the children bi-weekly. The assignment was to choose homework from a set of categories "inspired by Howard Gardner's eight human geniuses, and are physical, creative, intellectual, new experience, social, cultural, emotional, solitude, and community service":

> The implementation of the Journey Journal provided necessary freedoms for my students, in the forms of time, control, and freedom from judgment, to develop a strong uninhibited sense of self. My students were curious by nature and had the opportunity to explore their own curiosities, which allowed the world to open up to them. We were able to foster intelligent, observant, independent thinkers, who realized that the power to learn was within them, and that they just needed to spend the time investigating what interested them and then reflect on what they experienced and learned. My students learned to enjoy life purposefully, and developed an understanding that life and learning come hand in hand. (Class Paper)

It is not surprising, given the holistic foundations of this curricular culture, that many of the metaphors used by educators to describe the learner cluster around conceptualizations from the natural world, e.g., of the "many plants and flowers in a garden, each needing basic nutrients but each growing in its own unique way," of "bees gathering honey," or "butterflies flying from place to place." Another commonly used metaphor of how students learn is a variation on "an artist's palette, made up of various colors, a dab of this, a dab of that, all combining in a broad spectrum that needs to be utilized, explored, blended, re-blended, and sometimes turpentine away . . . and then started again" (Class Journals).

The teacher's role is crucial when the child is considered at the center of the process of education. Teachers, as older and more experienced, protect and nourish students' growth; they are guides in, rather than directors of, the process of education. They are active participants in their students' learning and in their own learning as well. A contemporary scholar of child-centered education holds the metaphor of teacher as an impressionist painter who "knows how to include and reconceptualize multiple theories into practice as she constructs her classroom without losing the foundation of child-centeredness, which is the valuing of children's needs and interests" (Tzuo, 2007, p. 39).

Words that teachers in this curricular culture generally use to refer to their roles include "gardener," "facilitator," "authentic co-learner," "role model," "resource," "nurturer," "personal and intellectual support system," "objective guide," "coach," and "mentor." One high school teacher regularly describes himself as "a river guide, accompanying [students] on a waterway which challenges, excites, and teaches them. I may steer the boat but I am as challenged and excited as they are" (Class Journal).

Advocates of this curricular culture believe that student motivation is self-sustaining and self-reinforcing; teachers' work largely consists of allowing each learner's motivation to continuously energize itself. By applying this principle, teachers can respond to each student's inner world and act as a bridge between it and the external world. It is this ability to provide students with access between the realms of internal and external reality that is the source of meaningful, creative learning. The role of the teacher, according to Gardner Murphy (1961):

> will not be fulfilled by turning over a thousand stones, but by enabling the child or youth to see in the stone which arouses his interest the history of this world, the evolution of its waters, atmospheres, soils, and rocks, prying into deeper meanings "just because they are there." (p. 27)

Characterized as passionate about students, the pursuit of knowledge, and knowledge itself, teachers who follow this orientation encourage the potential in every child and are responsive to all areas of need. They are exquisitely aware that learning depends principally on the relationships between themselves and their students, students and other students, students and content, and students and the context of the learning process. Moreover, teachers themselves must have a high tolerance for ambiguity and for the active (and sometimes messy) pursuit of learning; they must also have the love and patience to await the natural evolution of each individual's participation in the process.

Beliefs and Practices: Content and Context

One of the greatest areas of misunderstanding surrounding the culture of "Developing Self and Spirit" arises from discussions of curriculum content. Content generated by student interest does not, as many believe, typically mean that students only study what they want and when they want. While proponents of Neill's Summerhill model and similar alternative schools believe that students don't need to study anything until they are ready to—each in his own way, each in her own time—this is not in any way the norm.

The culture of curriculum, in practice, provides a broad array of content that is presented and processed in ways that encourage maximum student participation and creativity. Teaching is designed to allow and encourage students to question, to express themselves, to formulate and reformulate their ideas, and to make connections between the personal and the objective. What makes the topic of content particularly difficult to deal with in this curricular culture is the almost impossible task of separating how and in what environment the content is offered from the content itself.

The content offered falls into one of four specific categories: academics, athletics, arts and aesthetics, and service. Psychological, emotional, spiritual, and social growth are presumed to be a part of each content category.

The academic content gives students almost limitless opportunities for shaping and interpreting material to address their own interests and inclinations. In this way, curriculum integration is commonly practiced often through study across subject areas. Literature, philosophy, psychology, anthropology, sociology, theology, mathematics, and the sciences are all compatible with this mode of thought; there is, in fact, no academic subject matter that would be deemed unsuitable for exploration.

This curricular culture's holistic approach provides for the physical growth of all students no matter their specific athletic abilities. Proceeding from the premise of the unity of all aspects of the individual, children are encouraged to physically participate in one or many activities; in line with the desire to operate from a base of student interest, the opportunities are plentiful and varied. It is not unusual for even the smallest school to offer a broad choice of activities including from team sports such as basketball, football, soccer, track, and baseball, lacrosse, and field hockey. Individual sports activities are also available, again often in a variety that does not seem warranted by the number of potential participants; these may include swimming, bowling, golf, tennis, and horseback riding. There is a strong commitment to physical health and activity as an essential and pleasurable lifetime habit; while skill development and excellence are stressed in all student endeavors, ability is secondary to participation.

The arts are another essential component of content. Mirroring Plato's contention that aesthetic development was basic to the wholeness of the individual, opportunities in the visual, performing, and literary arts are many. Students are presented with on-going opportunities to paint, draw, build, sing, act, write, and otherwise enliven their participatory and appreciative aesthetic sensibilities. Such activities, moreover, are considered neither peripheral to the academic curriculum nor as extra-curricular; they are esteemed as an integral part of the general curricular offerings.

Service, within and outside of the classroom and school setting, is the fourth content area emphasized. Students are expected, as they mature, to take increasing responsibility for their own well-being and that of others. This content area takes many forms. Student governance is always a part of the content in a learner-centered orientation. In situations where schools serve a wide range of age or grade levels, cross-age tutoring, big and little sister programs, adopt-a-class programs, and peer tutoring are all common. Environmental responsibilities within the school community, such as gardening and recycling, are typical. Additionally, students often choose to contribute to their communities outside of school through the avenues of group or individual service projects. Long before service learning was an educational trend, it was commonplace in "Self and Spirit" classrooms and schools.

In sum, the goal for curriculum content provided in a holistic environment is to develop mind, heart, the body, and spirit. By modeling these curricular goals in the content provided to learners, the education in this culture of curriculum strives for a totality of purpose and method.

But whereas they are various forms of holistic education, the physical and social environment in the classroom is probably the most prescribed component of a learner-centered orientation to curriculum. The classroom itself—at the pre-school, elementary, high school, and university levels—is characterized by activity, motion, and conversation.

It is expected that learners will approach content through animated, practical engagement with subject matter, teachers, and peers. Educators in this curricular culture often abandon traditional textbooks in favor of primary source materials, human, and technological resources. The internal and external materiel brought to bear on learning is almost limitless; for instance, it is not uncommon for students to regularly interview members of the school or the larger community to gain information needed to solve a dilemma presented by classroom content. Neither is it unusual for the learner-centered classroom to have a number of non-teachers in attendance at any given time including parent volunteers, community members, staff colleagues, or older or younger students. Trips and excursions outside the school or classroom are a regular part of the learning environment: a park for study science, a community center to shed light on a project dealing with adult day care, or a grocery store as a setting for counting, measuring, and mathematics. To support students' interests and academic growth, libraries, computer technology, and other resource avenues are accessed more often and with greater regularity than is customary in traditional schools. These practices are consistent with the idea that the classroom is a part of the world and that students can and should partake of all the various stimuli and resources, human and material, available within it.

The classroom itself looks busy—as if many things are going on at one time—and that in fact is a fair representation of what actually occurs. One teacher, for instance, describes his fourth-grade classroom as one in which "the structure and content are flexible and varied, the expectations and focus are high, and the students are purposeful and engaged" (Class Journal). Cooperation is the norm, there is a balance of individual and group work, and interaction is based on dialogue and discussion, listening and sharing. How students *feel* about the material they are studying and learning is of great importance.

The physical context in which learning occurs must be comfortable—not grand, but comfortable—with adequate light, sufficient room in which to move about, and different areas where students can work alone or with others. The environment must, above all, be emotionally safe, caring, respectful and, thereby, conducive to experimentation and risk-taking. There is an assumption that the classroom *belongs* to the students, as a family and a community, and that it is their desire and responsibility to keep it usable and inviting. Contemporary educational philosopher Jane Roland Martin (1992) imagined holistic education within a "schoolhome." Francis Parker (1894/1937) described a school in three ways, as a "model home, a complete community, an embryonic democracy;" this curricular culture reflects Parker's vision through the physical and psychological environment found in the classroom and the school.

Beliefs and Practices: Curriculum Planning and Evaluation

The question of who develops curriculum in such a setting is in a sense simple to answer, for everyone affected—and everything imaginable—is involved in curriculum making. The curriculum plan itself is determined by the goals, ideals, visions, and values of this curricular culture. Specific programs of study, course work, developmental sequence and scope (in part) are a combined effort of professional educators (teachers and administrators), and subject matter specialists. They are also informed by the desires and needs of students, especially in terms of topics emphasized, depth and breadth of treatment, and the tangents and sequences of study. Teachers, teachers and students, students and students, and sometimes other parties integral to the successful realization of study and learning goals often negotiate the specific activities of the offered curriculum. Curriculum is planned and developed with as broad a brush as possible, allowing for maximum input and participation.

Curriculum making in this context, moreover, is never considered complete; it is under constant modification and revision to meet the developing needs of students through the discoveries and realities of society. Curriculum design is envisioned and enacted as a process, not as an end, for the ultimate goal is to continue the learner's inquiry to ever greater lengths and depths. Because of the ongoing use of multiple resources to animate learning, holistic progressive schools are often the first to incorporate new knowledge into their programs as they are not bound by texts of a set curriculum. Moreover, because the philosophical base of the culture is so strongly connected to the incorporation of all possible avenues of learning, it is also less likely than mainstream education to fall prey to a particular fad of curriculum composition, direction, or delivery.

While methods of assessment and evaluation are of on-going concern in "Developing Self and Spirit," standardized measurements designed to assess externally prescribed curriculum and outcomes are notably inappropriate when dealing with schooling that takes the student as its central focus. Holistic educators realize that the zealous urge to quantify learning creates an environment where the measures used become of greater import and interest than the goals that inform education itself.

Over time, beginning during the era of progressive education, different kinds of evaluation tools and instrumentation were designed to measure the broader concepts embraced by a student-centered curriculum. These alternatives were expected to measure not only student growth, but also growth among teachers and within the school itself, and changes in curriculum processes. Since teachers, students, parents, and administrators are all involved in creating the curriculum in this culture, it is considered essential that all be somehow involved in assessing and evaluating it.

Long before portfolio assessment and authentic evaluation strategies became popular in the latter part of the 20th century, their precursors were found in schools designated as "experimental." Students were involved in self-assessment from the youngest of ages and teachers and administrators were likewise expected to evaluate their own progress and growth. Reports to parents were anecdotal and extensive, focusing specifically on the development of the individual child. Academic grades were, to a large degree, done away with and classwork was evaluated less by testing and more by portfolio, performance, production, or presentation. Throughout all evaluative activities, it was clear that the process of enacting the curriculum took precedence over the content, for it was by way of the process that real learning occurred.

In schools that represent this curricular culture today, students are typically assessed in multiple ways, the majority of them non-standardized and authentic. Tests, when they are used, are most often teacher or teacher/student constructed and based on the specific problems upon which students are working. Assessment of students' academic achievement, focuses more on complex forms of problem solving than performance on standardized multiple-choice tests. Equally as important—to teachers, administrators, parents, and students—is the development of a positive attitude toward learning and school. Standardized, normed, objective tests such as the Iowa Test of Basic Skills, the California Test of Basic Skills, etc., are given when necessary for purposes of external evaluation by funding and/or accrediting agencies; the College Boards, SATs and like instruments are administered when needed for admission to institutions of higher education. Students from these schools perform well on all such measures.

Can students educated in such environments and assessed by "non-traditional" means measure up in the competitive world of jobs and university admissions? Experimental schools received scrutiny in a classic research study, known as the Eight Year Study, conceived and conducted by the Progressive Education Association in the late 1930s. Secondary school students from 30 experimental schools who entered college between 1936 and 1939 were paired and matched with students from more conventional institutions and evaluated on the basis of a variety of traits, including academic achievement. Arrangements had been made with the colleges, over 300 in number, to admit students from the non-traditional schools based solely on teacher recommendations and without regard to specific course credits or test results.

Regardless of the measures used to evaluate these students after college entrance or of the attributes measured, the graduates of the student-centered schools outscored their counterparts in every area, including academics (Chamberlin, Chamberlin, Drought, & Scott, 1942; Smith & Tyler, 1942). But perhaps, more importantly, the study highlighted that students from innovative schools seemed to "possess a higher degree of intellectual curiosity and drive, often demonstrated a high degree of resourcefulness in meeting new situations, and showed a more active concern with national and world affairs." An evaluator of the study concluded that schools from the less conventional approach send on to college "better human materials" (Cremin, 1961, pp. 255–256).

Although a large-scale study has not taken place in contemporary times, advocates believe that students are similarly successful in this curricular culture today. Educational research consistently demonstrates the worth of small class size, attention to the progress of each student, and high level of student engagement. However, it often is the case that many students in "Self and Spirit" schools do come from families highly supportive of their children's education.

Dilemmas of Practice

Teaching within the curricular culture "Developing Self and Spirit" requires educators to have exceptional dedication to students, to learning, and to process. They are obliged to be artists rather than efficiency experts, to be devoted to the act and acquisition of learning and desirous of increasing their own reserves of knowledge, and to be responsive to individual educational needs rather than prescribed, standardized goals and outcomes.

Those who work in such an environment must be dedicated to dealing with the whole child in all of his or her complexity as a social, emotional, academic, intellectual, spiritual, and practical being. Since students do not leave their other lives at the schoolhouse door, the realities of their personal existence outside of school must be recognized, appreciated, and dealt with on a daily basis. Additionally, holistic educators must acknowledge and contend with the broader social and political challenges of the society in which students reside. This demands both commitment and skill.

Teaching successfully in this curricular culture implies the ability to create and shape environments in which children are motivated to question, act, react, assess, evaluate, and question again. Teachers must be able to derive conundrums and problems from everyday activities and situations and, in order to do this well, they must have an understanding of each child as an individual and the intellectual possibilities of ideas and bodies of knowledge. Artistry emerges from the teacher's ability to match each child's experience with opportunities to grow cognitively, emotionally, socially, and spiritually through tasks that are challenging but not impossible.

Although the individual school district (or even state or the federal government) might provide the standards for curriculum development, the primary responsibility for program design resides with the teacher. Therefore, teachers must be skilled at, and enjoy, developing curriculum within the context dictated by the combined realities of the student and the classroom. This means that teachers must be able to grasp and utilize "teachable moments" as they occur within the every day moments of schooling.

Perhaps what is most important and demanding of all is for teachers to accept and embrace the vision and principles of the culture in which they work, for "Developing Self and Spirit" is more than a philosophy of pedagogy. This culture is intended to encompass the school in its entirety, not just in terms of curriculum content, teaching techniques, and assessment strategies but also in terms of its social life and organization. It is meant to extend beyond the walls of the school as well, and see itself in relation to the realities its students encounter at home and in the world outside of the educational institution. One cannot foster individual development only during school hours; this is a culture that presumes a shared and reflected conception of life itself.

But even when educators are ready to assume these enormous responsibilities, are passionate about teaching holistically, and develop the skills to teach successfully in this curricular culture, a major dilemma remains. As the school and classroom should be rich in resources or in access to resources, this becomes exceedingly difficult when the financial state of educational systems is in disarray. Also linked to larger issues of school finance is the question of class size—it is not easy to enact student-centered practice when classes are overly large and teachers work without support.

Critique

The strength of "Developing Self and Spirit" as a curricular culture lies in its holistic, fluid approach to learning—an approach that creates no unnatural barriers between the individual and the community, work and play, art and science. Education becomes an unfolding process that itself serves to stimulate learners' natural curiosity and encourages on-going and increasing involvement in life. However, as this postmodern concept of education is not only the antithesis of traditional industry-oriented, competitive, and teacher-centered classrooms, it is increasingly alien in the current climate of standardized curriculum and high-stakes testing. Therefore, common criticisms of this curricular culture must be acknowledged, but also interrogated, as a good many criticisms of "Developing Self and Spirit" stem from stereotypical notions about its beliefs and practices rather than from serious analysis. These misconceptions compel us to answer criticisms that would only have credibility if their premises were sound.

One frequently voiced concern is based on the mistaken notion that "Developing Self and Spirit" all but repudiates the importance of subject matter in the curriculum, relying only on individual interest and desire to shape learning. This misunderstanding has done more to discredit the culture than any other as it commonly leads to the assumption that students study what they want and when they want with benefit of neither supervision nor guidance. More accurately, in this curricular culture, teachers are charged with the responsibility for finding material suitable for learning through experience and then, after it is discovered, with utilizing it to build on students' earlier experiences so that their encounters will be as rich and full as is possible. What is at issue is an attempt to assure that student learning is not dependent upon the conventional academic disciplines but that it grows from connecting and transcending the disciplines in creative and cognitively defensible ways. Rather than dealing with separateness, the goal is to deal with wholes; instead of discrete bits of knowledge, the focus is on interaction and continuity.

A second stereotype of this curricular culture is that it rejects of all authority and simply celebrates untrammeled freedom. Undoubtedly, educators in "Developing Self and Spirit" do oppose authority that is externally imposed, the kind that impels through fear or compulsion engendered by an inequality of power. Their rejection of external authority, however, does not suggest that all authority be repudiated, but simply that it must come from more effective sources; it should be earned rather than assumed. Freedom, then, becomes not unfettered but dependent upon the exercise of intelligent judgment and responsibility in the assignment of authority to oneself or to others. Maxine Greene (1988) notes that only by way of education can people be

> provoked to reach beyond themselves in their intersubjective space. It is through and by means of education that they may be empowered to think

about what they are doing, to become mindful, to share meanings, to conceptualize, to make varied sense of their lived worlds. (p. 12)

A third common misapprehension about this curricular culture relates to outcomes for learners, suggesting that this culture's characteristic nature is such a misrepresentation of American life that graduates from holistic schools could not possibly function in a society based on competitive capitalism. Certainly, this curriculum downplays competition so that young people educated in this culture have less experience with the realities of competitive life. But to this concern, we might also ask, does it not benefit children as they grow to adulthood to deeply understand that people's accomplishments can be appreciated without evaluating them only in contrast to others? How can students be encouraged to be life-long learners if they work only for grades rather for than the intrinsic rewards and pleasures of learning?

A final criticism is the accusation of excessive individuality and the contention that this culture makes learners self-indulgent—that they are encouraged to care only for their wants and needs. Yet, such charges of blatant individualism fly in the face of a strong focus of "Developing Self and Spirit": the cooperative, problem-centered work within the process of schooling and the concomitant necessity of extending this work into the community itself. Advocates instead believe that the holistic process of education helps to develop individuals who are strong physically, spiritually, and intellectually (with a wide range of academic skills) so to become energetic, self-governing participants within the larger society.

Nonetheless, as a curricular culture emphasizes certain elements over others and cannot "do it all," there are issues for valid critique. A weakness in this curricular culture may be its lack of agreed-upon cognitive (or academic) end-products: there are no "goals" in the sense that we use the word other than the desire for well-educated, good people. It is taken on faith that learners have innate good sense and that—presuming they are guided by skilled teachers—they will choose wisely of the knowledge important for them to participate fully in society and to live well as individuals. We must ask if the learning process can fall prey to idiosyncratic interests of teachers and learners, directed by nothing more than vaguely articulated learning goals?

Moreover, although advocates of "Developing Self and Spirit" trust that with the right experiences, individuals will want to care about the world and each other, there is not an explicit sense of the common good in its social vision. There is a lack of critical emphasis on social realities and problems, for example fostering a critical look at racism—unless that endeavor bubbles up from students' interests. Additionally, children learning in this curricular culture truly experience an educational world without authoritarianism and competition, but they may not investigate the values of mainstream society in a critical way. In the words of an educator who observed a child-centered school:

The null curriculum was a critical engagement with the social, political, and economic contexts in which learning is connected. There was no evidence of teachers providing learning for the means of social reform. Also, there lacked a sense of connection to society. It was as if students and teachers were on hiatus from the realities of the world. (Class Paper)

Certainly, students in child-centered classrooms have the freedom to scrutinize texts or society and will receive the guidance for their studies and for critical analysis, but it also is their right not to grapple with such pursuits.

In conclusion, the dominant paradigm influencing schools today is one of imposition of goals and aims upon school communities, caring for products more than people, promoting business imageries rather than human ones. As society values measurement and accountability, constraint, regimentation, sameness, and the construed—it becomes increasingly indifferent to freedom and the natural. In contrast, this curricular orientation stems from a philosophy that presumes students' natural curiosity as opposed to believing in rewards and punishments for learning; it affirms the innate, genuine goodness of humankind to one that sees a need to somehow "make" people good in the face of evil. It may not be so much that the methods of "Developing Self and Spirit" are in such dispute, but rather, that current societal beliefs about the nature of children and humankind are so overwhelmingly out of step with the premises upon which this culture of curriculum rests.

References

Chamberlin, D., Chamberlin, E., Drought, N., & Scott, W. (1942). *Adventure in American education, Vol. 4: Did they succeed in college?* New York: Harper & Brothers.

Cobb, E. (1977). *The ecology of imagination in childhood.* New York: Columbia University Press.

Comenius, J. A. (1907). *The great didactic* (M. W. Keatinge, Ed. & Trans.). London: Adam and Charles Black.

Cremin, L. A. (1961). *The transformation of the school: Progressivism in American education, 1870–1957.* New York: Vintage Books.

Dewey, J. (1897/1981). *My pedagogic creed.* In J. J. McDermott (Ed.), *The philosophy of John Dewey* (pp. 442–454). Chicago: The University of Chicago Press.

Dewey, J. (1938/1963). *Experience and education.* New York: Collier Books.

Fishman, S. M., & McCarthy, L. (1998). *John Dewey and the challenge of classroom practice.* New York: Teachers College Press.

Fowler, B. (1930). President's message. *Progressive Education, 7.*

Froebel, F. (1887). *The education of man* (W. N. Hailman, Trans.). New York: D. Appleton.

Greene, M. (1988). *The dialectic of freedom.* New York: Teachers College Press.

Griffin, W. M. (1906) *School days in the fifties: A true story with some untrue names of persons and places, with an appendix, containing and an autobiographical sketch of Francis Wayland Parker.* Chicago: A. Flanagan.

Knowles, M. (1984). *Andragogy in action*. San Francisco: Jossey-Bass.

Martin, J. R. (1992). *The schoolhome*. Cambridge, MA: Harvard University Press.

Miller, J. P. (2007). *The holistic curriculum* (2nd ed.) Toronto: University of Toronto Press.

Miller, R. (2006). Educating the child's "inner power." Paths of learning. Retrieved from http://www.pathsoflearning.net/articles_Educating_Childs_Inner_Power.php

Moffett, J. (1994). *The universal schoolhouse*. San Francisco: Jossey-Bass.

Montessori, M. (1909/1964). *The Montessori method*. New York: Schocken Books.

Murphy, G. (1961). *Freeing intelligence through teaching*. New York: Harper Brothers.

Neill, A. S. (1960). *Summerhill*. New York: Hart.

Parker, F. W. (1894/1937). *Talks on pedagogics: An outline of the theory of concentration*. New York: The John Day Co.

Pearce, J. C. (1976). *The magical child*. New York: Dutton.

Robinson, K., & Aronica, L. (2009). *The element: How finding your passion changes everything*. New York: Viking.

Roehlkepartain, E. C., King, P. E., Wagener, L., & Benson, P. (2005). *The handbook of spiritual development in childhood and adolescence*. Thousand Oaks, CA: Sage.

Rogers, C. R. (1969). *Freedom to learn*. Columbus, OH: Merrill.

Rousseau, J. J. (1762/1911). *Emile*. London: J. M. Dent and Sons.

Samples, B. (1979). *The metaphoric mind*. Reading, MA: Addison Wesley.

Smith, E., & Tyler, R. W. (1942). *Adventure in American education, Vol. 3: Appraising and recording student progress*. New York: Harper & Brothers.

Steiner, R. (1973). *A modern art of education*. London: Rudolf Steiner Press.

Tzuo, P. W. (2007). The tension between teacher control and children's freedom in a child-centered classroom: Resolving the practical dilemma through a closer look at the related theories. *Early Childhood Education Journal, 35*(1), 33–39.

Whitehead, A. N. (1929). *The aims of education*. New York: Macmillan.

Chapter 7

Educating Through Occupations

Nancy Stewart Green and Pamela Bolotin Joseph

> An occupation is a continuous activity having a purpose. Education *through* occupations consequently combines within itself more of the factors conducive to learning than any other method.
>
> John Dewey, 1916, *Democracy and Education*, p. 309

On your visit to Township High School in a typical afternoon you would find a number of ninth graders working in small seminars, studios, and labs. Students rehearse excerpts from Studs Terkel's book, *Working*, in Ms. Porter's English class; tomorrow they will share their poetic or artistic representations of the characters in the book. In Mr. Lee's integrated math and science class, students listen to and ask questions of an engineer who explains real world math problems she encounters in her work. In fact, throughout Township High, all ninth-grade students are taking academic courses that focus on the question, "what is the meaning of work?"

In addition, for two semesters the ninth graders take in-depth courses focused on particular careers. Students in Mr. Simon's class on the construction industry meet with representatives of industry, unions, and the local zoning board as well as experts who explain the construction projects' impact on the environment. In this class, students will learn about the various trades in the industry and obtain practical knowledge about ordering and estimating materials. The course culminates in a joint project using basic design, woodworking, and electrical skills. This project will be displayed at a school-wide job fair at the end of the year.

But you would have to leave Township High and venture forth to various businesses, industries, and studios in the nearby metropolitan area to find the rest of the ninth graders. Several times a week, students visit businesses, work with mentors in the arts and industry, and do apprenticeships. Earlier, Mr. Simon's pupils visited job sites to see for themselves work in the construction industry. Depending on their classes' themes, students meet with journalists, authors, artists, musicians, and scientists in their work environments. For instance, those taking a course on teaching careers went to early childhood centers or schools and conducted interviews with teachers and teacher association leaders.

Three years ago teachers at Township High School decided to create schoolwide curriculum that makes connections between the world of work and academics so that *all* students could explore many kinds of occupations and could develop a critical understanding of work. Although only ninth graders experience a fully themed curriculum on occupations, some reconfiguration of curricular content took place throughout the school. For example, geometry class now includes an architecture unit co-designed by arts, science, and math faculty; students learn how architects use geometry and see first hand the factors involved in architectural planning. In biology class, medical and environmental researchers discuss problems posed in their fields. Social science teachers include labor history and economic systems in their American history and government courses and have frequent guest speakers to ensure that the curriculum stays focused on various real-world perspectives.

In subsequent years these ninth graders can opt to take more specialized courses in Career and Technical Education (CTE) geared toward specific occupations. Or, they can enroll in one of the "schools-within-a-school" or career academies at Township High that focus on the health professions, horticulture, media, banking and finance, or architecture and construction. No matter what paths students choose, Township High teachers try to provide students with substantial academic background in all career-oriented courses or programs.

§

This snapshot of Township High School contains elements of the philosophy and practices of the curriculum culture, "Educating Through Occupations." Advocates for this curriculum believe that study of occupations engages students in academic knowledge as well as connecting them with life outside the school, taking a view of vocational knowledge as "not just preparation for mere jobs but for occupations that enable a search for personal meaning, socioeconomic enhancement" and a critical understanding of work and society (Arenas, 2008, p. 378). In that sense, "Educating Through Occupations" is meant for all students, and not just for those who might enter the workforce soon after graduation.

Above all, "Educating Through Occupations" conveys a broad and inclusive meaning of occupation, rejecting narrow skills training in favor the integration of academic with work studies. Therefore it differs significantly from vocational education that primarily trains students to meet the needs of industry—despite shared practices in both orientations on "hands-on" work and apprenticeships. In addition, some theorists and practitioners envision a version of this curricular culture that focuses on critical understanding of economic systems, work conditions, and the industrial impact on the environment. A number of United States schools have incorporated aspects of "Educating Through Occupations" into their curriculum, although CTE has been the most popular and formalized enactment of this curricular culture in contemporary times.

Visions

This culture of curriculum draws both explicitly and implicitly from John Dewey's view of educating *through* and not *for* occupations:

> Though there should be organic connection between the school and business life, it is not meant that the school is to prepare the child for any particular business, but that there should be a natural connection of the everyday life of the child with the business environment about him, and that it is the affair of the school to clarify and liberalize this connection, to bring it to consciousness, not by introducing special studies, like commercial geography and arithmetic, but by keeping alive the ordinary bonds of relation. (Dewey, 1907/2007, pp. 90–91)

In the writings of Dewey and modern-day proponents about this curriculum, four themes emerge about its nature and aims:

- The unity of the curriculum with no separation between practical or experiential and academic learning;
- The development of whole persons who contribute to society as they continue to grow and learn throughout their lives;
- The contribution to democracy by providing an education of equal opportunity and that instills sympathetic understanding of other people's lives and work across social classes and backgrounds, and;
- The development of intelligent and even critical understanding of work and work conditions within society.

The first theme centers on the unity of the curriculum and the importance of removing the dichotomy between vocational and academic study (see Grubb, 1997).

> Vocational education, as [Dewey] conceived it, was not some peculiar kind of education that had to be constructed separate and apart from the cultural side of the curriculum. He called for an essential unity in the curriculum, informed by an elegant epistemology that took lived human experience as its inspiration. (Lewis, 1998, p. 291)

Further, Dewey "understood occupations as life activities that struck a balance between the intellectual and practical facets of existence" (Arenas, 2008,

p. 381). Connections to academic curriculum can be found in study of social activity—including industry and occupations—pertinent to the lives of students. Thus occupation, or vocation, must be "conceived broadly, as an organizer of many facets of our lives, not just our work lives" and "vocational knowledge" needed to not be "at the fringes but nearer the core of the school curriculum" (Lewis, 1998, p. 291).

But it is not just the subject of occupations that is important in this curriculum but the experiential nature of practical learning. Advocates describe how participation in the school and neighborhood through jobs and apprenticeships contributes to an individual's development of independent character:

> Activity calls for the positive virtues—energy, initiative, and originality—qualities that are worth more to the world than even the most perfect faithfulness in carrying out orders...the weak character will be strengthened and the strong one will not form any of those small bad habits that seem so unimportant at first and that are so serious in their cumulative effect. (Dewey & Dewey, 1915/1962, pp. 213, 215)

Also, participation in community fosters transformative experiences for intellectual and moral growth.

The second corollary emphasizes the personal development of individuals to become prepared, but not trained, for meaningful work. John and Evelyn Dewey (1915/1962) who documented numerous examples of this curriculum in their book, *Schools of Tomorrow*, wrote that "each individual should be capable of self-respecting, self-supporting, *intelligent* work" and to be "vitally and sincerely interested in the calling upon which they must enter" (pp. 177, 180). More recent proponents of this curricular culture embrace the notion that education should lead to personal fulfillment (Rehm, 1999; Rojewski, 2002), enabling students to examine work as part of a personal quest for meaning rather than as simply an onerous reality of life.

As well, proponents see a more utilitarian but nevertheless important personal significance of "Educating Through Occupations." They believe that within neighborhoods of generational unemployment and despair, occupational learning gives students a reason to come to school and allows them hopefulness for the future. Similarly, the Deweys (1915/1962) noted that in schools that stimulate children's "sense of responsibility for their community and neighbors," attendance improves and fewer children become delinquent (p. 158).

The third vision relates to how "Educating Through Occupations" contributes to participation in democratic society. The Deweys (1915/1962) saw that this curricular orientation creates a balance between the academic and the vocational curriculum; they argued that this balance has social importance because having two systems of education undermines democracy by essentially segregating students into two castes. They were adamant that "[t]here must not be one system for the children of parents who have more leisure and another for the children of those who are wage-earners" (p. 226).

> The academic education turns out future citizens with no sympathy for work done with the hands, and with absolutely no training for understanding the most serious of present-day social and political difficulties. The trade training will turn out future workers who may have greater immediate skill than they would have had without their training, but who have no enlargement of mind, no insight into the scientific and social significance of the work they do, no education which assists them in finding their way on or in making their own adjustments. (Dewey & Dewey, 1915/1962, p. 226)

By providing greater insight about occupations, including those that might be outside the experience of students or their families, learners will gain understanding about the work required, skills, and attributes needed for particular occupations. Further, as this curriculum would not privilege one kind of learning or one group of learners, it helps to create a society that meliorates inequality and supports equality of educational opportunity.

Finally, some supporters of "Educating Through Occupations" have a vision of students developing a critical understanding of work, labor conditions, and society. The Deweys (1915/1952) expanded their idea of "intelligent work" not only to include scientific understanding of processes but social understanding—including work conditions—so that workers will not be "blind cogs and pinions in the apparatus they employ" (p. 178). In *Democracy and Education*, John Dewey (1916) made a more direct connection between work education and a broader social vision; he wrote that education should lead to a "more equitable and enlightened social order"—one in which vocational education should "not subject youth to the demands and standards of the present system, but [utilize] its scientific and social factors to develop a courageous intelligence, and to make intelligence practical and executive" (Dewey, 1916, p. 319). In that way, curriculum would be intimately connected to contemporary social and economic life and study of work as a steppingstone to critical democratic citizenship.

As follows, such proponents emphasize attainment of political understanding of work and society (Kincheloe, 1999; Simon & Dippo, 1992). Critical educators believe that this curricular orientation must inspire interrogation of the nature of work and commitment leading to a larger movement toward social justice. Advocates of a critical form of "Educating Through Occupations" see education in a context of reform of the economic system that would give more voice to workers to become "an alternative to doctrinaire state socialism and unbridled free enterprise" (Kincheloe, 1999, p. 7). Through "a critical analysis of the social and political relations of production" (Arenas, 2008, p. 385), occupational education can be an "economic empowerment curriculum," helping to create self-conscious, questioning actors in the work force (Kincheloe, 1999, p. 183). Moreover, critical educators voice concern about the wider public dimensions of schooling, deploring the way in which schools and society foster inequality and perpetuates a culture of consumerism and competition.

To attain this critical vision of work education, students need to learn about alternative economic systems and resistance to "the systematic attempts to reduce [workers'] power." They should have "opportunities for meaningful and equal participation in the production process" and should have input into what is produced (Arenas, 2008, p. 384). Additionally, those taking the position that there is a need for a critical approach to "Educating Through Occupations" see vocational programs as logical places to investigate the relationships between production and the environment (see Arenas, 2008; Palmer, 1998).

As a whole, devotees of this curricular culture differ in their beliefs on how students should conceive of the wider world and act in it, yet they all agree that some version of social improvement is necessary. Whereas for some, societal enhancement means providing better opportunities for low-income students, for others, this curriculum means making society more equitable and producing compassionate, environmentally responsible citizens. Regardless of their ultimate goals for students, all those who favor this curricular orientation believe in a more generous and inclusive vision than the traditional notion of vocational skills training.

History

We cannot know the history of "Educating Through Occupations" without understanding how this curricular orientation developed in response to the more limited forms of vocational education for work skills preparation. John Dewey and other progressive educators had deep concerns about education that did not educate students to be citizens and to participate in the wider society. Work education bereft of strong academic foundations fulfilled Dewey's negative evaluation of trade education, with his concern that it would become: "an instrument of perpetuating unchanged the existing industrial order of society, instead of operating as a means of its transformation" into a society in which "the interest of each in his work is uncoerced and intelligent: based upon its congeniality to his own aptitudes" (Dewey, 1916, p. 316). These critics of vocational education would introduce alternative conceptions that would respect work but not target particular students for a narrow education.

As the United States changed from a primarily agricultural to an industrial nation in the mid-19th century, instead of honoring the tradition of basic literacy for citizenship, preparing students for the workplace became an articulated goal of public schooling for children of color and those from poor, working-class, and/or immigrant families. The earliest program of this kind was industrial education. White industrialists promoted it as a means for teaching industrial and agricultural skills to African Americans and Native Americans—ensuring that non-dominant classes would remain without the education for political power. Hampton Institute (founded in 1868) and Carlisle Indian Industrial School (founded in 1879) were early institutions in this effort. Industrial and agricultural education continued throughout the 20th century at Indian residential schools that also focused on deculturalizing Native Americans by separating children from families and forbidding language and cultural customs (Spring, 2009).

In the early 20th century, concern with the lack of preparation for employment and the supposed propensity to vice of urban working-class and immigrant youth led to a concerted movement for vocational training within public high schools. This system of curriculum differentiation would divide students between those deemed to be academically inclined and those who were considered unsuited for academic work. "The intellectual, moral, and even biological differences among turn-of-the-century adolescents were thought to be vast and immutable (Oakes & Saunders, 2007, p. 3).

Proponents of "social efficiency," who sought a more "rational," "functional" society promoted education that would parallel the lines of industry (Kliebard, 1995, p. 24) by sorting young people "by their evident or probable destinies" (Eliot in Tozer, Violas, & Senese, 1995, p. 115). This preparation would include agriculture and lower-level industrial skills for working-class males and gender-typed rudimentary skills for working-class women. Among the groups for whom vocational education was designed, women of all races and social classes had perhaps the most rigidly defined course offerings based on their "evident and probable destiny." Eventually, the sorting of students would begin as earlier as junior high school (Spring, 1997). The tracking system became so ingrained in schools systems that educational opportunity routinely was denied to broad segments of the population.

Educators and other stakeholders also posited that vocational education could have a positive social and economic impact. Booker T. Washington and his northern supporters sought to teach southern African Americans and Native Americans agricultural skills so they would stay on the land instead of moving to cities. And proponents of home economics, reflecting popular attitudes about the destiny of women and fears of social instability, sought to strengthen the family by teaching women home-related skills. Moreover, in these cases, curricula were designed without reference to the actual experience of young men who already were experienced farmers or the many young women who learned homemaking skills from their mothers.

Vocational programs often taught outmoded skills, failing to keep up with the needs of labor markets or keep pace with technological change. Nonetheless, high schools responded with unusual quickness to industry's need for clerical workers. At the same time that supporters argued for home economics programs, floods of young women (drawn largely from the middle class) were eager to take commercial education courses to learn skills that they would use in the burgeoning field of clerical work. Enrollments in commercial courses in public high schools grew from fewer than 15,000 students in 1890 to more than 300,000 students by 1920 (Rury, 1991, p. 149). Ironically, commercial education was not recognized as a truly vocational field—presumably because the main proponents of vocational education focused their attention on training for manual labor, especially of men.

Eventually, the demand for vocational education affected national policy. So great was the concern for work preparation programs in the era in which the United States identified itself as an industrialized nation and its leaders feared the superior technical training and industrial might of Germany, the federal government broke its tradition of non-involvement in education to allocate money for pre-college vocational education. The Smith-Hughes Act of 1917 provided funds for vocational education and guidelines for curriculum planning. The law also mandated the separation of vocational training and academics, emphasized skills useful for immediate employment, and required each state to provide a curriculum developed by a panel of experts from each industry. An outcome of the Smith-Hughes Act was to formalize the divide between working-class youth and "for those destined for college, leadership, white collar, and other intellectually-demanding work." This rationale seemed acceptable to many groups, including "manufacturers, unions, social reformers," and to educators "who believed that a differentiated curriculum would provide relevancy to students and reduce the number of students leaving high school early" (Oakes & Saunders, 2007, p. 5).

For decades thereafter, federal funding continued to support vocational programs and enrollment remained "relatively steady." But resistance from working class parents to programs preparing students for working class jobs was high (Grubb, 1989, p. 22). Students also did not passively accept their schools plans for them. For instance, although home economics programs were fairly popular in the rural South and Midwest, working-class young women in the industrial cities cared little for such studies (Rury, 1991, p. 142). In a number of cases, institutions established for a given workplace purpose were used by students for their own ends, usually to gain the skills to succeed in a higher-status occupation than that intended by the founders. Students at Hampton Institute (for agricultural and industrial training) desired to become teachers (Anderson, 1988); African American students at Lucy Flower Technical High School (a home economics school) in Chicago wanted to go to college (Green, 1986), and students at normal schools (for teacher training) sought liberal arts degrees. Within 50 years of their founding, these institutions with their fixed, practical curricula had been transformed into academic institutions.

However, during the same years of the growth of vocational curriculum for work training, progressive educators founded a variety of public and private schools based on, or incorporating aspects of, the Deweyan conception of "Educating Through Occupations." Many of the experiments in progressive education during the 19th and 20th centuries were imbued with the educational principles of this curricular orientation so that children learned experientially about occupations and engaged in work activities for the benefit of their schools and communities; such schools relied on surrounding rural, small town, and urban environments as the focus of knowledge and activities. Furthermore, these forms of occupational learning did not track students into career paths.

Schools in rural areas engaged children in the occupations of their communities, in particular, the science of agriculture (Dewey & Dewey, 1915/1962, p. 69). For example, for Marie Turner Harvey, founder of the Porter School in Kirksville, Missouri, guiding principles of education were that "the everyday life of the community must furnish the main content of education" and children experientially learned about gardening, cooking, poultry and animal husbandry "along with the three R's". The curriculum for literacy and mathematics reflected real-life problems relating to agriculture (Cremin, 1961/1964, pp. 293–294). The Interlaken School, a school for boys that existed from 1907 to 1918 (emphasizing the development of "manly boys" more than understanding of occupations) developed curriculum connected to the boys' work in gardening, farming, animal husbandry, carpentry, as well as supervised work in the school's self-sufficient heating and electrical plants (Dewey & Dewey, 1915/1962, Hamer, 1998).

In progressive schools established in towns children, explored the outdoors and their communities. Often these schools, unlike their urban counterparts, had land to build large facilities for vocational work. One such example began in 1889 when James Stout donated a great deal of money to the Menomonie, Wisconsin, school district for a system focused on industrial training. Although the arts and academics were included, the heart of the program was manual training—carpentry and iron-work for boys and fabrics and foods for girls—with physical education available for both genders. A newspaper editor of the time proclaimed: "Boys who might have become disciplinary problems elsewhere actually remained in school after hours to work in the machine and carpentry shops." This system became an influential model in the United States and Canada (Cremin, 1961/1964, pp. 145–146).

Another town example—the Organic School in Fairhope, Alabama, started by Marietta Pierce Johnson in 1907—featured a child-centered curriculum that included enjoyment of learning outdoors and manual work (Cremin, p. 147; Dewey & Dewey, 1915/1962, p. 26). As well, the Elementary School at the University of Missouri, guided by Professor Junius L. Meriam from 1905 to 1924, exemplified how a school can integrate the community and its industries into the curriculum (Dewey & Dewey, 1915/1962, pp. 35–40). For example:

Fourth grade students visited several grocery stores and created a list of products found in a grocery store as well as questions to ask a grocer. Students learned how foods were shipped and kept; they also learned about liquid and dry measures. A fifth grade unit of the lumber industry lasted twenty-four days and included four excursions—to the forest, the sawmill, the planning mill, and the lumberyard. Fifth and sixth grade students visited the tax collector's office, learning how, when, and why taxes were assessed and collected and what was done with the money afterward. Sixth grade students visited the coal mine after studying the production of coal. (Chidester, 2005, p. 154)

In addition to the Elementary School's other curriculum themes of stories and play, children had time each day for woodworking (including making furniture), metal work, weaving, and sewing to make things "useful or artistic" (Meriam in Chidester, 2005, p. 165).

Elements of "Educating Through Occupations" also made a presence in public and private urban schools. In 1883, Francis Parker, an innovative superintendent in Quincy, Massachusetts, became principal of the Cook County Normal School in Chicago. He instituted in its practice school students' investigations through "neighboring fields and along the lake shore"; as well, children "made the equipment they needed for their studies in science, nature study" and the arts (Cremin, 1961/1965, p. 133). John and Alice Dewey developed the Laboratory School in 1896 when John Dewey came as professor to University of Chicago. Its three types of curriculum featured occupations, social life, and forms of communication and inquiry (Cremin, 1961/1965, p. 140). So, too, at the City and Country School of New York City founded in 1914, Caroline Pratt created a curriculum that included occupations so that "the school eventually functioned as a self-sufficient community" with "jobs… linked to the curriculum as a natural outgrowth of student inquiry" and connected to academic learning (Semel & Sadovnik, 2008, p. 1751).

The Nines ran the school store, supplying the entire school with its supplies and materials: They were responsible for purchasing inventory and then selling it, and their curriculum was heavily influenced by economics, especially how the capitalist system works. The idea was less to make a profit than to serve the community and provide valuable learning experiences for the children. The Tens were responsible for all the hand-printed materials for the Sevens, like flash cards and reading charts. The Elevens ran the print shop and attended to all the school's printing needs: attendance lists, library cards, stationery, and stamps. The Twelves first made toys, then weavings, until they settled on the publication of a monthly magazine called The *Bookworm's Digest*, which reviewed new children's books. (Semel & Sadovnik, 2008, p. 1751)

The Deweys (1915/1962) also reported on the common practice of schools purchasing printing presses so that students learned typesetting and operated the presses; in this way they could "make English concrete" and provide needed materials for their schools (p. 61). Other examples in their study show how urban high schools integrated science and industry in a problem-based curriculum and how lives of children and their families improved because of the useful vocational skills taught to children, such as carpentry, cooking, and sewing (pp. 199, 152). Schools in urban areas, such as Chicago and Indianapolis, even integrated gardening into their curricula (Dewey & Dewey, 1915/1962, p. 68).

But the most famous experiment in "Educating Through Occupations" was the Gary Plan, begun when Willard Wirt, a committed follower of Dewey's "learning by doing" philosophy, became superintendent of the Gary, Indiana, Public Schools in 1907. Wirt wanted to make the school the center of the community by using each school facility at all hours, with "platoons" of students alternating between academic work and occupational instruction, outdoor activities, and arts and music. In the evening the facility was open for adult classes and community activities. Each school housed both elementary and high school programs, with hands-on occupational instruction for all ages, including making furniture for the school. The students, through their own labor, met the school's printing, electrical, painting, and plumbing needs; girls also did this work if they so desired (Volk, 2005, p. 40). By using each building at all hours and seasons, Wirt sought to make the schools economical but also to "make the school the true center of the artistic and intellectual life of the neighborhood" (Cremin, 1961/1965, p. 155).

The Gary Plan was the object of enthusiastic support—but more often from people outside the community. Observers praised it for "rousing children's curiosity," learning from peers across age-groups, and avoiding tracking so that only children of the poor would obtain industrial education (Cremin, 1961/1965, p. 157; Volk, 2005, p. 40). The Deweys wrote enthusiastically about the community created by both the manual work and democratic practices:

> Gary schools do not teach civics out of a textbook. Pupils learn civics by helping to take care of their own school building, by making the rules for their own conduct in the halls and on the playgrounds....Pupils who have made the furniture and the cement walks with their own hands, and who know how much it cost, are slow to destroy walks or furniture, nor are they going to be very easily fooled as to the value they get in service and improvements when they themselves become taxpayers. The health campaigns, the application work which takes them to the social agencies of the city, the auditorium periods when they learn more about the city, all give civics lessons that make their own appeal. The children can see the things with their own eyes; they are learning citizenship by being good citizens. (Dewey & Dewey, 1915/1962, p. 146)

Spurred by reports of the system's success both economically and pedagogically, other cities adopted this plan. "By 1929 more than 200 cities in 41 states had adopted it in part or in whole, and few other communities remained totally unaffected by its innovations" (Cremin, 1961/1965, p. 60).

However, this system also became the object of vitriolic opposition from its inception in 1907 through the 1920s. In New York City it was adopted in 30 schools, but it became so controversial (and so embroiled in city politics) that students, with the support of many parents and teachers, went on strike and rioted against their schools. Opposition stemmed from dislike of the longer school day as well as concern that academic subjects were being sacrificed to preparation for jobs. When the administration changed, the 3-year experiment with the Gary Plan was abandoned.

As one of the foremost examples of curriculum transformation in the educational history of United States, the Gary system serves as an example of the pitfalls of reculturing rapidly, from the top down, and without adequate "buy-in" from parents, students, and teachers. Despite the strong support of progressive educators, the elements of "time, trust, team, and training as necessary elements in order to have a chance at successful change" appeared not to have been present when school leaders implements the Gary system (Volk, 2005, p. 45).

By the end of the 1930s, even remnants of the platoon system were disappearing across the United States. Throughout much of the 20th century, vocational education as trade preparation made a strong presence in schools—generally intended for adolescents expected not to have college in their future. The progressive vision of occupations education never became the predominant model and the situation stayed the same for several generations of students.

However, prompted by another massive economic transition in the mid-1980s—this time to the post-industrial or "information" era and by renewed fears of foreign competition—vocational education again received national attention. Several years later, two federal initiatives in the 1990s supported the "new" vocational education—a form of education far more in line with Dewey's "Educating Through Occupations." The Perkins Act Amendments of 1990, the School-to-Work Act of 1994, and their reauthorizations in 1998 and 2006 increased financial support for vocational education and reversed the 1917 Smith-Hughes Act's provision of separating vocational and academic education. Moreover, they stipulated that vocational education should expose students to all aspects of an industry rather than focusing on a limited range of skills and that programs qualifying for funds under the act must be created at the local district level.

These federal mandates provided the impetus for programs to encourage collaboration among teachers, students, local businesses, and community leaders in the planning and evaluation of curriculum. With the intent of distinguishing this curriculum from the rejected skill-based education, the new legislation in 1998 also provided vocational education with a new name:

Career and Technical Education (CTE). With the impetus of federal support, school districts in all states began to offer courses and programs in CTE.

Yet, despite a new name and presumably different emphasis, it became apparent that CTE did not greatly improve the employability or the economic futures of its graduates. Studies in the following decades revealed that the incomes and employment rates for CTE graduates were lower than for those who completed college. But in contrast "vocational concentrators who *also* completed college preparatory academic courses had experiences much like those of their college prep peers" (Oakes & Saunders, 2007, p. 7). Such research provided evidence that CTE should be more in the Deweyan tradition (see Grubb, 1997):

> These findings, combined with shifts in the labor market, have led more and more educators and policymakers to believe that high schools should blur the distinction between college preparation and workforce preparation and prepare all students for *both* college *and* career. The thinking is that a combined approach would increase both the rigor and relevance of the high school curriculum, and, as a consequence, boost academic achievement, motivate students to stay in school, and improve their workforce outcomes. (Oakes & Saunders, 2007, p. 8)

Presently the idea that all students need to learn about occupations within an academic curriculum pervades contemporary state and national school reform initiatives and school practices.

There several current models for "Educating Through Occupations" in United States schools. *Career academies*—small learning communities (sometimes a school-within-a school)—focus on a career theme such as health, business, media, or technology and provide both technical and college prep courses. After the first career academy was initiated in 1969 as a school-within-a-school in Philadelphia, the number of career academies around the country grew steadily with a surge in the 1990s. In these schools, technical and academic teachers work together to integrate course material and work-based learning opportunities and college-prep courses are taught along with technical courses relating to the school's theme. The school forms partnerships with employers who mentor students, supervise internships, and provide financial support (Stern, 2001). Examples of current career academies include the W. B. Saul High School of Agricultural Sciences in Philadelphia, Maritime Academy Charter School (MACHS) also in Philadelphia, and Aviation High School (AHS) in Seattle.

Another approach to vocational education today has been the division of comprehensive high schools into *pathways* for which groups of students cluster according to their interests. These pathways are linked to occupations such as health sciences or engineering—all combining college preparatory classes with an introduction to a field of work (Stone, 2005).

Finally, there are reports of programs in academic literature, as well as in teachers' accounts of their practice, of *critical work education*. Although hardly reflecting a majority, some "Educating Through Occupations" teachers have built upon Dewey's belief that education should promote an intelligent, critical view of work conditions and systems—grounded in rigorous academic knowledge (see Kincheloe, 1999; Simon & Dippo, 1992; Steele, 2005).

Beliefs and Practices: Learners and Teachers

As do child-centered educators, the proponents of "Educating Through Occupations" believe that human beings seek meaning at each phase of their lives and that schooling should build on their curiosity and desire to learn. They affirm Dewey's belief that education should begin with learners' natural interest in practical life; otherwise, academic learning begins with abstraction, it has no significance to learners and the school becomes isolated from life. Dewey (1907/2007) refers to this as "waste in education":

> From the standpoint of the child, the great waste in the school comes from his inability to utilize the experiences he gets outside the school in any complete and free way within the school itself; while, on the other hand, he is unable to apply in daily life what he is learning at school. That is the isolation of the school—its isolation from life. When the child gets into the schoolroom he has to put out of his mind a large part of the ideas, interests, and activities that predominate in his home and neighborhood. So the school, being unable to utilize this everyday experience, sets painfully to work, on another tack and by a variety of means, to arouse in the child an interest in school studies. (pp. 89–90)

Advocates of this curricular culture propose that when there are connections between academic subjects and the "real world," students have reasons for learning and will actively and even passionately explore fields of study. For example, a CTE teacher noted that her students sometimes go far beyond the requirements, doing very ambitious projects: "Even for those students who aren't successful in school, who are struggling in three-fourths of their classes, sometimes a light goes on in marketing and they work hard and do great things" (Author's interview). Nevertheless, supporters of this curricular orientation also assume that students' motivation for learning stems from their desire to prepare for careers. They reason that learners' over-riding goals are to identify work that would be interesting, useful, and possibly lucrative.

Dewey and other progressive educators rejected the view that hands-on education was meant only for students destined for work in factories and trades; they believed that all students learn best by doing—but doing goes beyond practicing narrow skills to engaging in integrated, purposeful activity (Cremin, 1961/1964). In current times, too, advocates—including those identified with the field CTE—assume that all students, not just young people destined for jobs rather than college, need the skills used in the workplace. They contend that students who do well in academic courses often find their passion in occupational classes, discovering fulfillment in hands-on activities. But they also emphasize that "Educating Through Occupations" motivates students who have been turned off by conventional academic schooling.

Yet, educators in this curricular culture are not under the illusion that it is enough just to offer curricular content that is interesting or relevant as some students also need "psychic motivation or emotional self-confidence" to be successful in school. It is the students who have had difficulty in schooling, are more likely to be unemployed, and who feel disempowered that especially concern contemporary work educators. Such students need to be appreciated for their life experiences and strengths rather than to be considered as "deficient"; "the real challenge…is to assist young people in developing optimism in the face of entrenched hopelessness" (Lakes, 2005).

Beyond motivation, there are other premises about learning in this curricular culture. As in the real world, investigation of problems rarely stays on a theoretical level; problem solving is what people do in their occupations.

> The vocation acts as both a magnet to attract and as glue to hold. Such organization of knowledge is vital, because it has reference to needs: it is so expressed and readjusted in action that it never becomes stagnant. No classification, no selection and arrangement of facts, which is consciously worked out for purely abstract ends, can ever compare in solidity or effectiveness with that knit under the stress of occupation. (Dewey, 1916, p. 310)

As follows, the study of occupations provides a focus that enables learners to organize information in a more solid and lasting manner than any abstract system. Another key premise is that students learn best when dealing with real-world problems by negotiating with their peers in the search for solutions. Thus, learners no longer are thought of as mere imitators, but seen as capable of developing and solving problems. Finally, study of occupations lends itself to considering a plethora of questions related to all fields in the past and present—from agriculture, to architecture, to aerospace.

Overall, teachers in this culture of curriculum have multiple tasks: to keep students engaged, to make learning relevant, to stay informed of the world of work, and to figure out connections between occupations and academic content. As well, their roles include working with students in classes through innovative pedagogy, collaborating with colleagues across wide academic areas, and forming partnerships within communities.

To begin, teachers must conceptualize their roles quite differently from those who work from a transmission model or in more narrow forms of vocational education. To facilitate their students' active learning, they must be facilitators and coaches who see their students in a variety of contexts and have a fuller understanding of learners' various talents and interests. Teachers may provide crucial information but at the same time know how to quickly design and facilitate hands-on activities to lead students toward independent and creative thinking. For example a teacher in a marine science class explained what ensued when students created plans for a fish hatchery:

> I give them the problem and they accept the problem as theirs. In this class... they're one step beyond that. They not only accept the problem but they design the problem.... I give them the competencies they need to learn from doing the project, and then together we make sure that it matches. (Stern, Stone, Hopkins, McMillion, & Crain, 1994, pp. 51–52)

For the students who have low self-confidence, teachers need to be sure that there are many opportunities for successful completion of activities, paying attention also to students developing their social skills. Educators help students view themselves as empowered workers and thus they encourage students to participate, ask questions, and hold their own in classrooms and out in the community (see Gatto, 1991).

And because students need to learn about various professions or trades, teachers have to network with people in the community, invite guests to class, and make arrangements for field experiences—such as job shadowing. They also must find experts who have knowledge of the workplace and its problems. Teachers have an important role to communicate with community volunteers and find out what they can offer students and to let them know how to best support young people when they are doing activities in the field.

At the same time, teachers are called upon to significantly broaden their curriculum and pedagogy by gaining deeper knowledge of their own fields and seek connections between occupational and academic learning. Such growth may occur both independently and through collaboration in the development of curriculum materials.

Beliefs and Practices: Content and Context

The content of "Educating Through Occupations" is nearly limitless—shaped by students' interests in the world, e.g., house building, fashion design, music production. Moreover, content connects to academic disciplines throughout the arts, sciences, and technology as well as the more practical concerns of marketing, global economics, and environmental studies. Furthermore, content and context are firmly united. In a larger sense the context for learning in "Educating Through Occupations" is the world outside the school but even in classrooms, students are actively engaged in real-world issues. They create demonstrations of what they have learned and present them to their peers, teachers, and the public. They go on field trips to businesses, laboratories, hospitals, and environmental centers, bringing back what they have learned for discussion and integration in the classroom. A culminating activity could be an internship supervised by a mentor from the field.

This curriculum is consciously "modern," based on the here and now (and tomorrow) of students' lives and chosen to link studies to the social and economic milieu in which students find themselves. Students find out about occupations through observation, participation, and skills practice; they learn to solve problems, create their own mental constructs, and collaborate with others on real problems. But the content that students master may be of lesser importance than their growing ability to respond to problems and seek solutions—to "find out how to make knowledge when it is needed" (Dewey & Dewey, 1915/1962, p. 13).

Critical work education also fosters political analysis so that students understand economic systems and are encouraged not to accept misuse of power or exploitation of workers as acceptable or unalterable. This form of "Educating Through Occupations" may involve other experiential content for the purpose of empowerment. For example, role plays and drama workshops (based on Augusto Boal's forum theatre, whereby actors and audience interact) can be used to help marginalized youth "name their oppressions," act out and analyze their life experiences and their attitudes about learning, understand what it takes for "job readiness," and to "develop methods for appropriate alternative career planning" (Lakes, 2005).

It is assumed that the experiential aspect of the curricular content especially engages learners. For instance, unlike a very traditional geometry class that emphasizes memorization of theorems, in this curricular culture geometry would encompass practical problem-posing such as learning about "the concepts and skills to build roofs and frame walls that can withstand gale force winds" (Hoachlander, 2008, p. 24). The content also may include the creation of products. The students might develop a proposal for marketing a new product or be involved in a house renovation in their neighborhoods. While studying plants, students could make a garden, harvest vegetables, and sell their produce. Although specific skills do not drive the curriculum, helping young people to develop practical abilities is a welcome outcome, as would be students' decisions to pursue specific occupations because they developed passionate interests in them. Moreover, critical work education advocates hope that experiential learning will lead to "emancipatory knowledge" of occupations including "all aspects of production" and labor relationships, interrogating "market capitalism and large-scale industrialization," and understanding the effects of globalization (Arenas, 2008, pp. 384, 394).

The study of occupations does not have to take place only in industrial workplaces. Students can learn organizational skills and workplace values through community service in nonprofit organizations that exist for compassion and caring. Such examples include grassroots voluntary programs for youth to work for neighborhood improvement. In such settings, students can make an important contribution at the same time that they "learn a set of workplace values compatible with humanistic labor under democratic conditions" (Lakes, 1998, p. 316). An example of workplace learning is Apprentice Corporation, a performance company in Atlanta, Georgia, that provides dance training and performance opportunities for youth along with high expectations for discipline, responsibility, and respect.

In "Educating Through Occupations," academic content clearly is not neglected, but is integrated into projects in such a way as to make them more meaningful. Among the numerous examples of the integration of occupations and academic material is the perennial school store (possibly the most ubiquitous remnant of progressive education in public elementary schools) as a site for the practical application of arithmetic. But application of academics occurs also when students create a Web site to illustrate an aspect of history or conduct research and write reports to demonstrate results of a water-quality.

Undoubtedly practitioners of this culture of curriculum are encouraged by recent research that suggests that embedding academic subjects into occupations improves learning. For example, in an extensive study of mathematics education integrated into various field—agriculture, auto technology, business/marketing, health, and information technology—students who learned math through CTE courses performed better than their peers who did not learn math through integrated curricular content (Stone, Alfeld, Pearson, Lewis, & Jensen, 2006).

Beliefs and Practices: Curriculmu Planning and Evaluation

This culture of curriculum promotes creative and collaborative curriculum planning. As previously discussed, the curricular content must sensitively respond to students' interests and connect real-world problems with deep academic learning. But in "Educating Through Occupations," curriculum also is open to influences from outside the school setting. Because it links education to the real world, curriculum developers respond to a variety of societal changes, the local economy, and technological advances. Certainly, in the case of CTE, industry has been involved indirectly with curriculum planning when its representatives on commissions help create national and state learning outcomes and, more directly, by communicating their specific goals for CTE programs so that teachers are cognizant of the skills desired by business.

National agencies also contribute to curriculum planning. For example, the National Center on Education and the Economy (2006) published their goals for CTE programs. More directly, the federal government plays a role in CTE through financial backing, in particular, through the Perkins Acts of 2006. Although the federal support makes up just a fraction of CTE budgets, it accounts for the largest amount of federal support to high schools in the United

States and has a significant impact by providing funds and requirements to support innovation, to increase accountability, and to promote programs of study that link academic and technical content across secondary and postsecondary education (U.S. Department of Education, 2008).

Curriculum planning has followed the trend institutionalized in the Perkins Amendments to promote an integrated curriculum. In many CTE programs, academic teachers—teamed with vocational educators—are expected to integrate work-related material into their teaching. Besides exposure to business situations, teachers have broadened their ideas about planning through collaboration, e.g., when a group of high-school teachers worked to develop curriculum for a technical preparation program, this experience helped them collaborate to adopt new methods and, as one teacher said, it helped her "to break out of the mold of how you were taught" (Pauly, Kopp, & Haimson, 1995, p. 147).

In this curricular culture, assessment of students may encompass traditional measures of achievement in content areas, authentic assessment such as portfolios, and actual occupation-related products. This curricular culture's approach to evaluation has been influenced by vocational education's long tradition of authentic assessment of projects. CTE builds on this tradition to include demonstrations, products and services for sale, and student contributions to the community. Evaluation also takes place through employers' information to schools either about the students' apprenticeships or internships of the work of graduates whom they eventually hire.

Because legislators and business leaders see the economic significance of CTE, it has been subject to more external evaluation than most other curricular orientations. For example, researchers study high school programs to learn about graduates' educational attainments, large-scale studies have compared the income of CTE students with that of others in the general education track (Neumark & Rothstein, 2007, p. 125), and the success of career academies has been measured by income obtained by graduates when they entered the work force (Kemple & Willner, 2008). Such quantitative studies, however, provide only limited reflection of students' experiences and learning.

Dilemmas of Practice

Although John Dewey and progressive educators believed that children would learn and grow best when involved in real-life projects that drew from adult occupations, most instances of this curricular culture today occur at the high school level—primarily through CTE. Yet, certain ingrained characteristics of the typical United States high school present serious difficulties for curriculum enactment. To create environments that support this curricular culture, schools need to create "new structures," "opportunities for learning in multiple settings," "restructured coursework," and "integrated curriculum" (Oakes & Saunders, 2007, pp. 14–16).

The first of these obstacles, the standard organization of time (usually 40- to 50-minute periods) means that there are few opportunities for teachers to work with students for extended periods to allow more group work and projects. The traditional organization of the school day also severely limits the amount of time available to teachers to meet with colleagues for curriculum planning, brainstorming, and meaningful professional development. Some schools have addressed this problem by restructuring the day into longer periods, eliminating homeroom time to allow teachers to meet during school hours, or finding funds so teachers can be paid for planning time outside school hours—but each of these alternatives has its own difficulties. Career academies have tried to solve the problem by recruiting a group of teachers who work with a cohort of students, building in teacher planning time and allowing students to earn credit for two courses with extended classroom hours, but these alternatives require an unusual level of commitment from teachers and administrators (Stern & Stearns, 2007).

A second impediment to learning through occupations in contemporary high schools is the rigid division of teachers into subject-matter departments so that collaboration between teachers in different departments has been almost nonexistent. Besides the structural divisions of departments, the well-established hierarchy of subject matters, as well as the strong identification of high school teachers with their disciplines (Little, 1995, p. 58), has meant that even with the best intentions teachers have found it hard to cross subject borders, share perspectives, and collaborate.

As a result, academic teachers are unfamiliar with the academic scope of CTE teachers' work, have not taken the field seriously, and have welcomed CTE primarily as a holding place for their less able students. On one hand, academic teachers also have resisted what they think is "watering down" the curriculum with practical examples, but on the other, rarely have had experiences that could help them to make realistic connections between school and the world of work. As well, federal demands for CTE may seem threatening to academic departments. When vocational educators propose that the statistics or applied math be given credit within mathematics or that "Business English" qualifies for language arts credit—the specter of fewer courses (and eventually fewer teachers) for academic departments has caused alarm (Little, 1995, p. 68).

On their part, CTE teachers have resented the lower status of their field and the impression that their programs are "dumping grounds." They also count on academic departments to prepare students with the basics academic preparation but have been frustrated by having to take time from their own curriculum content when necessary to teach math or reading—difficult tasks in light of the few professional development opportunities that might show them how to integrate academic material into their curriculum (Wakelyn, 2007).

Thus it is a challenge to find instructors who are qualified in both technical and academic content and who can create and employ integrated curriculum. In short, curriculum integration is hard to do.

> Integration that is rigorous, authentic, and sustained is much more difficult than most of its advocates imagine. Constructing a rich, complex, cumulative integrated curriculum that simultaneously helps students master an academic discipline and apply it in a coherently defined domain demands time, expertise, and resources that are beyond the reach of most teachers. (Hoachlander, 1999, pp. 2–3)

Especially in the current educational climate focused on standardized tests, opportunities for professional development to learn more about curriculum integration have become diminished.

There also are programmatic difficulties encountered in implementing this curricular culture. Responsive to the Deweyan conception of "Educating Through Occupations" as appropriate for all students, CTE programs have been careful to recruit a wide range of students to avoid the stigma of serving only low-achieving students. However, some parents are concerned that an occupational program might result in diluted content and thus reduce their children's chances of getting to college. As one teacher recently noted, academic teachers and counselors may discourage top students from taking CTE courses (Author's Interview). Moreover, career academies have typically chosen students who have interest in school's focus, but at times this approach can be undercut by a district policy of using a lottery to place students or an open enrollment plan which reduces the school's input into which students attend. This happened at a career academy in Oakland, California, where "Many students come here [now] because the school is safe or because it's near to home, not because it's a health-oriented school," with the result that students may become dissatisfied with the program, thus lowering the community feeling within the school (Smith, 2008, p. 4).

A further dilemma for occupational programs is how to expand the involvement of business. Existing school-to-work programs generally are small and because of their manageability, have had success in finding employers able and willing to collaborate with them to provide career exposure, job shadowing opportunities, and sometimes paid internships for high school students. But expanding these contacts to a scale where they have an impact on a significant number of students is problematic (Pauly, Kopp, & Haimson, 1995, pp. 198–199). A major dilemma is simply that there are limits to what employers can, or have been willing to do. Beyond pressures for goal-setting, industry's relationship with schools has been minimal in terms of mentoring and involvement with students. The question of how to sustain authentic school-business partnerships is an ongoing concern.

Critique

Despite the expansive vision of creating vital educational experiences for all learners that underpins "Educating Through Occupations," by its very nature it is open to criticism that it offers a limited view of learning, learners, and the world. As well, the issue of which populations of students are being education through this curriculum remains. Hence we draw critique from several aspects of this curricular orientation: the learning theory upon which it is based and corollary assumptions about content, its underlying worldview, and the realities of its existence in today's schools.

First, we need to interrogate the belief that children primarily are interested in the material and materialistic world of occupations and hence be cautious about its widespread acceptance. Educational philosopher, Kieran Egan (1983), offers another perspective about what engages children's interests and questions Dewey's "self-evident truth" about focusing education on children's interests (p. 200).

> If one considers what most engages young children's minds it is surely stories about monsters, witches, dragons, knights, and princesses in distant times and places, rather than the subject matter, however actively engaged, of families, local environments, and communities. Indeed we might note that the everyday things around us are among the last things we come to appreciate intellectually. (p. 199)

Also, it is open to question if adults are placing their career concerns on young people before youth have discovered their identity and then their relationship to the world. At the same time, this approach has serious content implications. If students never explore the humanities—or only in piecemeal within novels or essays dealing with work or history of workers and technology—such a curriculum does not allow students to seek meaning or beauty as utilitarian purposes of life and studies must outweigh all others.

A corresponding criticism of "Educating Through Occupations" is that its focus is limited to the present world—finding sources of curriculum in occupations that are current and where opportunities for employment are anticipated. This world view is unequivocally materialistic, not giving much attention to the needs of human beings for spiritual or social growth. For example, although the curriculum stresses group work, it is for primarily instrumental ends: students have higher motivation to learn when they are working with their peers, and need to learn to collaborate for their roles in occupations.

> We train a side or an aspect of a person to prepare her or him for the world of work, but if we were limited as human beings to the world of work, we would deny the very possibility of the good life. Education concerns the whole person, empowering each of us with a sense of our integrity as individuals and as members of various communities…the marketplace is not the measure of humanity. (Kaplan, 1997, pp. 440–441)

Thus we ask, are educators in this curricular culture abdicating their responsibility to provide the young with a longer view of life, personal fulfillment, and democracy?

Also, because of its links to the occupations of the hour, this curricular culture can fail to foster consideration of social values implicit in the system for which it is preparing young people. For this reason, critical educational theorists have qualms about its uncritical attitude toward modern capitalism in the newest version of vocational education. The benevolent façade of occupational education deflects attention from the class-based economic system in which poverty is rooted and the changes needed in that system for genuine, widespread improvements in the living standards of the less advantaged segments of our society. Critical educators believe that it is necessary for young people to see alternatives to the business/industrial world as it is (Lakes, 1998). Nonetheless, in the literature of practices and research in CTE, the perspective of critical work educators does not reflect the mainstream ideology.

Finally, although many secondary schools do focus in some ways on careers, curriculum for students who plan to attend prestigious universities is based on rigorous academic learning according to traditional subject organization. So despite the possibilities of creating real-world curriculum of interest to all young people, parents have concerns about their children taking courses in CTE and fear that practical training will limit them to working-class jobs and that any dilution of academic preparation will hurt their children's chances of admission to the best colleges. And so, de facto tracking persists as CTE's population is far more likely to consist of students with lower socioeconomic status (Lewis & Cheng, 2006). As well, young women "still face significant discrimination and gender stereotyping when they attempt to participate in CTE programs" and are clustered into training programs that are traditional for women and, as a result, are less able to enter high wage careers" (AAUW, 2009, p. 1). If "Educating Through Occupations" is meant to level the playing field for young people of all backgrounds, it has clearly has a long way to go to realize that aim.

References

American Association of University Women (AAUW). (2009). *Career and technical education for women and girls*. Retrieved May 10, 2010, from http://www.aauw.org/act/issue_advocacy/actionpages/upload/CareerTechED1112.pdf

Anderson, J. D. (1988). *The education of blacks in the south, 1860–1935*. Chapel Hill: University of North Carolina Press.

Arenas, A. (2008). Connecting hand, mind, and community: Vocational education for social and environmental renewal. *Teachers College Record, 10*(2), 377–404.

Carl D. Perkins Vocational and Applied Technology Education Act Amendments of 1990 (Public Law 100-392). (1990). Washington, DC: U.S. Congress.

Chidester, L. H. (2005). *Junius l. Meriam's University Elementary School: Implications for prevailing interpretations of curriculum theories and practices past and present.*

Retrieved April 20, 2010, from http://www.coe.uga.edu/leap/adminpolicy/disserta-tions_pdf/LoriHopeChidester.pdf

Cremin, L. A. (1961/1964). *The transformation of the school: Progressivism in American education 1876–1957*. New York: Vintage Books.

Dewey, J. (1907/2007). *The school and society*. New York: Cosimo Classics.

Dewey, J. (1916). *Democracy and education*. New York: Free Press.

Dewey, J., & Dewey, E. (1915/1962). *Schools of tomorrow*. New York: E. P Dutton.

Egan, K. (1983). Social studies and the erosion of education. *Curriculum Inquiry, 13*(2), 195–214

Gatto, J. T. (Producer). (1991). *Classrooms of the heart*. [Videotape]. Retrieved from http://www.johntaylorgatto.com/bookstore/

Green, N. (1986). Remembering Lucy Flower Tech: Black students in an all-girl school. *Chicago History, 14*(3), 46–57.

Grubb, W. N. (1989). Preparing youth for work: The dilemmas of education and train-ing programs. In D. Stern & D. Eichorn (Eds.), *Adolescence and work: Influences of social structure, labor markets, and culture* (pp. 13–48). Hillsdale, NJ: Erlbaum.

Grubb, W. N. (1997). Not there yet: Prospects and problems for "education through occupations." *Journal of Vocational Education Research, 22*(2), 133–139.

Hamer, L. (1998). Caging wild birds: Making "real boys" into "real men" at the Inter-laken School, 1907–1918. *Educational Studies, 29*(4), 358–376.

Hoachlander, G. (1999). Integrating academic and vocational curriculum—Why is it so hard to practice? *Centerpoint*, No. 7. ERIC Document: ED433454.

Hoachlander, G, (2008). Bringing industry to the classroom. *Educational Leadership, 65*(8), 22–27.

Kaplan, A. (1997). Work, leisure, and the tasks of schooling. *Curriculum Inquiry, 27*, 423–451.

Kemple, J., & C. Willner. (2008). Career academies: Long-term impacts on labor market outcomes, educational attainment, and transitions to adulthood. *MDRC*. Retrieved May 10, 2010, from http://www.mdrc.org/publications/482/overview.html

Kincheloe, J. L. (1999). *How do we tell the workers?: The socioeconomic foundations of work and vocational education*. Boulder, CO: Westview Press.

Kliebard, H. M. (1995). *The struggle for the American curriculum 1893–1958*. New York: Routledge.

Lakes, R. D. (1998). Community service and workplace values: Toward critical peda-gogy. *Journal of Vocational Education Research, 23*(4), 311–323.

Lakes, R. D. (2005). Critical work education and social exclusion: Unemployed youths at the margins in the new economy. *Journal of Industrial Teacher Education, 42*(2). Retrieved May 10, 2010, from http://scholar.lib.vt.edu/ejournals/JITE/v42n2/lakes. html

Lewis, T. (1998). Vocational education as general education. *Curriculum Inquiry, 28*(3), 283–309.

Lewis, T., & Cheng, S-Y. (2006). Tracking, expectations, and the transformation of vocational education. *American Journal of Education, 113*(1), 67–99.

Little, J. W. (1995). Traditions of high school teaching and the transformation of work education. In W. N. Grubb (Ed.), *Education through occupations* (Vol. 2, pp. 57–81)). New York: Teachers College Press.

National Center on Education and the Economy. (2006). *Tough choices or tough times*. San Francisco: Jossey-Bass.

Neumark, D., & Rothstein, D. (2007). Do school-to-work programs help the "forgotten half"? In Neumark, D. (Ed.), *Improving school-to-work transitions* (pp. 87–133). New York: Russell Sage Foundation.

Oakes, J., & Saunders, M. (2007). Multiple pathways: High school reform that promises to prepare all students for college, career, and civic responsibility. In *Multiple perspectives on multiple pathways: Preparing California's youth for college, career, and civic responsibility*, 1–46. Los Angeles, CA: UCLA/IDEA. Retrieved May 10, 2010, from http://www.idea.gseis.ucla.edu/publications/mp/index.html

Palmer, J. (1998). *Environmental education in the 21st century: Theory, practice, progress and promise*. New York: Routledge.

Pauly, E., Kopp, H., & Haimson, J. (1995). *Homegrown lessons: Innovative programs linking school and work*. San Francisco: Jossey-Bass.

Rehm, M. L. (1999). Vocation as meaning making narrative: Implications for vocational education. *Journal of Vocational Education Research, 24*(3) 145–159.

Rojewski, J. W. (2002). Preparing the workforce of tomorrow: A conceptual framework for career and technical education. *Journal of Vocational Education Research, 27*(1). Retrieved from http://scholar.lib.vt.edu/ejournals/JVER/v27n1/rojewski.html

Rury, J. L. (1991). *Education and women's work*. Albany: State University of New York Press.

School to Work Opportunities Act of 1994. Public Law 103-239. (1994). Washington, DC: U. S. Congress.

Semel, S. F., & Sadovnik, A. R. (2008). The contemporary small school movement: Lessons from the history of progressive education. *Teachers College Record, 110*(9), 1774–1771.

Simon, R. I., & Dippo, D. (1992). What schools can do: Designing programs for work education that challenge the wisdom of experiences. In R. I. Simon (Ed.), *Teaching against the grain: Texts for a pedagogy of possibility* (pp. 121–136). New York: Bergin & Garvey.

Smith, T. (2008). *Striking the balance: Career academies combine academic rigor and workplace relevance, 1-5*. National High School Center. Retrieved May 11, 2010, from http://www.betterhighschools.org/docs/MDRC_CareerAcademiesSnapshot_08-11-08.pdf

Spring, J. (1997). *The American school 1642-1996* (4th ed.). New York: McGraw-Hill.

Spring, J. (2009). *Deculturalization and the struggle for equality: A brief history of the education of dominated cultures in the United States* (6th ed.). New York: McGraw-Hill.

Steele, L. (2005). Sweatshop accounting. *Rethinking Schools, 19*(1). Retrieved April 24, 2010, from http://www.rethinkingschools.org/archive/19_01/swea191.shtml

Stern, D. (2001). *Career academies and high-school reform before, during, and after the school-to-work movement*. Laboratory for Student Success, the Mid-Atlantic Regional Educational Laboratory. ERIC document: ED474217

Stern, D., & Stearns, R. (2007). *Combining academic and career-technical courses to make college an option for more students: Evidence and challenges (Multiple perspectives on multiple pathways: Preparing California's youth for college, career, and civic responsibility*, Paper No. 13). Los Angeles: University of California.

Stern, D., Stone III, J., Hopkins, C., McMillion, M., & Crain, R. (1994). *School-based enterprise: Productive learning in American high schools*. San Francisco: Jossey-Bass.

Stone, J. D., Alfeld, C., Pearson, D., Lewis, M. V., & Jensen, D. (2006). *Testing the value of enhanced mathematics learning in career and technical education.* National Research Center for Career and Technical Education. Minneapolis: University of Minnesota.

Stone, J. R. (2005). The neglected majority—revisited. *Journal of Vocational Education Research, 21*(2). Retrieved from http://scholar.lib.vt.edu/ejournals/JCTE/v21n2/pdf/stone.pdf

Tozer, S. E., Violas, P. C., & Senese, G. B. (1995). *School and society: Historical and contemporary perspectives* (2nd ed.). New York: McGraw-Hill.

U.S. Department of Education. (2008). *Department of Education Fiscal Year 2008 Congressional Action.* Washington DC: U.S. Department of Education.

Volk, K. S. (2005). The Gary Plan and technology education: What might have been? The *Journal of Technology Studies, 31*(1), 39–48.

Wakelyn, D. (2007). *Retooling Career Technical Education.* Issue Brief, National Governors' Association for Best Practices. Retrieved May 12, 2010, from http://www.nga.org/Files/pdf/0706TECHED.PDF

Chapter 8

Connecting to the Canon

Pamela Bolotin Joseph

The prime object of education is to know what is good.... It is to know the good in their order. There is a hierarchy of values. The task of education is to help us understand it, establish it, and live by it.... A liberal education aims to develop the powers of understanding and judgment. It is impossible that too many people can be educated in this sense, because there cannot be too many people with understanding and judgment.

Robert Maynard Hutchins, 1953, *The Conflict in Education in a Democratic Society,* pp. 353, 354

In Mr. Thomas's English classroom at River West High School, his 11th-grade students walk through the door and see a reminder in big letters on the white board: "Seminar Day!" Several students know that today they will work on group projects with Mr. Gerald's American history students and participate in seminar later in the week; after checking in with Mr. Thomas, they leave for the class next door. The students who remain quickly form a circle, placing their nameplates on their desks. Mr. Thomas's pupils are getting ready to discuss an interpretive question from a book they have all finished reading, *To Kill a Mockingbird,* by Harper Lee. For this class, the students will focus on the question that Mr. Thomas will pose to them: Why did Atticus Finch choose to defend Tom Robinson?

The teachers selected this classic American novel, somewhat ubiquitous to United States middle and high school English classes, because it has beautiful but accessible language, complex narrative and characters, links literature to history, and has emotional impact as students read about prejudice, injustice, and hatred through the eyes of a young girl, the narrator Scout. As are many classic works of literature, *To Kill a Mockingbird* is a story about good versus evil as well as heroism, courage, and nobility.

Just before the seminar begins, Mr. Thomas checks the students' "entrance tickets" to show that they have given more thought to the plot and characters before coming to class. Then he reminds the students of the norms of discussion—rules they have reviewed previously. When Mr. Thomas asks the seminar question, he allows students a few minutes to think about possible answers and to take notes before speaking. The beauty of this question is that there is not one right answer and the character's motives are open to debate. During the discussion, students express divergent ideas about what was the catalyst for Atticus's decision, whether his motives were really noble, and if he made the best decision for his family. Other students talk about the character's determination, what it takes for people to take such risks, and if they could imagine themselves doing "the right thing." At the end of the discussion—when all felt that they had the chance to share their ideas—Mr. Thomas asks his pupils to evaluate how the discussion went that day, for example, did everyone get to participate? Then he tells the students to write a brief exit slip, either to explain the idea they will think further about as a result of the discussion or if classmates expressed viewpoints that changed their understanding of the novel.

For several years Mr. Thomas and Mr. Gerald have been colleagues at River West High School, but in different departments (English and Social Studies). After Mr. Gerald attended a summer Paideia institute on intellectual dialogue in the classroom, he decided to incorporate Socratic seminars into his teaching practice. However, since class size is usually large, he felt that he could be a successful facilitator if class size could be more optimal for seminar participation: 15–20 students. This prompted Mr. Gerald to ask Mr. Thomas if he would be willing to explore team-teaching an interdisciplinary course of American Studies. Mr. Gerald figured that if they could combine classes, they each would have opportunities to lead small seminars. Their administrators helped them by scheduling their classrooms next to each other and making sure that both teachers had shared periods for teaching and planning.

Mr. Gerald grounds his American history course on historical research, e.g., how to study primary sources and evaluate evidence—in this instance, learning how people have worked to change social and political institutions. He especially wants students to deeply know history, and that includes knowledge of African American civil rights leaders and lawyers, such as Charles Hamilton Houston and Thurgood Marshall. Mr. Gerald's history classes also hold Socratic seminars around such texts as Henry David Thoreau's "On Civil Disobedience" and Martin Luther King Jr.'s "Letter From Birmingham Jail." Mr. Thomas similarly teaches his subject's academic goals, such as understanding the perspectives of characters, plot structure, and voice. He also teaches skills of essay writing for assignments necessary in both classes. Previous to today's seminar, students have written and shared their work about how individual characters in *To Kill a Mockingbird* have grown (or not grown) in their understanding and sympathy. Mr. Thomas has found many works of American literature that illuminate history; for example, he will introduce students to poets and authors of the Harlem Renaissance such as Langston Hughes and Zora Neale Hurston. Moreover, Mr. Gerald and Mr. Thomas have asked other teachers at their school to help them introduce art and music into their curriculum. Now both teachers provide opportunities for students to obtain deep understanding about social change and racism—as well as other historical themes—through art, novels, stories, autobiographies, poetry, music, plays, and film.

Although the situation is not ideal—as Mr. Gerald and Mr. Thomas both wish they could have more flexibility with a larger classroom with a moveable wall and block scheduling to have longer class periods—they have been pleased with the arrangement and see the benefits for students and themselves well beyond the original intention of creating seminars with smaller class size. They hope that more teachers at River West High School will offer humanities curriculum.

§

Educators who teach in the culture of curriculum we call "Connecting to the Canon" describe similar curriculum as portrayed in the above scenario—classrooms in which their students become engaged with classic works of literature, drama, or philosophy, grapple with complexity of these classics, and awaken to the moral and intellectual possibilities within their own lives. There is a fundamental premise stated within the writings of all those who affirmed this curricular orientation hundreds of years ago and those who value it today: a time-honored, stimulating curriculum centered upon the universal truths and persistent quandaries of humankind, aimed at developing understanding of the best way to live one's life, is the ideal education for all students.

Four themes predominate whenever and wherever we find this culture of curriculum: the need to transmit knowledge, the wisdom within exemplary intellectual or artistic works, the humanizing potential of study, and, learning as power—as mastery and as a commodity that allows individuals access into the dominant society. This curricula has many labels and variations: academic rationalism, the canon, classical education, core curriculum, cultural literacy, general education, great books, humanities, liberal studies, the liberal arts tradition, Paideia, and perennialism. It is most frequently referred to (especially at the university level) as liberal education.

Proponents of liberal education curriculum believe that when individuals attain deep understanding of age-old existential quandaries, they will become well rounded, moral, and wise; moreover, they will become liberated from living merely by habit and unexamined belief because liberal education "[opens] the personality to change and questioning" (Nussbaum, 2004, p. 47). In that sense, this orientation is a "progressive idea" because it "involves a freeing of the mind and the expression and cultivation of the self—as opposed to training for some station in society and equipping with a narrow range of workplace skills…" (Miller, 2007, p. 186). Within this orientation,

> [T]he ideal of the educated person has come to mean a person of intellectual formation, one who possesses knowledge in depth and breadth, one who possesses the knowledge and skills of citizenship, and who is

respectful of others and caring toward them, and one who is enabled to engage in thoughtful action. (Mulcahy, 2009, p. 484)

Educators who favor this curricular culture's express faith in liberal education to humanize students by cultivating spirituality, moral sensitivity, self-understanding, intellect, rationality, discipline, the powers of good judgment, and knowledge about of how to live deliberatively and humanely as good citizens (see Joseph, 2010). Furthermore, they see liberal education as a catalyst for creating "a crucial public culture" that facilitates "active participation in debate" (Nussbaum, 2004).

Visions

Unique to this culture of curriculum is the significance of a reservoir of cultural consciousness of classic Euro American knowledge and the necessity for all students to have access to it. Learners become the link between the past and the future, assuring the continuance of the cultural values, beliefs, and behaviors. Advocates have faith in a common core of education—shared experiences, ideas, and values—to allow individuals to live deliberately and humanely within their communities and society. The inherent social vision embodies the expectation that education will provide respectful yet autonomous individuals who behave according to the culture's moral code.

The heart of these visions is the value of continuing cultural heritage from generation to generation based on the tenet that discovered wisdom should not be abandoned; our lives can be enriched by contemplating the questions posed and resolved through the ages. It is believed that that young people have a great deal to learn from the experiences and understanding of their elders and ancestors and their ideas that have stood the test of time.

Other intertwining aims include the development of cultural memory and identity. Advocates of "Connecting to the Canon" believe that memory is important and that the teaching of cultural heritage provides knowledge of a common narrative (Thernstrom, 1985; Bloom, 1994). Bruner (1996), aware of the danger of affirming one historical voice, nevertheless explained the worth of historical memory:

> But ignore for a moment the pomposity of the self-appointed spokesmen for undisputable universal truths. For there is a compelling claim on this side too. It inheres in the deep integrity, for good or evil, with which any larger culture's way of life expresses its historically rooted aspirations for grace, order, well-being, and justice. (p. 69)

However, it is not enough to learn just from the personal experiences of elders or direct advice; there are bodies of knowledge that represent "collective cultural activity" (Bruner, 1996, p. 22). Rich historical, literary, artistic, philosophical, and political sources engender the most important inquiries and wisest answers. From generation to generation, classical sources persevere because of their greatness of substance and form.

Yet, transmission of cultural values is not a passive phenomenon. We do not just read or hear about cultural wisdom and become wise. Rather, we must each attain cultural knowledge through our individual connections to narratives of conflict, of triumph over adversity, of hope. We learn not just from accepting the values within the stories from our cultures, but through discovering a personal relationship to these stories, lessons, and drama.

Supporters of "Connecting to the Canon" have a moral vision for individuals. W. E. B. DuBois epitomized this aim when he wrote: "the object of all true education is not to make men carpenters, it is to make carpenters men" (1903/1965, p. 46). DuBois argued for an education "that would broaden the mind and spirit rather than narrow them" and would "turn the soul—the mind, heart, and spirit… toward the true, the good, and the beautiful" to "cultivate the art of living for individuals and communities" (Hansen, Anderson, Frank, & Nieuwejaar, 2008, pp. 446, 449). Becoming human inevitably involves the development of character (including self-discipline, spirituality, and compassion) and the cultivation of intellect and rationality. Education becomes "a transformation of a person's mind and character" (Adler, 1977/1988, p. 234) and the fully educated person is one who achieves "the powers of rationality, morality and spirituality" (Hutchins, 1953/1970, pp. 352–353). Such vision is conveyed in contemporary times when a ninth-grade English teacher tells parents at an open house, "I will make your children work very hard—but they will learn what it means to be *human* (Author's observation).

In this tradition, value transmission must include reflection. The idea that we should take ideas and values on faith or accept them without examination is not a part of this worldview. Studying the best that the culture has to offer also means challenging the beliefs and values held dear by the culture, developing the intellectual tools to consider, interpret, and test these values. Autonomous thinking is an important goal.

But rationality is not the only goal. Proponents of this curriculum believe that rigorous education in the humanities leads to the development of habits of the mind and eventually to habits of the heart, to the strengthening of character or humane feelings. Hence, a university president extols liberal education in a commencement address because it "cultivates the intellect and expands the capacity to reason and to empathize" (Levin, 1995, p. 61). Advocates of home schooling write that "a genuinely classical education developed a particular kind of disciplined heart and mind" (Wilson, Callihan, & Jones, 1995, p. 9).

Moreover, access to this education permits the acquisition of cultural capital. Through mastery of appropriate cultural knowledge, students can leave school and go out into the world and relate to others who also know "the right stuff." Students who obtain cultural capital have the "goods"—the assets of having a culturally sanctioned education. Often the belief system of "Connecting to the Canon" includes the creed that students need to feel at home, to negotiate, and to comprehend the prevailing culture. Having the wherewith-all to understand classic cultural references (including humor) allows individuals to "fit into" society or to feel "less alienated from the mainstream" (Ross, 1989, pp. 47–48). Hirsch (1987) writes about cultural literacy as a commodity—"common currency for social and economic exchange in our democracy, and the only available ticket to full citizenship" (p. 13)—and that lack of cultural literacy excludes learners from full social participation.

Any system of education that tracks students into vocational fields without providing them first with a rich intellectual and spiritual education needed for living and for citizenry would be abhorrent both for learners and for society. Wood (1998), a spokesperson for democratic education, refers to cultural capital as necessary "to better equip students to participate democratically" in his concern that a "political underclass" results from "differentiated knowledge acquisition" (p. 188). Consequently, this culture of curriculum upholds a democratic vision that all young people are *entitled* to have a liberal education (Adler, 1977, 1982). As Robert Maynard Hutchins (1953/1970) declares, "If all men are to be free, all men must have this education. It makes no difference how they are to earn their living or what their special interests or aptitudes may be" (p. 354). Correspondingly, Martha Nussbaum (2004) argues that the liberal arts model educates women to question their roles in societies that oppress females and instead prepares them to become leaders.

History

The idea of liberal education stems from ancient Greece and the Socratic tradition of intellectual and moral training to prepare individuals to participate as citizens within a democracy. Greek and Roman Stoic philosophers also argued for liberal education as preparation to become world citizens by gaining the ability to understanding different cultures and recognizing the humanity of other people. Most of all, liberal education is meant "to be pursed as an end in itself"—in "contrast to a 'mechanical' education whose purpose is to be practical or useful" (Miller, 2007, p. 184).

In the history of liberal education as enacted in the United States, the theme of democratic participation continued to be a rationale whereas education for multicultural understanding has had far less emphasis. Learning from exemplary traditional sources of knowledge influenced American curriculum in the past and continues to do but, for the most part, the key justification has been enculturation—for students to understand and connect to dominant cultural heritage. For this reason, we characterize this curriculum orientation as "Connecting to the Canon."

This culture of curriculum for European American colonists first appeared as schooling for religious literacy. The desire for reading and understanding the Bible was the fundamental justification for schooling. Laws requiring support of schooling passed by the Puritans contained the rationale that people themselves must have knowledge of the Bible so that they could ascertain "the true sense and meaning of the original" and that "learning may not be buried in the grave of our fathers" (Massachusetts, Law of 1647). After the religious influence upon this culture of curriculum dissipated in many American schools, the desire for rigorous scholarship—especially the search for meaning of truth and virtue within a religious context—continued in many parochial schools across America (see Gutek, 1974; Efron, 1994) with interest expressed in some secular private and public schools as well (Haynes, 1993).

A second potent influence upon the maintenance of this culture of curriculum was the intellectual tradition of the Enlightenment, emphasizing ancient Greek educational philosophy that virtue and rationality must be taught in order to have an educated citizenry who would see the worth of democracy and work to preserve it. These assumptions stirred Jefferson's argument for liberal education (including the study of Latin, Greek, English, geography, and mathematics) for an educational elite that would furnish leaders—who would thoroughly appreciate and thus safeguard rights and liberties within a democracy. It was a like sentiment for liberal education that W. E. B. DuBois embraced for developing a "talented tenth" of African Americans.

Over time, liberal education curriculum was recommended for secondary students who could obtain a college education; notably, in the United States in the late 19th century, the influential report (1892) of the Committee on Secondary School Studies (the Committee of Ten) proposed an academic liberal curriculum since most high school graduates would have prepared for the university. To the present day, support for a classical curriculum (debated as a course of study for all young people and not for just an elite group) centers on the notion that each generation must be exposed to the great ideas of Western Civilization to have renewed appreciation and understanding of virtue and freedom (Finn & Ravitch, 1985; Hughes, 1993).

But also, in the 19th and early 20th centuries, a distorted version of this culture of curriculum existed. Classical studies—particularly in Greek and Latin language and later, any course of study that was extremely challenging and involved extensive memorization—gained favor because of the belief that arduous work, especially memorization, strengthens the mind. No belief in education for virtue, critical thinking, or democratic ideals—but "faculty psychology"—a psychological rationale emphasized the metaphor of the mind *as if* it were a muscle—influenced curriculum (see Pinar, Reynolds, Slattery, & Taubman, 1995, pp. 75–77; Kliebard, 1987, p. 6) and captured the imagination of the public, scholars, and teachers. Although the banality of such curriculum eventually came under attack from various critics and the classical approach became widely discredited, the metaphor of mind as muscle never has completely disappeared from American cultural thinking (e.g., in public debate about lowered academic standards and in films about education such as *Dangerous Minds*).

Another deceptive version of "Connecting to the Canon" was the history of American curriculum exclusively for assimilation—for creating citizens who could identify with a new nation, its customs and institutions. One version of this culture of curriculum we could aptly name "Forging Cultural Identify," the other, "Compelling Enculturation."

The nationalist interpretation of "Connecting to the Canon" began at the birth of the United States as an independent nation. Statesmen and educators passionately believed in "a truly American education that would not mimic European traditions and that would create a "deliberate fashioning of a new republican character... committed to the promise of American culture" (Cremin, 1976, pp. 43–44). The widespread use of textbooks by Noah Webster and later McGuffey created the legends of American heroes and leaders. The forging of cultural identity was considered crucial for those who lived under monarchy in America and in Europe; conservative American political values, as well as sexist and racist stereotypes, permeated the moral and political lessons in textbooks (see Elson, 1964; FitzGerald, 1979).

In the first several decades of the 20th century in many public schools, teaching cultural heritage meant only cultural transmission and assimilation, especially for poor and working classes, people of color and non-Anglo ethnicity. In the name of cultural transmission, immigrants and their children were "Americanized" by curriculum taught through rote drill about facts of American history and work habits. Also, the United States government continued to take Native American children from their families in order to become "deculturalized" and to learn the traditions of the dominant culture—more often than not, experiencing training in manual labor and the prohibition of native languages (see Spring, 1994). In such manifestations of "Connecting to the Canon," no hints of intellectually stimulating curriculum remained nor did the democratic ideal of providing educational opportunity survive.

Education for enculturation, bereft of an intellectual and moral core, became commonplace in nearly all American schools by the 1920s. Because of anti-intellectualism in American culture (Hofstadter, 1962) and the association of a classical education with elitism (Kliebard, 1987), curricula situated in classic Western Civilization works of literature, history, and philosophy dwindled, although instances of liberal studies continued in high schools who prepared students for the more academic universities.

Then, in the mid-20th century and again in the 1980s, stinging critiques of what was considered mind-numbing curriculum, e.g., courses to help students win friends or "adjust" to life (Kliebard, 1987), led to a revival of interest in classic studies, first in American universities and a generation later in secondary education. The critics' remedy for vacuous curriculum was a rich education in the humanities. Proposals for curricula with potent intellectual and moral visions and clear ties to classical knowledge eventually entered into public dialogue and found some supporters. Some classrooms and schools implemented these curricula, but classical studies in the humanities never predominated in American schooling.

More recently, liberal education curriculum appeared at the center of a national controversy about required curriculum at universities, often referred to as "The Culture Wars." In multicultural America, competing voices in schools and universities argued whether or not the dominant approach to teaching great bodies of knowledge—primarily the tradition of White, male, Western European thought—is appropriate for all students and particularly for women and people from non-dominant cultures. The Culture Wars created polarities of thought with little expressed interest in learning from other cultural traditions (Banks, 1993). However, demands for culturally appropriate education sparked heated discussion and sporadically influenced curriculum in public schools and universities; outcomes included required courses in multicultural education for college students and the creation of culturally relevant schools such as African-American academies in public school districts.

Critics of the Eurocentric, male-dominated curriculum pointed out that "traditional" curricula "ignored most of the groups that compose the American population whether they were from Africa, Europe, Asia, Central and South America, or from Indigenous North American peoples" (Levine, 1996, p. 20). African American authors were "invisible" on Mortimer Adler's list of classic literature (Forrest, 1990) and "the culture and experience of [African Americans] have been virtually excluded from treatment in the textbooks and curricula of the educational system" (Anderson, 1990, p. 3). Furthermore, "women were excluded from the lives of scholarship—as from 'significant' subject matter, as from positions of authority and power—when the basic ideas, definitions, principles, and facts of the dominant tradition were being formulated" (Minnich, 2005, p. 78). Although Adler (1977/1988) wrote that "the list of the great books results from the most democratic or popular method of selection" (p. 320), he did not take heed of the work of those from non-dominant cultures ignored or rejected by classicists.

As well, the Culture Wars contested the accuracy of world views and history. Feminist and Afrocentric scholars challenged the idealization of European intellectual tradition, contending that it embodied a history of dominance, oppression, and ethnocentrism. Defenders of the Western Civilization tradition responded by discrediting competing versions of history and insisting that "the victims of oppression have always been able to find a transforming and strengthening vision within the literature and thought of Europe" (Hughes, 1993, p. 150). As the nature of core curriculum widened to include more than what prior generations deemed classical sources, the works of Plato, Dickens, and the *Constitution* would be joined writings of Marx and Engels, W. E. B. DuBois, Willa Cather, and Toni Morrison.

Currently, required readings in K–12 and higher education do reflect more works by women and non-Europeans than they did several generations ago and at some universities, there are required courses so that all students have exposure to other than the male, Western tradition. Recommended reading lists and curriculum guides for literature demonstrate increasing diversity. The high school recommended readings list from the National Endowment for the Humanities includes several African and African American authors among its primarily European American list. However, although William Shakespeare, Charles Dickens, Nathaniel Hawthorne, and John Steinbeck may be routinely taught in U.S. schools, in many instances high school curricula interweave traditional classics within a broader curriculum of literature written by Toni Morrison, Maya Angelou, Richard Wright, Ralph Ellison, Amy Tan, Maxine Hong Kingston, Sandra Cisneros, Bernard Malamud, Sherman Alexie, Louise Erdrich, and Leslie Marmon Silko. Once more, the works of these culturally diverse authors have been deemed "classics." Certainly, the notion of canon has not been stagnant.

But, despite the gradual additions of works that diversify the male, Euro-American world view, the transformative vision of multiculturalists does not prevail in this curricular culture; it has not become a norm that there is value in learning and scrutinizing the wisdom and experiences of many cultures and not just one (Banks, 1993; Levine, 1996). The idea of European American canon has expanded and consequently humanities curriculum has become more diverse, but liberal education on the whole does not deeply teach about the experiences, traditions, worldviews, and values of non-Western cultures.

Beliefs and Practices: Learners and Teachers

Seemingly, curriculum for cultural transmission calls forth images of passive learners—empty vessels—into which educators pour cultural literacy and standards of behavior. However, the metaphor of learner as receptacle does not convey how proponents of this curriculum think about students; rather, they insist upon active mental engagement, thinking, questioning, and stimulation of the imagination.

Descriptions of learners imply that cognitive development is an interaction of the student's own knowledge and the stimulation of the environment. Adler (1977/1988), who strongly espoused this curricular culture, refers to "the activity of the student's mind" and fused learning canon with sentiments akin to Piagetian psychology in describing the student: "But because he is a living thing, and not dead clay, the transformation can be effected only through his own activity" (pp. 278, 234).

Despite their dynamic cognitive portrayal, students with natural curiosity, the desire for knowledge and the ability to learn according their own inclinations customarily are not depicted by those who write about this curriculum.

Instead, the belief system holds that young people need to be led, stimulated, and coached because learning, the development of intellect, is arduous work.

A reappearing metaphor occurs in the continual dialogue of "Connecting to the Canon"—learners as athletes. Although the belief in the mind as muscle may have vanished as a serious model for learning theory, advocates of this curricular orientation explicitly portray genuine learning as discipline, struggle, strengthening, expanding, and training—replete with pain (Adler, 1977/1988; Pelton, 1985). But, as do athletes, learners often rise to the challenge and find satisfaction in mastery.

Finally, a major corollary in beliefs about students is that this education is not out of the reach of any learner and all can benefit from classic curriculum. Advocates believe that all young people are capable of learning and growing from the powerful ideas within a humanities curriculum and it is their right to have this knowledge; poor children and not just those from affluent families should read the poetry of Robert Frost, Langston Hughes, and Walt Whitman (Kozol, 1991). Furthermore, supporters of the humanities curriculum affirm that students who have experienced the "hard knocks" of life—of poverty and abuse—are even more apt to identify with the conflicts and truths in the powerful stories and metaphors in great works of literature, drama, and philosophy; and, they have even more to gain than the elite, not only from acquiring cultural capital, but from the liberating knowledge therein (Shorris, 1997).

To believe that all learners can master a classical curriculum—despite their lack of innate interest in it—and to consider the content of the curriculum as impenetrable without struggle, it follows that the teacher must have a crucial role in this culture of curriculum. Students cannot grasp powerful ideas and relate their own moral struggles to lessons from the past without teachers' intervention and creativity. Teachers actively mediate between learners and content.

We see that this culture of curriculum holds two metaphors for teachers: elders and masters. Teachers as elders are wise people who have thought deeply and well; they have the knowledge that must be "patiently and imaginatively" conveyed to the current generation (Broudy, 1984, p. 23). Teachers as masters have pedagogical expertise to know how to lead learners to wisdom through inquiry and personal connection.

Educators who work within this culture of curriculum know that they cannot depend on materials to be intrinsically exciting enough to engage learners, so their first task is to interest students in the content. Teachers also must play to their audience as performers or storytellers to spark learners' engagement with classical content. However, teaching does not rest with performance. Educators must have deep understanding of subject matter and tremendous insight about teaching.

Teachers' roles are as questioners, guides, and coaches. Teachers use "discussion, induction, discovery, dialogue, debate, and a variety of procedures [called] heuristic;" teachers help students learn how to learn (Broudy, 1984, p. 26). For example, a teacher in a Catholic high school typifies his practice:

> I teach by the Socratic method—posing question and not giving answers.... I see myself as a facilitator...an active questioner.... My metaphor for my role as a teacher is "devil's advocate." For example, when I teach religion, I show the kids the supposition that disproves God exists and then go on from there...a little knowledge can take you away from God and a lot of knowledge can take you back.... I rely on my study in philosophy to give me empowerment and mastery as a teacher.... I also help kids to become questioners; they learn that it's okay to question and okay to doubt. (Author's interview)

This educator's question-posing suggests the Socratic tradition of critical examination of conventional thinking: unsettling questions that lead to disequilibrium, to "intellectual bewilderment, devastation, and even rage" (Purpel, 1989, pp. 78–79). Although teachers themselves may not always have answers to ultimate questions, in this culture of curriculum, teachers encourage doubt, guide learners through their bewilderment, but ultimately lead students toward meaningful answers and affirmation of values. In this culture of curriculum, students are not left in confusion.

Beliefs and Practices: Content and Context

The content of "Connecting to the Canon" depends upon a platform of subject matter so that learners will have an essential background in language arts, mathematics, science, history and geography. Through teachers' guidance and coaching, students develop skills for critical reading, writing, speaking, and problem-solving. Advocates believe that this learning eventually gives students the ability to comprehend, and apply to their own lives, the ideas and values within exemplary works of cultural wisdom (Adler, 1982, Broudy, 1984, Frazee, 1993). Content, as the repository of wisdom, receives the greatest emphasis within this culture of curriculum.

Advocates discuss several features that indicate a classical source of wisdom:

- *Thickness* so that "every sentence contains an idea...the whole work covers acres of thought and feeling" and these thoughts and feelings may convey to us new ways of thinking about ourselves and the world around us;
- *Adaptability,* our learning about the situations of others long ago must cast light on our present predicaments or about existence itself;
- *Endurance* so that "a work has withstood long and intense criticism";
- *Creativity* in that "it is a seminal work that anticipated the future or bridged two phrases of development of disciplines";

- *Artistry*—"a superb elegance or lucidity of form";
- *Pedagogic value* "with good returns for the time invested in study." (Barzun, 1991, pp. 124–135; Broudy, 1984, p. 23)

The study of history, philosophy, drama, art, and religion—as well as myths and heroic stories in which forces of good and evil do battle—becomes the content that leads to the acquisition of wisdom (Barzun, 1991). The content is chosen, not because it is immediately accessible or clear, but because it stretches learners intellectually, artistically, and morally. The curricular content also should convey social and political knowledge. Cultural wisdom is found within complex and sometimes enigmatic stories, speeches, art, plays, or, in the logic of mathematics and the ethical dimensions of the sciences.

Humanistic study is characterized by the idea that human beings have choices, that they may be tested and have opportunities to demonstrate courage and persistence, even when confronting the power of nature and God (or gods). It is assumed that great storytellers tell us something important about living as human beings and about perseverance. Neither mastery of bodies of factual knowledge (despite the popularity of E. D. Hirsch's lists for cultural literacy) nor direct moral indoctrination (such as character education's didactic use of literature to point out admirable traits) is considered appropriate for the studying the humanities. Rather, this curricular culture facilitates ethical inquiry (see Simon, 2001):

> Teachers guide students to discuss moral dilemmas embedded within studies across the curriculum…. In particular, students learn about the consequences of making moral decisions and how fictional characters as well as real people make choices with awareness that a moral question is at stake. Through this process, students ponder the effect of moral, immoral, and amoral actions upon themselves and others, empathize with and appreciate the perspectives of others (their classmates as well as those of fictional characters or historical figures), and construct their understanding of what it means to be a moral human being. (Joseph & Efron, 2005, p. 531)

Of special importance is the study of history. We acquire wisdom and knowledge of culture through historic memory. Advocates of this culture of curriculum stress the need to learn the discipline of history so we can see the interconnectedness of events and ideas so we can better learn what shaped our cultural heritage—"to understand fully who we are today and how we came to be that way" (Thernstrom, 1985, p. 78). Narrative is important for "framing accounts of our cultural origins" and for the "cohesion of a culture" (Bruner, 1996, p. 40). Educators also believe that content must be taught so that learners have deep understanding of the cultural-historical significance of literature to fully appreciate its meaning (Graff, 1979/1995, p. 123).

Many canon-based programs purposely choose integrated curriculum (see Miller, 2007) so that learning becomes multi-dimensional, deeper, and richer, e.g., integrating literature, art, and drama into the study of history to learn about personal perception and experience. For instance, a Humanitas program taught in high schools organized interdisciplinary curriculum within conceptual topics as courses, for example, "Women, Race, and Social Protest" and "The Protestant Ethic and the Spirit of Capitalism" (Aschbacher, 1991, p. 16). The core curriculum at Central Park East Secondary School was utilized to develop themes through organizing questions such as "how do people achieve power?" and "how do people respond to being deprived of power?" in cross-disciplinary classes such as humanities-social studies (Wood, 1992/1993, pp. 47–48).

Most likely, we would recognize this culture of curriculum by its classroom milieu of a forum, ideally with few enough students to facilitate active discussion among all the participants and frequent feedback from the teacher. In Paideia schools across the United States, as well as in numerous classrooms in which teachers facilitate Socratic seminars, teachers guide students to scrutinize texts and to articulate reasoned positions based on deep understanding and not merely opinion (see Hess, 2009; Moeller & Moeller, 2002; Roberts & Billings, 1999).

Educators writing about the context of learning refer to the image of "a community of scholars" (Adler, 1977/1988; Aschbacher, 1991). Classrooms with core curriculum are depicted as scenes of "back-and-forth interaction among groups of students and between students and the teacher" (Hirsch, 1993, p. 25). Teachers sit with the students at a table or in a circle. Although teachers may be masters in subject-matter depth, they also are seeking answers to quandaries; they pose "genuine questions" that lead to "interpretive discussion" with an exchange of ideas (Haroutunian-Gordon, 1991).

Although in such seminars, students are actively engaged in questioning and answering questions, such discussions do not happen spontaneously. Working individually or in small groups, students prepare for discussion through careful reading and the teacher's coaching. In this curricular culture today, reading of texts is still crucial, but technology has a role in facilitating students' in-depth study by providing resources in history, the sciences, and the arts. The follow-up to discussion also is an integral feature of canon classrooms as students develop essays and projects linked to issues raised in seminars.

Beliefs and Practices: Curriculum Planning and Evaluation

The predominant influence upon curriculum development is the norms about content—the beliefs held by educators and parents about what knowledge and traditions that children should receive. Such norms often are deeply imbedded and resistant to change; inclusion of contemporary and multicultural sources happens very slowly. The consistency of literature curricula in American high schools (see Applebee, 1990) up to recent times reveals this conservative approach. In particular, The Great Books Foundation has been reluctant to vary from their deeply rooted traditions; there are few women or authors outside the traditional canon on their readings lists. A good many decisions about curricular content stem from the knowing or tacit acceptance of sources believed to connect young people to cultural wisdom.

In this culture of curriculum, teachers appear in the circumscribed center of curriculum planning. The multitude of decisions about what ideas, themes, and questions to emphasize comes from educators' academic strengths and interests, their professional goals, and their understanding of what is meaningful to young people. The pivotal role of teachers in orchestrating the curriculum is supported by the presumption of their expertise in subject matter and pedagogy. Those schools adopting thematic integrated curriculum encourage collaboration in which teachers themselves become a community of scholars as they work in interdisciplinary committees to decide on concepts and questions as they plan curriculum for the year (Aschbacher, 1991). Yet, as movement toward a core national curriculum in the United States gains momentum in the 21st century, curriculum planning for the canon may indeed become more proscribed.

Teachers also are at the heart of the assessment process. Despite some call for standardized testing of knowledge standards (Hirsch, 1993), most of the advocates of liberal education place faith in teachers as masters to assess what their students have learned. Demonstration of learning occurs through individual writing of essays through papers and examination; such essays often require students to take a position and argue using evidence to support their positions. Teachers also evaluate students' knowledge through Socratic questioning or as students engage in debate. In some classes, students illustrate they have learned important ideas and quandaries through the creation of art and drama. Instructors also may utilize portfolio assessment as students collect their essays and art illustrating their intellectual and perhaps moral growth.

However, assessment practices do not appear to include evaluation of the curricular content itself. The ardent belief in the accumulated wisdom within presumably great moral, intellectual, and artistic sources thwarts re-evaluation of the universality of a classic or whether or not it should endure. Rather, it is suspect that individuals or even a generation of individuals should make serious changes to choices of content that may have evolved over decades, hundreds and even thousands of years. The basic premise about curriculum evaluation simply is this: the content is good (for learners) because it is good (because it has endured). Critical examination of the worth of the curriculum usually does not take place in this culture of curriculum.

Dilemmas of Practice

Teachers choosing to initiate "Connecting to the Canon" as the culture of curriculum in their classrooms face several dilemmas. These predicaments relate to the crucial knowledge and skills needed to become a superlative practitioner, the controversial nature of subject matter, and the unpopularity of this curriculum in contemporary America.

The first dilemma is whether or not practitioners have or will invest in the remarkable depth of content and pedagogical knowledge needed to assume their roles as teachers in this culture of curriculum. The richness of their knowledge of the humanities, their talent as a superb questioners, and their capacity to engage students in content would require an extensive and continual liberal arts education and instructional preparation.

To achieve excellence in this curricular approach, teachers need deep knowledge of a variety of areas. They should have strong grounding in the humanities, of narrative and historical context, knowledge of symbols, dramatic devices, and themes. Integrated curriculum would require teachers to work collaboratively across academic fields. Furthermore, teachers' own education would be deficient without keeping abreast of scholarship reflecting an expanded notion of human experience that is increasingly becoming more inclusive, e.g., ethnicity and gender must be considered if curricular content is chosen because of its potential for universality. Even when curricular choices emphasize the Eurocentric tradition, teachers are called upon to include some works by women (see Whaley, 1993) and people from non-dominant cultures (Graff, 1992; Forrest, 1990) in order to teach what it means to be human to a diverse student body.

In conceptualizing this curriculum so that it reflects contemporary scholarship, teachers must have knowledge of political perspectives within great cultural works to help their students see through such lenses. Obliteration of political issues not only creates one-dimensional interpretations from the dominant culture's world view, it robs students of opportunities for critical thinking and perspective-taking. For example, Graff (1992) explains how teaching the politics of *Heart of Darkness* takes students beyond existential themes to include a focus on cultural dominance and racism. Such scrutiny of art, literature, sciences, and social sciences might call for enriched education of teachers if they themselves had received an apolitical education in the humanities.

Besides needing tremendous subject matter depth, teachers in this culture of curriculum must know how to engage students with content. Great works of literature, history, and philosophy may initially be inaccessible to many students. The fleeting visual imagery of popular culture and technology requires little intellectual stamina (see Finn, Ravitch, & Fancher, 1984); the great books do not automatically reflect the immediacy of contemporary children's or adolescents' lives. So, to "know their audience," teachers must stay savvy, current, and responsive to their students' interests and lives and be conversant with the popular culture enjoyed by their students. More importantly, practitioners need to be sensitive to their students' personal struggles to better guide them toward discovering meaning in their studies. Such a task means that educators must make a deep commitment to their own learning—from Shakespeare to rap music—to connect learners to the classics.

Another dilemma facing practitioners is dealing with explosive controversies over the content of this curriculum. Educators choosing to teach within this culture of curriculum could encounter opposition from the political conservatives who fear both teachers' autonomy in choosing content and children's learning of critical thinking skills (Elliott, 1994). Or, caught in the crossfire of the Culture Wars, educators would have to articulate their visions and account for their decisions to teach primarily from the cultural wisdom from the European American tradition or to defend their efforts to broaden the canon and make it more multicultural.

Finally, we consider the dilemma that educators who desire to connect students to cultural wisdom encounter adverse public perception about the nature of this culture of curriculum. Popular culture and media often portray "Connecting to the Canon" as caricature, as an elite curriculum full of "dead" allusions and information. Within the current climate of schooling with its emphasis upon basic literacy and skills for employment, such curricula gets little support from national or state school reform efforts. Despite the growth of the Paideia school movement and more frequent use of Socratic seminars in classrooms, this is not a popular curricular orientation and "American society...exhibits a striking ambivalence towards the traditions" of liberal education (Schneider, 2004, p. 6). That this culture of curriculum has not persisted as a dominant culture of education in the United states resides in its dissonance with American culture's anti-intellectualism, preference for the new to the old, novelty to tradition, fascination with scientific methods and technology above humanities and narratives of human experiences, and preference for the practical over the theoretical. Finding support for this culture of curriculum surely is an uphill battle.

Critique

There are three inter-related areas regarding critique of "Connecting to the Canon." The first involves inherent contradictions that call into question whether its goals are attainable, the second refers to the nature of knowledge or wisdom, and the third dimension concerns the issue of power related to the decisions made as to what engenders wisdom.

Critical inquiry begins with examining the fundamental vision. If the main goal of this culture of curriculum is to learn what it means to be human, can we recognize this outcome? How can we know about qualities of character that are "within a person?" Will we find out if learners become adults who have acquired wisdom? Clearly, it is difficult to appraise intangible consequences.

Calls by advocates to educate both the hearts and minds of learners also call for scrutiny. Can this curriculum teach learners to lead moral lives through knowledge acquisition? Advocates only discuss affect when they discuss how students connect emotionally to content, e.g., having empathy with young Hamlet's dilemma. Moreover, teachers' roles are essentially cognitive—to stimulate, provoke, and broaden—and to make learners work hard; such teachers command the respect of students but compassion and friendship are not mentioned. Although teachers may demonstrate that they care about students by helping them reach their intellectual potentials, there is no focus here on students engaging with their hearts with the community, other learners, or in caring relationships with teachers. Noddings (1994) defined moral dialogue as a relationship of "deep concern for the other" (p. 5); thus, we can say that this culture of curriculum has dialogue about moral dilemmas, but it does not generate "moral dialogue."

We also must reflect on the nature of knowledge in "Connecting to the Canon" and the ramifications for learners. Curricular content is traditional and resistant to change; proponents judge contemporary cultural sources as unworthy, except as a catalyst for students' engagement. The conservative nature of the curriculum raises several concerns about choices of content and visions for the learner and society.

First, we need to be circumspect about upholding classics as the only appropriate study. Conservatism resists the new, exciting, different, and challenging—closing off sources that may also tell us about what it means to be human. Garber (1995) warns us:

> What is disturbing is the risk that the back-to-basics emphasis of self-appointed guardians of literary and critical values will render respectable a dismissiveness about new ideas that amounts to a doctrine of anti-intellectualism. Just as the now classical was once "popular," the now "high" was once "low" and threatening—Impressionist painting, film noir, jazz, Mozart, Wagner. But art, as writers from Sophocles to Marlowe to Baudelaire to Joyce to Woolf to Morrison have always known and shown, is threatening. It is about transgression, and daring, and engagement. (p. 55)

We should rightfully be concerned that the substance of content becomes static as a particular set of values and ideas is taught from generation to generation with little modification.

However, we might soften this criticism that classicists fear the new by remembering the difficulty in recognizing a potential classic among contemporary sources. Bruner (1996) suggests that interpretation of narrative construal is "deeply affected by cultural and historical circumstances." Thus, contemporary readers responding to the immediacy of the context can misconstrue literature's worth because they may not yet have an appreciation for the richly insightful and potentially enduring themes it contains. We simply may not be able to see the existential themes in drama, art, literature, or history that portray events in our immediate world.

We must also ask, can this curriculum educate people to be responsive to current social conditions and the dynamics of cultural change? If students are not encouraged to construct their own understanding of the world, is their vision not shaped and limited by the perceptions of previous generations? As Moretti (1993) concludes, "Any pedagogy not focused on the intellectual empowerment of the young is ultimately dysfunctional. We don't want to teach the young the right history. We want to teach them to create histories of their own" (p. 124).

Even though the underpinning belief of this curricular culture is a vision of liberating intellect, "Connecting to the Canon" also holds a conservative ideal of enculturation and cultural identification. Advocates for this culture of curriculum strongly suggest that young people not only embrace the guidelines for conduct deemed exemplary throughout the generations, but they should learn to see themselves as part of the culture's common narrative. Can we connect learners to cultural wisdom but also have them become autonomous—to critique their culture and its values? Ultimately, it is far more likely that learners, as they become insiders within the cultural tradition, will defend rather than challenge or reject traditional values.

Moreover, besides resisting innovation, this curricular culture ordinarily rejects insight from sources outside the mainstream cultural heritage and sanctions European-American intellectual and artistic dominance over others. This is not a benign or unbiased occurrence, despite advocates' insistence upon neutrality. Critics of this curricular orientation attack the narrowness of the themes and materials deemed worthwhile or classic; they argue that knowledge becomes extremely limited when we only value a particular world view, in this case, the predominantly male Eurocentric canon. A mono-cultural educational system "closes us off to all other possibilities of human experience" (Asante, 1992, pp. 22–23). Thus, the classic educational position, in particular, ignores non-Western intellectual, spiritual, and moral contributions.

In a curriculum that represents the Western worldview, the themes of rationalism and individualism predominate. In contrast, for example, African culture places a "heavy emphasis on emotional intelligence" and the belief that "the world is not limited to the physical senses or intellect"; it also values "unity," "collective works," and "cooperative economics" and has an "ethos of communalism" (Durden, 2007, pp. 26–27). When students learn only the canon, the result is the omission of oral traditions, holistic education with its emphasis upon harmony of spirit, mind, and body, connectedness, relationship between humans and environment, and the concept of multiple realities (Okur, 1993; Reagan, 1996; Saucerman, 1988; Collins, 1991; Allen, 1998). Moreover, in the liberal education canon, African or indigenous historical perspectives on colonialism and forced diaspora is a null curriculum.

In American schools and universities, the Western Civilization tradition not only was taught to students of all cultural backgrounds, it was taught as the superior wellspring of wisdom—presented as "civilization itself," as universal, as the "norm and the idea" (Levine, 1996, p. 20; Okur, 1993, p. 92; Minnich, 2005, pp. 37–38). Although learners may benefit from having the "cultural capital" of "wisdom" from the dominant culture, what effect does denial of cultural heritage have upon learners who have to negate or remain ignorant of their own? Paula Gunn Allen wrote that "contemporary Indian communities…believe that the roots of oppression are to be found in the loss of tradition and memory because the loss is always accompanied by a loss of a positive sense of self" (Allen, 1988, pp. 14–15). The relegation of other cultural traditions to a realm of not-human and not-civilized not only manifests arrogance, it leads to cultural annihilation. It is no wonder that Asante (1991) described an education in the European traditional culture as death for learners from others cultural backgrounds.

Notwithstanding, it stands to reason that deep knowledge of more than the dominant Western tradition could be taught in schools and still we would have curriculum congruent with "Connecting to the Canon." Swing (1995) observes that there is the traditional Eurocentric humanities curriculum in which all students—regardless of their cultural backgrounds—receive the cultural capital of the dominant culture; or one could offer a displacement curriculum in which the world view of the minority culture displaces the dominant (traditional, Eurocentric) cultural focus. Yet, other models exist: a bi-cultural configuration that recognizes both the dominant culture and the most significant minority culture with the aim to help students live within both their worlds; or, an interactive bi-cultural model that shows the influence of both dominant and minority cultures upon each other. It is clear, however, that incorporation of a multitude of cultural traditions into a curriculum would not be feasible because a potpourri of cultural knowledge is inconsistent with the deep understanding called for in this culture of curriculum.

In conclusion, there are several reasons why this culture of curriculum is deficient as a mono-cultural model. If we connect to a single intellectual and moral tradition and do not attain a deep and rich knowledge of at least another culture's wisdom and experience, it is unlikely that we can have a standpoint to critically examine dominant beliefs and values; accordingly, we cannot vigorously appreciate the wisdom of the canon because we have not genuinely challenged it. Also, lack of scrutiny may mean that not only do we have difficulty modifying our beliefs and actions in light of real and changing social conditions, moreover, it is "tunnel vision" and "racial chauvinism" (Moses, 1991, p. 87) to assume that one culture has the best answers, the one true story, the only keys to civilization. To give our students the "goods" to navigate in a diverse and inter-connected world, this culture of curriculum must acquire wisdom from sources beyond a dominant worldview and cultural narrative.

References

Adler, M. J. (1977/1988). Reforming education: The opening of the American mind. New York: Macmillan.

Adler, M. J. (1982). *The Paideia proposal: An educational manifesto*. New York: Macmillan.

Allen, P. G. (1988). Who is your mother? Red roots of white feminism. In R. Simonson & S. Walker. (Eds.), *The Graywolf annual five: Multicultural literacy* (pp. 13–27). Saint Paul, MN: Graywolf Press.

Allen, P. G. (1998, April). *Native American construction of knowledge*. Paper presented at the American Educational Research Association, San Diego, CA.

Anderson, T. (1990). *Black studies: Theory, method, & cultural perspectives*. Pullman: Washington State University Press.

Applebee, A. N. (1990). *Book-length works taught in high school English courses*. ERIC Clearinghouse on Reading and Communication Skills. ED318035

Asante, M. K. (1991). Afrocentric curriculum. *Educational Leadership, 49*, 28–31.

Asante, M. K. (1992). Learning about Africa. *The Executive Educator, 14*, 21–23.

Aschbacher, P. R. (1991). Humanitas: A thematic curriculum. *Educational Leadership, 49*, 16–19.

Banks, J. A. (1993). The canon debate, knowledge construction, & multicultural education. *Educational Researcher, 22*, 4–14.

Barzun, J. (1991). *Begin here: The forgotten conditions of teaching & learning*. Chicago: University of Chicago Press.

Bloom, H. (1994). *The Western canon: The book and school of the ages*. New York: Harcourt Brace.

Broudy, H. S. (1984). The uses of humanistic schooling. In C. E., Finn, Jr., D. Ravitch, & R. T. Fancher (Eds.), *Against mediocrity: The humanities in America's high schools* (pp. 15–29). New York: Holmes & Meier.

Bruner, J. (1996). *The culture of education*. Cambridge, MA: Harvard University Press.

Collins, P. H. (1991). *Black feminist thought*. New York: Routledge.

Cremin, L. (1976). *Traditions of American education*. New York: Basic Books.

DuBois, W. E. B. (1903/1965). The talented tenth. In F. L. Broderick & A. Meier (Eds.), *Negro protest thought in the twentieth century* (pp. 40–48). Indianapolis, IN: Bobbs-Merrill.

Durden, T. R. (2007). African centered schooling: Facilitating holistic excellence for Black children. *The Negro Educational Review, 58*(1–2), 23–34.

Efron, S. G. (1994). Old wine, new bottles: Traditional moral education in the contemporary Jewish classroom. *Religious Education, 89*, 52–65.

Elliott, B. (1994). Education, modernity and neo-conservative school reform in Canada, Britain, and the US. *British Journal of Sociology of Education, 15*, 165–185.

Elson, R. (1964). *Guardians of tradition: American schoolbooks in the nineteenth century*. Lincoln: University of Nebraska Press.

Finn, Jr., C. E., & Ravitch, D. (1985). The humanities: A truly challenging course of study. In B. Gross & R. Gross (Eds.), *The great school debate: Which way for American education?* (pp. 308–309). New York: Simon & Schuster.

Finn, Jr., C. E., Ravitch, D., & Fancher, R. T. (1984). *Against mediocrity: The humanities in America's high schools.* New York: Holmes & Meier.

FitzGerald, F. (1979). *America revised: History schoolbooks in the twentieth century.* New York: Vintage Books.

Forrest, L. (1990, December 3). Mortimer Adler's invisible writers. *Chicago Tribune.* Http://articles.chicagotribune.com/1990-12-03/news/9004090924_1_black-boy-invisible-man-great-books

Frazee, B. (1993). Core knowledge: How to get started. *Educational Leadership, 50,* 28–29.

Garber, M. (1995, October 29). Back to whose basics? *The New York Times Book Review,* 55.

Graff, G. (1979/1995). *Literature against itself: Literary ideas in modern society.* Chicago: Elephant Paperback.

Graff, G. (1992). *Beyond the culture wars: How teaching the conflicts can revitalize American education.* New York: W. W. Norton.

Gutek, G. L. (1974). *Philosophical alternatives in education.* Columbus, OH: Charles E. Merrill.

Hansen, D. T., Anderson, R. F., Frank, J., & Nieuwejaar, K. (2008). Reenvisioning the Progressive Tradition in Curriculum. In F. M. Connelly, M. H. Fang, & J. Phillion (Eds.), *The Sage handbook of curriculum and instruction* (pp. 440–459). Thousand Oaks, CA: Sage.

Haroutunian-Gordon, S. (1991). *Turning the soul: Teaching through conversation in the high school.* Chicago: University of Chicago Press.

Haynes, C. C. (1993). Beyond the culture wars. *Educational Leadership, 51,* 30–34.

Hess, D. E. (2009). *Controversy in the classroom: The democratic power of discussion.* New York: Routledge.

Hirsch, Jr., E. D. (1987). *Cultural literacy: What every American needs to know.* Boston: Houghton Mifflin.

Hirsch, Jr., E. D. (1993). The core knowledge curriculum — What's behind its success? *Educational Leadership, 50,* 23–30.

Hofstadter, R. (1962). *Anti-intellectualism in American life.* New York: Vintage Books.

Hughes, R. (1993). *Culture of complaint: The fraying of America.* New York: Oxford University Press.

Hutchins, R. M. (1953/1970). The conflict in education. In J. W. Kelly & S. P. Kelly (Eds.), *Foundations of education in America: An anthology of major thoughts and significant actions* (pp. 351–356). New York: Harper & Row.

Joseph, P. B. (2010). Liberal education curriculum. Iin C. Kridel (Ed.), *Sage encyclopedia of curriculum studies* (pp. 542–543). Thousand Oaks, CA: Sage.

Joseph, P. B., & Efron, S. (2005). Seven worlds of moral education. *Phi Delta Kappan, 86*(7), 525–533.

Kliebard, H. (1987). *The struggle for the American curriculum 1893–1958.* New York: Routledge & Kegan Paul.

Kozol, J. (1991). *Savage inequalities: Children in America's schools.* New York: Crown.

Levin, R. C. (1995). Liberal education and the western tradition. *Yale Alumni Magazine, 58,* 61–63.

Levine, L. W. (1996). *The opening of the American mind: Canons, culture & history.* Boston: Beacon Press.

Massachusetts School Law of 1647. (1973). In H. S. Commager (Ed.), *Documents of American history, Vol. 1* (9th ed., p. 29). Englewood Cliffs, NJ: Prentice-Hall.

Miller, A. (2007). Rhetoric, paideia and the old idea of a liberal education. *Journal of Philosophy of Education, 41*(2), 183–206.

Minnich, E. K. (2005). *Transforming knowledge* (2nd ed.). Philadelphia: Temple University Press.

Moeller, V., & Moeller, M. V. (2002). *Socratic seminar and literature circles for middle and high school English.* Larchmont, NY: Eye on Education.

Moretti, F. A. (1993). Who controls the canon? A classicist in conversation with cultural conservatives. *Teachers College Record, 95,* 113–126.

Moses, W. J. (1991). Eurocentrism, Afrocentrism, & William H. Ferris' *The African Abroad. Journal of Education, 173,* 76–90.

Mulcahy, D. G. (2009). What should it mean to have a liberal education in the 21st century? *Curriculum Inquiry, 39*(3), 465–486.

Noddings, N. (1994). Learning to engage in moral dialogue. *Holistic Education Review, 7*(2), 5–11.

Nussbaum, M. (2004). Liberal education & global community. *Liberal Education, 90*(1), 42–47.

Pelton, C. L. (1985). Education reform: A teacher responds. In C. E. Finn, Jr., D. Ravitch, & P. H. Roberts (Eds.), *Challenges to the humanities* (pp. 159–173). New York: Holmes and Meier.

Okur, N. A. (1993). Afrocentricity as a generative idea in the study of African American drama. *Journal of Black Studies, 24,* 88–108.

Pinar, W. F., Reynolds, W. M., Slattery, P., & Taubman, P. M. (1995). *Understanding curriculum: An introduction to the study of historical and contemporary curriculum discourses.* New York: Peter Lang.

Purpel, D. E. (1989). *The moral & spiritual crisis in education: A curriculum for justice and compassion in education.* New York: Bergin & Garvey.

Ross, K. (1989). Bringing the humanities to the lower achiever. *English Journal, 78*(7), 47–48.

Reagan, T. (1996). *Non-western educational traditions: Alternative approaches to educational thought and practice.* Mahwah, NJ: Erlbaum.

Roberts, T., & Billings, L. (1999). *The Paideia classroom: Teaching for understanding.* Larchmont, NY: Eye on Education.

Saucerman, J. R. (1988). Teaching Native American literature. In J. Reyhner (Ed.), *Teaching the Indian child: A bilingual/multicultural approach* (pp. 189–201). Billings, MT: Eastern Montana College.

Schneider, C. G. (2004). Practicing liberal education: Formative themes in the reinvention of liberal learning. *Liberal Education, 90*(2), 6–11.

Shorris, E. (1997). *New American blues: A journey through poverty to democracy.* New York: W. W. Norton.

Simon, K. G. (2001). *Moral questions in the classroom: How to get kids to think deeply about real life and their school work.* New Haven, CT: Yale University Press.

Spring, J. (1994). *The American school 1642–1993* (3rd ed.). New York: McGraw-Hill.

Swing, E. S. (1995). Humanism in multicultureland: A comparative looking glass. *Educational Foundations, 9,* 73–94.

Thernstrom, S. (1985). The humanities and our cultural heritage. In C. E. Finn, Jr., D. Ravitch, & R. T. Fancher (Eds.), *Against mediocrity: The humanities in America's high schools* (pp. 66–79). New York: Holmes & Meier.

Whaley, L. (1993). *Weaving in the women: Transforming the high school English curriculum*. Portsmouth, NH: Boynton/Cook.

Wilson, D., Callihan, W., & Jones, D. (1995). *Classical education & the home school*. Moscow, ID: Canon Press.

Wood, G. H. (1992/1993). *Schools that work: America's most innovative public education programs*. New York: Penguin Books.

Wood, G. H. (1998). Democracy and the curriculum. In L. E. Beyer & M. W. Apple (Eds.), *The curriculum: Problems, politics & possibilities* (pp. 177–198). Albany: State University of New York Press.

Chapter 9

Sustaining Indigenous Traditions

Tarajean Yazzie-Mintz

> Our minds keep the remembrance of oral tradition, the histories of our ances-
> tors, the images of our grandparents, and even the memories of their memories.
> We are spiritually connected to our past, our present, and our future.
> Linda Skinner, "Teaching through Traditions," 1999, p. 121

In a classroom at Miner Elementary School in western New York, 19 first
graders are clearing their desks in preparation for Ms. Jones' Seneca language
and culture class. Ms. Jones, a member of the Seneca Nation, enters—pushing
her utility cart holding all the curriculum materials she needs to teach a lesson about the Seneca language and culture. The students turn at their desks to
watch her entrance, punctuated by her singing a song to the tune and rhythm
of the "Meow Mix" commercial song—all familiar sounds except that she is
singing the song using Seneca words to describe the movements of a cat. The
children sing along with her as she floats to the front of the classroom to post
her language materials on the board. They all sing the song twice and then
they switch to *London Bridge*, also in Seneca. When they finish she turns
around to face the students and greets them with Seneca words that translate
to: "I am thankful that you are all well."

Ms. Jones' entrance into Miner Elementary classrooms 3 years ago did
not happen so fluidly. Initially teachers and parents resisted her presence and
the idea of the language and culture program in the school. White parents
believed that if their children participated in this language and culture program, achievement (measured by standardized assessments) would decline.
Teachers at Miner Elementary, many of whom are not of Seneca descent, also
assumed that, despite the proximity of the school to the heart of the Seneca
nation, this new Seneca language and culture program would become a dis-
traction from their own instruction. Even some Seneca parents thought that
either the Seneca language should not be taught in school or that the language
and culture would conflict with their Christian religion and beliefs. It was
natural for this resistance to be passed on to the children in the classrooms at
Miner Elementary School.

Miner Elementary is located just off one of the Seneca Nation's five reservations in New York State. Ms. Jones was hired to teach Seneca language and culture in this school that educates both Seneca children and non-Native children. In this first-grade classroom there are 13 White students, 2 African American students, and 4 Seneca students. Ms. Jones believes that as this school resides geographically next to the reservation, it is necessary for all children who attend the school to learn about their relationship with the tribal nation; moreover it is important for Seneca children's identities to be validated in a school community that previously did not acknowledge the proximity of the Seneca ancestral and contemporary political borders. To choose not to address this relationship would be an act of ignoring the Seneca Nation's existence and therefore the existence of the Seneca students attending Miner Elementary.

Although Ms. Jones teaches children of different social, racial, and ethnic identities, many of them became novice readers and elementary speakers of the Seneca language within the first 3 years of the program. In addition, as the Seneca language is taught to the children, they also learn Seneca history, structures of government, and basic knowledge about traditional practices situated within geographic and culturally defined spaces—such as the ceremonial lodge called the longhouse. Teaching to a racially and culturally diverse student population is a challenge, as Ms. Jones is continuously perfecting her approach, incorporating a new explanation about the Seneca longhouse, or the Seneca calendar, or meaning of words (seasons) and action (how to ask another child to play) within related conversations. The instructional complexity emerges from and is shaped by the diversity of ways in which Seneca people live in contemporary Seneca society and in relationship with non-Seneca society. For example, in a lesson about longhouses, she checks her students' knowledge: "Do all Seneca people attend longhouse ceremonies?" She confers with the children to create an opportunity for them to demonstrate their knowledge and understanding that, today, some Seneca people continue to practice their traditional ways and others do not.

There is an underlying rationale for teaching the Seneca language and culture to elementary school children: this language is no longer spoken in many homes, nor is it taught within the local Seneca community. The result is that the Seneca language is disappearing, and with it, unique cultural and social practices of the Seneca. While the majority of students in Miner Elementary School are from racially and culturally White backgrounds, their engagement in these lessons provides a rich experience about the social and cultural context surrounding their town and school. Once more, this program provides the possibility of developing a new generation—of both Seneca and non-Seneca peoples—who know the language and culture and care about sustaining Seneca traditions.

Curricular programs such as the Seneca culture and language program address the lack of awareness among mainstream society about contemporary American Indian life, struggles, and contributions. Front and center are the lives, language, and ways of being contemporary Seneca people. Indigenous existence is not relegated to the past within a history lesson, but is placed in the present through dynamic and interactive instructional discussions. In powerful ways, the history of the Seneca people is used to inform the present state of government, language, identity and geographic location within the students' daily life routines. The fact that many of these school children traverse political and geographic boundaries of reservation/non-reservation on a daily basis without knowing of their importance is unthinkable to Ms. Jones. An obvious fact to Ms. Jones and other Indigenous educators is that land is central to mapping knowledge about the world, relationship with other peoples, and our connection to ancestry and history. She knows that, ironically, it was land and definitions of boundaries (reservation/non-reservation) that were exchanged for education and for social and health services stipulated in many treaties between Indigenous nations and the U.S. government. The boundaries that children and teachers cross on a daily basis are foundational and historical in the formation of instructional spaces created by the Seneca language and culture program.

§

The Seneca language and culture program is an example of the on-going work in communities within or near American Indian, Alaska Native, and Native Hawaiian communities. However, the notion of sustaining Indigenous culture and language within and across tribal nations is not solely the occupation of tribal nations/villages. In this case, the perpetuation and success of the Seneca language and culture depends upon the acceptance of non-Natives in non-Native controlled schooling, environments, and structures. Across the United States there are many more Indigenous teachers, schools, and communities attempting to maintain their respective Native languages and traditions. Non-Native teachers have joined in the efforts to teach in schools in ways that make contributions to local communities. Curricula to sustain Indigenous traditions are varied, but ultimately should result in the acquisition of knowledge, ways of being, and living defined by Native peoples.

The opening vignette in this chapter reveals some important themes and assumptions embedded within this curricular culture's purpose of sustaining Indigenous traditions. These include:

- The preservation of Native identity;
- Revitalization and empowerment of individuals as members of Native nations through acquisition of Indigenous knowledge imparted within contextual spaces;
- Native language as the vehicle for enacting sustained traditional actions and connection to the past;
- Relationship with nature and people; and most importantly;

• Recognition of Indigenous knowledge as foundational to defining purposes of education for Native youth.

Cultural and linguistic traditions are at the heart of "Sustaining Indigenous Traditions." Youth and adults are positioned to ensure that Indigenous nations continue to exist through (re)enacting tradition (such as speaking their Native tongue). Schools envisioned by this culture of curriculum are spaces in which traditions can be taught as content knowledge (for example, Seneca government and history) with children in relationship with one another and their teachers. Advocates of this curricular culture represent a diversity of tribal nations, languages and cultures.

Visions

This curricular culture is rooted in the notion that educators are tapping into Indigenous traditions and knowledge bases that are to be preserved. Advocates hold that Indigenous youth are to be educated and socialized to learn, understand, and utilize Native knowledge and language, so as to participate in Indigenous social, cultural, and political systems. "Sustaining Indigenous Traditions" is envisioned as upholding preexisting knowledge and processes rather than an attempt to merely shape and change Indigenous cultures for the purposes of educational success. Sara Keahi (2000), a Hawaiian educator, articulates a vision of this curricular culture:

> ...key ideas important to our Native culture that supports the needs of Native Hawaiians to utilize our own resources, to help ourselves, to learn our Native Hawaiian language, to become knowledgeable about our ancestors' culture, to become active participants, not merely passive observers, of all things Hawaiian, and to look to ourselves to solve our own problems. (p. 56)

Curricula constructed under the framework "Sustaining Indigenous Traditions" positions Indigenous communities as holders and controllers of knowledge and processes for learning. Therefore, knowledge shaping the curriculum is situational, emergent from geographical and historical locations and events, and serving to support varied educational purposes.

For this curriculum to flourish, it is necessary to envision schools as a part of communities, rather than seeing communities as a part of schools' purposes. Practitioners of this curricular culture have stated visions that encourage schools to adapt curriculum and instruction to Indigenous traditions rather than merely incorporating culture into an existing curriculum or instructional framework inconsistent with the culture (Cajete, 1994; Swisher & Deyhle, 1988, Yazzie, 1999, 2002). Adapting curriculum includes placing

Indigenous voices as primary voices of knowledge and tellers of historical phenomena. Fenelon and LeBeau (2006) describe a curriculum model responsive to Lakota and Dakota teaching and learning, highlighting four areas within the social sciences that must be addressed:

- Indigenous history;
- Cultural understanding or "Indian" worldview;
- Contemporary sociological structures;
- Social justice struggles. (p. 23)

An Indigenous perspective and epistemological stance shape this curricular culture (Fenelon & LeBeau, 2006) and thus knowledge held by different tribal and Indigenous groups cannot be understood as universal, although the Lakota curriculum model, for example, may highlight a broad spectrum of shared Indigenous ideals. Others envision the purpose of this curricular culture as guiding efforts to improve education and instructional access for Native students at various ages (Cajete, 1999; Skinner, 1999).

To sustain Indigenous cultures, a curriculum must be inclusive of multiple visions and approaches, while also addressing the academic learning needs of the individual student. For some, the curriculum should address societal issues of language and culture loss, self-esteem, and/or serve as a response to understanding and resisting historical oppression (Fenelon & LeBeau, 2006; Hermes, 2005). And still for others, a curriculum whose purpose is to sustain Indigenous traditions will serve as the means to enhance academic achievement, serving as a tool for learning mainstream content. Ultimately, this curricular culture should create viable opportunities for Indigenous peoples to know, enact, and recreate Indigenous knowledge and ways of being within contemporary Native and mainstream society. The curriculum can also produce knowledgeable non-Natives who then can also support achieving the vision.

Educators believe that Indigenous language and culture models for education must be inclusive of Native and non-Native thinkers engaged in learning Native history, culture, language and art forms (Ah Nee-Benham & Cooper, 2000, p. 11). Emergent practices away from Native lands, such as in cities, support educational efforts to diversify standard curriculum taught in schools. Moreover, educators anticipate that knowledge must emerge from sound theories about learning and teaching, and include connections to global technological societies. Educators who want to engage in the curriculum which sustains Indigenous traditions must see that knowledge is located within particular spaces, such as geographic locations. Cajete (1994) writes:

American Indian people's inherent identification with their Place presents one of the most viable alternative paradigms for practicing the art of relationship with the natural world. American Indians have consistently attempted to maintain a harmonious relationship with their lands in the face of tremendous pressures to assimilate. Traditionally, Indian people have expressed in multiple ways that their land and the maintenance of its ecological integrity are key to their physical and cultural survival. (p. 81)

For example, Navajo people consider that learning and life development take place within the four sacred mountains: Mount Blanca (San Luis Valley, CO), Mount Taylor (near Grants, NM), San Francisco Peaks (Flagstaff, AZ), and Mount Hesperus (La Plata Mountain Range, CO); land and knowledge are viewed as interconnected. Other tribal communities have similar beliefs about what knowledge can be taught and when and where teaching can happen; there is a time and a place for the teaching of this curricular knowledge. For example, for the Seneca, there are stories that can be taught and told during particular times of the year (e.g., winter stories and summer stories). Among the Lakota and Dakota traditionalists, learning and teaching begins with formal acknowledgment of relationship to all ("all of our relations") before the learner can seek knowledge inward (Fenelon & LeBeau, 2006). Space, time, and orientation—and their relationship to varying types of knowledge—are key components envisioned within this curricular culture. These elements also influence different types of teaching and learning to take place within a curriculum developed to sustain Indigenous traditions. It would not make sense to attempt to arbitrarily change "tradition" for the sake of convenience of the instructor. The specialized knowledge of time, place, and epistemological orientation of Native worldviews are essential in the discussion about a curricular culture that strives to sustain Indigenous traditions. While "Sustaining Indigenous Traditions" holds that knowledge is place-based, learning is also envisioned as a practice that must include intercultural understandings of science, language, and struggles and survival.

While the majority of discussions about this curricular culture target schooling practices on or near Native lands, reservations, and villages, there are on-going efforts to include this curricular culture's vision within urban contexts where the majority of American Indian students reside. In urban contexts it seems that efforts to envision a culture-based curriculum are complex. Still these endeavors share the vision and ideals of connection to individuals' homelands, traditions, language and practices, as well as making important distinctions among multiple tribal traditions, languages, and cultures. The objective in learning environments located away from designated homelands is to support the growth and development of Native identity and belonging. Curriculum scholars continue to document learning, teaching, and curricula in urban settings to contribute to how culture-based curricula can be envisioned and implemented.

History

This curricular culture began not just as a curriculum for learning in schools, but as a curriculum imparted by families for cultural survival. To understand its emergence, one must understand the ways in which education has been destroyed and rebuilt over multiple generations since Europeans arrived in North America. Ultimately, one must understand how curriculum was shaped from on-going struggles and tensions to define educational practice for and by Native peoples (Lomawaima, 1999, 2000; Lomawaima & McCarty, 2006). Over time this curricular culture has taken many forms, shaped by developers, purpose, and historic era.

Indigenous communities—as cultural, social, and political nations—implemented curricula to sustain Indigenous traditions before (and after) colonial contact. Among the diverse groups of Native nations, families socialized their youth, preparing their nation's next generation of leadership, teachers, healers, and enforcers of social control. Members of families and extended kinship played central roles in the education of the children. Community at large mirrored a social structure in which the central socializing agent, the family, operated. For example, within families there were social roles in place to provide initial "training" for leadership or to carry out disciplinary consequences which then would translate into official roles in community at large.

Through a curricular practice of apprenticeships, youth watched and acquired knowledge of industry (e.g., hunting, gathering, and cooking) and the social institutions (e.g., selection of leadership or definition of gender roles) around them. The curriculum to sustain Indigenous traditions was central to each Indigenous nation's ultimate survival. Inevitably, contact with colonizing immigrants from European countries spurred social changes in tribal nations' social and cultural structures—(re)shaping generations through the contemporary era.

This culture of curriculum has been strongly influenced by the politically, socially, and culturally imposed structures of numerous and varied non-Native nations. Western groups introduced educational theories, processes, and systems, which interfaced but operated in stark contrast to the existing Indigenous ways of learning, ways of knowing, and philosophies. The most damaging attack to Indigenous curriculum was the act of removal of thousands of Native children from their central socializing agents—their families and communities. Placed in industrial boarding schools, Native children's Indigenous education was systematically blocked. For generations beyond the late 1800s, children were schooled and socialized by institutions initially developed by religious organizations and then practices were improved upon somewhat by the U.S. federal government under the Department of War.

Early Western beliefs about how to effectively educate (civilize) Native children included the idea that they should not be exposed to their own Native cultural, linguistic, historical, and local knowledge sources. Exposure to

Indigenous life ways and knowledge was believed by White educators to be a detriment to the child's ability to be socially and culturally transformed into individuals characterized as non-Indian. The boarding school curriculum was created to spread the tradition of White European ways of life and eliminate Native traditions. Commissioner of Indian Affairs, Thomas J. Morgan (1889), articulated the Western belief that education of these youth should "begin with them while they are young and susceptible, and should continue until habits of industry and love of learning have taken the place of indolence and indifference" (Morgan, 1889, cited in Prucha, 1973, p. 225). Schooling designed by the U.S. government was characterized as an education for extinction, to educate in such a way that Native people would no longer see them as Native peoples (Adams, 1995). However, studies demonstrate that while Indigenous youth were torn from their families and communities, they continued to maintain familial, tribal, and Indigenous ties despite efforts to remove tribal and family influences (Child, 1998; Lomawaima, 1994).

Early efforts to counter assimilationist thought were enacted by Native children themselves. In federal boarding schools, children taught their peers their traditional practices, values, stories, and language (Child, 1998). Other children simply refused to participate in the school's activities or to follow orders—and many simply ran away. Young children used resistance as a way of defying explicit and implicit curricula whose purpose was to transform them from being Indian to becoming more like White people. Children who taught and socialized younger Native children in their various traditions were the pioneers of this curricular culture. They sought to sustain connections to their Native communities and roots by fighting against the loss of their identity, language, and cultures. Historians of Native education have documented these acts of resistance and self-determination (Lomawaima, 1994).

When schools initially underestimated the stamina of these youth and their ability to subvert and resist Western school structures and routines, Native youth continued to perform prohibited practices such as speaking one's native language, sharing cultural stories, and reaffirming Native identities. Students created a counter curriculum resulted in practices which sustained an Indigenous identity. Shaped by historical events and responses to forced educational practices, these brave efforts of peer socialization often worked successfully against these schools' official curriculum.

Like the counter curriculum enacted by Native youth in boarding schools, "Sustaining Indigenous Traditions" can be viewed as a counter curriculum to mainstream assimilationist curricula (Adams, 1995; Dejong, 1993; Lomawaima & McCarty, 2006; McCarty, 2002). While the notion of sustaining Indigenous traditions may be perceived to be located within the power of Indigenous communities, the development of curricula supporting these very traditions *in schools* were not always in the control of Native people. Using Native culture and language within formal school settings was theorized to be beneficial to achieving the goal of assimilation. In fact, Indigenous cultures and languages were used during the 1920s as a part of the continued educational agenda set forth by the U.S. government (see Meriam Report, 1928). Moreover, educational historians Lomawaima and McCarty (2006) highlight curricular discussions which determined "where and when Indigenous cultural practices might be considered benign enough to be allowed, even welcomed within American life" (p. 6). In other words, educators who believed in assimilation practices determined the validity of this curricular culture and decided when it would be appropriate to integrate Indigenous language and knowledge in the formal school setting. Often, practices in this curricular culture were allowed if knowledge taught contributed to the goals of the school.

In more recent times, influenced by the wave of multicultural education emerging from the civil rights era, schools have been created across the United States in cities (including Milwaukee, Buffalo, Tulsa, St. Paul, Albuquerque, and Seattle) to provide greater educational access to Native children and families. In these schools, educators attempt to implement curriculum focusing broadly on Native language and culture, values, beliefs, and pan-Indian practices (including participation in Pow-Wow social or competition dance events). These schools represent contemporary attempts to enact the curricular approach of "Sustaining Indigenous Traditions" by instructing youth with instructional philosophies, processes, materials, and assessments that are responsive and relevant to the Native families and children living in urban settings. In these contexts one might find several Native languages taught, or arts and crafts, or history and stories rooted in specific tribal nations' traditions.

For example, the American Indian Magnet School in St. Paul, Minnesota, describes itself as a "school emphasizing individual learning styles to support a strong academic foundation and cultural base." Its curriculum includes the teaching of Lakota and Ojibwe languages, as well as incorporating broad notions of American Indian culture in literacy practices (American Indian Magnet School, 2008). This school was created in the early 1990s, and in 2006 the school enrollment had a diverse student population, consisting of 33% American Indian, 23% Asian American, 11% Hispanic/Latino, 24% African American, and 9% White (Caucasian) (St. Paul Public Schools Data Center, 2008). While historically the curriculum was created primarily to educate Native youth, schooling options have evolved to include a racially mixed population of learners. Today, it is common to witness the inclusive nature of this curricular culture. A variety of students can learn about Indigenous groups, issues, languages, and perhaps join in the movement to revitalize Indigenous communities wherever they may reside in contemporary society.

Beliefs and Practices: Learners and Teachers

To understand and enact this curricular approach, educators need to understand and value Native ways of being; that is, they must know intimately how economic and social factors shape the learner's instructional preparedness and thus engage experts in the local community who are recognized as holders of specialized Indigenous knowledge. Teachers in formal school settings must be able to make connections to historical experiences, knowledge, and socio-cultural context found in families, tribal traditions, and community whether they be located on reservations or far from Native lands (Yazzie-Mintz, 2007).

Educators who implement this curriculum believe that the process of learning starts when the child is very young and can continue throughout the learner's lifetime. At times, children may not be conscious that they are learning content of an established curriculum to sustain Indigenous traditions. Babies of Indigenous nations, for example, are often welcomed into their respective tribal ceremonies (the curriculum). The exposure to Native language, song, story, and other practices of Indigenous knowledge in ceremony is a supporting act of cultural survival. When learners reach a level of maturity, they can truly appreciate the purpose of being present and acquiring knowledge that is to sustain their traditions.

While students of other racial and ethnic backgrounds may benefit from this curriculum, the primary purposes of this curriculum are to be responsive to the needs, interests, competencies, and motives of Native children and their tribal survival. Because of these purposes, instruction is in the hands of knowledgeable teachers of the community, rather than someone who is from outside of the culture. But again, it is important to note that there are exemplary non-Native teachers who have faithfully embodied a curriculum that supports learning of Indigenous traditions.

Learners will not always know the ultimate goals and objectives of this curriculum; however, most often they will enact the curriculum prior to understanding its full impact on their identity, sense of belonging, and social and intellectual development. There is an assumption that as young learners grow, they will develop deeper understandings of their traditions, stories, and songs. For example, the interpretation of Navajo folk tales, such as the coyote stories, become more complex as learners develop throughout their lifetime; eventually, they will use the coyote trickster tales to explain or theorize about social or political events in the contemporary world. With this understanding of both education and curriculum, teachers can adapt their instructional approach to be inclusive of specific local knowledge.

Advocates of "Sustaining Indigenous Traditions" believe that students hold significant knowledge stemming from interactions with family, community, and with the natural world; to strengthen instruction, educators work intently to incorporate this knowledge into classroom content and pedagogy. Curriculum theorists, developers, and practitioners understand that students for whom this curriculum is intended may come to the classroom (or other learning environments) with little to no knowledge about Indigenous knowledge systems, history, language, culture, morals, values, or interests.

Moreover, only in recent research (emerging throughout the 1990s) have scholars—through studies of dropouts, achievement, and youth culture outside of school—gained better understanding of Indigenous students' motivations. Educational researcher Donna Deyhle (1998) found that Navajo youth's motivations for learning are shaped by resistance to White domination. Further, learning to interpret their popular culture's preoccupation with rap and heavy metal music demonstrates that Navajo youth are complexly shaped by their continuous analysis of their cultural context and beyond. In this work, Navajo youth are not viewed as coming to the act of sustaining traditions as empty vessels, but rather as skilled interpreters of culture, contemporary society and power structures. Although Native youth may not conduct their "reading" of their learning and social contexts from an Indigenous world view, they may be engaging in "reading" their world from a complex combination of multiple social and political lenses. As follows, to engage students in learning Indigenous curriculum requires that teachers are knowledgeable of the multiple ways in which tribal knowledge, culture, and language can emerge in the learning context.

Still, some educators in schools implementing a curriculum that sustains Indigenous tradition believed that students engage in straddling two worlds, the Native and the White. This thinking has been described as deficit thinking because it does not more complexly consider students' abilities, interests and motives for engaging in this curriculum. Many students who will be taught within this curricular culture fall along a continuum of knowledge about their respective Indigenous traditions. Some have been raised steeped in their respective tribal tradition whereas others have been raised outside of tribal traditional spaces and practices. Teachers' approaches must respond to the students' level of readiness and prior exposure to this knowledge; skilled teachers might gauge students' knowledge and generate lessons with their experiences in mind. The teacher's role is to make the knowledge interesting and relevant to the lives of the students who emerge from a wide and diverse range of backgrounds. Authentic content and outcomes will depend greatly on the teacher's initial observations and impressions of the students' level of knowledge of tradition, and also their own knowledge, motivations, and interests. But while developing and implementing this curriculum is complex, any teacher can implement a curriculum to sustain Indigenous traditions in some way. Some instructional acts may address issues defined as surface exploration of traditions and some may deepen a learner's understanding about the nature of Indigenous knowledge systems—referred to as Indigenous epistemologies.

Teachers can take steps to ensure that both students and content are addressed in meaningful and purposeful ways. Educators working within this curricular culture will embrace ties with the local community, know who within local communities holds Indigenous knowledge about specialized practices, and continue to be learners of cultures alongside their students. Practitioners who work to sustain Indigenous cultures believe that teachers have the capacity to build important partnerships with parents, local organizations, historical societies, and universities and colleges. How teacher generate and foster these connections serves as models for their pupils to also engage in insightful intellectual exchange with local elders, the holders of knowledge.

Within Native communities an elder is viewed as an expert on tribal nation philosophy, ecology, biology, or history; similarly, a teacher in a formal school setting might be viewed as having knowledge and expertise about a language, mathematics, and science or U.S. history. For example, Ms. Jones, the Seneca language teacher described in the opening of this chapter, continues to maintain strong partnerships with the Seneca tribal office that funds and supports language learning opportunities with elders in the Seneca community. She also has called on her own study of Seneca history and traditions through participation in her nation's longhouse ceremonies and celebrations. Finally, she draws her elementary students into the learning through song—singing songs in the Seneca language mixed with contemporary and recognizable tunes that invite her students into the lessons. Certainly, great commitment is necessary to establish viable programs within school environments, which often have little resources dedicated to this type of curriculum.

How teachers facilitate learning depends upon depth and breadth of knowledge of the content. Often teachers facilitate cultural teachings in the Native language or by modeling traditional practices. A high school science teacher, Jack Seltzer, working with Navajo youth in Monument Valley, Arizona, started a garden which yields Indigenous plants of Navajo people (Toomer-Cook, 2006). Embedding horticulture within the high school science official curriculum has contributed to the revitalization of particular plants on the land, important knowledge in the classroom, and connections between the school and local community. Through this project the teacher fosters important relationships among younger and older Navajo generations; these two generations participate in an act that, for both, revitalizes Navajo farming traditions. As a non-Native teacher, Seltzer's motivations are based on the hope that he, too, can contribute to the continuation of cultural practices, beliefs, and traditions of Navajo people. Teachers who implement this curricular approach have moral as well as academic beliefs about sustaining Indigenous traditions. Educators who use this curriculum become embodiments of knowledge; they act, learn, and teach based on how they have been gifted the knowledge. "Teacher as an embodiment of curriculum" is a critical metaphor that helps highlight the notion that to sustain Indigenous traditions, one must be the embodied experience of the knowledge itself.

Another example of this curricular culture is the Cherokee language work of Tahlequah, Oklahoma, teachers who impart language and culture to a population of preschool through second-grade students. Their approach to sustaining Cherokee tradition is to place this language as the primary source of knowledge in the curriculum. Teachers, who embody and enact the language, facilitate learning using an immersion approach starting when children are young.

The students learn the language through social, physical play, and instructional interactions. These teachers' roles are multifaceted. If they are to achieve their goal of producing fluent Cherokee speakers who will sustain Cherokee traditions, the teachers must develop language-learning approaches, materials, age-appropriate literature, and science and math activities. Teachers must create opportunities to expose these youth to multiple and rich language use.

The work of Ms. Jones, Jack Seltzer, and the Cherokee language immersion teachers demonstrate the scope and depth of knowledge that teachers need to have when teaching cultural knowledge. Their work is richly informed by knowledge of history as well as contemporary political and social structures under which Indigenous peoples live. Moreover, to implement this curriculum, teachers should be prepared to seek out experts on local knowledge; through the act of bringing these individuals to the classroom, teachers create an opportunities to learn alongside their students. It is not unusual to witness teachers who have given their entire lives to the effort of sustaining Indigenous traditions; they are deeply internally motivated and externally enact their curricular goals on a daily basis inside and outside formal schooling contexts. Within this curricular tradition, learners and teachers are holders and actors of knowledge, and it is their vocation and purpose to ensure knowledge of Indigenous traditions is passed on to new learners and teachers.

Beliefs and Practices: Content and Context

The beauty of a curriculum that sustains Indigenous traditions is its knowledge that can be taught across the standard curriculum of schools and to different levels of student ability and experience. Within this curricular culture the subject matter generally rests upon two foundational areas: (a) enacting knowledge rooted in Indigenous cultural traditions and practice (e.g., songs, food, language, ceremonies, stories); and (b) deepening knowledge rooted in the study of history, governance, and geography. Some supporters of this curricular orientation also believe that content of this curriculum should be inclusive of learning a respective Indigenous language (which simultaneously serves as a tool for instruction).

When teachers and students examine the socio-historical context in relationship to the Indigenous ways of thinking—referred to as Indigenous epistemologies—they engage in an implicit study of Indigenous traditions that is dynamic, alive, and contextual. The content must be taught in a way that teaches learners that to sustain Indigenous traditions, one must see and experience the dynamic nature of the knowledge taught, rather than interpreting it as static and unchanging. For instance, as a part of a project implemented by Jerry Lipka and a group of Native Alaskan teachers, students in Alaskan villages learned about how water and fishing rights affect their way of life. Knowledge about water and fishing rights can be taught as a part of a history lesson, but is also profoundly shaped by local telling of history and enactments of tradition. Ojibwe children might learn the processes of growing and harvesting rice, or Navajo children might learn to speak the Navajo language so that they have the opportunity to participate in Navajo governance as adults, or the education of Lakota youth may draw upon the primacy of relationship with relatives, humans and non-human beings. Educators who enact this curriculum instruct in and outside of formal schooling settings. We can see in these examples how learners enact and deepen their knowledge of Alaskan Native, Ojibwe, Navajo, and Lakota traditions. This curriculum, formal and informal, can be enacted in schools as well as within families and communities.

The subject matter is taught in informal and formal learning contexts, and through systematic approaches as well as exploratory methods. Within structures of schooling, the subject matter of this curriculum can be delivered in specialized classrooms referred to as pull-out or push-in programs. The opening scenario featuring Ms. Jones, for example, describes a "push-in" program, wherein the teacher brings the curriculum to classrooms, rather than students coming to a special classroom taught by a "culture teacher." Another context in which this curriculum is implemented is the regular classroom environment. General education teachers might infuse ways of sustaining Indigenous traditions into lessons across the school's standardized curriculum, such as incorporating Indigenous knowledge, methods of questioning, and processes of investigation into math, science, the arts, language arts, and social studies. For instance, teachers can create language arts lessons that may include reading about different tribal nations. Another possibility might be to have learners read stories written in a Native language. The important consideration about content and context of this curriculum is to keep in mind themes related to contemporary issues. Focusing on topics—such as documenting and writing about the tribal elections or studying issues related to family and health care—is a powerful way to help learners construct understanding of their tribal identities and structures.

Throughout this curricular approach, there is a strong focus on how the nature of Indigenous knowledge and experiences change in relation to the context. The context in which Indigenous knowledge is developed, transformed, and maintained is an important consideration in developing this curriculum for particular learners in situated contexts. For example, a science class engaging in inquiry about recycling may link the inquiry with learning core Navajo values (e.g., living in beauty with the natural environment). As a follow-up to this initial science inquiry, the learners can connect Navajo values with living and recycling in rural versus urban settings. Knowledge about recycling is dependent upon context; in cities, people routinely recycle by placing their items in a green or blue bin curbside. In Navajo communities, families cannot simply place a bin outside their homes, rather, they must engage in recycling efforts that are much more active and intentional. The learners' discussion about how recycling takes place on and off the Navajo reservation develops understanding of concepts such as Nationhood, geography, and governance.

The study of science principles can be inclusive of theories and tenets emerging from an Indigenous perspective. The content must be connected and must deliver opportunities to make meaning of global issues within the local context of an Indigenous nation.

Often educators hold the assumption that what should be taught under this curricular framework is merely what "looks" Native. This understanding of Native-based curriculum might define content as the process of making colorful beadwork, or cooking traditional foods. Additionally, in a music class the content taught might be Indigenous music appreciation focusing on different forms such as contemporary rock songs with political messages about land, mother Earth and resistance, or listening to a traditional healing song with a message about relationship. In contrast, educators implementing a curriculum to sustain Indigenous traditions focus their instruction on generating deeper understandings of what it means to be a Native person in a contemporary, technological world. Content must be introduced hand-in-hand with the teaching of critical analytical skills to investigate the different types of knowledge represented within the curriculum.

Beliefs & Practices: Curriculum Planning and Evaluation

The curriculum within this culture is designed, developed, and implemented by teachers who draw upon the expertise of students, other teachers, families, and community members. The curriculum is determined, negotiated, co-constructed, and evaluated by multiple members of the educational community. Because this curricular culture seeks to develop and sustain Indigenous knowledge and practices, what knowledge should be taught is often determined by groups of people rather than one individual. Part of the discussion in curriculum development includes asking critical questions such as: What cultural knowledge should be taught and by whom? When can Indigenous knowledge be taught, and where? The final negotiation among curriculum developers is to define processes for measuring or evaluating knowledge acquisition—an assessment process.

In some learning environments located on reservations, land allotments, or isolated villages, the curriculum may be shaped by a tribal curriculum developer or a group of recognized holders of tribal knowledge and/or elders. These experts are identified to design tribally specific curriculum to be taught in schools located within their tribal political boundaries.

Native communities may decide, as a nation, that Indigenous knowledge must be taught in schools located within the political boundaries of their nations. For example, the Cherokee Nation of Oklahoma determined it important to design, develop and implement a Cherokee language immersion program. This program was established in response to the Nation's study of language speakers; findings of their study indicated that only a small percentage of their population is fluent in the Cherokee language marking their language on the road to rapid extinction. The Cherokee immersion program and curriculum were therefore developed to address the critical need to generate a new generation of fluent Cherokee language speakers.

This curriculum development process emerged from a Nation level of involvement, but the curriculum to sustain Indigenous cultures can also be developed by individuals who do not reside in schools located on Native lands. For example, a teacher of Lakota heritage residing in Phoenix, Arizona, may be the only educator in the school who holds knowledge of a Native language and cultural practice. In this case, the teacher may collaborate with a colleague to develop an integrated study of United States history—allowing both educators to deepen their knowledge and extend their pedagogy by both focusing on the integration of Lakota history within the study of U.S. history and teach history through the perspectives of different tribal people's creation stories. Both curricula are developed by creative and knowledgeable teachers, who embody the desire to create knowledge for their students that engages them in deeper and nuanced understandings of historical telling and representation. This curriculum developed for a history class in Phoenix, Arizona, may not result in the survival of the Lakota people, like the Cherokee immersion program, but it will bring attention to the existence of Lakota people as members of United States contemporary society.

This curricular culture operates both inside and outside of the standards-based education paradigm. For the Cherokee language program, evaluation is internally monitored, and for the history curriculum, the teachers may make explicit connections to Arizona state standards in history. One curriculum operates outside of state standards and the other must be cognizant of state standards in history. Many advocates of this curricular culture believe that content and practices taught in public schools should align with standards required by the state. Alignment of the curricular goals and implementation with state standards serves as a legitimizing practice, while at the same time curricular goals can also advocate for specialized knowledge applicable for developing or supporting students' sense of tribal identity.

The viability of this curriculum developed for formal school settings depends greatly on students' academic achievement on standardized assessments. The curricular culture has better chances of remaining in the school if the knowledge and practices of Indigenous culture curriculum supports measurable increased academic engagement and performance among the students. Many teachers and researchers currently are in the midst of this conversation and make many attempts to show the connection between the curricular objectives and academic achievement measured by standard testing practices in schools. For example, educational researchers Jerry Lipka, Nancy Sharp, Barbara Adams, and Ferdinand Sharp (2007) documented the processes used by teachers to incorporate Alaskan elders' knowledge in a geometry lesson entitled, "Patterns and Parkas." The teachers used an expert-apprentice model in which students worked with and observed closely elders create a rhombus from a rectangle. They describe the instructional process:

> Making parka patterns pieces has the potential to enrich the math curriculum. In our approach, students create their own patterns, often similar to those used in their community. Through this process of making pattern sets, the students gained insight into geometric relationships. This process of students making patterns differs from using already made, consumer-oriented pattern pieces, which skip the important step of observing how the geometric shapes are related to each other.... (p. 102)

This instructional process makes purposeful use of local experts in curriculum development, and the elders' expert knowledge and practices are infused with a schooling process within the school environment. Children in this classroom are shown models of how to learn from a knowledgeable member of the community; as well, they experience a rich geometry lesson in which mathematical understanding of geometric shapes is taking place. To implement content within this context requires creative insight into the learning potential of mathematical thinking, coupled with deep knowledge and familiarity of local context, expertise, and ways of being. The curriculum developed by teachers and local elders is interdisciplinary, the success of which is dependent upon multiple actors in the educational process.

The learners' knowledge is evaluated on several levels: by the teacher through observations, by the use of a teacher-made test, and by the elders who provide immediate and constant feedback as the learners make their parka patterns. It is possible to envision and enact a systematic evaluation process when implementing a curriculum to sustain Indigenous traditions. Developers with forethought may save time by providing clear and concise evaluation criteria, so that the curriculum is not derailed due to political debates about the nature of the knowledge and the measures assessing knowledge taught. More and more tribal nations are beginning to design their own measures of competence and knowledge acquisition. Such measures are meant to provide evidence of the rigor and effectiveness of their locally defined curricula. As is the case for many curricula developed for school contexts, a curriculum to sustain Indigenous traditions is highly politicized, and certainly has multiple stakeholders overseeing, observing, and evaluating the purposes and outcomes of such a curriculum.

Dilemmas of Practice

Those who envision this educational practice have reported that teachers find the pressures of formal school structures—such as the official curriculum, assessment procedures, and goals inherent in public education practices—difficult to overcome when implementing a curriculum focused on sustaining

Indigenous traditions. Teachers may find it difficult to balance a philosophical commitment to sustaining Indigenous traditions with the traditions of knowledge defined by mainstream society and our current testing culture.

Another challenge within this curricular culture is to serve Native student populations while at the same time understanding the multiple historical, social, political, and cultural outcomes of an educational system (structure, curricula, pedagogy, and instructional process) implemented by Native *and* non-Native teachers in schools. The practice of Indigenous culture-based curriculum and instruction represents a continued struggle and search for balance between non-Native teaching ideals (mainstream learning purposes, approaches, and outcomes) with Indigenous epistemologies (living philosophies, ways of being, and educational strategies unique and relative to each Native Nation's historical and political contexts). More to the point, while American Indians are categorized under one racial category, teachers may have difficulty addressing distinctions among diverse tribal traditions, customs, knowledge, and life ways. It may be easier to treat American Indian topics as an over-generalized topic than to address distinct tribal knowledge and practices distinctly and respectfully. So while teachers may be invested in sustaining tribal traditions, language, and cultural ways within contemporary times, they must also address educational needs of their respective student populations (who might be Native or non-Native) within unique "situated contexts" (Hermes, 1999). There is the tendency to over-generalize curricular theory and practices across tribal nations, rather than to focus locally within tribe; this practice is also a dilemma for tribal peoples committed to educational practices that revitalize or sustain Indigenous knowledge.

Geography (e.g., the physical location of the school or classroom) presents a dilemma within this culture of curriculum; that is, geography and enacted knowledge are intimately intertwined. Particular learning activities are associated with particular spaces; where education takes place has meaning. For example, in an elementary school on the Navajo reservation, a hogan, a traditional dwelling, was built to become the classroom for teaching and learning about Navajo culture and language. In this school, the hogan becomes both the space in which the curricular culture is enacted and a central focus of the curricular knowledge taught.

Teachers are socialized to take on the notion that learning and teaching only happens in schools. Native educators and educators who work with Native communities recognize that learning and teaching can happen in places outside of schools, and that learning can be facilitated by teachers who are not certified by the state. The belief that only certified teachers hold sound instructional knowledge is problematic for tribes (and educators) that desire to teach and revive a quickly dying language. Proponents of this curricular culture believe that experts—fluent speakers of language for example—hold knowledge to be taught, and while certification can be bestowed on individual teachers they cannot simply go out and learn to speak Cherokee fluently.

Therefore in planning for this curricular culture, what counts as qualifications to teach is often a focus of debate.

Another assumption held by teachers, administrators, and parents is that if one is Native then that individual naturally desires to sustain her traditions. A dilemma of practice for teachers is addressing parental concerns and resistance when considering implementing a curriculum to sustain Indigenous traditions. It is not wise to assume that all Native peoples support this curricular approach in or outside of schools.

Influence of mainstream educational philosophy also creates tensions regarding educational outcomes—often leading us to a narrow definition of success. Within this worldview, the educational conversation is about content and outcomes measured primarily as achievement in the subjects of math, reading, and science. Native/Indigenous communities do not operate or exist without these dominant educational approaches; in fact, our communities have the capacity to embrace the notion of competition, individualism, technology, and personal achievement. The dialogue within Native communities includes speaking about innovation in Native educational communities. Innovation is referred to as implementing effective instructional and learning strategies, or best practices, which can reflect dominant educational discourses and structures of educational institutions because the measures of effective and best practices are dominant assessment tools.

Our work to sustain Native traditions within the dominant culture of curriculum is at odds with desired outcomes for Native people—to be simultaneously a member of an Indigenous/tribal nation and to be recognized as a full member of dominant White society as evidenced by access to all of its benefits and rights and privileges. How can our imagined Native culture-based educational systems result in the same outcomes as a dominant education? How might Native curricula empower students to learn in ways that are measured as successful? Should the approach be evaluated by measures that are inherently assessing mainstream instructional outcomes?

Critique

Critics of "Sustaining Indigenous Traditions" believe that the goals, purposes, and implementation of this curricular culture are unrealistic in this standards-driven era of American schooling and impractical for full participation in contemporary American society. Native language and culture are central components of this curricular culture; critics believe that language and culture are not sufficient knowledge to be taught to students who must compete and work within a world that prioritizes social, political, and economic communication in the English language. This curricular culture directly engages local and Native knowledge systems and ways of being in acts of schooling; these purposes and approaches contrast sharply with mainstream educational thought. Critics believe that an education to sustain Indigenous traditions relies on a narrow purpose of schooling, and therefore this curriculum is not appropriate or beneficial to all citizens. This curriculum requires specialized knowledge including, but not limited to, the ability to speak, read, and write in a Native language. Critics point out that there are not enough teachers who hold the expert knowledge required to enact the curriculum effectively and widely across multiple communities on and off Native lands and reservations. In addition, school systems and the teacher preparation pathways to the profession must also fully implement this curricular culture. Yet, the current educational system that supports teacher training is not set up to properly train teachers to implement this culture of curriculum. In fact, teacher education programs focused on this curricular culture are fairly new, and Indigenous theories guiding this practice are yet to be developed, published, and more fully debated among curriculum scholars.

Indigenous communities are different and distinct from one another and language and cultural traditions, in turn, are different and distinct. As this is the case, how can this curricular culture be educationally responsive to large numbers of Native communities representing diverse backgrounds and knowledges? How to educate students from different cultural and linguistic backgrounds emerges as a blind spot for advocates of this curriculum; deciding which Indigenous language, culture, and knowledge should be taught must be determined. Currently such decisions are made within local and tribally specific communities situated on reservations, land allotments, or villages. Urban multicultural contexts like Chicago, Los Angeles, Milwaukee, and New York City—cities in which large numbers of Native families reside— are often left out of the curriculum development and implementation discussion. This curricular culture then does not address the educational, cultural, and linguistic needs of Native students across different backgrounds and in different educational contexts.

From the critique of "Sustaining Indigenous Traditions," a few critical questions emerge: What aspects of culture or language should be taught in schools serving more than one tribe? What approaches can educators take to ensure authenticity of the Indigenous culture when curricular content is taught out of tribal context? What steps can be taken to avoid reinforcing stereotypes about Native peoples, such as over-generalization of customs, language, and culture across distinct tribal nations? These questions highlight potential pitfalls of this curricular culture, in terms of what should be taught, how to ensure cultural authenticity, how to avoid stereotyping and caricaturizing Indigenous cultures, and who should enact those cultures.

References

Adams, D. (1995). *Education for extinction: American Indians and the boarding school experience, 1875–1928.* Lawrence: University Press of Kansas.

Ah Nee-Benham, M. K. P., & Cooper, J. E. (Eds.). (2000). *Indigenous educational models for contemporary practice: In our mother's voice*. Mahwah, NJ: Erlbaum.

American Indian Magnet School. (2008). *American Indian magnet school "our mission"* Retrieved July 25, 2008, from http://www.aims.spps.org/home.html

Cajete. G. (1994). *Look to the mountain: An ecology of Indigenous education*. Skyland, NC: Kivaki Press.

Cajete, G. (1999). The Native American learner and bicultural science education. In K. G. Swisher & J. W. Tippeconnic III (Eds.), *Next steps: Research and practice to advance Indian education* (pp. 135–160). Charleston, NC: ERIC.

Child, B. (1998). *Boarding school seasons: American Indian families, 1900–1940*. Lincoln: University of Nebraska.

Dejong, D. H. (1993). *Promises of the past: A history of Indian education*. Golden, CO: North American Press.

Deyhle, D. (1998). From break dancing to heavy metal: Navajo youth, resistance, and identity. *Youth and Society, 30*(3), 3–31.

Fenelon, J. V., & LeBeau, D. (2006). Four directions for Indian education: Curriculum models for Lakota and Dakota teaching and learning. In I. Abu-Saad & D. Champagne (Eds.), *Indigenous education and empowerment: International perspectives* (pp. 21–68). New York: Rowman & Littlefield.

Hermes, M. (1999). Research methods as situated response: Toward a First Nations' methodology. In L. Parker, D. Deyhle, & S. Villenas (Eds.), *Race is ... race isn't: Critical race theory and qualitative studies in education* (pp. 83–100). Boulder, CO: Westview Press.

Hermes, M. (2005). Complicating discontinuity: What about poverty? *Curriculum Inquiry, 35*(1), 9–26.

Keahi, S. (2000). *Advocating for a stimulating and language-based education: If you don't learn your language where can you go home to?* In M. Nee-Benham & J. E. Cooper (Eds.), *Indigenous educational models for contemporary practice: In our mother's voice* (pp. 55–60). Mahwah, NJ: Erlbaum.

Lipka, J., Sharp, N., Adams, B., & Sharp, F. (2007). Creating a third space for authentic biculturalism: Examples from Math in a cultural context. *Journal of American Indian Education, 46*(3), 94–115.

Lomawaima, K. T. (1994). *They called it prairie light: The story of Chilocco Indian school*. Lincoln: University of Nebraska Press.

Lomawaima, K. T. (1999). The unnatural history of American Indian education. In K. G. Swisher & J. W. Tippeconnic III (Eds.), *Next steps: Research and practice to advance Indian education* (pp. 1–32). Charleston, NC: ERIC.

Lomawaima, K. T. (2000). Tribal sovereigns: Reframing research in American Indian education. *Harvard Educational Review, 70*(1), 1–21.

Lomawaima, K. T., & McCarty, T. L. (2006). *To remain an Indian: Lessons in Democracy from a century of Native American education*. New York: Teachers College Press.

McCarty, T. (2002). *A place to be Navajo: Rough Rock and the struggle for self-determination in indigenous schooling*. Mahwah, NJ: Erlbaum.

Meriam, L. (Ed.). (1928). *The problem of Indian administration*. Baltimore, MD: John Hopkins University.

Prucha , F. P. (1973). *Americanizing the American Indians: Writings by the 'Friends of the Indian' 1880–1900*. Cambridge, MA: Harvard University Press.

St. Paul Public Schools Data Center. (2008). Information about a school. Retrieved July 25, 2008, from https://mis.spps.org/data_center/index.cfm?CFID=559673&CFTO KEN=79843165

Skinner, L. (1999). Teaching through traditions: Incorporating languages and culture into curricula. In K. G. Swisher & J. W. Tippeconnic III (Eds.), *Next steps: Research and practice to advance Indian education* (pp. 107–134). Charleston, NC: ERIC Clearinghouse on Rural Education and Small Schools.

Swisher, K., & Deyhle, D. (1988). Adapting instruction to culture. In J. Reyhner (Ed.), *Teaching American Indian students* (pp. 81–95). Norman: University of Oklahoma.

Toomer-Cook, J. (2006). Top teacher blends old, new. *Desert Morning News* (Salt Lake City, UT). Retrieved July 3, 2008, from http://findarticles.com/p/articles/ mi_qn4188/is_20060730/ai_n16648027

Yazzie, T. (1999). Culturally appropriate curriculum: A research-based rationale. (pp. 83–106) In K. G. Swisher & J. W. Tippeconnic III (Eds.), *Next steps: Research and practice to advance Indian education.* Charleston, NC: ERIC.

Yazzie, T. (2002). *Culture deep within us: Culturally appropriate curriculum and pedagogy in three Navajo teachers' work.* Unpublished doctoral dissertation. Cambridge, MA: Harvard University.

Yazzie-Mintz, T. (2007). From a place deep inside: Culturally appropriate curriculum as the embodiment of Navajo-ness in classroom pedagogy. *Journal of American Indian Education, 46*(3), 72–93.

Chapter 10

Deliberating Democracy

Edward R. Mikel

> A democracy is more than a form of government; it is primarily a mode of associ-
> ated living, of conjoint communicated experience…. Since a democratic society
> repudiates the principle of external authority, it must find a substitute in volun-
> tary disposition and interest; these can be created only by education.
>
> John Dewey, 1916, *Democracy and Education*, p. 319

It is the second day of September at Lookout Middle School in a working-class
area of a large midwestern city. An ethnically and racially mixed group of
58 sixth graders files into a double classroom where their two teachers greet
them. Both Ms. Bryant and Ms. Reed are assigned to their respective departments—one is in language arts-social studies and the other in math-science.
The students will be in this class for five 4-hour block periods each week.

This is the first of 4 consecutive days of curriculum planning and organizing for this block class. After attendance is taken and the random banter of
early adolescents has subsided, Ms. Reed announces the next days' agenda
and explains:

> This year we will be doing something quite different with your—with
> *our* curriculum—in this language arts and social studies block. We won't
> start by trying to figure out what's language arts and what's social studies;
> we're going to concentrate on only what you are concerned about, what
> you think is important, and what everyone together thinks is important.

This organizing process is hardly spontaneous or ad hoc. It comprises a
set of structured activities over four days intended to carve out and set in
place the building blocks of a term-long curriculum, including a set of thematic areas of study and the substance of the first area of study: key learning
activities, designated knowledge and skill outcomes, potential resources, and
procedures for assessing the progress of students' learning and evaluating the
curriculum.

The design and planning process starts with students individually and pri-
vately answering three organizing levels of questions in sequence:

- Who are you? What are you like? What are your interests, problems, needs?
- What questions or concerns do you have about yourself?
- What questions or concerns do you have about the world you live in?

The six-graders' questions about their own lives are: "When will I die?" "Will I 'make it' in life?" "Will I achieve my goals?" "Would I be scared if I had to go to war?" "Am I really like what other people say I am?" Then, they pose these questions about the world: "What will happen to the world (greenhouse effect, ozone, air pollution, rain forests, etc.)?" "Will there ever be world peace?" Why do insane people have rights?" "Why do people hate Blacks?" "Will prejudice ever end?" "Why do we use money?" "Why do we need a president?"

A central activity begins on the first day and lasts well into the second. Small groups compile their individual responses to the self and world questions—no one was compelled to share self questions or world concerns. Ms. Reed and Ms. Bryant go from group to group, helping to facilitate the activity. Students chart the frequently asked questions, but note rare or unique ones as well. The activity continues with groups noting the convergence of self and world questions. Through deliberation and consensus, each group then names two or three "organizing centers" such as "Jobs, Money, Careers," "Death and Dying," "Living in the Future," "Environment and Health," "Conflict," and "Sex, Life, Genetics."

On the third day, deliberations move from small groups to the whole class. With chart-paper listings of small groups' work posted around the double classroom, students need to decide upon one organizing center to use for the first unit and make suggestions for subsequent units. Students vote by raising their hands for as many ideas that they like. After the votes are cast, Ms. Reed excitedly announces, "We have our first unit—'Living in the Future!'"

Day three of planning ends and day four begins with another small group activity: selecting the self and world questions to be addressed that coincide with the first organizing center and then developing a first description of learning activities. Teachers and students also identify outcomes of knowledge and skills that should result from learning activities. They decide that it is important to have knowledge about current events and history, cultures, anatomy, health, statistics on population growth, and technology. They also choose to develop skills of critical thinking, research, writing, graphing, map-reading, communication, and using computers.

Finally, students and teachers begin to establish a process to check daily on students' grasp of key ideas and understandings across the several activities of study. They further work to devise a means by which students can have a significant role in evaluating the unfolding curriculum as well as their own learning goals and achievements.

§

These 4 days in the sixth-grade classroom illustrate defining elements of the democratic culture of curriculum: deliberation of curriculum design and democratic process in learning activities. This is a recreated account of what its originators call "integrative curriculum." Beyond the resolve to create interesting and significant learning experiences, the overriding intent of this curriculum is to "design the core" of democratic education (Beane, 1997; Brodhagen, 2007; Brodhagen, Weilbacher, & Beane, 1992). Education that allows students to understand and to experience the process of democratic decision making is at the core of this culture of curriculum.

Visions

The curricular culture, "Deliberating Democracy," holds three principal visions that capture the form and spirit essential to what has been called strong or participatory democracy, a tradition that has struggled over time against the conventional more restrictive, less inclusive, and more narrowly political-electoral versions: (1) *democracy as animated by idealized values that together seek the well-being of all individuals within a vital and healthy community;* (2) *democracy as organized around shared authority and mutual responsibility;* and (3) *democracy as reliant upon knowledge that is open to alternative sources and ends.*

Democracy is about decision making in groups and the conditions of relationships, values, and activity, and structures which enable this process to be democratic. This requires that *all members of the group be significantly (ideally, equally) engaged in both the making of and abiding by decisions on matters affecting the group as a whole.* Furthermore, decisions are to be made in *full regard for the suitability and good effect of those decisions on the lives and futures of all members.*

Democracy invokes a moral imperative that permeates all our social arrangements and interactions—including life in schools, as Dewey (1916) argued in the words opening this chapter. It is experience directed toward a set of "idealized" values that we must live by as a people and take as the primary guide to our life in community (Apple & Beane, 2007a, 2007b). The core values and principles of democracy together make up a complex of social, political, and moral "goods" for individuals and the community as a whole: freedom, autonomy, and pluralism, as well as equality, caring, and justice. Likewise,

> Democracy connotes wide-ranging liberty, including the freedom to decide one's own destiny. Democracy means social and civil equality and a rejection of discrimination and prejudice. Democracy embraces the notion of pluralism and cultural diversity. It welcomes a wide range of perspectives and lifestyles, moving different social groups toward peace-

ful coexistence or respectful integration. Democracy represents the ideal of a cohesive community of people living and working together and finding fair, nonviolent ways to reconcile conflicts. (Gastil, 1993, p. 5)

Underneath all layers of democratic participation, from routine daily life through society's momentous events, is what Dewey and others have called the "democratic faith." This is an unshakable belief in democracy as the best mode of social life, one which captures the full allegiance and dedication of all those who experience it. To hold this faith is also to believe in the inherent capacity and goodwill of all members to make their experiment in democracy work in best way humanly possible. Faith in fellow members of a democratic community keeps alive the critical vision of mutual responsibility and shared authority.

A democratic society may be seen as a "commonwealth" of "little publics," including even schools and classrooms (Dewey, 1916; Parker 1996a). Little publics of several types—schools, churches, neighborhood associations, civic groups, recreational and sports clubs, business and political organizations—are nested within the larger realms of little publics of the same type, of related and distant types, and, ultimately, of larger national and global societies. Members of little publics can learn and practice the democratic arts of participation intensively within that primary community. But to ensure that society becomes and sustains itself as a commonwealth of democracy, members of all small publics must participate as fully as possible in the affairs of the larger society.

Within democracy "as a way of life" as Beyer (2001) claims, the continuing question is "how we regard others, how we make choices, and how we foster more widely shared decision making, in the process diminishing inequalities of power and influence" (p. 158). Collaboration, in turn, cannot abide the naked exercise of power as standard practice, but depends upon participants feeling and exercising responsibility toward one another.

Formal knowledge can serve as a cornerstone of this wider participation and, thus, of fundamental processes of the commonwealth of democracy. Knowledge becomes at once a vital private and public holding. The pertinent vision is one of knowledge that is open to alternative sources and ends, just as any fully democratic project would be. Many writers have underscored the open and generative nature of learning and knowledge in the democratic culture of curriculum. Apple and Beane (2007a, 2007b), Beyer (1996b), Sehr (1997), and Parker (2003) point to requisites of knowledge and learning in the democratic culture of curriculum: the free flow of ideas; forums for public discussion to create, clarify, and reevaluate positions and perspectives; opportunity and ability to locate relevant information and to uncover multiple interpretations: habits of critical reflection and analysis by which to examine assumed reality conveyed in written, spoken, and image texts; awareness of the complexities and interconnections of major public issues to each other past and present;

and the give and take of deliberation among conflicting beliefs and social perspectives that can enlighten peoples' understandings and give rise to more just decisions about how to live together democratically.

Providing a common knowledge assumes neither a uniform nor monolithic shape enforcing a single "regime of truth." Indeed, it may encompass parts that are quite divergent, from origins quite diverse. Its unifying force lies in the evolving conversation it provokes and sustains, and the contingent and transitory moments of shared understanding it expresses.

In *Democracy and Education*, Dewey (1916) referred to three vital process of democracy: *association, communication,* and *deliberation*. Democratic association entails the conscious seeking out of the "numerous and varied interests" that lie behind actions—undertaken or contemplated. Democratic communication is, in Dewey's words, "vitally social or vitally shared" and allows each person—or primary affiliation group or local community—to experience the perspectives of others in their public spheres, and by that connection to develop understanding and appreciation for others' experience and understanding of the world.

Deliberation is the hallmark of democratic life. Just as full and free association imparts awareness of alternative paths and communication, deliberation ultimately charts the course mutually taken together. Deliberation may form the nucleus of decision making, but democratic deliberation cannot exist apart from the daily practices, continuing relationships, and persisting values that inhere in communication and association as the warp and woof of democratic society (Englund, 2006; Miller, 2005, 2007; Parker, 2003).

History

The notion that schools should become completely democratic cultures has made only a very limited appearance in the history of American schooling. The traditional culture of schooling places the source of knowledge and authority within texts and teachers; there are few examples of children and adolescents fully participating in determining the course of their education as a deliberative body. The democratic concept of freedom is even somewhat dissimilar to the philosophy of child-centered schools. What distinguishes this curricular culture is its social-political emphasis upon the group process of deliberating the curriculum rather than individuals making choices that mainly affect their own course of study.

Although it is natural to assume that this curricular culture would adopt as its model the American political system, its history is rooted in a far more expansive form. The philosophical-political origins are in a broader, fuller concept of democracy and democratic experience, one far more reminiscent of the New England town meeting than a larger representative government. Democratic educators reject the limited, representative form of democracy because it is "weak"—not strongly participatory.

Historically, there have been discourses about inequality (a primary condition of society throughout human history) that have informed the understandings within this curricular culture. All ventures in democracy have necessarily faced questions of the moral rightness of social and economic structure—not to mention the unmistakable practical effects on public participation of substantial inequality among groups and individuals.

This has been an American problem as well. Various writers have questioned the norms and traditions of the American system of democracy, characterizing them as "weak" rather than "strong" (Barber, 1984), "protectionist" rather than "participatory" (Pateman, 1970), and "limited" instead of "inclusive" (Mansbridge, 1983).

As well, throughout history, there have existed fears of "pure" democracy. As Nathan Tarcov (1996) points out, the ancient Greek root of the term, rule by the *demos* does not translate as "rule by all" but, rather, "rule by the many," the many being the poor or common people. To the extent that the demos, the many poor or common folk, may exercise rule in their narrow class self-interest, their rule becomes a very real threat to the unequal wealth, social privilege, and political influence held by aristocratic or other elite groups.

American political history also has been influenced by this fear. David Sehr (1997) traces the origins of this weak and non-participatory system to the Federalist constitutional design and, further, to the preeminence of Hobbes and Locke in the heritage of Anglo American political thought. The Federalist constitutional design was intended to embody an antipathy toward direct democracy. This design also provided for the formal guarantee of many fundamental freedoms such as those of religion, speech, and the press, and security against unrestricted government incursion into citizens' private lives. But the freedom of direct popular participation in government was also feared as a looming threat to individual liberties, particularly that liberty to acquire property and wealth. The exercise of this liberty in colonial times had led to dramatic inequalities in wealth and privilege, a system buttressed by a popular social ideology of unlimited opportunity for success, and of assumed "natural differences" in ability giving rise to the evident imbalances (Sehr, 1997).

This curricular culture owes much to the writings of John Dewey, who made conscious the relationship between schooling and democracy. Dewey's theoretical formulation of democracy and education was intended to overcome what he termed the "either-or dualisms" formed of oppositions between the ideas of ends and means, of individual and society, of child and curriculum, assumed to be fixed and absolute. What was critical for Dewey (1938) was how present experience could engender the realization of growth in future experience. Where present experience does so, future experience becomes "deeper and more expansive" in quality. The developmental effects of present experience do not happen accidentally, of course, but through a deliberate reconstruction of the meaning of present experience.

The reconstruction of experience for true individual and collective growth can happen, in Dewey's view, only under certain social arrangements—the characteristics of which having been previously ascribed to "strong democracy." To be sure, the reconstruction of experience for growth does, and indeed must, occur in all social spheres, including schools, but democratic arrangements must be sufficient to permit an authentic personal and collective reconstruction of experience for further growth and heightened democracy.

In spite of common values and beliefs, democratic progressivism as an educational movement—over its historical course and in its contemporary expressions—exhibits a clear tension between alternatives taken to realize the hope of education for democracy. Dennis Carlson (1997) characterizes this tension as existing between "two overlapping but distinct" currents of thought and practice: *democratic pragmatism* and *social reconstructionism* (that we, in this book, consider as separate but related curricular cultures). Carlson notes that, while offering decidedly alternative approaches to the democratic project in public education, the two find common roots in Dewey's writings and practice.

Democratic pragmatism and social reconstructionism have adopted independent, though intersecting paths (Carlson, 1997). In the former, participation primarily means active engagement and it anticipates emerging forms of community that may become quite novel. In the latter, participation chiefly refers to commitment to new forms of community that are radical departures from what is presently known. In short, there are opposing perspectives in the two projects that have led to substantial differences in their enactment. Both promote the freedom to participate directly and fully in public life. But the pragmatists presume that ends will be determined in the course of examining positions and circumstances; the reconstructionists presume that positions will be determined in the course of examining ends and circumstances.

Despite schooling's often stated goal to teach about American democracy, it is difficult to find any clear historical examples of schools and teachers that have attempted education aimed at strong democracy and using the means of full, direct participation of all involved. For these examples, it is necessary to look at a loosely connected array of initiatives within the democratic wings of the educational progressivism movement, approximately 1880 to 1940 (Carlson, 1997; Cremin, 1961; Reese, 1986). However, a number of important advocacy projects, school- and classroom-based efforts at change, and theoretical writings did press for an education governed by such principles as freedom for public participation, direct self-governance, social and political mutuality, and just and caring community (Apple & Beane, 2007a, 2007b; Carlson, 1997; Darling-Hammond, 1996; Parker, 1996a).

The progressive commitment to democratic education and curriculum stretched into the 1960s, a time when the federal role in promoting new directions in schooling blossomed. Admittedly, it has stayed a minority concern among change projects over the last three decades—when federal and state monies and mandates have supplied the highest octane fuel for school change and reform. Yet, democratic curriculum and schooling remain the aim of a dedicated number of school people, activist parents and community members, professors, consultants, and curriculum developers (Meier, 2003; Miller, 2005; Schultz, 2007). Democratic education also flourishes in classrooms and schools influenced by integrative curriculum models such as that developed by Brodhagen, Weilbacher, and Beane (1992) and in alternative private and public schools which endorse the democratic process as the most important aspect of learning.

The idea of democratic education also has been encouraged through sharing of ideas and support through journals, newspapers, and networks. These resources have been very helpful to democratic educators: the urban education journal *Rethinking Schools*; the journal *Democracy and Education*; *Teaching Tolerance*, a magazine for educators published by the Southern Poverty Law Center; the Institute for Democracy in Education; the Institute for Democratic Education in America; the Center for Powerful Education; Educators for Social Responsibility; the Coalition of Essential Schools; and the informational and program organizing Web site of the Forum on Democracy and Education. Such exchange of ideas and support have nurtured and sustained those who have kept the democratic vision alive.

Since the recent turn of the century the democratic culture of curriculum has been beset with the corrosive influences of the standardization and regimented testing regime promoted by the No Child Left Behind legislation passed early in the George W. Bush administration and by the Race to the Top (RTTT) project of the Barack Obama administration headed up by Education Secretary Arne Duncan. Social studies, the humanities, and integrated curriculum, areas especially suited to education democratic life and citizenship have been increasingly marginalized by the national movement (Hunt, 2008; McGuire, 2007; Renner, 2009). Educational leadership, in national and state policy and particularly at the school level, is needed on behalf of democratic education, to legitimize those classroom processes inherent to democratic learning and relationships and to protect and expand those spaces in the school and in the community where curricular or extra-curricular activity can foster democratic interaction, dialogue, and concern for the well-being of all (Apple & Beane, 2007a, 2007b; Finn & Meier, 2009; Pryor, 2008).

Beliefs and Practices: Learners and Teachers

As a Deweyan laboratory of democracy, the classroom can approach the model of an ideal democratic small group (Gastil, 1993). Such groups are relatively sovereign over the conduct of their own affairs, and distribute authority equally among all members of the groups. Even in the best of circumstances, of course, classrooms can only approximate democratic small groups in this sense. They are highly subject to the direction of legally authorized school boards and administrators. Teachers have superordinate standing as "first citizens" of the classroom community, and rightly so, by virtue of being adults, their professional qualifications, and their status as the agents of the overseeing school authority. Yet, even within this circumscribed democracy, authority and relationships can be significantly altered from the norm. Students can take on active roles as citizens of the classroom community, exercising explicit determination over the substance and processes of learning for their benefit and that of their fellows.

Power to determine what constitutes meaningful learning is redistributed more equally among teacher and learners, and the roles of teacher and learner are not so rigidly distinguished. This assumption of shared authority reflects a primary democratic faith in the individual and collective capacity of all people to create possibilities for resolving problems and achieving commitments affecting the community as a whole.

How is this shared authority exercised? The short answer is—in everything. Whereas it can be said that even in classrooms that would not be considered democratic, teachers will negotiate some learning procedures (e.g., choices of activities), in the democratic curricular culture the most crucial issues of learning involve determination of content; it is not assumed that the teacher or an external authority has the right to make this decision.

As is evident in the earlier example of integrative curriculum, choosing the substance of learning takes a strongly democratic character beginning with the primary experience of the learner and moving out toward sanctioned knowledge including expected outcomes of the official curriculum. From the original questions and concerns put forth by learners come the constituents of learning: the overarching themes and component questions, topics and particulars of study, and the vocabulary and methods for inquiry. These are negotiated against official mandates from school, district, and state authorities, but hold first importance.

Openness in knowledge and learning are vital to the democratic curricular culture. Not all the constituents' knowledge and skills may be fully open to collective determination, but a substantial number of them must be—in respect to major units of study and on a continuing basis—for the culture of curriculum to count as democratic.

In none of its areas, academic or social, does a democratic curriculum expect all students to arrive at the same learning in the same way. Much of what goes on in a democratic curriculum is comprised of distinct and occasionally quite dissimilar learnings of individual students and small workgroups. Yet, it is taken for granted that from all these efforts together, from the different paths and resources, a core of shared learning and expectations will emerge. Students will be responsible to each other and to the teacher as the legally and morally responsible adult to help create this common core of learning and to come to know it well. They will also take away from their efforts some things they have learned deeply that their peers have not.

An example of how democratic curriculum-making depends upon the quality of relationships between teacher and learners, and among learners, is provided by Susan MacKay's (1997) essay about "nurturing dialogue and negotiation" in the primary classroom. In the spirit of the democratic culture of curriculum, MacKay attempted to make a radical departure from her approach to curriculum in prior years, an approach which she considered child-centered, but later realized had neither centered control in the children as individuals nor in them as members of a classroom learning community. She reflected upon her practice:

> My classroom was organized around areas for math, reading, writing, art, science, blocks, and dramatic play. We sat in circles. I let the children talk. I went home at night and spent hours cleverly connecting thematic units. If we were studying frogs, we read frog books, sang frog songs, did frog math, made frog art, wrote frog stories, and observed real frogs, until we completed the 'What We Have Learned About Frogs" on our KWL chart and moved on to our next topic. Slowly, painfully, this year I realized that by organizing and connecting everything we did for them, I was denying the children opportunities to work in ways they were perfectly capable of working. Even if the idea for the frog theme had been generated by the children's genuine interest in frogs, I had taken away any hope for a true democratic experience by proceeding to make all the plans for their work—denying them the opportunity to participate meaningfully in the decisions that would affect their learning. (p. 20)

It is clear that MacKay originally skirted around the possibility of her children composing their own learning in significant ways. They had negligible control over the ideas and questions of interest, methods, and objects of study. She did not take the democratic teacher's role of facilitation, guidance, support and encouragement, coordination, and final arbitration; nor she did not allow her children to play the defining elements of this role for themselves and for their peers.

Ultimately, in MacKay's account (1997), she cast aside the false choices she had given her children in favor of authentic choices over learning they could make for themselves—as individuals and with each other. Each child's learning was to find its way into the nexus of what the class was learning as a whole—becoming, ultimately, this classroom community's shared core of knowledge. Growing up in support of this open-ended determination of curriculum was an infrastructure MacKay referred to as an "arrayed repertory" of resources offering many possibilities. The repertory included:

> ...all the available materials at any of the areas in the room or in the school, ideas born from the children's stories or other literature, and also any ideas or materials the children brought from home. It remained important for

me to help the children make connections with each other.... I began to perceive group activities as opportunities to expand the group's reper-tory instead of opportunities for me to inject my own thematic agenda.... We focused as a whole group on tools which would expand the available repertory and enhance the children's individually chosen areas of work. (1997, p. 22)

MacKay also found ways in which to "problematize and question" those per-sonal choices collectively, so that they became the "very stuff" of the curricu-lum itself.

Democratizing the curriculum meant her "truly negotiating" the curricu-lum with the children as well as by the "children among themselves." MacKay (1997) concluded that the patterns of relationships "around all learning" and ongoing reflection "upon those relationships" over time became the very heart of the curriculum. And that "our fates" in learning were bound together in "dialogue." The teacher thus becomes, as Thomas Kelly (1994) has termed it, a "catalyst for collaboration."

The relationships of democratic association that Ms. MacKay created for her children fostered their growth as mutually responsible learners; they were responsible to themselves to find a primary course of personally significant learning and to assist in the meaningful learning of others. Through this reciprocal engagement, points of intersection and common focus are discov-ered—and the class together fashions a core of shared knowledge.

The force of root values and principles in the democratic culture of cur-riculum decisively affects the character of learning for individuals and the entire classroom community. Teachers and students alike are deeply engaged together in the enterprise of seeking to discover, understand, and create. They aim to employ their learning in the service of further knowledge and appre-ciation, creative expression, and worthy action in human society, the living world, and the physical domain.

Beliefs and Practices: Content and Context

All the preceding examples of this chapter show in one way or another how democratic curriculum moves beyond the boundaries of the usual school sub-ject areas into the sort of dynamic and varied inquiries undertaken within the formal disciplines of knowledge. As Beane (1997) points out, the school sub-jects are "institutionally based representations of disciplines" that "deal with a boundaried selection of what is already known within them" (p. 39). The disciplines do assume a particular lens (or analytic orientation) on the world and favor certain investigatory techniques by which to interpret phenomena. Yet, because of the freedom of inquiry within these disciplines, the range of specific topics addressed, questions posed, and methods employed are quite wide and the boundaries of disciplined inquiry are quite fluid—thus, heightening the curriculum's democratic potential.

Many of the most salient instances of the democratic culture of curriculum are from the social studies and humanities, or from integrated curriculum studies. This is not surprising in view of the primary orientation of this culture to the political and social dimensions of knowledge. Studies of the social world are thus natural candidates for this curriculum, perhaps focused on the activity of making knowledge within a community of scholars or lay people (Hunt, 2008; McGuire, 2007; Renner, 2009; Schultz, 2007).

The Center for Study of Responsive Law offers the curriculum, *Civics for Democracy: A Journey for Teachers and Students* (Isaac, 1992). The curriculum intends to bridge the gap between classroom and community experience so that students may become—in the present and the future—"skilled citizens" who practice civics to overcome apathy, ignorance, greed, or abuses of power in society at all levels. Participatory civics for democracy requires "knowledge of history, understanding of civic rights and strategies, and sharing in a growing civil culture of regular participation" (p. v). *Civics for Democracy* provides stories of students who have worked for positive change within citizen movements: civil rights, labor, women's rights, consumers' rights, and environmental movements. Also included are descriptions of the techniques of participation: direct actions, citizen lobbying, legal actions, ballot initiatives, and uses of the media. Finally, possible activities for students to undertake in their schools or communities are sketched out. The concept of civic participation assumed in this curricular content obliges all citizens to work to create conditions for association, communication, and commitment that foster responsive, and fair deliberation crucial to a vital democracy.

In addition, historical events may offer rich opportunities to consider the nature of democracy. A case in point, the democratic curriculum would study the Civil War as a period of intense struggle over the course of society and governance—testing the "great experiment" in democracy. It is a crystalline case for curriculum to come to grips with the perpetual controversies of democracy expressed in conflicts great and small.

Central topics in the democratic curriculum, such as the Civil War, are well-served by democratic deliberation because they require careful gathering or generation of knowledge, thorough explanation, and insightful interpretation. As topics are pursued in that manner, a fund of knowledge will reveal itself in numerous ways: how a student frames a problem, searches for related information, uses reference materials and data bases, seeks diverse viewpoints, judges the strength of arguments, interprets primary documents, adjudicates competing interpretations, creates arguments, and weighs alternative courses of action (Englund, 2006; Grant, 1996; Parker, 1997, 2003, 2005).

Mark Gerzon (1997) argues that, indeed, conflict is at the heart of democracy. Conflict gives democracy its vital pulse, although a pulse that can race out of control. The core challenge of citizenship, according to Gerzon, is learning to engage well in conflict. He believes that the most controversial issues in the American school curriculum, e.g., sex education, creationism, multicultural literature, school prayer, and the religious content of holiday music concerts can become appropriate topics for study.

Accordingly, we may view the school as an unsurpassed forum for providing opportunity both to learn democratically and to discover how to live democratically (Apple & Beane, 2007a, 2007b; Meier, 2003; Parker, 1997, 2005; Ritchie, Tobin, Roth, & Caruso, 2007). There are many classroom and school-wide issues that call for community decisions: rules of conduct, administrative and logistical matters, and allocation of resources to extracurricular activities. How can these decisions best be made? Walter Parker (2003) calls for developing what he terms the "deliberative arts" of democracy. Among these arts are the many facets of joint problem-solving—listening as well as talking, grasping others' points of view, and using the common space to forge positions with others rather than using it only as a platform for expressing opinions.

Many teachers have substantially democratized curricula in the science, mathematics, and technology, and have employed content material from trade books, news sources, and historical documents (Beyer, 1996b; Sehr, 1997; Wood, 1992). A school can choose to both open the math, science, and technology courses more to the activity of the related disciplines, to applications to the everyday world by trained professionals and practitioners, and to the experience of nonspecialists with mathematical, scientific, and technological knowledge and skills.

We imagine a scenario that demonstrates the richness of a democratic curriculum in mathematics, sciences, and technology: The math curriculum would encompass a rich core of knowledge, including accounts of major historical developments of the ways in which people have used mathematics. Teachers would encourage understanding that knowledge is neither static nor uncontested by showing how fresh discoveries in the world of mathematics are now commonplace—such as the invention of non-Euclidean geometry, differential calculus, and discrete analysis. Their colleagues in the sciences could explore similar achievements, such as Copernican astronomy, or quantum and relativity theory. In addition, teachers would emphasize contemporary theoretical debates that are fueled by continuing research discoveries, such as whether plants can produce food in the absence of light, if life exists on Mars, and how likely it is that dinosaurs were warm-blooded.

All math, science, and technology courses would also invest a good deal of time introducing students to applications of this knowledge by non-research professionals and technical specialists—people such as engineers, accountants and actuaries, forensic chemists, environmental analysts, pollsters, transportation planners, and others. Finally, the courses would offer a number of detailed cases on the use and non-use, understanding and misunderstanding of mathematical, scientific, and technological principles in the every day lives of people who are professionals or technical specialists in these areas. Content cannot be considered apart from process. In democratic curricula it is important for all students to be aware of what others are doing—that, in other words, there is full (democratic) communication among the projects as they develop (Beane, 2002; Grant, 1996). Students can learn from each other and from the teacher, getting advice on how to proceed, information about useful resources, and suggestions on how they might best represent and convey what they had learned through their models, writings, and artifacts. It is also important to note that all learners have equal opportunity to participate in all forms of learning: model-building, fact-finding, analyses, and summary discussions, writings, and media presentations, although individuals may concentrate on one or several these activities.

The learning in which they engage is comprehensive, thorough, and insightful because it springs from and is organized around powerful questions meaningful to all, singly and collectively. Because this is a community whose members are invested in learning, many resources, methods, and perspectives are brought to bear: Through the core of shared knowledge held by the whole classroom community and the unique personal achievements of each individual, what is gained is so much the richer and deeper.

In an important sense, democratic knowledge and curriculum arises in the free, open, inclusive, and responsive communication that is the lifeblood of democratic society (Criddle, Vidovich, & O'Neill, 2004; Finn & Meier, 2009; Pryor, 2008). In the democratic culture of curriculum such communication across the formal disciplines and corresponding realms of the everyday social world makes possible a full exchange of ideas, imagination, understanding, and purpose. Knowledge rises, extends, changes direction, and falls under the force of evolving consciousness and transformed understanding.

The content of learning is also shaped by the interpretive context in, which it arises, and often has the reciprocal effect of reshaping that context in ways that participants might not have envisioned. Democratizing curriculum and education means in its broadest sense, connecting learning in the classroom with the use of knowledge in settings near and far, now and into the future. It is in this sense of a democratic curriculum that Kelly (1997) suggests the descriptors "outreach-oriented" and "connectionist." By the former term, Kelly means an advocacy of school learning which is "authentic"—that is, learning which, in a disciplined way, addresses problems and an audience beyond the school. By the latter, he refers to teaching and learning that is "multi-dimensional, interdisciplinary, context-conscious." This "relational vision of teaching and learning integrates the head, the heart, and the hands" (p. 8).

Among the intended areas of learning in a curriculum may be that of the social life of the classroom itself. Teachers consider the analysis of classroom relationships and values an important goal. To this end they use classroom meetings, the definition of rules and expectations, peer mediation of disputes, and, not infrequently, the creation of a classroom constitution. Of greatest concern is how such classroom regularities as decision-making procedures, status systems, affective relationships, and social control processes presently shape or could possibly influence the varieties of experience and learning that might arise (VanSickle, 1983; Beyer, 1996b; Goodman, 1992).

Formal education has long been acknowledged as preparing young people for life beyond the school, in the present and for their future as adult workers, community members, heads of families, and especially as citizens (Biesta, 2007; Parker, 2005; Westheimer & Kahne, 2004). In the Deweyan view of education, learning as the reconstruction of experience, particularly those experiences that relate to future adult roles, cannot take place outside of a shaping context of social arrangements and activity. The democratic culture of curriculum, therefore, takes foremost a social-political stance to learning in classrooms, schools, and in all matters of curriculum.

Beliefs and Practices: Curriculum Planning and Evaluation

It is not unreasonable to consider planning and evaluation the center of the democratic culture of curriculum. This curricular culture assumes no preeminent content but considers planning as a process at the heart of its functioning. Democratic curriculum is constantly in a state of formation; knowledge and learning are continuously reconstituted out of the deliberations that constitute planning and evaluation.

Deliberation is democratic to the extent that its participants associate freely and communicate openly and fully. Participants are those individuals who are affected by these deliberations, primarily the teachers and students. Ideally, all participants would have equal power and resources, and indirect participants, e.g., teachers' aides, administrators, communities members, have some claims on the deliberative process. To be sure, there is a legitimate differentiation in authority between teachers and students, and often, indirect participants are insufficiently recognized. The process, therefore, must be constantly monitored and calibrated so as to avoid imbalances of power and neglect.

Democratic deliberation turns on the shifting balance of mutuality and diversity (Englund, 2006; Finn & Meier, 2009; Parker, 2003). Participants assume at least some irreducible differences and conflicts, but have faith that other participants will do their best to find common ground. Above all, planning and evaluation within a democratic culture of curriculum must be entirely open and inclusive, deeply creative as well as critically minded, and ever alert to those emerging intersections of value and interest that might grow into commonalities of thought and action.

Teachers are, by legal authority and professional training, more than equal partners in planning and evaluating the curriculum. In addition to their own interests and judgment about the direction and content of the curriculum, they must represent policies and voices of those in the school organization and surrounding community who have a stake in the curriculum.

Curriculum planning might involve many stakeholders in a deliberative process that widens the concept of planning from a linear model of goals and objectives to broad and inclusive discourse about the nature of knowledge, instruction, and community (Carlheden, 2006; Finn & Meier, 2009; Henderson, 2001). A multitude of questions could be asked about, for example, in an elementary language arts curriculum: What is good literature? What proportion of material should come from each of the major literary genres, for example, or, better, how much from the traditionally underrepresented or non-Western traditions? Should curriculum be chosen for breath of coverage or to depth? Should primary sources be utilized rather than excerpts? What should be the roles of direct instruction, experiential activities, community-based learning, and direct contact with working authors? How much planning should be oriented to the families and communities the school served? Is it important to know about the languages other than English spoken there, and the various religious, social, family, and aesthetic values and practices observed? Is it important to ensure that the children's developing literacy is directed to understanding the roots and possible resolution of issues before the local community? Do children who come with different strengths need to be treated differently in respect to how their learning is assisted or guided?

Students can be key players in curriculum planning but also work with the larger community. Elliot Wigginton (1988) has discussed the role of students in planning and producing a magazine for a Foxfire project involving the use of the community as a primary source for their learning and of the content represented in the final product. Such democratic curriculum planning takes into consideration understanding of the community's needs and interests. What Wigginton claims for Foxfire projects would be true in principle for many forms of democratic, community-based learning, service learning, action or advocacy learning, and cultural or historical studies.

Students not only can participate meaningfully in planning the curriculum, but also in conducting evaluation of their own learning and that of peers. Brodhagen (1995) emphasizes the importance of students' setting goals for their learning over both the short and long term, frequent checks by teachers of their classes' ongoing progress, unit and quarterly reviews of the quality and effectiveness of activities undertaken by students and teachers, the roles to be played by students, teachers, parents, and, the collaborative assessment of each student's achievements over the designated grading periods. VanSickle (1983) has noted the positive effect on classrooms when students not only instruct and advise one another, but also when they participate in formative evaluations of one another's success in academic and social realms.

Evaluation seeks to confirm that students are fulfilling their dual responsibility of engaging in the path of most meaningful personal learning and making their learning available to their peers. In this way, a common core of knowledge is forged but it does not constrain substantial learning of a strongly personal nature. In the democratic culture of curriculum, evaluation and planning are situated right in the midst of the classroom locale: the "small public," so to speak, that the classroom constitutes. Evaluation is focused first, therefore, on learning and the learner, but is broad enough to encompass other curriculum matters. Multiple approaches used in authentic evaluation of student learning also can be expanded upon to address specific curricular questions concerning teaching and teachers, content and resources, and context and environment (Neill et al., n. d.).

For example, a teacher in a traditional subject area (not an integrated, fluid curriculum) would invite students to play a key role in determining class activities, to continue to evaluate these activities, to negotiate the pace of moving through the text, and to decide how much homework was needed in order to help all students to be successful.

As the democratic culture of curriculum gives such great importance to participatory governance and collaborative decision making at all times, planning and evaluation assume a pivotal role: to set the conditions under which the other defining beliefs and practices concerning teachers and learners, content and context are enacted. The reciprocal nature of planning and evaluation is critical as well. Certainly, evaluation is essential to understanding how well we have done what we set out to do, but good planning is necessary to imagine what we might do in future efforts from what we have learned from our past and continuous experiences.

Dilemmas of Practice

Teachers wishing to build a democratic culture of curriculum in their classrooms face a number of dilemmas. Schools have not generally been showcases of or laboratories for democratic practice; there are numerous formidable institutional forces in place that resist and undercut teachers' attempts to become strongly democratic in the practice of curriculum. Not the least among these is the typically hierarchical nature of decision making in schools. In many senses, teachers are considered simply to be agents of higher seats of authority. It is not within teachers' purview, according to this ideology, to make significant decisions about curriculum, either independently or in concert with their students—or, for that matter, with any other stakeholders or interested parties such as colleagues, parents, or community members. So, the first constraint is the predominant institutional culture of official authority over curriculum.

For teachers who wish to push the current boundaries of authority in order to become more democratic, there is the reality of what students have come to expect about the way schooling is supposed to operate. The longer students have been in school, the more likely they are to have adopted the conventional beliefs and assumptions about authority over the curriculum. Students can become quite suspicious when offered the possibility to participate in a significant democratic experiment in their classroom. There is need to span the wide and deep chasm between authority usually attached to the teacher's role and that accorded to the students. It is easy for teachers, especially when they are new to classroom democracy, to unintentionally subvert democratic principles via habits that die hard and are often difficult even to recognize. A process of extensive re-socialization is generally necessary for teachers and students alike.

Putting democracy into practice requires time and energy that is both of a different type and appears often to be irrelevant to he real task at hand. The premium placed on deliberation and collective decision making in the democratic culture of curriculum can seem, even to the teacher, to be more than is really needed. And, in fact, a truly thorny dilemma for teachers is to find a viable balance between planning and evaluation activities and study activities. To be sure, there is a tripartite responsibility to be fulfilled: individuals to self, the classroom group to the core knowledge of its community, and all participants to the available knowledge and perspectives of the larger world, especially those likely to be less visible or less acknowledged.

Numerous scholars (Beyer & Liston, 1996; Meier, 2003; Finn & Meier, 2009; Parker, 1996b; Pryor, 2008) all point to the need to locate deliberations over curriculum planning and evaluation in a broad context of a range of stakeholders who are invested in the breadth and quality of education that young people receive. It is the power of such deliberations, the authors argue, that gives rise to an education that is developmentally appropriate, morally sensitive, culturally relevant, academically rich, and linked to what lies beyond the school. But these authors also acknowledge the great difficulty and usual failure to bring representatives of stakeholder groups into serious curriculum deliberations. Teachers must help build curriculum from what matters to young people and to all these constituencies. Moreover, they must exercise their own commitments and sense of responsibility to the multiple approaches to knowledge in and beyond the academic world and to the knowledge held within society's many communities and cultures.

All this coordination of experience, interest, and purpose depends upon sustained and ordered interaction conducted in the democratic spirit as well as by democratic precepts. Learning how to balance concerns, allocate time, and especially how to invest heavily in the earliest phase of a curriculum development in order to reap increased learning later are teaching skills acquired only with arduous experience.

Teachers who manage to forge democratic curricula for their classrooms often stand out as rather peculiar, if not alone, in their schools. Although it has been proven important for teachers not to feel or be alone in their endeavors, teachers who work democratically frequently see themselves in a decided minority in their schools. They may be the object of spoken or silent resentment or dismissal for their natural popularity with students or considered irresponsible for giving up so much of their authority in favor of putting forward students' ideas, intentions, and capability for self-direction. Also, democratic teachers often find themselves asking for resources beyond textbooks, opportunities to modify the daily schedule, and support to move learning into settings outside their classrooms. For all this expansive attitude toward alternative sources, modes, instruments, and ends of learning that a democratic curriculum may engender, teachers should be prepared to face the consequences of teaching democratically within traditionally hierarchical and sometimes more narrow-minded institutions.

Critique

The democratic curricular culture is oriented to the political and social dimensions of the educational process and invites critique focused upon purposes or aspects of schooling that are seen as undervalued in the democratic culture. Such critique would forward the argument that no classroom can sufficiently approach the conditions of a viable small group democracy: in reality the classroom can have relatively little autonomy or sovereignty and does not distribute authority among its members to reach a state of equality. As a result, in trying to establish a local community of knowledge and learning, this curricular culture can be charged with failing to nurture student and teacher individuality and not introducing students enough to those specialized areas of knowledge that comprise the highest levels of formal education. Finally, the democratic culture may be seen as too feeble to seriously challenge the conditions of inequality or injustice in society whose forces continually corrode those insufficient attempts to remedy them.

It is certainly true that the classroom can never be anything close to a sovereign small group democracy. Teachers have significant ascribed and legal authority over students. Perhaps more important, the curriculum is not really an open proposal. Through tests, guidelines, specification of textbooks and other resources, and/or direct oversight, the curriculum of any classroom will be substantially determined. A best, the mandated curriculum will be diluted, amended, or deflected in certain of its components. Given the reality of schools—high teacher-student ratios, steep workloads, limited resources—it is practically impossible for the democratic curriculum to validly accomplish it primary aims: significant individual preference in learning, critical awareness of the larger world, and shared participation in a core of highly valued knowledge.

In fact, the latter aim is best sought through a curricular culture whose orientation is not so broad or so non-academic as the democratic culture.

"Deliberating Democracy," in its broadest reach, serves the philosophy of general education. In its narrower terms, this culture of curriculum may serve a comprehensive social studies or humanities program. But it cannot begin to address induction into the specialized bodies of knowledge and communities of scholars that is concern of formal education at its most advanced levels. Students who participate in the democratic culture may be quite ill equipped to take their studies further.

On another score, by presuming that the curriculum should revolve around a constructed core of shared knowledge, the democratic culture forfeits the opportunity to stimulate authentic individual growth, especially of learners, but not inconsequentially of teachers either. The goal of optimizing personal development cannot co-exist with any pretense toward a curriculum that requires something of everyone in common.

Finally, any attempt at local democracy will surely wither in the face of anti-democratic forces—overt and implicit, great and small—from the larger society that permeates the institution of schooling. By far, the better lessons in democracy would be achieved by systematic inquiry into the conditions of inequality, injustice, and exclusive privilege that undermine attempts at strong democracy in any locale or at any level of contemporary society. While classroom and school social conditions and those of the surrounding community may prompt learning and even supply cases in point for study of the concrete failings of democracy in everyday institutions, it would be highly self-deceptive to believe that any classroom could reinvent itself enough so thoroughly as to become an example of democracy worth studying.

In sum, in this culture of curriculum the role of the classroom is to provide a venue for learning about the most noble trials of democracy, wherever and whenever they have existed, and to intelligently uncover the shortfalls of modern institutions which only pretend democracy. It is hardly the responsibility or the potential of classrooms to become micro-democracies in the strong sense of the concept.

References

Apple, M., & Beane, J. (Eds.). (2007a). *Democratic schools: Lessons in powerful education* (2nd ed.). Portsmouth, NH: Heinemann.

Apple, M., & Beane, J. (2007b). Schooling for democracy. *Principal Leadership, 8*(2), 34–38.

Barber, B. (1984). *Strong democracy*. Los Angeles: University of California Press.

Beane, J. (1997). *Curriculum integration: Designing the core of democratic education*. New York: Teachers College Press.

Beane, J. (2002). Beyond self-interest: A democratic core curriculum. *Educational Leadership, 59*(7), 25–28.

Beyer, L. (1996a). Introduction: The meanings of critical teacher preparation. In L. Beyer (Ed.), *Creating democratic classrooms: The struggle to integrate theory and practice* (pp. 1–26). New York: Teachers College Press.

Beyer, L. (Ed.). (1996b). *Creating democratic classrooms: The struggle to integrate theory and practice.* New York: Teachers College Press.

Beyer, L. (2001). The value of critical perspectives in teacher education. *Journal of Teacher Education, 52*(2), 151–163.

Beyer, L., & Liston, D. (1996). *Curriculum in conflict: Social visions, educational agendas, and progressive school reform.* New York: Teachers College Press.

Biesta, G. (2007). Education and the democratic person: Towards a political conception of democratic education. *Teachers College Record, 109*(3),740–769.

Brodhagen, B. (2007). The situation made us special. In M. Apple & J. Beane (Eds.), *Democratic schools: Lessons in powerful education* (pp. 83–106). Portsmouth, NH: Heinemann.

Brodhagen, B., Weilbacher, G., & Beane, J. (1992). Living in the future. *Dissemination Services on the Middle Grades, 23*(9), 1–7.

Carlheden, M. (2006). Towards democratic foundations: A Habermasian perspective on the politics of education. *Journal of Curriculum Studies, 38*(5), 521–543.

Carlson, D. (1997). *Making progress: Education and culture in new times.* New York: Teachers College Press.

Cremin, L. (1961). *The transformation of the school: Progressivism in American education, 1876–1957.* New York: Vintage Books.

Criddle, E., Vidovich, L., & O'Neill, M. (2004). Discovering democracy: An analysis of curriculum policy for citizenship education. *Westminister Studies in Education, 27*(1), 28–41.

Darling-Hammond, L. (1996). The right to learn and the advancement of teaching: Research, policy, and practice for democratic education. *Educational Researcher, 25*(6), 5–17.

Dewey, J. (1916). *Democracy and education.* New York: Macmillan.

Dewey, J. (1938). *Experience and education.* Bloomington, IN: Kappa Delta Pi.

Englund, T. (2006). Deliberative communication: A pragmatist proposal. *Journal of Curriculum Studies, 38*(5), 503–520

Finn, C. & Meier, D. (2009). E pluribus unum? *Education Next, 9*(2), 50–57.

Gastil, J. (1993). *Democracy in small groups: Participation, decision making, and communication.* Philadelphia: New Society Publishers.

Gerzon, M. (1997). Teaching democracy by doing it. *Educational Leadership, 54*(5), 6–11.

Goodman, J. (1992). *Elementary schooling for critical democracy.* Albany: State University of New York Press.

Grant, R. (1996). The ethics of talk: Classroom conversation and democratic politics. *Teachers College Record, 97*(3), 470–482.

Henderson, J. (2001). Deepening democratic curriculum work. *Educational Researcher, 30*(18), 18–21.

Hunt, E. (2008). A vision of powerful learning in the social studies: Building effective citizens. *Social Education, 72*(5), 277–280.

Isaac, K. (1992). *Civics for democracy: A journey for teachers and students.* Washington, DC: Essential Books.

Kelly, T. (1994). Democratic empowerment and secondary teacher education. In J. Novak (Ed.), *Democratic teacher education: Programs, processes, problems, and prospects* (pp. 63–88). Albany: State University of New York Press.

Kelly, T. (1997). Perspectives on democratic pedagogy and selected educational innovations. *Democracy and Education, 11*(3), 7–12.

MacKay, S. (1997). Planting the seeds for a critical pedagogy by nurturing dialogue and negotiation in the primary classroom. *Democracy and Education, 11*(3), 18–31.

Mansbridge, J. (1983). *Beyond adversary democracy.* Chicago: University of Chicago Press.

McGuire, M. (2007). What happened to social studies?: The disappearing curriculum. *Phi Delta Kappan, 88*(8), 620–624.

Meier, D. (2003). So what does it take to build a school for democracy? *Phi Delta Kappan, 85*(1), 15–21.

Miller, R. (2005) Toward participatory democracy. *Paths of Learning.* Retrieved August 16, 2009, from http//www.pathsoflearning.net/articles_Toward_Participatory_ Democracy.php

Miller, R. (2007). What Is democratic education? *Paths of Learning.* Retrieved August 16, 2009, from http://www.pathsoflearning.net/articles_What_Is_Democratic_ Education.php

Neill, M., Bursh, P., Schaeffer, B., Thall, C., Yohe, M., & Zappardino, P. (n.d.). *Implementing performance assessments: A guide to classroom, school, and system reform.* Cambridge, MA: The National Center for Fair & Open Testing.

Parker, W. (1996a). Introduction: Schools as laboratories of democracy. In W. Parker (Ed.), *Educating the democratic mind* (pp. 83–100). Albany: State University of New York Press.

Parker, W. (1996b). Curriculum for democracy. In R. Soder (Ed.), *Democracy, education, and the schools* (pp. 182–210). San Francisco: Jossey-Bass.

Parker, W. (1997). The art of deliberation. *Educational Leadership, 54*(5), 18–21.

Parker, W. (2003). *Teaching democracy: Unity and diversity in public life.* New York: Teachers College Press.

Parker, W.C. (2005). Teaching against idiocy. *Phi Delta Kappan, 86*(5), 344–351.

Pateman, C. (1970). *Participation and democratic theory.* Cambridge, UK: Cambridge University Press.

Pryor, C. (2008). Dilemmas of democratic thought for educational leadership: Considerations of social justice scholarship. *Teacher Development, 12*(4), 279–288.

Reese, W. (1986). *Power and the promise of school reform.* Boston: Routledge & Kegan Paul.

Renner, A. (2009). Teaching community, praxis, and courage: A foundations pedagogy of hope and humanization. *Educational Studies, 45*(1), 59–79.

Ritchie, S., Tobin, K., Roth, W., & Caruso, C. (2007). Transforming an academy through the enactment of collective curriculum leadership. *Journal of Curriculum Studies, 39*(2), 151–175.

Schultz, B. (2007). "Not satisfied with stupid band-aids": A portrait of justice-oriented democratic curriculum serving a disadvantaged neighborhood. *Equity and Excellence in Education, 40*(2), 237–269.

Sehr, D. (1997). *Education for public democracy.* Albany: State University of New York Press.

Tarcov, N. (1996). The meanings of democracy. In R. Soder (Ed.), *Democracy, education, and the schools* (pp. 1–36). San Francisco: Jossey-Bass.

VanSickle, R. (1983). Practicing what we teach: Promoting democratic experiences in the classroom. In M. Hepburn (Ed.), *Democratic education in schools and classrooms* (pp. 49–66). Washington, DC: National Council for the Social Studies (Bulletin No. 70).

Westheimer, J., & Kahne, J. (2004). What kind of citizenship? The politics of educating for democracy. *American Educational Research Journal, 41*(2), 237–269.

Wigginton, E. (1988). What kind of project should we do? *Democracy and Education, 3*(1), 1–9.

Wood, G. (1992). *Schools that work: America's most innovative public education program.* New York: Dutton.

Chapter 11

Confronting the Dominant Order

Mark A. Windschitl and Pamela Bolotin Joseph

Education as a force for social regeneration must march hand in hand with the living and creative forces of the social order. In their own lives teachers must bridge the gap between school and society and play some part in the fashioning of those great common purposes which should bind the two together.

George Counts, 1932, *Dare the School Build a New Social Order?*, p. 375

Ms. Garrison teaches a block course of English and social studies for sixth graders in a middle school serving a diverse, largely working- and middle-class community in a moderate-size city. One fall, while thinking about how to approach the required Central American unit of study, Ms. Garrison noticed an article in the local newspaper about Jennifer Harbury, a Harvard-trained lawyer who for some years worked to assist immigrants from Central America, including refugees from the Guatemalan civil war.

Ms. Garrison learned that Harbury had become involved in the struggle of Native people and other *campesinos* for justice from the feudal agrarian conditions and oppressive central government. Harbury eventually married freedom fighter, Commander Everardo. His later disappearance in combat led Harbury to attempt to elicit information from the United States government about her husband's fate. She eventually charged that Everardo was captured and tortured by a Guatemalan army colonel on the payroll of the Central Intelligence Agency of the United States.

When Ms. Garrison read about Jennifer Harbury's hunger fast to call attention to her need for information about her husband, the story "touched her heart" and she thought it would similarly touch her students as well. She recognized that Harbury's story showed the very human side of conflict and struggle that generally have been portrayed in textbooks only in limited and abstract political terms, often unrelated to emotions and experiences that her students could understand.

Ms. Garrison designed her Latin American curriculum unit around the people, events, and issues surrounding the Harbury article. Her students studied in detail the lives and circumstances of the people categorically labeled "guerrillas," *campesinos*, and "Indians," and learned about the dire material conditions under which the people struggled and about their voicelessness in public affairs. Her students also learned about the strength of the people's determination, their dedication to attaining a better life, and their personal devotion to family, comrades, and neighbors. The unit developed further with a classroom visit by the reporter who wrote the original newspaper article and, with a letter-writing campaign to the chair of the American Foreign Relations Committee. The class also sent copies of those letters to Jennifer Harbury. The unit culminated in a classroom visit by Harbury herself, who was touched by the students' letters on her behalf. Activities within the unit steadily flowed from one to another—taking the form of writing, discussions, and projects. Students engaged in combinations of artwork, background writing, collection of artifacts, and presentations by students to their peers and, occasionally, to their families and community members.

The introduction of this unit stirred much uncertainty in Ms. Garrison. She was unsure initially about becoming involved with the guerrillas' struggle. She was uncertain about the wisdom of centering her curriculum on a topic of such political controversy involving a strident challenge to United States policy and the conduct of federal officials. And, she was not convinced whether the focus of her teaching should be on engaging students as directly as possible in such affairs, in preparing and encouraging them to become activists.

As the class moved further along with the unit, Ms. Garrison herself became involved in solidarity activities with the guerrillas' cause and became convinced of the rightness and importance of Jennifer Harbury's project, of the Guatemalan liberation movement, and of the challenge to American foreign policy and CIA operations. She no longer had qualms about teaching with the purpose of encouraging students to take action in making the world a better place.

What emerged while enacting the unit was a striking new direction in Ms. Garrison's pedagogy. She utilized the social terrain of the lives of her young adolescent students to name issues of fairness, justice, oppression, and freedom in order to correspond to what was presented in the curriculum's formal content. She also introduced a multitude of media—painting, collage, model, music, and sculpture—for students to more expressively capture the particulars of action, thought, and feeling which weave throughout the everyday lives and strivings of the people they studied. She worked to ground abstractions of social, economic, and political relationships to make them comprehensible and infused with personal meaning.

At the end of the unit, Ms. Garrison believed that her students deeply understood, as part of human existence, the notions of justice, liberty, security, and dedication to cause; her curriculum essentially addressed the question of what it means to be human, to live humanely, and to strive for the human rights of all. Ms. Garrison now declares that she is proud to be teaching, through her curriculum, the critical importance of activism to the future of democracy and to the well-being of all people.

§

This description represents the actual experience of an educator who transformed her role as a teacher and her curriculum work. Ms. Garrison's emerging goals and practice reflect many elements of the curricular orientation, "Confronting the Dominant Order."

Although the word confrontation customarily evokes images of discontent, assertiveness, and angry response, this chapter employs the concept of confrontation not as an arbitrary act with aggressive overtones but as reasoned action taken as a result of deep reflection. This kind of action and the illuminated state of reflection that prompts it arise from critical awareness of existing social, political, and economic conditions and the belief in the possibility that society can be transformed to ensure that all people have the access to a free, fair, and humane life. Although we describe this curricular culture as critical, in essence, we are guided by our understanding of it as a curriculum of liberation (liberatory pedagogy), arising from multicultural, feminist, and critical pedagogies.

Visions

"Confronting the Dominant Order" encompasses several visions, first of confrontation, and then, of transforming individuals, schools, and society. But to explain these visions, we must first understand how advocates of this culture of curriculum characterize the dominant order and why it is necessary to confront it. The underlying view of this curricular culture describes a world in which there are imbalances of power and privilege brought about by social, political, and economic dynamics. Obstacles to freedom, liberty, and empowerment stem from unequal access to knowledge, resources, and opportunity—much of this connected to racism and other forms of discrimination.

Another conviction in this worldview is that oppressed people themselves unintentionally contribute to the perpetuation of unequal power relationships. Acceptance of the existing social, political, and economic order may take the form of hopelessness—people feel that they are controlled by "outside forces" and cannot imagine how they can come together and bring about change" (Greene, 1988, p. 25). Or, acceptance may mean that people become satisfied with their situation, however limiting. The power dynamic that brings about this uncritical acquiescence is explained by the term "hegemony."

> The concept of hegemony refers to a process in which dominant groups in society come together to form a bloc and sustain leadership over subordinate groups. One of the most important elements that such an idea

implies is that a power bloc does not have to rely on coercion. (Although at times it does....) Rather, it relies on *winning consent* to the prevailing order, by forming an ideological umbrella under which different groups who usually might not totally agree with each other can stand. The key to this is offering a compromise so that such groups feel as if their concerns are being listened to... but without dominant groups having to give up their leadership of general social tendencies. (Apple, 1996, pp. 14–15)

The hegemony of cultural influences—including popular culture, media, government, business, and science—persuades individuals that their constrained reality, the status quo, is normal and right. Individuals thus do not feel compelled to question their experiences or to ask if society's norms are just (Giroux, 1997, p. 12).

Among the cultural influences that maintain existing social, economic, and political relationships is schooling (Anyon, 1980/1994; Bowles & Gintis, 1976). Those who support "Confronting the Dominant Order" view education as a non-neutral enterprise in which traditional schools reproduce dominant societal structures. Some students acquire the knowledge needed for their successful admittance into dominant society whereas others are denied this cultural capital. The mechanisms of reproduction reside in classroom practices such as tracking (which is never liberatory and are unsupported by research in learning) and unequal access to resources such as books, technology, and excellent teachers.

Critical advocates have metaphors for traditional schools as banks or factories. Knowledge is deposited "as a gift bestowed by those who consider themselves knowledgeable upon those whom they consider to know nothing" (Freire, 1973/1990, p. 58) and students are seen as products narrowly trained to be contributors to the work force (Apple & King, 1983). Even when students resist the explicit and hidden curriculum that reinforces political, social, and economic values, they do not obtain a critical, self-conscious education that will prepare them to alter the cultural dialogue and bring about change.

The traditional ethos surrounding student evaluation emphasizes control and uniformity. People external to the classroom create the testing standards and the tests, suppressing any meaningful evaluation strategies that should rightfully be based on intimate knowledge of young people. Teachers are "de-skilled;" their evaluation input is not necessary in this kind of schooling (Apple, 1982, p. 71). Standardized test scores label students, often reflecting allocations of social class, ethnicity and other attributes (Cherryholmes, 1985, p. 64).

Schools and traditional foundations of knowledge embody institutional racism, classism, and sexism, often derived from the pernicious ideology of essentialism—sorting people as if they had innate abilities according to the group to which they belong—pre-determining potential (or lack of) for achievement. As follows, by their femaleness, women are stereotyped as emotional, superficial, or math-impaired. Other inferior characteristics are attributed to African Americans, Asian Americans, Latinos, and members of the gay community. Although popular culture and other social institutions serve to reinforce and perpetuate these limiting stereotypes, schools are one of the worst offenders, often combining a pathological indifference to students' individuality with institutional practices to sustain an educational underclass.

Accordingly, schools influence individual personality development. They reward students for learning subject matter, but not for questioning it, thereby working against the development of critical, autonomous, and confident learners. Schools also can limit learners' aspirations. Young people can acquire very restricted understandings of their own identities and potentialities; they do not imagine themselves as effective, creative, or self-actualized (Wardekker & Miedema, 1997, p. 49). When these limited self-definitions become internalized, students, like other marginalized members of society, tend to express fatalistic attitudes toward their situation, a fatalism sometimes interpreted as docility.

Despite their worldview that harshly characterizes how schools limit learning and hope, advocates of "Confronting the Dominant Order" have visions of what schools can do (Weiler & Mitchell, 1992). They believe that education can be re-directed toward individual transformation and social action that changes the status quo. Transformation takes place as students learn to use their own intelligence to take control of their lives. It begins with understanding of the identity of self and recognition that individuals are shaped by their experiences with class, race, gender, or other socially defined identities; these realizations begin the process of empowerment. Once more, liberatory pedagogy has a goal of "enable[ing] both students and teachers to develop a critically conscious understanding of their relationship with the world...." (Freire & Shor in Au, 2009, p. 22) and thus aims to create a critical learning community.

Ideally, schooling should give each child the uncompromised opportunity to develop into a self-determining and rationally acting person by way of self-reflection, analysis, and criticism, all within an environment of mutual respect and trust. The possibility for self-determination must not be limited by material power, ideologies, or prejudice. The school provides opportunities for taking action to improve social conditions and to help students see themselves as social, political beings with rights to access the legitimate systems of influence in schools, their workplaces and communities.

Empowerment is more than an individual or psychological event, it has a double reference: to the individual and to society. The freedoms and human capacities of individuals must be developed to their maximum, but individual powers are linked to democracy in the sense that social improvement must be the necessary consequence of individual betterment (Giroux, 1993, p. 10). The ultimate aim for individuals working together is to build the kind of society that makes possible growth and development for everyone. Individual transformation, in this theory of action, leads to social transformation.

This culture endorses principles of personal liberation, critical democracy, social equality, and a recognition of the political and partisan nature of knowledge, human learning, and the educational process (Aronowitz & Giroux, 1985; Banks & Banks, 1993). The primary purpose of education is to teach about the broader contexts of citizenship, shared political power, and the dignity of human life (Gay, 1995). Education provides students with the "knowledge, character, and moral vision that builds civic courage" (Giroux, 1993, p. 18). This curricular philosophy serves to break down the master narrative of Eurocentrism and penetrates the grand myth that the United States society is a homogeneous, unitary cultural system. As a pedagogical strategy, it recognizes that the democratic tradition is a worthy ideal, but an imperfect experiment and an unfinished agenda that is characterized by struggle within and between multiple groups (Gay, 1995).

Because traditional education lacks a language of possibility about how schools can play a major role in shaping public life (Giroux, 1993), "Confronting the Dominant Order" requires that a new language be spoken—a language of critique, hope, and possibility. It calls for moral discourse in which the ideals of justice and compassion become the referents for all conversations, analyses, and actions.

History

Although the notion of "Confronting the Dominant Order" seems outside the mainstream of American educational tradition, we need to remember that confrontation and the expulsion of what was deemed a source of oppression—British curtailment of political and economic liberty—made a forceful presence in schooling and various educative agencies at the beginning of the American nation. "The real revolution," wrote historian Lawrence Cremin (1977) "had been essentially a matter of popular education" (p. 38). Committees of Correspondence, revolutionary pamphlets, newspapers, and sermons educated people about the need to confront and overthrow British rule. Furthermore, colonial "teachers used the lectern to nurture ideas of independency, while students organized symbolic actions ranging from burnings in effigy to boycotts of tea" (Cremin, 1977, p. 38). After the revolution, education in the United States reflected the desire for community (Cremin, 1977) and identification with conservative principles (Elson, 1964) as former revolutionaries sought to create and not overturn traditions. Never again did confrontation of political and economic dominance typify American education.

Curriculum for confrontation re-emerged in the 20th century, emanating from dissatisfaction with political, social, and economic conditions and structures. Social ferment of 1900–1920 in response to "a marked intensification of industrialization, immigration, urbanization, and bureaucratization" included many educational activities involving protest of existing conditions—literature, journalism, lectures, debates, study groups, and classes for adults. Moreover, curriculum for confronting the dominant order was taught to working-class children in Sunday schools for organized by socialists who wanted to instill a respect for labor (Teitelbaum, 1990, p. 33).

The Depression of the 1930s brought doubt about the American economic system, and some prominent educators considered the role of schools for teaching about the need for change and promoting different political and economic values. Addressing the Progressive Education Association in 1932, George Counts galvanized the audience with his call to "face squarely and courageously every social issue, come to grips with life in all of its stark reality, establish an organic relation with the community, develop a realistic and comprehensive theory of welfare, [and] fashion a compelling and challenging vision of human destiny" (Counts in Cremin, 1961/1964, p. 259). In the call for revamping society, Counts was "the Thomas Paine among early social reconstructionists" (Benne, 1995, p. xxii).

In the 1930s, although education with an avowed purpose of reforming society did not become a major thrust of progressive education (and certainly not of mainstream education), the ideas that Counts raised became the center of educational discussion in a small but important publication, *The Social Frontier*. The journal emphasized that schools should point out the excesses of the capitalist system and take the lead in rebuilding society. Many of the writers for *The Social Frontier* were neo-Marxist, explaining social conditions in terms of class struggle. Most importantly, the social reconstructionists writing for that publication examined how schools taught acceptance of social institutions (Giarelli, 1995), leaving an important intellectual legacy for more contemporary social theorists and educators. The journal also provided critique of its positions, e.g., contributors frequently noted the problem of indoctrination (Giarelli, 1995) and the journal published dialogue that opposed neo-Marxist views of social conditions (see Dewey, 1936/1939).

Also, during that time, a major curricular effort to confront the American economic system in the 1930s was the publication of a popular series of social studies textbooks for children and adolescents authored by Harold Rugg. Rugg believed that "the social studies should introduce students to controversial social, economic and political issues" (Carbone & Wilson, 1995, p. 65). Despite the fact that Rugg never argued for the end of capitalism, his espousal of a balance between planned economies and free enterprise and his emphasis upon class differences eventually caused him to be branded as a subversive (Carbone & Wilson, 1995). By the Second World War, Rugg's textbook series were pulled from schools.

Although some confrontation of social, economic, and political conditions within educative platforms occurred in the 1950s in response to the threat of nuclear war (Benne, 1995, p. xxiv), the social protest movements of the 1960s as well as the civil rights and Vietnam War protest movements in the 1960s and early 1970s became catalysts for re-visioning schools as instruments for social change. Efforts to educate young people about social injustices occurred within freedom schools and "teach-ins" on campuses. In addition, critics of society's disregard for children wrote critical analyses of schooling, one example being Jonathan Kozol's grim exposé of urban schooling's inequality and racist educational practices. Clearly, at the end of this era, schools were no longer viewed as neutral but as mirrors of social institutions as well as potential educative forums for analysis and contention.

Another sort of confrontation called into question traditional notions of knowledge and education; this was the philosophical movement known as postmodernism. This paradigm received some attention by the mid-20th century and academic and societal acceptance by the 1980s, becoming an important theme in curriculum studies and educational research to the present day (Slattery, 1995). Postmodernism contested traditional intellectual authority (Doll, 1993), opposing the scientific, rationale view that the world is knowable, orderly, and controllable. Rather, it focused on the social construction of knowledge—individuals' personal interpretations of experience and interpretations as influenced by positionality, e.g., social class, gender, and race, by the chaotic, spontaneous aspects of experience, and by artistic representations of reality (Slattery, 1995). Ultimately, the postmodern paradigm was an intellectual revolt against official knowledge—the basis by which dominant social groups made policy decisions affecting the lives of those not in power.

The feminist movement also challenged the nature of knowledge and education. Conscious-raising groups in the latter part of the 1960s—influenced by earlier civil rights work and revolutionary political thought—led to women's studies courses and the rise of specific feminist literature throughout the next decades. In accordance with postmodernism, feminists called into question the epistemological question of the source of the claims for knowledge and truth and the role and authority of the teacher. They also interrogated the concept of difference by recognizing that women from different backgrounds—affected by their positions influenced by social class, race, and ethnicity—have had diverse experiences (Weiler, 1991, p. 459).

Another powerful influence upon American social theorists and educators was the movement for popular education that put into practice the idea that people who are not part of the powerful elite can, in fact, take control of their education and their lives. Brazilian educator Paulo Freire advocated education for "critical consciousness" to make it possible for disenfranchised people to create social change by understanding the social and economic forces that enslave them. Friere's *Pedagogy of the Oppressed*, first published in 1973, has become "a basic text" for "a critical method of instruction" (Spring, 1991, p. 149). Another educator who demonstrated how to teach for critical awareness was Myles Horton who created Highlander Folk School. Although this school for adult education began in 1932, it was a mainstay in fostering dialogue about social change for many years and influenced educators of all levels (Ayers, 1995).

Throughout the 1970s and the following decades, the development of a theory and practice labeled critical pedagogy became an umbrella for scrutiny of schools and society relating to treatment of women, people of color, working classes and the poor—although some social theorists and educators view feminist and multicultural pedagogy as counterparts rather than as subsumed by critical pedagogy. As a liberatory philosophy of education, critical pedagogy was shaped by various international theorists about education, schooling, and society about how schools "seem to legitimize class inequalities" and how education prepares the young for their place in a class-divided, sexist, and racist social order." Critical scholars also demonstrated that even students resist the school environment and messages (hidden and explicit) of schooling (Purpel & Shapiro, 1995, pp. 99, 105).

Curricular scholars such as Henry Giroux, Michael Apple, Maxine Greene, David Purpel, and Svi Shapiro—among many others—have written about the importance of using analysis as a platform to action, especially in creating a philosophy that encompasses hope (Giroux, 1997, pp. 218–229). Peter McLaren (1989) synthesizes this vision:

> Critical pedagogy resonates with the sensibility of the Hebrew symbol of "tikkun," which means, "to heal, repair, and transform the world...." It provides historical, cultural, political, and ethical direction for those in education who still dare to hope. Irrevocably committed to the side of the oppressed, critical pedagogy is as revolutionary as the earlier views of the authors of the Declaration of Independence: since history is fundamentally open to change, liberation is an authentic goal, and a radically different world can be brought into being. (p. 160)

Practitioners have joined together with a hope for a better world, such as Rethinking Schools groups, to confront and change racism and intolerance in schools while others have written about methodology needed to change classrooms to teach for equity and justice (Bigelow, Christensen, Karp, Miner, & Peterson, 1994). George Counts's question for educators—"do they dare to disturb the social order?"—still resonates for those who champion a curriculum intended to confront the status quo.

Beliefs and Practices: Learners and Teachers

In the critical culture of curriculum, learners are considered individuals with unique personal histories that are dynamic, rich with the respective influences of family life, peer relationships, and popular culture. These histories do not simply influence knowledge, dispositions and interests, they form the interpretive lens through which students view the world. Learners bring with them into the classroom their cultural expectations, experiences of social discrimination or of privilege, life pressures, and their strengths in surviv-ing (Wallerstein in Shor, 1987, p. 33). Students are "the best interpreters of their social worlds" and "when given the chance, students search for meaning within their own lives" (Schultz, 2007, p. 173). Additionally, advocates believe that "students are willing and able to make change in their lives and the lives of others no matter how complex the circumstances and how vast the barriers may be" (Schultz, 2007, p. 175).

Pedagogy is seen as a site of discourse among participants—teachers and students—whose identities are multifaceted, often contradictory, and always in process (Weedon, 1987). A critical culture means that teachers and students question how their personal identities as social beings influence their relation-ship with what is taught. This curricular culture values alternative ways of knowing the world as well as the roles of aesthetics, emotion, and personal relationships in the creation of knowledge. Its vision casts knowledge as a value-laden social construction, comprised of equal status contributions from multiple cultural sources and groups (Gay, 1995).

There also is a role for rational thinking in this curricular culture, but knowledge as a set of universal, objective principles is not consistent with this culture's vision, nor is the view of knowledge-seeking as a value-free, dispassionate search for truth. Teachers and students not only work together to understand the content of the disciplines, but to examine how powerful mechanisms in society control their access to versions of knowledge, how these mechanisms control expectations and aspirations in individuals, and how individuals, in turn, may take action of their own to influence society. Together, teachers and students scrutinize the bedrock, taken-for-granted assumptions of education, e.g., the epistemological basis of subject matter, how knowledge is produced, interpreted, validated and promoted, the pur-poses of schooling, and relationships among stakeholders in the educational enterprise.

The scrutiny of oneself and society leads to empowerment—the ability to think and act critically. When students are empowered, "they have knowl-edge of their social, political, and economic worlds, the skills to influence their environments, and humane values that will motivate them to participate in social change to help create a more just society and world" (Banks, 1992, p. 154).

Teachers are seen not as detached classroom technicians; they are "trans-formative intellectuals"—"engaged critics" who play an active role in shaping curriculum.

> They do not operate from an aloof perspective that legitimizes the separa-tion of facts from values. The understand the nature of their own self-for-mation, have some vision of the future, see the importance of education as a public discourse, and have a sense of mission in providing students what they need to become critical citizens. (Giroux, 1993, p. 15)

Thus teachers are "partisans, not doctrinaire." They believe something, say what they believe and offer their beliefs to others in a framework that always makes it debatable and open to inquiry (Giroux, 1993, p. 15). Teachers have "authority" in the classroom but are not "authoritarian" (Shor & Freire in Au, 2009).

Teachers prudently reveal themselves to students so that students are free to react to the personal history of the teacher. This is essential to stimulate dialogue—the primary vehicle for learning in the critical classroom. Dialogue—a crucial feature of the critical culture—often develops around profound personal experiences that are not necessarily shared by teachers and students. While teachers do not have the moral authority to speak for others whose experiences they do not share, they can speak—about and to—the experiences of racism, sexism, class discrimination and other concerns as historical and contingent issues that affect public life (Giroux, 1993, p. 35).

Dialogue

> Freire's conception of dialogue, then, also speaks to the particular relationship between students and teachers within his conception of critical, liberatory pedagogy. Within his framework, students and teachers are not automatically "equals" in that their relationship is not completely horizontal. Rather, within Freirean pedagogy, the teacher in fact maintains authority and directiveness in the learning process. (Au, 2009, p. 223)

Within this curricular culture, teachers have the responsibility to:

- Model and reinforce non-judgmental responses,
- Respond to student ideas and do not ignore or dismiss them when they are voiced,
- Incorporate student experiences into their teaching and connect them where appropriate to the curriculum,
- Show students that they are not alone and without help, and
- Ensure that students are confident and relaxed enough to voice their concerns.

Teachers may also try to stimulate and provoke a changed consciousness in students through vivid demonstration. One memorable example is third-grade teacher Jane Elliott's social experiment in her homogeneous (White) classroom in a small town in Iowa in which the children began to grasp what it was like to face prejudice because of race. Her simulation allowed some children special privileges whereas others had restrictions in which they were forbidden the use of drinking fountains and playground equipment, were not allowed to play with children unlike themselves, and were continually reminded of their lack of intelligence—all depending upon whether the children had blue or brown eyes (Peters, 1987).

Another provocative classroom account is Bill Bigelow's teaching of

Columbus's "discovery" of America. Bigelow began by coming into class one day and absconding with a student's purse, announcing that he had "discovered this purse." His students' disconcerted response becomes a catalyst for their thinking about unfairness. These high schoolers also became angry at the traditional textbooks' descriptions of discovery as Bigelow provided primary documents revealing the brutality of the European contact with Indigenous peoples. Eventually, the students questioned all sources of knowledge, including the teacher's contributions, as they began to obtain a critical approach to learning and knowledge (Bigelow, 1989).

A high school teacher who designed a simulation about prejudice in response to her students' discriminatory behavior to a substitute teacher explained why interrupting learners' complacency—and not just teaching about prejudice—is so important to her:

> I can tell my students about my disappointment in them, talk about discrimination and prejudice, teach what happens when cultural groups are oppressed and subject to racist remarks and actions... but I want them to construct their own meaning around this. This isn't something that I can teach. I do believe, however, that I can create some sort of simulation to get at the heart of this and open up dialogue and hopefully begin the process of respecting and valuing diversity. (Class Journal)

In addition to being provocateurs, teachers' tasks are to find out what the students know, help them reflect on this knowledge, and to set it into a larger context in order to help them make connections (Freire, 1973/1990). In turn, educators constantly modify their own knowledge through the reflections of the students. Learners—no longer docile listeners—are now critical co-investigators in dialogue with the teacher. There is a reciprocal process of dialogue so that students also educate teachers. "There are not teachers and students, but teacher-students, and student-teachers" (Freire, 1973/1990, p. 67).

Beliefs and Practices: Content and Context

In this curricular culture, content means the organized and systematic depiction to learners of the things about which they want to know more (Freire, 1973/1990). Through dialogue, the teacher re-presents that knowledge to students from whom it was first received—not as a lecture, but as a problem (Freire, 1973/1990). Investigations bring tentative viewpoints and answers that stimulate more questions, self-awareness, and an incrementally more conscious, mature approach to these questions. The content thus renews itself.

Because many student-generated issues involve immediate and emotional themes, a structure is needed to prevent anxiety and the articulation of resentments. Issues are recast as a concrete representation—in story, photograph, skit, collage, or song—with many sides in order to avoid polarizing points of view. These representations, called "codes," mediate discussions about topics that are too overwhelming or threatening to address directly (Freire, 1973/1990, p. 106). The codes do not provide solutions, but are capable of prompting discussion about solutions and strategies from the class. Finally, the problems suggested will not be overwhelming, but should offer possibilities for group affirmation and small actions toward change. Action, or follow-through to the consequences of reflection, is essential to learning.

Themes also play a significant role in the critical classroom. Themes are abstract terms which are anchored in people's common, lived experiences. Themes such as dominance and liberation, silence, and justice are investigated in relation to concrete experiences in the learner's world through such questions as: What are examples of dominance? What forms can silence take? How do people liberate themselves? Teachers and students can use photographs, drawings of people interacting, even "found objects" to be stimulants for dialogue. These objects can be cultural artifacts, advertisements, tools, toys, labels, clothing—anything that supports students' understanding of the environment.

This culture of curriculum de-emphasizes the compartmentalization of subject areas. Science, mathematics, and literature, for example, cannot be examined as stand-alone fields of study that remain uninfluenced by one other. Because social studies is a composite of several disciplines involving social constructions (e.g., political science, economics, history), it is easy to use conceptual frameworks from those disciplines to examine, for example, how funding for disease research is determined by politics rather than by science, or, how female and Black contributions to literature have been systematically suppressed throughout American history.

This cycle of reflection and action is referred to as the *praxis* of knowing. Plans for action evolve from students' understanding of problems as well as from visions of better conditions. Students can practice taking action through in-class role plays, and action competencies such as reporting a problem, filing a complaint, fighting for funding or adopting an issue such as unsafe conditions around a neighborhood business (Shor, 1996, pp. 42–43). As students test their analyses in the real world, they begin a deeper cycle of reflection that includes input from their new experiential base. Reflection and action are both necessary. Reflection without action is idle chatter, verbalism; action without reflection is activism—"action for action's sake" (Freire, 1973/1990, p. 77).

Not all of class time can be given over to the examination of the students' lived experiences; at times, the teacher will select specific content for students to examine. Freire believes that it is "unthinkable for a teacher to be in charge of a class without providing students material relevant to a discipline." He explains that objects of study should fuel the teacher's curiosity. "They stimulate my curiosity and I bring this enthusiasm to my students. Then both of us can illuminate the object together" (Shor & Freire, 1987, pp. 212–213). For example, a liberatory educator writes:

As a social justice educator in a language arts classroom, I look for stories where the protagonists refuse to accept "their place" in society; I try to find fiction and nonfiction about people who disrupt the script society set for them. I want students to see that history is not inevitable, that there are spaces where it can bend, change, become more just. (Christiensen, 2009)

Content would include the social/historical products of revisionist scholarship as well as insiders' viewpoints. Attention is given to the historical and scholarly contributions of diverse individuals and events rather to than the trivial, isolated and exotic aspects of non-dominant peoples (Banks, 1990; Hilliard in Gay, 1995). Marginalized people who have been silenced throughout history are given voice and allowed to tell their own stories—challenging the status quo situation in which they have been represented as victims, servants to society, passive participants, second-class citizens, and imperfect imitations of European, Anglo male models (Gay, 1995).

Another avenue for critical pedagogy is environmental studies, particularly focused on ecojustice. Environmental degradation affects the Earth and all living beings and has to be understood as an important component of healing and repairing the world.

Approaching social transformation through the optic of ecosocialist pedagogy deepens this pedagogical project since it challenges teachers to recognize their embeddedness in globalized social relations of exploitation and how these relations are linked to an embodied social and political geography of environmental inequity and crises. (McClaren & Houston, 2004, p. 36)

Environmentalism also is a way to draw in students—who may be concerned about their immediate world—to move from the local to a more global orientation in understanding the effect of environmental devastation.

This curriculum is rich with primary sources—social commentaries, newspaper articles, personal memoirs, original artifacts, literary treatises, biographies, and artistic impressions—empowering learners to interpret historical events for themselves. Students learn how events are experienced by many different people; examination of multiple sources generates multiple realities. When original documents are not available to help students construct an unfiltered image of a particular discipline, commercial textbooks may be one of the few print resources available to students; then, students must be taught to critically examine sources, becoming aware of both historical and social constructions subject to the economy of publishing agencies and forces outside of school (such as state governments) that render certain texts legitimate objects of knowledge.

The definition of "text" in the critical classroom includes anything that carries a message. Popular culture is a serious object of study because it is suffused with text and exerts a powerful influence on the ways students mediate, relate, resist, and create their own cultural forms and forms of knowing (Giroux, 1993). Instruction also consists of helping students how to read critically; for example, Kohl, in his essay (1995), "Should We Burn Babar?" suggests that children can become conscious of classism and racism—even in apparently benign animal stories. Students also can also be taught to imagine how to challenge and resist dominant versions of the text. Simon (1992) describes teaching *The Merchant of Venice* by including an interpretation of Shylock in a performance in the Yiddish theater—not as an anti-Semitic caricature, but as a character showing defiance of anti-Semitism (pp. 101–120).

Although the classroom environment is a crucible for dialogue, expression, and even confrontation, a sense of community and trust must first be created. When students describe "good classes" in this curricular culture, they talk about places where construction of meaning happens in a context that honors supportive relationships, previous experiences, and multiple cultural and linguistic realities. Furthermore, the good classroom is a forum for critical analysis of the world that allows for the further development of solutions (Rivera & Poplin, 1995). Similarly, topics and techniques are welcomed that honor feelings as well as the intellect such as role-playing, simulations, drama, song, and poetry, readings, journals, brain-storming, and classroom celebration (Belenky, Clinchy, Goldberger, & Tarule, 1986).

To a great extent, the critical pedagogy classroom is democratic. Clearly, an authoritarian classroom or one in which teachers impose their beliefs rather than allowing students to examine them would shut down dialogue.

Democratic classrooms become incubators for students seeking to improve their world since they strive to center and adjust the school around the needs of the children rather than forcing students to conform and adapt to something already established without them in mind. (Schultz, 2007, p. 173)

Teachers and students must be partners in all aspects of learning about themselves, their worlds, and about changing the world as they pose problems and questions.

Beliefs and Practices: Curriculum Planning and Evaluation

In this curricular culture, teachers seek to invest students in their own learning by involving them as co-authors of the curriculum. It is believed that learners are competent to play a role in course development and in doing so, join with teachers in knowing the joys and difficulties of intense intellectual activity (Shrewsbury, 1987). Teachers invite students to generate ideas, to negotiate subject matter, and to find resources outside the school setting, e.g., to move into the community to gather documents, conduct interviews and make observations as part of the learning process. Curriculum development stems not from students' trivial preoccupations, but from an informed sense of "What should I be paying attention to here?" (Giroux, 1993, p. 14).

Planning begins with teachers discovering concerns that run through learners' conversations. Teachers try to situate themselves in the students' culture—to comprehend their literacy, aspirations, the stuff of their daily lives, while taking into account their students' cognitive and emotional states. To identify themes, teachers listen attentively to students, not only during class, but during breaks and outside the classroom.

Because curriculum constantly evolves from student issues, teachers cannot measure fulfillment of predetermined objectives or test outcomes. Evaluation in a problem-posing environment concerns examining a broad spectrum of student's abilities to articulate issues, generate their own learning materials, redefine their views of the world, and take risks to act in their daily lives. Through a variety of means, teachers try to continually ascertain if students understand the root causes of problems, whether student action on problems are effective, and especially, what special insights learners gain about themselves and the groups of which they are members.

These determinations cannot be made solely using terminal assessment techniques, but rather, by qualitatively evaluating the on-going work of students. Whether or not critical insights are being realized by learners is evidenced through discussions, role-plays, presentations to the class, oral arguments, position papers, letters to support social action, and other products of inquiry. Group work can be evaluated and honored as the product of a collective of learners rather than being parsed into individual components for "scoring." The purpose of evaluation is to provide feedback about communicative skills, content knowledge, and above all, critical insights about the content. Teachers evaluate not only processes of reflection but also the action taken by learners in the action-reflection-action cycle; their continuous evaluation functions as a guidance process as well as an indicator of accomplishment. Evaluation can take several forms: narratives from the teacher, written self-critiques by students during the reflection process, interviews and observations by the teacher, by peers, or by community members who have been affected by student attempts at transformative action.

In the critical culture, assessment is conducted in the best interests of the students. It means providing guidance to learners for the purposes of opening a universe of possibilities for their future and as a means of supporting critical thinking and powers of reflection. Evaluation rewards creativity and encourages diversity. As in the design of instructional experiences, evaluation takes into account the individual students' life experiences and identity. And, in contrast to traditional evaluation which so often marks the dead end of a unit of study, critical evaluations are a springboard for a continuing, more complex, cycle of reflection-action-reflection.

Dilemmas of Practice

We begin with the obvious when considering dilemmas of practice in "Confronting the Dominant Order": teaching radical curriculum—challenging cherished premises and myths about society—is not only an unpopular stand, in many places it would be anathema. Without a community that tolerates political activism and without the support of administration, teachers most likely would not feel safe to "disturb the social order." Even in a more sympathetic environment, teachers and students may find that exposing and objecting to unequal power relationships within their own schools may meet with resistance; it is one thing to challenge politics in Guatemala and quite another to confront the decision-making process on one's own turf.

Still, even when teachers find themselves in situations that are not hostile to confrontational and liberatory pedagogy, their task remains difficult. A radical version of the world calls for investigations of racism and classism, and works for fundamental changes in values and institutions. Can those who have not understood the experience of being marginalized develop empathy for those who have been oppressed? Can people with privilege work against their self-interest? Members of dominant social groups are more than willing to believe in the American dream and consider as true that the dream is readily available for all. Only with great difficulty can we teach to suspend individuals' beliefs about deeply imbedded social mis-understandings and myths, about a "democratic story about itself that is so enveloping and sentimental" (Shor, 1996, p. 23).

Teachers also are likely to discover that students resist doing critical analysis (Ellwood, 1993; Shor, 1996). Students often have little experience in such thinking or social action, have no language to imagine the concepts of this curriculum, bring "no transformative agendas to class," and furthermore, "old habits die hard" (Shor, 1996, pp. 19–27). Critical theorists fear that the oppressed, who have adapted to the structure of domination in which they are immersed, often become resigned to it; they prefer the security of conformity in a state of familiar "unfreedom" to the unfamiliar situation produced by freedom and the implications it carries for personal responsibility (Freire, 1973/1990, p. 32).

Furthermore, the essential elements of "Confronting the Dominant Order"—dialogue followed by individual and group actions—are dependent upon many factors:

- Internal class dynamics, e.g., length of time students have been together in class, whether they are from the same or different linguistic backgrounds and their level of trust,
- Students' understanding of the barriers to change,
- Internal feelings—level of self-confidence created through problem-posing, through other life-settings and prior roles and experiences in their culture, and
- Support mechanisms of students' families, communities, and work environments (Moriarty & Wallerstein, 1983).

Another impediment to this curricular culture may be the circumscribed worldview of teachers themselves. Often, school administrators and teachers are silent to each other and to the students about racial segregation, racism, and sexism (Lave, 1996). Many teachers are not even aware of privilege and oppression in their own lives. How then can they hold serious conversations with children about such pervasive yet unperceived phenomena (Rivera & Poplin, 1995, p. 235)? Although awareness of teachers' own positions and biases could develop from teacher education, it is not likely that colleges of education will support such a "radical shift" in teacher preparation (Purpel & Shapiro, 1995, p. 113).

Finally, literature about this culture of curriculum reveals a discontinuity between theory and guidelines for practice in K–12 education; there have been myriad arguments about theory, but sophisticated dialogue about method has been scarce. Despite substantial accounts of critical pedagogy curriculum (Bigelow, 1988; Davidson, Hammerman, & Schneidewind, 1997; Lee, Menkart, & Okazawa-Rey, 1998) and some thoughtful attempts to combine theory and practice, especially application of Freirean critical pedagogy (Rivage-Seul, 1987; Peterson, 1991, Frankenstein, 1992), the question of whether or not the critical approach can be developed in the direction of a viable program of instruction has not been satisfactorily addressed. Moreover, deliberation about the nature of curriculum and pedagogy has not been brought to the "area of public concern and public debate" by critical theorists (Bell & Schniedewind, 1987; Purpel & Shapiro, 1995, p. 111).

Critique

Critique of "Confronting the Dominant Order" raises many issues emanating from the variant ideas within this curricular culture, its pedagogical implications, and its worldview. Several of these concerns reflect long-standing differences among proponents of this curricular culture. Issues have been raised as well by advocates through their own self-reflection; for those who propose critique of education and society, it has been reasonable for them to question their own purposes and practices.

The first element in our critique pertains to the theoretical complexity of this curricular culture. Although the differences among the critical, feminist, and multicultural pedagogies are often simply a matter of emphasis, in several ways these three contributing philosophies are incommensurate. Feminist theorists claim that the goals of liberation and political transformation espoused in critical pedagogy are not attainable without exploring one's own privileged position and the existing conflicts among the oppressed groups themselves; they also call into question the privileged position of white male theorists (Weiler, 1991; Weiler & Mitchell, 1992) and recognize the importance of students feeling connected along with the concepts of family, friendship, nurturing, and goodness (Rivera & Poplin, 1995, p. 233). Critical theorists associate the roots of racial domination with capitalism (and its elaboration as a world system) and see the problem of racial inequality in schooling subsumed under the general rubric of working-class oppression, whereas multiculturalists view racism as a separate, more powerful dynamic (McCarthy, 1988). There are inherent tensions among feminist, multicultural and critical perspectives that thwart portrayal of this culture as a congruent whole. Even within each of feminist, multicultural, and critical pedagogies there are ideological differences or unresolved tensions (see Rivera & Poplin, 1995, p. 223; Garcia, 1994, pp. 86–87).

The varying explanations of social dynamics, ideas about practice, and ultimate goals make imagining consistent pedagogical practices that remain true to theory a daunting task. Clearly, this culture of curriculum calls for living with tensions inherent in dialectic thinking, fluid explanations of social phenomena, and the complications of human interaction; it demands that teachers be intellectuals who can grapple with complexity. This outcome is questionable in light of American society's apathy to radical social reform, the pursuit of quick fixes for educational solutions, and the frequent procedure-oriented approaches suggested in teacher education.

The second component of this critique comes from response to the question, should "Confronting the Dominant Order" be the singular curricular orientation for children and adolescents? To this question, we give a mixed answer. First, the idea of infusing curricula with critical analysis, concern for identity, and social action surely elevates education to a moral and intellectual enterprise. However, we have quandaries about what becomes left out (the null curriculum) when concepts in academic subjects are chosen to "fit" into this paradigm.

A critical approach to teaching subject matter does not provide students grounding in a discipline because it does not necessarily teach the conceptual frameworks and skills for learners to become thoroughly competent (see Frankenstein, 1992). Likewise, students exposed only to this curricular culture may not know the joy of learning associated with the creation of knowledge and deep mastery of a domain. Although proponents of the critical culture may not make the claim that it is the only viable approach to curriculum, we certainly think it is reasonable that content (be it mathematics, science, or literature), as a vehicle for critical analysis and for revealing privilege and oppression, must at least teach learners to understand certain content fundamentals. We cannot neglect the task of helping students become literate by, instead, spending most of the teaching time on political analysis (Shor & Freire, 1987, p. 212).

In other ways, the content of this curricular orientation may limit students' attainment of cultural capital, of a full, rich education that gives them an even playing field, the means and competence not just to enter—but to confront—the dominant order. Grounding learning in the students' own life experiences is desirable in any educational system, but making it the de facto curriculum closes doors that students may not realize should be opened. Furthermore, we question if featuring popular culture as a vehicle for mediating student learning may be a mere capitulation to the shallow, immediate interests of children as consumers. The critical culture seems to circumscribe a null curriculum that disparages, by its absence, the classic works of literature, science, and the arts as culturally-bound constructions with questionable validity and of little relevance to the students' own life situations. We are concerned about the logic of those holding this extreme position and realize that some critical curriculum workers would say that classic works may take their place alongside the suppressed and unrecognized contributions of authors, scientists, philosophers, and artists from the non-dominant cultures—that emphasis is properly reapportioned to the classics, not denied them.

Finally, many aspects of "Confronting the Dominant Order" have a distinctly negative character (Wardekker & Miedema, 1997). This curriculum's emphasis upon inequities, dominance, distortion, and grossly imperfect social situations provokes unsettling quandaries: Does the critical culture crush hope and re-enforce young people's despair? Does its harsh economic explanations of self-interest provoke cynicism? Can students resist the pessimism that they may feel when they cannot easily change the world? Moreover, does attention to power differences within this curricular culture become a barrier to community? Can young people who are acutely aware of political, social, and economic inequities imagine working with others across class, race, and gender borders to create a just and humane society?

Although Freire may have "vehemently opposed teachers imposing their knowledge on students" (Au, 2009, p. 225), educators who themselves see the worth of the critical culture nevertheless have some doubts about the imposition of their values and a negative worldview upon young people (Ellsworth, 1989). Their qualms mirror the long-standing debate among social reconstructionists since the time of George Counts relative to indoctrination (Dewey, 1936). For example, a new elementary teacher writes that "although I regard myself in many ways as a critical [pedagogue], I see the students' needs and interests as paramount over my own and see my role more as a provider of background and support, rather than as the general marching my troops into the fray of social struggle" (Class Journal). Ellwood (1993), then a high school teacher in an urban classroom, writes about imposition of the teacher's worldview upon students, poignantly asking, "can we really look through our students' eyes?"

> I have gradually begun to see how invested many of my students are in the classic American dream.... I was reminded that my students must hold fiercely to the conviction that they can make it.... Still, I did not entirely understand that some students saw social critique as threatening, and why. Have I at times fed feelings of despair in some young people by asking them to examine society critically? Critical pedagogues might argue we should encounter such despair by mobilizing our students to action... if you accept my argument that the classroom is an imperfect democracy with the teacher retaining a degree of power that cannot be denied, must we not also accept the possibility that we will push our students toward analyses that are not empowering after all? (Ellwood, 1993, pp. 76–77)

The opportunities for mis-application of critical pedagogy are many. Students can come away from this kind of experience with the sense that everyone is oppressing them, that every form of authority is constrictive, that all codified knowledge is relative, suspect, and of little personal value. Young students who begin their critical understanding of the world by being introduced to concepts of fairness and equality can be baffled by the particulars of what constitutes practices of unfairness. If some classmates come from more economically advantaged families, are they the oppressors? Is it always bad when someone has more of something than someone else? Determining who is oppressed and in what way requires that students consider in-depth triangulations of values, circumstances, and theoretical explanations; can young learners think with such complexity rather than choosing simple condemnation?

Also, the fact that many students do not share the same ethnic, social, racial, and linguistic backgrounds as their teachers may lead to cultural incongruencies in the classroom which can mediate against actualizing curricular goals. Incompatibilities are evident in value orientations, behavioral norms, and expectations, and styles of social interaction, self-presentation, communication and cognitive processing (Bennett, 1990; Gay, 1991; Spindler, 1987). The classroom sharing of experiences can lead to a sense of commonality, but in settings in which students come from differing positions of privilege, the sharing of experience may cause resentments and defensiveness rather than build solidarity. In these circumstances, a collective exploration of experiences leads not to a common knowledge based on sameness, but to the tensions of articulated differences (Weiler, 1991).

In conclusion, the greatest concerns about this culture of curriculum are its complexity and negativity. Is there so much emphasis on the intricacies of theory that this culture remains outside the imagination of most educators? Do ideas about difference eclipse conversations about how to accomplish egalitarian schools and a just and humane society? Does pessimism overshadow hope? Can proponents of "Confronting the Dominant Order" articulate a vision that can enter public discourse and initiate curriculum change? Without the articulation of a clear, convincing, and confident vision, we believe that this culture of curriculum may be doomed to its label as "radical" and disregarded, rather than being viewed as a viable alternative for education.

References

Anyon, J. (1980/1994). Social Class and the Hidden Curriculum of Work. In J. Kretovics & E. J. Nussel (Eds.), *Transforming urban education* (pp. 253–276). Boston: Allyn and Bacon.

Apple, M. (1982). *Education and power.* London: Routledge & Kegan Paul.

Apple, M. W. (1996). *Cultural politics and education.* New York: Teachers College Press.

Apple, M., & King, N. (1983). What do schools teach? In H. Giroux & D. Purpel (Eds.), *Moral education and the hidden curriculum: Deception or discovery* (pp. 82–99). Berkeley, CA: McCutchan.

Aronowitz, S., & Giroux, H. A. (1985). *Education under siege: The conservative, liberal and radical debate over schooling.* Hadley, MA: Bergin & Garvey.

Au, W. (2009). Fighting with the text: Contextualizing and recontextualizing Freire's critical pedagogy. In M. W. Apple, W. Au, & L. A. Gandin (Eds.), *The Routledge international handbook of critical education* (pp. 221–231). New York: Routledge.

Ayers, W. (1995). Popular education: Teaching for social justice. *Democracy & Education, 10,* 5–8.

Banks, J. (1990). Citizen education for a pluralistic democratic society. *The Social Studies, 81,* 210–214.

Banks, J. (1992). A curriculum for empowerment, action, and change. In K. A. Moodley (Ed.), *Beyond multicultural education: International perspectives* (pp. 154–170). Calgary, Alberta: Detseling Enterprises.

Banks, J. A., & Banks, C. A. (1993). *Multicultural education: Issues and perspectives* (2nd ed.). Boston: Allyn & Bacon.

Benne, K. D. (1995). Prologue: Social reconstructionism remembered. In M. E. James (Ed.), *Social reconstruction through education: The philosophy, history, and curricula of a radical ideal* (pp. xxi–xxvii). Norwood, NJ: Ablex.

Belenky, M. F., Clinchy, B. M., Goldberger, N. R., & Tarule, J. M. (1986). *Women's ways of knowing.* New York: Basic Books.

Bell, L., & Schniedewind, N. (1987). Reflective minds, intentional hearts: Joining humanistic education and critical theory for liberating education. *Journal of Education, 169,* 55–77.

Bigelow, B. (1988). A new kind of classroom: Critical pedagogy in action. *Rethinking Schools, 3*(1), 4–5.

Bigelow, B. (1989). Rediscovering Columbus: Re-reading the past. *Rethinking Schools, 4*(1), 1, 12–13.

Bigelow, B., Christensen, L, Karp, S., Miner, B., & Peterson, B. (1994). *Rethinking our classrooms: Teaching for equity and justice*. Milwaukee, WI: Rethinking Schools, Ltd.

Bennett, C. (1990). *Comprehensive multiculural education: Theory and practice* (2nd ed.). Boston: Allyn & Bacon.

Bowles, S., & Gintis, H. (1976) *Schooling in capitalist America*. New York: Basic Books.

Carbone Jr., P. F., & Wilson, V. S. (1995). Harold Rugg's social reconstructionism. In M. E. James (Ed.), *Social reconstruction through education: The philosophy, history, and curricula of a radical ideal* (pp. 57–88). Norwood, NJ: Ablex.

Cherryholmes, C. (1985). Theory and practice: On the role of empirically based theory for critical practice. *American Journal of Education, 94*, 39–70.

Christiensen, L. (2009). Teaching for joy and justice. *Rethinking Schools, 23*(4). Retrieved March 26, 2010, from http://www.rethinkingschools.org/archive/23_04/joy234.shtml

Counts, G. S. (1932/1970). Dare the school build a new social order? In J. W. Noll & S. P. Kelly (Eds.), *Foundations of education in America: An anthology of major thoughts & significant actions* (pp. 335–339). New York: Harper & Row.

Cremin, L. A. (1961/1964). *The transformation of the school: Progressivism in American education 1876–1957*. New York: Vintage Books.

Cremin, L. A. (1977). *Traditions of American education*. New York: Basic Books.

Davidson, E., Hammerman, J. K., & Schneidewind, N. (1997). Education for equity: Acting on critical consciousness. *Democracy & Education, 12*, 39–42.

Dewey, J. (1936/1939). Educators and class struggle (J. Ratner, Ed.). *Intelligence in the modern world: John Dewey's philosophy*. New York: The Modern Library.

Doll, Jr., W. E. (1993). *A post-modern perspective on curriculum*. New York: Teachers College Press.

Elson, R. M. (1964). *Guardians of tradition: American schoolbooks in the nineteenth century*. Lincoln: University of Nebraska Press.

Ellwood, C. M. (1993). Can we really look through out students' eyes? An urban teacher's perspective. *Educational Foundations, 7*, 63–78.

Ellsworth, E. (1989). Why doesn't this feel empowering? Working through repressive myths of critical pedagogy. *Harvard Educational Review, 59*, 297–324.

Frankenstein, M. (1992). Critical mathematics education: An application of Paulo Freire's epistemology. In K. Weiler & C. Mitchell (Eds.), *What schools can do: Critical pedagogy and practice* (pp. 237–264). Albany: State University of New York Press.

Freire, P. (1973/1990). *Pedagogy of the oppressed*. New York: Continuum.

Garcia, E. (1994). *Understanding and meeting the challenge of student cultural diversity*. Boston: Houghton Mifflin.

Gay, G. (1991). Culturally diverse students and social studies. In J. P. Shaver (Ed.), *Handbook of research on social studies teaching and learning* (pp. 145–156). New York: Macmillan.

Gay, G. (1995). Mirror images on common issues: Parallels between multicultural education an critical pedagogy. In C. Sleeter & P. McLaren (Eds.), *Multicultural education, critical pedagogy, and the politics of difference* (pp. 155–189). Albany: State University of New York Press.

Giarelli, J. M. (1995). The social frontier 1934–1943: Retrospect and prospect. In M. E. James (Ed.), *Social reconstruction through education: The philosophy, history, and curricula of a radical ideal* (pp. 27–42). Norwood, NJ: Ablex.

Giroux, H. A. (1993). *Border crossings: Cultural works and the politics of education.* New York: Routledge.

Giroux, H. A. (1997). *Pedagogy and the politics of hope: Theory, culture, and schooling, a critical reader.* Boulder, CO: Westview Press.

Greene, M. (1988). *The dialectic of freedom.* New York: Teachers College Press.

Kohl, H. (1995). Should we burn Babar? Questioning power in children's literature. In H. Kohl (Ed.), *Should we burn Babar? Essays on children's literature and the power of stories* (pp. 3–56). New York: The New Press.

Lave, J. (1996). Teaching, as learning in practice. *Mind, Culture, and Activity, 3,* 149–164.

Lee, E., Menkart, D., & Okazawa-Rey, M. (1998). *Beyond heroes and holidays: A practical guide to K-12 anti-racist, multicultural education and staff development.* Washington, DC: Network of Educators on the Americas.

McCarthy, C. (1988) Rethinking liberal and radical perspectives on racial inequality in schooling: Making the case for nonsynchrony. *Harvard Educational Review, 58,* 265–279.

McLaren, P. (1989). *Life in schools: An introduction to critical pedagogy in the foundations of education.* New York: Longman.

McClaren, P., & Houston, D. (2004). Revolutionary ecologies: Ecosocialism and critical pedagogy. *Educational Studies, 36*(1), 27–45.

Moriarty, P., & Wallerstein, N. (1983). *Teaching about nuclear war: A positive problem-posing strategy.* San Francisco: Catholic Archdiocese (Commission on Social Justice).

Peters, W. (1987). *A class divided: Then and now.* New Haven, CT: Yale University Press.

Peterson, R. E. (1991). Teaching how to read the world and change it: Critical pedagogy in the intermediate grades. In C. E. Walsh (Ed.), *Literacy as praxis: Culture, language & pedagogy* (pp. 365–387). Norwood, NJ: Ablex.

Purpel, D. E., & Shapiro, S. (1995). *Beyond liberation & excellence: Reconstructing the public discourse on education.* Westport, CT: Bergin & Garvey.

Rivage-Seul, M. K. (1987). Peace education: Imagination and the pedagogy of the oppressed. *Harvard Educational Review, 57,* 153–169.

Rivera, J., & Poplin, M. (1995). Multicultural, critical, feminine and constructive pedagogies seen through the eyes of youth: A call for the revisioning of these and beyond: Toward a pedagogy for the next century, In C. Sleeter & P. McLaren (Eds.), *Multicultural education, critical pedagogy, and the politics of difference* (pp. 221–244). Albany: State University of New York Press.

Schultz, B. D. (2007). "Not satisfied with stupid band-aids": A portrait of a justice-oriented, democratic curriculum serving a disadvantaged neighborhood. *Equity & Excellence in Education, 40,* 66–176.

Shor, I. (1996). *When students have power: Negotiating authority in critical pedagogy.* Chicago: University of Chicago Press.

Shor, I., & Freire, P. (1987). *A pedagogy for liberation*. South Hadley, MA: Begin & Garvey.

Shrewsbury, C. M. (1987). What is feminist pedagogy? *Women's Studies Quarterly, 15,* 6–14.

Simon, R. I. (1992). *Teaching against the grain: Texts for a pedagogy of possibility.* New York: Bergin & Garvey.

Slattery, P. (1995). *Curriculum development in the postmodern era.* New York: Garland.

Spring, J. (1991). *American education: An introduction to social and political aspects* (5th ed.). New York: Longman.

Spindler, G. D. (1987). *Education and cultural process: Anthropological approaches.* Prospect Heights, IL: Waveland Press.

Teitelbaum, K. (1990). Critical lessons from our past: Curricula of socialist Sunday schools in the United States. *Curriculum Inquiry, 20*(4), 407–436.

Wardekker, W. L., & Miedema, S. (1997). Critical pedagogy: An evaluation and a direction for reformulation. *Curriculum Inquiry, 27,* 45–62.

Weedon, C. (1987). *Feminist practice & postructuralist theory.* Oxford, UK: Basil Blackwell.

Weiler, K. (1991). Freire and a feminist pedagogy of difference. *Harvard Educational Review, 61,* 449–474.

Weiler, K., & Mitchell, C. (1992). *What schools can do: Critical pedagogy and practice.* Albany: State University of New York Press.

Chapter 12

Envisioning Peace

Pamela Bolotin Joseph

Bringing up the subject of an education for peace in such critical times as these, when society is continually threatened by the possibility of war, may appear to be the most naive kind of idealism. I nonetheless believe that laying the foundations for peace through education is the most effective and the most constructive way of opposing the war...

> Maria Montessori, 1949/1972, *Education and Peace*, p. 42

Even before entering Mr. Raphael's combined fifth and sixth grade classroom in Valley Elementary School, "Welcome" signs in various languages greet visitors in the hallway. Inside Mr. Raphael's classroom, students' work decorate the walls as do pictures of Mother Earth, the Dalai Lama, other peace workers, a sign with the words "shalom," "salaam," and "peace" as well as proverbs from many nations selected by the children. A large map pinpoints the nations from where children and their families emigrated; a colorful chart displays languages spoken by the children's families. The room also displays an American flag, a class flag created by the children, and individual flags replete with personally significant symbols made by each child. The most prominent sign in the classroom is "Insult Free Zone." Mr. Raphael notes that "the reason that is the biggest sign is I think it's most important for them to be in an emotionally safe environment."

Mr. Raphael takes care to create a culture of peace in his classroom. For example, when children have disagreements, problems are worked out at peace tables. Holding class meetings to solve problems through dialogue is an important aspect of class. Mr. Raphael trains students as mediators on the playground and all the children seek to find win-win solutions. The children also experience a peaceful classroom milieu as Mr. Raphael helps them to honor each other's backgrounds and to treat each other with kindness and respect. Helping children to learn about interdependence is important to Mr. Raphael and thus all children have meaningful jobs in the classroom; some even take turns being interior decorators so that they are responsible for creating an inviting classroom environment. The children and their teacher also participate in planting and maintaining school gardens and working with the school's extensive recycling program. Mr. Raphael believes that "this environment is theirs and they have to learn to care about this environment if I expect them to learn about the larger environment outside." Chiming Tibetan bells to mark transitions between activities also fosters a peaceful classroom atmosphere.

In addition to cultivating a feeling of peace, Mr. Raphael wants his students to understand the ramifications of violence and models of nonviolent conflict resolution in the wider world. He often invites community members to speak with the children, such as Hiroshima and Holocaust survivors, so that children can grasp the horrors of war. So, too, his students read about historical and contemporary peacemakers and have conducted email interviews with people in various countries who are involved in peace processes. The children illustrate their learning through art projects, presentations, and role-playing.

This classroom is not unusual at Valley Elementary School. Several years ago, Mr. Raphael and his colleagues began a series of meetings to figure out how they could create a noncompetitive, emotionally safe, and peaceful environment. Their goals were not only to help children learn how to get along better with each other but also to care for each other and the school community by creating respectful policies for all aspects of school life—including how all adults treat children. Valley Elementary teachers believe that they have to model peace and not just teach a peace curriculum. Staff and students also have participated in a pro-peace demonstration, peace days, and taking an anti-bullying pledge. Children, staff, and administrators continually refer to the school's Four R's: respect, relationship, responsibility, and rights. Moreover, they have begun to understand that these principles not only guide their relationships with each other but also help them to envision their relationships with others far beyond the school community.

Valley School's focus on nonviolence and peace education has led to an academically rigorous curriculum, particularly in the areas of social studies and science. This has meant that children study history and contemporary culture with attention to peace movements, non-violent social change, human rights, gender equity, eco-justice, and, conversely, dominance, power, structural violence, and environmental degradation. Curriculum content also involves the study of and appreciation for many cultures and the development of a global perspective. Another strong curricular focus is media literacy; for example, teachers help children to interrogate the militarism in society and efforts by media producers to disregard the quality of life for all living things. Earth stewardship is another important theme in the curriculum and has led to serious study of ecology and sustainability as well as social action projects in which children work along side of their teachers, administrators, and families to create an environmentally sustainable school and community.

§

These descriptions of Mr. Raphael's classroom (see Joseph & Duss, 2009) and the Valley School's curriculum highlight important themes of the curricular culture of nonviolence or peace education—what in this book we call "Envisioning Peace":

- Recognition and rejection of violence, including violence to all living beings and the Earth,
- Critical awareness of injustice and social justice and a corresponding respect for human rights and environmental stewardship,
- Resolving differences through dialogue, and
- Imaginative understanding of peace.

This curricular culture demands that students gain deep knowledge of academic disciplines and critical thinking skills so that they can deeply understand the world. It also requires that students understand and appreciate peace. Ultimately, this curricular culture calls for teachers to stimulate in students a moral sensibility in which they desire to live in peace and harmony with each other, all human beings, and the natural world.

Visions

Advocates of "Envisioning Peace" depict its curriculum as transformative experiences that leading to a desire to live justly and peaceably. Peace education focuses on how humans should live together and treat each other (Snauwaert, 2008)—encouraging an ethical stand to counteract the prevailing worldview of tolerance for violence that exists in many societies and schools (Danesh, 2006; Miller, 2003). Accordingly, peace education is a form of moral education (Joseph & Efron, 2005).

Peace educators believe that the only hope of saving humankind and the Earth is to "to end the violent nature of our existence" (Shapiro, 2002a, p. 44) through the process of education in which "the conflict-based worldviews which inform most of our educational endeavours are replaced with peace-based world views" and "consciousness of the oneness of humanity" (Danesh, 2006, pp. 58, 67). The essential premise of peace education is the need to cultivate a worldview that supplants acceptance of war, conquest, competition, and domination with a vision of cooperation, nurturance and peace (Mische & Harris, 2008). As follows, peace educators feel a sense of mission beyond the transformation of one classroom or school: "Peace education should be directed not only toward the maturation of the individual but toward the coming of age of the human species" (Reardon, 1988, p. 53).

The inherent visions of this curricular culture correspond to the four interconnected themes of peace education curriculum. Viewed on a continuum, individuals first embrace nonviolence, commit to social justice, learn the skills of nonviolence, and, ultimately, imagine a world of peace (see Lederach, 2005; Harris & Morrison, 2003).

First, peace education rests on the premise that people must come to systematically understand the nature of violence and to remove its hold upon the individuals and cultures. Peace educators do not have an excessively optimistic vision of the world. Rather, they perceive societies permeated by institutional violence, militarism, and domination in which children learn competition and war as social norms (Danesh, 2006; Mirra, 2008) and metaphors of war and conflict shaping the discourse of daily life (Reardon, 1989). So, too, peace educators are aware that many societies enculturate their young to believe that it is permissible for males to dominate females, for one race to dominate another, for adults to have unquestionable control over children, and for humans to believe it is their right to exploit Earth's resources (Eisler, 2007; Mische & Harris, 2008).

Peace education then is proposed as a way to counteract "horrific forms of violence, like ecocide, genocide, modern warfare, ethnic hatred, racism, sexual abuse, domestic violence...." (Harris, 2004b, p. 5) including "the devastating impact of human violence upon the Earth, its ecosystems, and the various species that inhabit it" (Harris & Mische, 2002, p. 1). This means to recognize relationships of dominance that occur in families, schools, and societies and to call attention to violence in all forms of human interactions.

The second vision in "Envisioning Peace" is awareness of and opposition to injustice. This component extends recognition of violence to critical examination of oppression, dominance, militarism, and environmental degradation (Harris & Morrison, 2003). Peace pedagogy calls for complex understanding of the roots of conflict and for those who are better off to critically analyze their privilege. It connects teachers to "a powerful tradition of critical teaching which can enable students to recognize and understand the taken-for-granted presence of inequality and injustice in their lives and its links to anger and violence" (Shapiro, 2002a, p. 46). Moreover, it requires people to individually and collectively take stands to end brutality oppression in private and public spheres, including gender inequity (Eisler, 2007) and violence toward the natural world (Selby, 2000). Thus, a number of peace education theorists link critical pedagogy and peace education (Rivage-Seul, 1987; Shapiro, 2002b; Synott, 2005).

Concomitantly, "Envisioning Peace" demands social and eco-justice by means of affirmation of human and environmental rights (Bowers, 2004; Brock-Utne, 2000; Harris & Morrison, 2003; Reardon, 1989, 1997; Selby, 2000; Snauwaert, 2008). This calls for both legal and moral support for protecting human fulfillment, freedom, and dignity and the ecological health of the planet. Peace would require "the application of universal ethical principles at all levels of government and leadership" (Danesh, 2006, p. 68) and that international standards on human rights become the basic operating rules of most societies, assuring respect for the dignity, integrity and identity of all persons and people. Life would be sustained by a biologically diverse and healthy natural, planetary environment. In sum, world peace would mean the realization of comprehensive and authentic human security. (Reardon, 2001, p. 3)

This vision for peace education provides individuals with knowledge of codified documents such as *The Universal Declaration of Human Rights, Declaration on the Rights of the Child,* and *The Earth Charter,* for the purpose of helping people to understand their rights and the rights of others—and to realize that non-violence can be a norm and not an aberration.

The third vision, resolving differences through dialogue, means development of commitment and capacity to resolve conflict without violence. Although proponents of peace education understand that human beings continually will face conflict as they deal with each other, that "conflict is ubiquitous" (Harris & Morrison, 2003, p. 29), they believe that people can learn to resolve conflicts without violence. When teaching a "pedagogy of peace" (Joseph & Duss, 2009; Harris, 1990; Shapiro, 2002a), educators stimulate students' "understanding of our real differences, capacity for compassionate attentiveness, ability to live with our differences, and willingness to engage in meaningful dialogue" (Shapiro, 2002a, pp. 46–48).

Resolving differences without violence and with respect toward others calls for changes in thinking from a conflict as "something that has to be won" to peacemaking: "mutual adaptation, reconciliation, and active cooperation/integration" (Boulding, 1988, pp. 141, 142). The skills of conflict resolution, or peacemaking, cultivate and require "compassion, caring, nurturing, and friendship" (Harris, 1996). The process is important because not only does it create dialogue, it helps individuals to understand each other's perspectives and to develop relationships. Peacemaking in itself may be conceived as a transformative and creative process of "personal and social change" (Lederach, 2005, p. 29).

The fourth vision in "Envisioning Peace" is an imaginative understanding of peace. This means more than thinking about peace as the absence of war but as the development of a peace paradigm that includes language, behaviors, structures, and images of peace (Galtung, 1969; Mische & Harris, 2008; Reardon, 1989).

Most of all, we have to change our major metaphor. The prevailing metaphor for human struggle, achievement, and transcendence—warfare—emerging from patriarchy, might well be changed to the metaphor of labor and birth, human development and maturation, emerging from a more fully human, androgynous paradigm. (Reardon, 1988, p. 52)

Before people can learn how to make peace, they must understand and feel what peace means and educators and parents must take every opportunity to provide environments that nurture peace, for children to engage in peace-building (Harris & Morrision, 2003). Once more, peace should be taught and understood as a dynamic process that requires creativity and courage (De Bie, 2007; Eisler, 2007).

Peace educators must provide opportunities to affirm a way to "transcend the cycles of violence that bewitch our human community" (Lederach, 2005, p. 4) by cultivating "moral imagination" that encompasses knowledge of the complexity of living in peace, capability for empathic relationships with others, and the courage of taking risks to make peace possible (Lederach, 2005, p. 29). Through moral imagination, it is possible to believe that peace is possible, even in times when it seems inconceivable.

History

Peace education has a long and rich history, but one that has been "hidden" (Stomfay-Stitz, 2008), neglected, and seldom found in educational histories read by teachers or the public. This curricular orientation today, an established and growing international field of interdisciplinary scholarship, owes much of its existence to remarkable advocacy for nonviolence—even at times when the endorsement of peace education was unpopular or ferociously opposed as its goals and practices often have been far outside those of traditional education.

Peace education in the United States is intrinsically linked to centuries of initiatives and movements that condemned war and militarism, beginning with the early influence of historical peace churches—the Brethren, Mennonites, and Quakers—that consistently upheld the tenets of nonviolence and paths to peace (Harris & Morrison, 2003) and refuted the need for war. An early proposal, "A Plan for a Peace Office for the United States" written by physician and statesman Benjamin Rush, included the appointment of a Secretary of Peace; the plan had wide dissemination when Benjamin Banneker—scientist, inventor, and correspondent with Jefferson about the evils of slavery and racism—strongly supported Rush's proposal and published it in his *Farmers Almanac* in 1793 (Stanford, 2008, p. 24). Rush also advocated for ending capital punishment, militarism, and for the establishment of free public schools that would teach pacifist principles (Howlett, 2008).

In the first several decades of the 1800s, peace proponents formed numerous peace societies and wrote many tracts in newspapers and journals about the importance of peace for the benefit of society, some proposing the need to educate children about peace. The Massachusetts Peace Society, established in 1815, published a journal until 1827, *Friends of Peace*. The American Peace Society, founded in the 1820s, created its own journal, *The Advocate of Peace*, which included a section especially written for children. Another peace crusader, Elihu Burritt, was a prolific writer and activist for peace during the 1840s and the next several decades; he advocated peace education, abstinence from all wars, and world peace. Moreover, by the 1830s, several colleges and universities offered peace curricula. War protests also occurred, for example, opposition to the War of 1812 and Henry David Thoreau's protest of the Mexican American War made famous through his essay, *Civil Disobedience* in 1849 (Harris & Morrison, 2003; Howlett, 2008; Stomfay-Stitz, 1993).

But amidst a period of crusades for peace, the United States experienced a brutal Civil War (1860–1865). Many peace proponents sided with abolitionists who were against the inherent violence of slavery but nevertheless refused to join in violent conflict, often serving as conscientious objectors working in hospitals (Curti, 1936). The response to the horrors of war prompted renewed peace efforts in the following years. For example, Alfred Love, a Quaker, founded a pacifist organization, the Universal Peace Union, in 1866. This organization focused on international peace and expressed concern about militarism by objecting to military parades, ceremonies, and monuments. It also took the position that schools should not allow military training for boys nor textbooks that "glorified war." In 1867, Quakers formed The Peace Association of Friends in America to rekindle their peace work and reprinted their earlier anti-war literature war highlighting portraits of pacifists and peace activists— with some of this writing intended for an audience of young people. In this vein, peace movements after the Civil War had begun to focus on educating children for peace and avoiding miseducation for war (see Howlett, 2008).

In the early years of the 20th century there was "remarkable interest in peace and an equally remarkable growth of organizations dedicated to the cause of peace" including participation in peace conferences by a wide spectrum of American society (Osborne, 1985, pp. 33–34). To some extent sparked by the Hague Peace Conferences in 1899 and 1907 that heralded a strong interest in peace throughout the world (Barash & Webel, 2009), these peace groups "were inspired by a new, optimistic international outlook in social reform and driven by concern over the increasing militarism of the industrialized powers" (Zeiger, 2000, p. 54). During these years, not only religious pacifists but also mainstream members of society embraced peace advocacy. In 1902 textbook publisher Edwin Ginn began publication of an International Library to advance knowledge about peace and in 1910, he established the International School of Peace that became the World Peace Foundation. Andrew Carnegie, who provided considerable support for building the Peace Palace at The Hague, created the Carnegie Endowment for International Peace to promote international law and understanding and to study the causes and effect of war (see Stomfay-Stitz, 1993). Another significant illustration of peace concern was the establishment of the Nobel Peace Prize in 1901.

This time also marks the beginning of a peace education movement that was embraced by peace activists and teachers, especially women educators.

A major development for peace education was the founding of the American School Peace League (ASPL) in 1908 by Fannie Fern Andrews, a former public school teacher (Stomfay-Stitz, 1993; Zeiger, 2000). Unlike other peace groups, the ASPL focused entirely on education. This organization for teachers, high school students, teacher educators, and the public aimed "to promote, through the schools and the educational public of America, the interests of international justice and fraternity" (Crum, 1953, p. 51). By 1913 "the League had 37 state branches and was supported by the National Education Association (NEA), the National Society of School Superintendents, and the U.S. Commissioner of Education" (Osborne, 1985, p. 35).

The ASPL brought its issues to the attention of many state and county teachers' associations and the NEA (Crum, 1953, p. 52). One interest was the creation and commemoration of Peace Day to mark the beginning of the first Hague Peace Conference. Another focus was antimilitarism, especially male-oriented glorification of war (Zeiger, 2000, p. 58). The ASPL and other peace groups fought against military training in schools and were successful in nearly every state that tried to implement military drills for boys in physical education (Zeiger, 2003, p. 167). "The transformation of school curricula from a war to a peace orientation was as the heart of their work with concern about the effect of militarism on schools and children" (Zeiger, 2000, p. 56).

A noteworthy outcome of the League's work was the 1914 publication of *A Course of Study in Good Will*, a 400-page curriculum guide for elementary and junior high children. Children in younger grades were instructed in conflict resolution, how to be respectful to others, and how to become peacemakers. Older children learned about a "human brotherhood" and international relations. Other features of this curriculum include themes of diversity and tolerance through readings from Western and non-Western sources, the study of men and women who had "a selfless dedication to the common good" (e.g., Clara Barton, Louis Pasteur, Florence Nightingale), and concern for the natural environment and kindness to animals. Moreover, this curriculum "opened up roles in the curriculum for women and people of color" as well as immigrants (Zeiger, 2000, pp. 55–61). The ASPL's curriculum was prescient in its approach that is in keeping with current peace education curricula that highlight peace role models. It also emphasized diversity and tolerance by respecting difference and showed that "interdependence must be essential to peace" (Zeiger, 2000, p. 60).

Still, "this certainly was no radical curriculum" but focused on "values of obedience, law, and deference to authority... and harmony...." Moreover, "nowhere in the curriculum did the authors make room for heroes of dissent, the unruly or the civilly disobedient—no William Lloyd Garrison, no Henry David Thoreau, no fugitive slaves, no anti-imperialists" (Zeiger, 2000, p. 62). Also, these peace educators believed in international solutions to prevent war, but did not go so far as to renounce war unconditionally or see the need to join alliances with socialists and trade unionists who advocated a general strike in response to the outbreak of war (Osborne, 1985, pp. 35–36).

Despite the desire for some members to have the ASPL identify with pacifists and protest the Untied State's entrance into World War I, Andrews, who was head of the organization, unilaterally announced that the ASPL fully supported the war. Correspondingly, the second edition of the *Good Will* curriculum came out in 1918 with a new title: *A Course in Citizenship and Patriotism.* Still teaching about conflict resolution and peacemakers, this version no longer taught that war itself was "immorality," but it was the actions of Germany, such as its "invasion of an innocent nation," that embodied immoral action. The revised edition also adopted the "feverishly patriotic language of Anglo-American nationalism" (Zeiger, 2000, pp. 64, 65).

Then again, peace educators including Andrews herself were under "constant suspicion, and often direct attack, as subversive and unpatriotic" (Osborne, 1985, p. 39). In many school districts, teachers were forced to take loyalty oaths and it became "not even permissible to remain neutral or silently critical: Teachers were expected to be active supporters and military boosters." A well-known example was Mary McDowell, a Quaker teacher in the New York public schools, who was tried and fired in 1918 "for conduct unbecoming a teacher" (Zeiger, 2003, p. 167). At the outbreak of the war, it can be said that peace movements were "swimming against the tide" and that the peace education movement experienced failure because the "the patriotism and nationalism that the schools were designed to provide in the first place proved to be far stronger than any attempts to teach international goodwill" (Osborne, 1985, pp. 36–37).

In the years following World War I, the impulse for peace could be discerned via the formation of the League of Nations—an organization for international understanding and curtailment of militarism—which was important to many U.S. peace advocates even when the United States refused to join it. Also following this war, novels and later films that showed the horror of war were well received by the public and peace movements continued to attract membership. Peace education efforts in the United States resumed after World War I "though at only a fraction of its former scale" (Osborne, 1985, p. 37). The peace education work that continued had two foci: diminishment of militarism in schools and curriculum as well as international friendship.

Progressive educators in the years between the world wars objected to authoritarian instruction that impeded critical thinking and, as in earlier times, opposed military training in schools often brought in through physical education (Stomfay-Stitz, 1993, p. 119). A Committee on Militarism in Education was formed to fight against the establishment of compulsory military training in colleagues and high schools (Osborne, 1985, p. 38). John Dewey, who also objected to militarism in schools, questioned textbooks that expressed a "militant nationalism" and instead wanted curriculum to foster "feelings of respect and friendliness for other nations and peoples of the world" (Howlett,

1982, 440, 441). Various curriculum projects of the time emphasized world citizenship and understanding. Among these were: a textbook, *Adventures in Citizenship: Literature for Character* (1928); the NEA Yearbook *Social Change and Education* (1935) that taught about human rights; *The Story of Nations* (1934) which focused on the importance of peace; and, *Educating for Peace* (1940) contained various curriculum units which examined militarism and promoted world peace. The theme of international understanding was highlighted in the 1937 *Yearbook of the National Society for the Study of Education* (Osborne, 1985, pp. 38–39). Additionally, several religious groups in that era published peace curriculum with an international perspective including the Society of Friends (Quakers) and the Jewish Peace Fellowship (Stomfay-Stitz, 1993, pp. 79–80, 107, 109–113).

Any optimism for a world without war diminished by the mid-1930s as nations revealed their imperialistic intentions and war preparations. During the era of World War II, peace movements in the United States faced harsh realities and lost momentum (Hermann, 1992, p. 888). It became especially difficult to support peace education when it was considered "subversive" and peace educators thought of as "un-American" (Tudball, 2003, p. 21). However, a minority of peace activists continued to be "absolute pacifists" (Hermann, 1992, p. 887) who became conscientious objectors (often because of their religious backgrounds), serving on farms and in hospitals when war came (Hermann, 1992, p. 887; Mascari, 2006).

The period immediately following World War II became a crucial era for major peace initiatives and education for nonviolence as the world responded to the experiences of battle, genocide, and atomic warfare. Thus the United States joined the United Nations, established in October 1945 with the rationale to:

> Save succeeding generations from the scourge of war, to reaffirm faith in the...dignity and worth of the human person [and] in the equal rights of men and women, to establish conditions under which justice and respect for the obligations arising from treaties and other sources of international law can be maintained, and to promote social progress and better standards of life in larger freedom. (Preamble, *United Nations Charter*, 1945).

In November 1945, a conference convened to intentionally establish a vehicle to promote a culture of peace, to establish the "intellectual and moral solidarity of mankind." The work of this conference became the formation of UNESCO—the United Nations Educational, Scientific and Cultural Organization. UNESCO was charged with:

> ...promoting collaboration among nations through education, science and culture in order to further universal respect for justice, for the rule

of law and for the human rights and fundamental freedoms which are affirmed for the peoples of the world, without distinction of race, sex, language or religion. (Constitution, Article 1, 1945, UNESCO)

UNESCO also developed a global Associated Schools Project Network that focused on studying four themes: "world concerns and the role of the United Nations, education for sustainable development, peace and human rights, and intercultural learning" (Davies, 2008).

Then in 1948, The United Nations adopted the *Universal Declaration of Human Rights* and the General Assembly ordered it to be "disseminated, displayed, read and expounded principally in schools and other educational institutions" (United Nations, 1948) within all countries. A later important UN initiative in 1959, the *Declaration of the Rights of the Child*, focused on nurturing children and defending their rights to security, education, protection from harm, and discrimination—that children should be "brought up in a spirit of understanding, tolerance, friendship among peoples, peace and universal brotherhood." Peace education advocates thereafter had international sanction for aims of their work as well as educational resources (United Nations, 1959).

In the United States during the decade following the formation of the United Nations, there was little emphasis on curricula specifically called peace education. But nonetheless, the field continued to develop materials emphasizing the interdependence of nations and value of peace for the welfare of individuals and the planet. One trend was the development of global education in the social studies field for "preparing students for citizenship in a global age" and "international cooperation for the common good" (Stomfay-Stitz, 1993, p. 168). Another direction, nonviolent conflict resolution, did not become a feature of schooling in the 1940s and early 1950s, but later became a theme in peace education during the time of the Civil Rights era. With inspiring examples of Gandhi's and Martin Luther King Jr.'s non-violent social activism, peace educators began to focus not only on the goal of peace, but on the strategies to bring about a peaceful society and world (Stomfay-Stitz, p. 168). Even through the cold war years saw the formation of international peace movements and peace protests against atomic testing and warfare, in the United States the marking of peace advocates as subversives that began during World War II "continued through the 1950s, during the years of communist witch-hunts and McCarthyism" (Tudball, 2003, p. 21).

The 1960s and the 1970s were decades in which people organized for peace with marches, peace protests, and civil disobedience. There were intensive efforts to end both the racist violence against peoples in American society and the United States' wars in Viet Nam, Laos, and Cambodia. These peace movements encountered extreme hostility, despite their eventual achievements (see DeBenedetti, 1980; Wittner, 1984). In response, "peace education in the sixties may have been submerged and visible only at brief moments or perhaps merged with world affairs or citizenship education—a reflection of prevailing trends" (Stomfay-Stitz, 1993, pp. 182–183).

The idea of intentionally educating children to work for a peaceful world gained ground in the early 1970s. Maria Montessori's fervent advocacy for peace in education became better known, not only because of the growing popularity of Montessori schools but through the U.S. 1972 edition of her book, *Education and Peace*, originally published in Europe in 1949. Others signs of a peace education renaissance in this decade was the publication of *Education for Peace* by the Association for Curriculum Development and Supervision, the *Handbook on Peace Education* published in 1974, and the formation of the Peace Education Network (Stomfay-Stitz, 1993, pp. 200, 202, 205). This network allowed U.S. peace educators in elementary and secondary schools to "share and enrich their respective efforts, work toward defining and systematizing the young field, and encourage its introduction into schools" (Reardon, 1988, p. 7).

Peace curriculum in the 1970s broadened its focus. The study of global independence increasingly became part of the social studies curriculum (Hicks, 2003, p. 267), leading to a planetary perspective (Stomfay-Stitz, 1993, p. 207). And, setting the stage with the creation of "Earth Day in 1970, several conferences sponsored by the United Nations and other international organizations declared the crucial need for a value-based environmental education to educate about interdependence, change behaviors, and stimulate activism" (Gough, 2006, p. 73); however, in these years, environmental education curricula stayed more of a grassroots effort than part of school curriculum (Postma, 2006, pp. 4–5). Finally, another important influence on peace education was Freire's 1973 book, *Pedagogy of the Oppressed*, which helped peace educators to focus on development and human rights education (Reardon, 1988, p. 6).

The resurgence of peace education in the 1970s also must be understood in light of the growth of feminist movement. As the peace education movement began to focus on the dynamics of building peace, several primary concerns of feminism—awareness of oppression, honoring historical contributions of women, and the importance of caring—provided important themes for education. The intertwining of peace education and the women's movement seemed a natural connection to feminist peace educators who called for examination of militarism and war's effect on women and children, the study of women who have been exemplary role models for peace, and for changing societal metaphors of militarism toward those that reflect human relationships. These formative ideas about the linkage between feminism and peace education would continue to develop in the next decades (see Brocke-Utne, 1985; Boulding, 1995; Noddings, 2008; Reardon, 1988).

During the decades of the 1980s and 1990s, peace education truly became a recognized area of scholarship with the publication of many conceptual and practice-oriented books and journals, proliferation of peace programs in universities, and numerous Web sites developed by peace organizations that introduced themes of peace education and provided curriculum examples (see Stomfay-Stitz, 2008). Peacebuilding—to create a culture of peace in class-rooms and schools (Harris & Morrison, 2003)—particularly thrived in Montessori schools and some public and private schools; peacemaking—to learn how to resolve conflicts peacefully—received the endorsement of many public school districts concerned about violence in students' lives (Harris, 1990, p. 254). Global education continued to be a direction of peace education—aided by technology that allowed sharing of experiences and data by children and adults throughout the world. Moreover, the environmental justice movement focusing on "connections between human/civil rights and environmental issues" began in the mid 1980s (Li, 2006, p. 2464) and "fostered the language of sustainable development" and influenced environmental education curriculum (Postma, 2006, pp. 6–8).

For teachers who want to become peace educators in the 21st century, there is a multitude of resources. Scholars and practitioners have formed organizations, sponsored conferences, and have written numerous books on the theory and practice of peace education as well as the related disciplines of ecological, global, human rights, and conflict resolution education. Several journals publish conceptual and practice-based accounts of peace education and peace education initiatives as well as ecojustice education; these include: *Peace and Change: A Journal of Peace Research, Journal of Conflict Resolution, Journal of Peace Research*, the *Journal of Peace Education, Journal of Environmental Education, Canadian Journal of Environmental Education*, and *Green Teacher*. Moreover, there are many Web sites for peace education theory and curriculum such as those created by Montessori educators, UNESCO, the Global Campaign for Peace Education (GCPE), and the *Encyclopedia of Peace Education*.

Peace education currently is a vibrant, inspirational, and growing field of study. Notwithstanding, awareness of the current vitality of this field must be tempered with recognition that "peace education has not really taken hold in school systems around the world" (Harris, 2008, p. 5). There have been few grand scale attempts to envision or create peaceful schools which cultivate relationship rather than competition, and oftentimes this curricular orientation is ignored or neglected by conventional school systems and teacher education programs.

Beliefs and Practices: Learners and Teachers

In "Envisioning Peace," educators hold several assumptions about human nature and learners: that "all people have the capacity or potential for individual peacefulness, this capacity can be developed as a consequence of social learning processes," and educational experiences can be designed "to achieve increased individual peacefulness among all or most students" (Sommerfelt & Vambhein, 2008, p. 80). Peace educators believe in students' natural goodness and that children can be socialized to become peaceful and to value peace. Ultimately, they hope to "motivate students to value nonviolence" and to "seek nonviolent means for dealing with [potentially violent] situations" (Harris, 1990, p. 269).

As peace education's goal is to create a world in which people can curb aggression, behave cooperatively, and solve conflicts without violence (Sommerfelt & Vambhein, 2008, pp. 82, 80), individuals need to attain peacefulness within themselves—corresponding to "Gandhi's concept of 'ahimsa', where a non-violent mind is the basis for non-violent actions" (Sommerfelt & Vambhein, 2008, p. 80). As follows, teachers need to attend to their own and to children's development of peacefulness and inner peace (Carter, 2004; Harris, 2004a).

To be peace educators, teachers need to have a deep understanding of peace—not only to teach *about* peace but to become role models who embody the attributes of peace. Advocates describe the qualities held and exemplified by peace educators as spiritual in nature, defining spirituality as encompassing "love and compassion, patience, tolerance, forgiveness, contentment, a sense of responsibility, a sense of harmony" (Whang & Nash, 2005, p. 89). Teachers must competently nurture and compassionately care for students and show how conflicts can be resolved justly and without anger. That is not to say that teachers must strive to be perfect models for whom peace is easy; they also need to cultivate authentic relationships with students and share their own struggles to live peaceably.

An essential premise of peace education is that children must be cherished and respected. Ideally, this process begins at home and continues into the school, but when children have known aggression or violence, they especially need an experience of peace and hope in their schools (Harris, 1996, p. 63). To encourage "children to be peaceful within themselves, with others, and in the environment," educators must: "respect the intrinsic nature of each child, prepare learning environments to meet the physical, intellectual, emotional, and spiritual needs of the children, and provide sensitive, knowledgeable adults to guide the process" (McFarland, 2004, p. 24). Advocates note the importance of peace education in the early years "to reach children before they even begin to develop the prejudices and stereotypes" (Schimmel, 2009, p. 65). Further, they believe that young children "have come to recognize that peace is a preferred state of being" and that "it is desirable to resolve conflicts in a manner beneficial to all parties" (Crawford, 2005, p. 321).

Yet, despite their allegiance to a philosophical tradition rooted in beliefs about human goodness and humans' "true identity" of nonviolence (Synott, 2005, p. 9), peace educators are acutely aware of humankind's propensity toward conflict and violence. They are sensitive to the horrors of violence and feel a constant urgency to counter violence in the lives of children, teach them to solve conflicts peacefully, and help them to become peaceful people. And, they believe that without intentional enculturation into the ways of peace, young people can be socialized into violence and accept that violence is innate (Weigert, 1989, p. 40).

For educators to "create in children's minds a desire to learn how nonviolence can provide the basis for a just and sustainable future" (Galtung, 1976 in Harris & Morrison, 2003, p. 11), they must challenge students' acceptance of violence in their lives, in their school, and in this world. When students believe that violence is a natural way of being or an innate part of human nature, "the first pedagogical task is to help them to see that there is a logical flaw in the reasoning of the statement" (Weigert, 1989, p. 40). Challenging learners' beliefs does not take place in a didactic fashion, but through democratic approaches that encourage students to share their ideas. "Meaningful educational dialogues depend on teachers' humility" and teachers should acknowledge that the complex issues of peace, war, and ecology seldom elicit unmistakable answers (Li, 2006, pp. 2466–2467). And so, educators may share their values and insights about peace and violence for critical examination by the students rather than pretending to be neutral (Harris, 1990; Reardon, 1988). As well, teachers need to help children feel comfortable to talk about the violence they encounter in their lives and help them to heal from their hurtful experiences (Harris, 1996; Morris, Taylor, & Wilson, 2000).

Peace education begins with children's awareness of peace for their own needs and interests and expanding to consciousness of the value of peace in all situations. This occurs as children gain "a working understanding of the complex topics of peace and conflict" (Crawford, 2005, p. 321). Eventually, older students are capable of an increasingly sophisticated grasp of conflict resolution processes (Johnson & Johnson, 2005) and a critical understanding of conflict and structural violence as well as their own agency (see Bajaj, 2008). A "peace pedagogy requires teachers to establish a continuous process of questioning, challenging, acting, and reflecting upon behaviors conducive to peace" by challenging learners "to see the world in new ways and hence creates cognitive dissonance in [their] minds" (Harris, 1990, p. 269). As in other curricular cultures in which teachers act as questioners, peace educators must obtain academic breadth in subject areas that support the study of human rights, peacemaking, peacebuilding, and environmental sustainability.

In "Envisioning Peace," its foremost vision of "ending the violent nature of our existence" influences educators' beliefs about their missions, responsibilities, and the process of educating children. People who become peace educators believe that violence is avoidable and have a passionate dedication to non-violence and human rights. They need to hold a "deep and motivating belief in the universal and fundamental worth of the human person," to be "committed to democratic values and skilled in democratic practice," and to affirm the core values of "environmental sustainability, cultural diversity, human solidarity, social responsibility, and gender equity" (Reardon, 1999, pp. 12–14). Moreover, peace educators must be able to deal with an ongoing tension or ambiguity as they balance their grim awareness of violence and war with the hopefulness of working for peace.

Peace educators' obligations lead them to take moral and courageous stands as human beings and as educators:

> They should be citizens who support and defend social justice, reject politically correct discourses that promote individual and structural hypocrisy, who courageously dedicate their talents, time and resources to eradicate all forms of oppression, and who labor to build ethically diverse communities devoid of fear, tension and suspicion. They should be agents of peaceful coexistence who validate others' narratives of suffering, assume ownership of their group's actions towards other groups, and who genuinely seek to develop empathy, trust, and other peaceful dispositions in their work and social interactions. They should respect life and the dignity of each human being without discrimination and prejudice. (Ndura-Oudraogo, 2008, p. 47)

Thus, for some peace educators, teaching peace and nonviolence is an extension of their agency and their personal identities as activists (Joseph & Duss, 2009, p. 204).

Although people may choose to be peace educators because of their calling—to bring about "the social, political and economic transformation that would comprise a culture of peace" (Reardon, 1999, p. 8)—this vocation may demand a process of self-development in which individuals become self-aware and critically sensitive to the needs of communities, cultures, and the environment. Montessori believed that teachers themselves should go through "an inner, spiritual preparation" to fully serve children and to become peace educators (McFarland, 1999). Becoming an advocate for peace therefore may be viewed as a process, not only of becoming a peace educator but of the moral, spiritual, and political development of teachers themselves.

Beliefs and Practices: Content and Context

The curricular content of "Envisioning Peace" is holistic, multidisciplinary, and interdisciplinary across wide bodies of subject areas. The fields of history and science are fundamental to this curricular culture but educators also find resources from the humanities (literature, poetry, drama, and art) and from social sciences (geography, political science, and international studies). And although it is difficult to imagine an entire mathematics curriculum taught within peace education, nevertheless, this subject provides an important knowledge base for the studies of political, economic, and environmental issues of war, peace, and human rights. Still, teachers of any subject area can support peace education by educating for peacemaking and peacebuilding in their classrooms.

Peace education literature describes content as composed of five interconnected and sometimes overlapping curricula (Haavelsrud, 2008; Joseph & Efron, 2005; Morrison, 2002):

- Peace Studies
- Human Rights Education
- Global Education
- Environmental Education
- Conflict Resolution

Each has a wealth of curriculum materials and could be considered a separate area, however, peace education may need to include all of these components to offer learners the opportunity for a deep understanding of peace in their lives and in the world.

Peace Studies

Peace studies aims to cultivate a deeply emotional understanding of peace and appreciation for the people and actions that build peace. This curriculum has been the historically focused on "teaching *for* peace and educating *about* peace" (Brock-Utne, 2009, p. 213). Yet, at the same time, peace studies attempts to stimulate abhorrence of violence as the result of critical examination of militarism and the dangers and experiences of war.

Teaching about peace includes exploring the meaning of inner peace and peace in this world through discussions, written reflections, and artistic representations (dela Torre, 2008). For example, an assignment for a high-school humanities class was asking students to be nonviolent for 24 hours and to reflect on their experiences (Joseph & Duss, 2009). Teachers also encourage students to imagine a peaceful classroom and school and what it would take to create such environments. Peace studies curriculum includes historical accounts, literature, and film to provide stories of how people have worked for peace as well as readings on nonviolence (see Carter & Clay-Robinson, 2009; McCarthy, 2002). In all of the above examples, teachers encourage students to engage in dialogue about the meaning of peace rather than use didactic instruction (see Galtung, 2008).

To provide opportunities for students to experience peace through their emotions and imagination, this curriculum includes meditation so that students may experience peace within themselves and engage in "deeper reflection" (Sommerfelt & Vambhein, 2008, p. 82). Teachers also have employed art and music as a way of cultivating children's commitment to peace, for instance, by participating in peace choirs and designing peace logos. Educators have encouraged the development of peace pledges in which children and teachers promise to make peace through nonviolence, kindness, and respect for others and the environment (Joseph & Duss, 2009).

Peace studies curriculum (especially for older children) likewise includes critical thinking about acts and patterns of violence. Students study images and metaphors of violence in media and culture. They investigate the reasons for why wars start, what they accomplish, and what could have been alternatives to war (Joseph & Duss, 2009). They find information about the number of wars "raging in the world," child soldiers, children who have died in war, and children's health issues because of exposure to chemicals (Soto, 2005, pp. 92–93). Students also research terrorism, gender violence and genocide—expressing their learning through projects and creative expressions (Joseph & Duss, 2009). Such curriculum mirrors Montessori's belief that to bring about peace, people need to understand "the complex phenomenon" of war and to develop "a science of peace" so that they can "understand events" and not feel "overwhelmed" (Montessori, 1949/1972 pp. 73, 34).

Human Rights Education

Human rights education, a crucial component of "Envisioning Peace," cultivates critical understanding of the roots of conflict. This field of peace education incorporates the content of critical pedagogy and critical multicultural education so that students study, domination, oppression, structural and symbolic violence, and power within communities, nations, and the world (Bajaj, 2008; Jennings, 2009). It also informs students about human rights as "standards that outline the conditions necessary for people to live in full dignity" (Jennings, 2009, p. 66) and helps them to investigate the denial of rights and ways to address injustice (Tibbetts, 2002). But despite a multitude of resources including Amnesty International, Project Human Rights Education, and UNESCO, human rights education often is a neglected element of peace education (Jennings, 2009) and "many students and teachers do not know about human rights or international instruments that protect human rights" (Suárez, 2007, p. 59).

Peace educators argue that children and adolescents need a deep foundation of human rights education for which "the United Nations provides the norms and standards for the pursuit and protection of the fundamental rights of all people (Reardon, 1988, p. 39). These rights are sanctioned in: *The Universal Declaration of Human Rights, The Convention on the Rights of the Child, The International Covenant on Civil and Political Rights, The International Covenant on Civil and Political Rights, Convention on the Elimination of All Forms of Discrimination Against Women, International Convention on the Elimination of All Forms of Racial Discrimination,* and *Convention on the*

Prevention and Punishment of the Crime of Genocide. Awareness of these declarations cannot be taught by merely reading a paragraph in a textbook or by a one-time lesson; rather, the principles of these documents need to be infused throughout the curriculum and become the basis of interdisciplinary inquiry and commitment (Suárez, 2007, pp. 59–61). Knowledge of human rights permits students to "recognize the human rights dimensions" to problems and conflicts and to consider "potential responses" including their own roles as advocates (Tibbitts, 2002, p. 165).

Through current news events, documentaries, films, and literature, this curriculum has many sources for helping students to realize denial of and advocacy for human rights. Educators can infuse "developmentally appropriate" historical and contemporary accounts across the curriculum to examine injustice (Crawford, 2005; Lucas, 2009). When possible, the curriculum needs to include local dimensions. For instance, the study of Japanese internment camps and forced removal of Native American children to boarding schools can be documented by historical resources as well as by community members who can speak to how such eradication of rights affected them or their families. Topics that demonstrate denial of human rights and injustice stemming from the family experiences of the students should especially be considered to help students to develop an understanding of international human rights (Bajaj, 2008). As well, this curriculum can explore the rights of children and adolescents within the context of home, peer groups, school, and society so that students know that human rights pertain to their own lives.

Global Education

Global education focuses on multicultural understanding, international relationships, and peaceful coexistence and develops a knowledge base to explore world-wide social, political, and economic problems such as "unfair trade relations, racial discrimination, terrorism, militarization, and environmental degradation" (dela Torre, 2008, p. 6). Furthermore, global education allows schools "to help students to understand how cultural, national, regional, and global identifications are interrelated, complex, and evolving" (Banks, 2009, p.108).

This field of peace education holds a number of ethical principles: "humans are equal regardless of identity or status"; "human behavior is culturally and not racially determined"; "all humans posses basic rights" but have "world-centered obligations" and "all individuals must actively engage in meeting human needs"; "humans need to establish a worldwide civic culture" and have "a caring and ethical relationship to the land and water and all living creatures and plants" (Kirkwood, 2001, pp. 10–11; Kirman, 2003, p. 94). Global education curriculum is based on recognizing and respecting essential values: the "oneness" or "connectedness" of humankind," "interdependence of all people within a global system," "respect for the environment," appreciation of diverse cultures and religions, and "multiple perspectives—a belief in the educative value of considering differing views on any issue" (Pike, 2000, p. 65; dela Torre, 2008, p. 6).

Based on the metaphor of a global village, global education involves study of and participation in the world community, interdependency, and "improving the quality of life" for all humans and the Earth (Hendrix, 1998, p. 305). Historically, the learning outcomes for global education have been "perspective consciousness," "knowledge of world conditions," "cross-cultural awareness of the world's diverse value systems and societal frameworks," understanding of "global system dynamics," and "knowledge of choices or alternatives to current management patterns" (Cook, 2008, p. 894).

Global education especially calls for the study of geography so that students can visualize human commonalties as well as world problems rather than trying to only understand abstractions. This subject is a building block as it offers: "breadth (everything happens somewhere and is affected by location); universality (whatever happens affects the earth in large or small ways); and opportunities for integration with other disciplines" (Kirman, 2003, p. 94). For example, beginning with geography and then involving other subject areas, students can investigate why people become refugees and why displacement of populations is a global, environmental, and human rights issue. Geography also allows connections to students' own histories as children study the migrations of families throughout the world and learn about the reasons why migration was chosen or forced upon people.

Global education provides other opportunities for multidisciplinary curriculum. Students can learn about universally held human values through literature, poetry, art, drama, music, and dance. Students need to learn the history, experiences, and viewpoints of people in various countries to permit empathic understanding of human rights issues involved in conflict (Langager, 2009). The subjects of science, mathematics, and social science allow for in-depth investigations of world problems, for instance, "to gather statistics from international sources on conditions such as the distribution of food, calorie intake, and child mortality" (Brock-Utne, 2000, p. 134).

Environmental Education

As in other areas of peace education, environmental education creates an interdisciplinary curriculum undergirded by ethical principles. To teach environmental education as depicted in this curricular culture, peace educators strive to develop their students' "environmental consciousness and identity" which includes both "eradication of views that reproduce violence" as well as "respect for all forms of life" (Morris, 2002, p. 580; Sauvé, 1996, p. 25). Although environmental education often is considered a distinct curriculum within peace education, it best can be understood by depicting its relationship to peace studies, global, and human rights education.

As in peace studies, this curriculum provides opportunities to cultivate emotional and aesthetic understanding, in this case, by giving children "a conscious connection to place" to develop an ecological identity (Pelo, 2009, p. 30). It is also hoped that students will experience "a sense of wonder"—"the sheer delight in being alive in a beautiful, mysterious, bountiful world" (Orr, 1992, p. 86). But appreciation and sense of wonder is not an end in itself but a bridge to environmental literacy, critical inquiry, and commitment (Li, 2006, p. 2466).

The parallel with global education is environmental education's ecological perspective that links the needs of individuals to those of the planet (Selby, 1999, p. 137). It also includes "a sustaining ethical commitment to care for the future generations: and to plan for sustainable development "to restrain human greed and selfishness" (Li, 2006, p. 2465). Environmental peace educators are aware that "the ecological crisis is the paramount issue that faces all of humanity" (Bowers, 2004, p. 48). They perceive at the root of environmental calamity "a cultural crisis—a direct outcome of the dominant western mechanistic worldview with its … scientific notions of separation and domination" (Selby, 2000, p. 88). A global perspective's themes of interdependence and unity—among humans and between humans and nature—counteract modernist concepts.

Above all, environmental education within "Envisioning Peace" stems from a critical pedagogy and human rights perspective within the environmental or ecojustice movement (Mikel, 2010) which "vigorously strives to replace the shortsighted not-in-my-backyard (NIMBY) mentality with a more inclusive not-in-any-one's-backyard (NIABY) ethical endeavor" (Li, 2006, p. 2465). It also "strives to question and rectify the existing interrelated economic, political, and legal systems which fail to recognize the intricate connections between human rights/civil rights and environmental issues" (Li, 2006, p. 2464). As in human rights education, educators draw from and use "as a heuristic" sanctioned international documents such as *The Earth Charter* "with its core principles of the recognition of the importance and value of all forms of life" (Corcoran, 2004, 113). Further, this curriculum has to be a catalyst for questioning and challenging "dominant socio-economic systems" (Bowers, 2004, p. 56; Sauvé, 1996, p. 24). To facilitate such transformative learning, environmental educators encourage students' critical and systemic thinking, belief in the possibility of change, and agency to effect change (Jucker, 2004, pp. 21–22).

The curriculum of environmental peace education is theme-based and experiential. Within interdisciplinary units and year-long studies, students explore the connections between humans and the environment, global interdependency, and environmental degradation, and the conditions of human and non-human life (Crewdson & Perlmutter, 2003; Selby, 2000). Learning activities may include simulations, such as students playing roles that represent perspectives of people who are affected by global warming (Bigelow, 2009, pp. 21–22). But more often, educators seek real-life activities in which students work in communities to learn the impact of human activity on the environment, to deepen their understanding of scientific principles, and to be aware of their own agency through ecological stewardship projects.

Environmental educators also focus on developing ecological communities within schools. Creating a school as a basis for serious environmental education can involve children, parents, and teachers learning about native plants as well as creating and sustaining gardens throughout school grounds; vegetables could also be raised in school gardens so that students learn the growing process and enjoy the results (Mikel, 2009). So, too, could the school community learn about ecology by conducting an "audit" of energy use and waste and working to "overturn a culture of unthinking wastefulness and energy consumption" (Selby, 2000, p. 93). But the bigger picture of a school's environmental efforts has far greater meaning than specific activities in themselves:

> Schools aspiring to a darker shade of green would seek to inform their organization, relationships, and processes of change with basic ecological principles: strength in diversity; continuous movement and fluctuations; energy flows, cycles, and undulations; countless forms of partnership; co-evolution through the processes of creation and mutual adaptation. (Selby, 2000, p. 91)

Moreover, environmental peace educators would strive to establish schools "in which care for others and the earth becomes the matrix in which adults and children live" with the aim of "encouraging students' expression of care" (Smith, 2004, p. 91).

Conflict Resolution Education

As a response to school violence, conflict resolution education is the most widely used form of peace education in the United States. It emphasizes peacemaking skills to "resolve conflicts in constructive and nonviolent ways" (Johnson & Johnson, 2005, p. 288) and helping students to be able to see others' perspective and control anger. The underlying assumption of the conflict resolution field is that peacemaking involves building skills, developing "a craft, a set of disciplines to be learned" (Boulding, 1988, p. 146).

This area of peace education teaches "the principles of conflict resolution" and how to follow "a problem-solving process" (Garner, 2008). Specifically, students are taught: communication skills, interpersonal and small group skills, negotiation, consensus decision-making, collaboration, anger management, problem solving, perspective taking, creative thinking, and mediation (Johnson & Johnson, 2005). An important feature of many conflict resolution programs is peer mediation to train students to become mediators. Conflict resolution skills must be built over the long term as "it takes considerable practice to master the cooperation, controversy, and peacemaker procedures at a level where they are automatically used without conscious thought or planning" (Johnson & Johnson, 2005, p. 290). Although classroom teachers may individually teach conflict resolution skills in their classrooms or as a separate course, the need for an entire school to commit to helping all of its students learn how to solve conflicts peacefully is apparent, as students interact with others throughout the day.

Oftentimes, conflict resolution education has been introduced into schools as violence reduction programs. Less frequently, conflict resolution education has been integrated into the academic curriculum. Teachers of younger children illustrate peaceful conflict resolution through fiction, nonfiction, and poetry (Carter & Clay-Robison, 2009; Roberts, 2005); secondary teachers help students to consider the violent effects of communication failures via examples in classical and contemporary works of drama and fiction. In history and social studies classes, students can study processes by which nations and groups work out conflicts through examples from history and current events (Johnson & Johnson, 2005; Joseph & Duss, 2009; Tudball, 2003).

Montessori education regularly incorporates conflict resolution into the context and curriculum of the classroom. Common to the Montessori classroom are peace centers or tables for students to provide "a quiet, sanctioned place for frustrated participants to cool off individually and then come together to work out differences collectively." Students in Montessori schools are encouraged to role play by using puppets to "verbalize their feelings to one another without having a direct confrontation" and to practice social skills. Children also are taught how to use "visual cue or mnemonic activity to help them remember steps in conflict resolution." Another important feature of these classrooms is a peace book, "a type of collaborative journal that is kept on the peace table and serves as a record of conflicts and resolutions between pairs of children" created in pictures and words. The peace book not only helps children to work together to solve their problems, it can be shared and help other children work out their disputes (Crawford, 2005, pp. 324, 326, 327).

Another educational effort to integrate conflict resolution into curricular content has been the work of Educators for Social Responsibility (ESR), in particular, its peaceable classroom model which focuses on cooperation, communication, appreciation for diversity, the healthy expression of feelings, responsible decision making, and conflict resolution. ESR offers lesson plans from pre-kindergarten through high school—from managing conflict to understanding the nature of conflict (http://esrnational.org/).

§

Although peace educators affirm that these five components of peace education together provide a deep understanding of peace, they realize that a multi-dimensional curricular content would be insufficient unless they continually address context—taking heed of the lived experience of students in classrooms and schools. "The objective then becomes one of not just teaching peace, but ultimately of transforming the classroom into a peaceful learning environment" (Crawford, 2005, p. 322) to create a culture of peace.

Peace education needs to be taught so that students understand *and* feel peace by experiencing "authentic teacher modeling" and an environment where they "feel safe and supported in their efforts to work cooperatively and resolve conflicts in a harmonious manner." Students "deserve to learn about [peace education]...in a way in which the words that they hear about peace corresponds fully with the behaviors, tone, and values that they see represented in their classrooms" (Crawford, 2005, pp. 322, 327). Such classrooms celebrate all diversity, invite collaboration, and feature peaceful transitions (Joseph & Duss, 2009; Miller, 2003).

Peace educators also highlight the need for democratic classrooms (Harris, 1996; Shapiro 2002a) without competition and domination (Brock-Utne, 2000). In democratic classrooms, there are opportunities for "the continual process of seeking others' perspectives and involvement in consensus building" (Joseph & Duss, 2009, p. 191). Also, in such classrooms, teachers can help their students to think about "competitive structures," "develop their own interests" and "acknowledge their pursuits," and "imagine a transformed society" (Brock-Utne, 2000, p. 136).

However, it is difficult to transform students' beliefs if they experience a peaceful classroom in an otherwise hostile setting. Thus it is far better when not just one classroom teacher but a school commits to creating a peaceful environment.

> It is not easy to work for [the goals of peace education] in the normal competitive school system. Even though these goals are frequently proclaimed by formal schooling, the structures of grading and individual achievement and competition do not promote cooperation and self-worth in practice. (Brock-Utne, 2000, p. 136)

Educators therefore must create peaceful schools that run counter to their more typical competitive and conflict-based nature (Danesh 2006; Goldstein 2005; Jeffries 2000) with their cultures of "otherness, conflict, competition, aggression, bullying and violence" (Danesh, 2006, p. 57). In such schools, adults would model peaceful, noncompetitive relationships with each other and create structures that foster respectful relationships even in times of conflict. Schools as caring communities also are welcoming places for families and community members and focus on children's social-emotional well being, building and sustaining relationships, and collaborative decision-making (Battistich, Solomon, Watson, & Schaps, 1997; Brion-Meisels, Brion-Meisels, & Hoffman 2007; Schaps, 2003). Such milieus require profound changes to assumptions about schooling including "the design of the social and physical environment, lines of authority and communication, and expectations about outcomes" (Miller, 2003).

Beliefs and Practices: Curriculum Planning and Evaluation

As the curricular culture of peace education strongly emphasizes the cultivation of values and imagination, the ultimate visions of this curricular culture must guide the curriculum planning process. Thus educators need to ask, what curricular experiences do students need so that they develop the "capacities for care, concern, and commitment" (Reardon, 1988, p. 76) to reject violence and become advocates for peace, human rights, and environmental stewardship? Clearly, individual development and "transformation to a peaceful world" depend upon "a set of skills" (Gervais, 2004)—such as critical thinking and conflict resolution—to be able to analyze social problems, discern cultural influences that promote violence, recognize alternative perspectives, and resolve conflicts respectfully. Furthermore, to learn how to be peace advocates and stewards, students need to have deep content knowledge across the curriculum.

Curriculum planning in this curricular culture depends upon educators' academic expertise and resourcefulness. Teachers have available unit and lesson plans from UNESCO and other peace and environmental organizations, but as the curricular content of "Envisioning Peace" is multidimensional and interdisciplinary, it can best be developed collaboratively among educators who have different academic strengths—especially when planning for curriculum across grade levels and subject areas.

Assessment of learning should reveal complex mastery of knowledge, skills, and values. Educators can evaluate students' understanding of concepts from subject areas and skill development—the ability to resolve conflicts, work collaboratively, and solve problems (Hägglund, 1996, Harris, 2004b; Johnson & Johnson, 2006). However, because peace education involves students' comprehensive investigations—such as causes of war and global environmental problems—as well as their participation in social action and stewardship projects, short-term measurement is inadequate. Instead, portfolios of students' investigations, reflections, and creative expressions can better document authentic learning. Most importantly, assessment must be democratic and noncompetitive; a traditional grading system does not honor the spirit and values of peace education (Weigert, 1989, pp. 45–46).

But, it is not easy or perhaps even possible to assess accomplishment of the ultimate goals of "Envisioning Peace" (Harris, 2004b). Educators can analyze students' reflections and creative works to document consciousness and acquisition of peace values, but overall the "capacities for peacemaking...cannot be limited to the achievement of specific objectives of quantifiable goals" (Reardon, 1988, p. 61) and the "tests and exams normally used in schools are unsuitable for the evaluation of peace education outcomes, because they do not evaluate a state of mind" (Bar-Tal, 2002, p. 34).

There are however, several approaches for evaluating implementation of peace education curricula. One way is to examine school curriculum to assess the quality of students' experiences. Such evaluation could take into consideration to the extent in which curriculum and pedagogy work to foster "critical thinking, emotional insight, creative experience and constructive action, peaceful communities" (Danesh, 2006, pp. 164–165.) Evaluation thus centers on how well teachers and chosen content communicate peace education's themes and values. For example, researchers have developed a continuum for global education to assess the extent that schools emphasize "global social justice over global competitiveness" "tolerance over chauvinism" or "critical thinking" over passive acceptance of information (Mundy & Manion, 2008, p. 945). There also has been significant research on the context of peaceful and caring classrooms demonstrating that students in such environments feel a sense of community, experience social-emotional growth, and develop ethical behaviors (Battistich et al., 1997); such studies serve as examples of how schools committed to peace education can evaluate their cultures. Furthermore, researchers can undertake longitudinal studies to find out if former students become peace advocates and environmental stewards, although such information would not be attainable in the normal course of classroom or school evaluation of curriculum.

Dilemmas of Practice

As is the case of all curricular cultures that challenge ingrained patterns of curriculum, educators' greatest dilemmas can be to figure out how to weave peace education into the fabric of schooling. This is a particularly difficult struggle for a variety of reasons. First, there is apathy or hopelessness about endemic violence experienced in families, communities, and within the world—frequent portrayals of violence in the media lead to numbness rather than outrage. Similarly, there is "public skepticism and resistance to ecological crises" which thwarts efforts for teaching environmental and global in the mainstream curriculum (Li, 2008, p. 2466). Another barrier to acceptance of peace education is school's and society's quick-fix mentality that rejects holistic responses in keeping with an integrated form of peace curriculum (Jeffries, 2000, p. 19). Finally, there is the political reality that peace education "represents an implicit challenge to authority" and "is open to criticism from established interests within society with a vested commitment to the status quo" (Page, 2004, p. 16).

But even when educators can establish peace curriculum in their class-rooms and collaborate with colleagues to develop peace-oriented schools, there still may be ongoing dilemmas that peace educators will encounter:

One quandary for peace educators is how to balance between the dis-heartening reality of violence in students' lives and/or in the world and the optimism for the possibility of peace. To focus on the horrors of oppression, degradation, and violence robs students of hopefulness. But to ignore a criti-cal edge is to pay no heed to the histories of conflict and human rights (Bajaj, 2008). Therefore, to "teach peace as something more than sentimental kitsch is to help students see how inseparable is the dream of peace from construct-ing a more just world" (Shapiro, 2002, p. 46). Certainly, the complex nature of peace education requires peace educators to balance between such dichoto-mies. However, as peace itself is an imprecise ideal, educators need to be com-fortable with ambiguity and embrace the tensions that are at the heart of peace education (Miller, 2003).

Peace educators also need to balance between their seemingly conflicting roles. They need to be role models of peace and fairness who do not conceal their pro-peace ideals and activism. And, they must develop non-didactic democratic pedagogy because they cannot teach critical thinking by pros-elytizing. The conundrum for peace educators is that they cannot attempt to indoctrinate nor can they be disinterested (Reardon, 1988, p. 23). Peace educa-tors have to develop a pedagogy that encourages critical investigations and a multitude of perspectives and yet ensure that students have opportunities to explore how peace efforts can make possible the healing of a violent world.

In addition, the histories that students bring to the classroom and school may create challenges. Although peace education may take place in communi-ties in which children think of war as something quite distant from their lives, others may "carry the heavy yoke of painful historical memories" having either personally experienced or have family members who have been refugees from war, have known genocide, and have lived in cultures with histories of violent inter-ethnic or religious conflicts. When working in classrooms in which stu-dents hold "collectively and deeply entrenched beliefs about the 'other side'," peace education strategies need to be modified. In particular, conflict educa-tion programs need to be expanded because they "focus mainly on individu-als acquisition of conflict resolution skills and on the resolution of historical interpersonal rather than historically rooted collective conflicts...." (Salomon, 2002, p. 38). Peace education taught in communities in which students have known intractable conflicts calls for educators to develop knowledge of the conflicts—whether they stem from experiences of students who have known gang violence or of immigrant students whose families have been members of conflicting groups. Teachers must become especially skillful in cultivating dialogue in the class and may need special training in conflict resolution and reconciliation strategies to deal with sensitive issues and interactions in their classrooms.

Critique

"Envisioning Peace" is a complex curricular orientation that seldom proposes simplistic fixes to the urgent problems that confront humanity and the Earth. Consequently, to do justice to its complexity is an enormous task for peace educators aspiring to create classroom or school-wide curriculum. Because of its depth and scope, peace education offers extensive choices for content knowledge, skill building, and cultivation of advocacy; it holds numerous possibilities for creative, multidisciplinary, and integrated curriculum planning. Still, peace education, "like the notion of peace itself, is a contested concept" and "is open to so many different political interpretations" (Brock-Utne, 2000, p. 132; Danesh, 2006). Scholars of peace education have offered critique either because this multidimensional field is too complex and unfocused or, conversely, because its complexity is not adequately recognized.

By developing peace education as a conceptual umbrella—"intentionally devised to be open to various interpretations and to accommodate various viewpoints" (Brock-Utne, 2000, p. 133)—the field is open to collaborative work for dealing with various problems associated with violence. And yet, some scholars express concern that peace education's interdisciplinary fields of study "have not always come together to form an organic whole" (Hirao, 1987, p. 59) and that there "is a clear need for a theoretical framework of peace that will bring together these divergent—yet interrelated—objects and concepts" (Danesh, 2006, p. 56). Lack of an integral structure for peace education makes it challenging to decide on essential goals and strategies. Only to some extent have scholars addressed fragmentation in cross-disciplinary dialogue about peace, global interdependence, conflict resolution, human rights, and ecojustice—although some call for more conversations about interrelationships and removal of barriers separating thematic areas (see Hicks, 2003; Selby, 1999). In sum, these issues about the nature of peace education continue to be raised as areas of concern.

Nonetheless, peace educators must "understand the complex nature of their endeavors" (Harris & Morrison, 2003, p. 175) for peace education to "effectively address its promise as a field of inquiry and grounded practice" (Bajaj, 2008, p. 138). In previous decades, critique of peace education highlighted the inadequacy of teaching peace merely as the absence of war (Galtung, 1969; Montessori, 1949/1972; Reardon, 1988). In a similar vein, more recent appraisals center on peace educators' failure to integrate critical studies by unproblematically teaching peacemaking and peacebuilding skills (Bajaj, 2008; Gur-Ze'ev, 2001). Scholars maintain that without including critical inquiry or attending to issues of justice in peace education, peace education is ineffective because it leads to "frustration and disillusionment" rather than to "transformative agency" (Bajaj, 2008, p. 139). Similarly, earlier efforts of peace educators who "lacked...either a critical perspective or a critical stance" have been judged to be unsuccessful because when "they had to remain non-controversial, they condemned themselves to ineffectiveness" (Osborne, 1985 p. 37). Peace education thus needs to "ensure that the issues of power are central to collaborative dialogues (Soto, 2005, p. 95) and to "introduce students to issues of asymmetrical power relations, structural violence, and how principles of human rights can inform action amidst such a context" (Bajaj, 2008, p. 139). As in the words of a high school teacher of nonviolence curriculum:

Everyone's always saying, just make peace, and the response is you can have a cold peace where nobody is killing everyone else, but you can still have tremendous injustice and violation of human rights. I tend to think in terms of justice and peace. (Joseph & Duss, 2009, p. 195)

Another point for critique is that peace education is deficient in thoroughly addressing diversity as a social justice issue. For instance, researchers note that when global education teaches "awareness of others," it may instead "foster a them/us mentality" if teachers do not emphasize the themes of "global interdependence and social justice" (Mundy & Manion, 2008; p. 960). Moreover, environmental educators may neglect teaching about environmental injustice and human rights, particularly the exploitation of environments where people live in poverty (McClaren & Houston, 2004; Selby, 2000). A parallel criticism focuses on peace education's failure to consider issues of justice stemming from racism and exclusion of African American viewpoints (Berlowitz, Long, & Jackson, 2006).

The other key critique involves the inherent idealism—even utopianism (Gur-Ze'ev, 2001)—of peace educators' expectations. Even among ardent proponents, including Maria Montessori (1949/1972), concerns have been expressed about naïveté in light of horrific conditions:

I am continually astounded and dismayed by the persistence of murderous violence in the world. Humanity seems to be trapped in a deepening spiral of hatred, vengeance, and militarism that will ultimately lead to the horrible destruction of life on this planet. (Miller, 2003)

The notion that peace is possible is currently being challenged across the glove in [numerous countries]. In the U.S., children and youth are criminalized and pathologized and frequently witness violence. Young children are now exposed to a world where war and conflict are everyday occurrences. (Soto, 2005, pp. 92–93)

Therefore the enormity of violence puts into perspective peace educators' goal to transform beliefs so that individuals and groups will reject violence and embrace peace and justice, "to turn the unthinkable into mainstream views," and "to jump the barrier between beliefs/awareness and living practice" (Jucker, 2004, p. 20). Likewise, a concern has been raised of the "logic of targeting schoolchildren or individuals instead of adults or communities" as the long-term effects of peace education for children and adolescents are undocumented (Sommers, 2003, p. 173). As well, recognition of violence within school cultures casts a pall on peace educators' hopes. When schools mirror society's "institutionalized race, class and gender biases" (Jeffries, 2000, p. 19) and are scenes of "structural violence" (Galtung, 2008), it becomes even more difficult for peace educators to create transformative experiences for students and uphold their own idealism. But perhaps the most formidable concern relating to idealism is the issue of motivation (Gervais, 2004, p. 210). Even if individuals come to believe in nonviolence and have learned peacemaking skills, will they have the desire and will to become peacemakers and peace advocates? This, of course, is an unanswerable question that peace educators must continually face.

Peace educators have to live with the dichotomy of hope and despair (Harris, 2004a, Miller, 2003), continually facing an existential quandaries about their acute sensitivity to violence and their belief in and hope for peace (Joseph, 2010). To "avoid frustrations about the lack of their direct ability to make the world more peaceful," peace educators must realize:

They sow seeds that may germinate in the future to produce new levels of peace strategies and degrees of consciousness about the problems of violence that plague human existence. In teaching about peace and violence they take one small step towards creating a less violent world, and they should appreciate the importance of that step...Peace educators may not be changing the social structures that support violence, but they are attempting to build a peace consciousness that is a necessary condition for creating a more peaceful world. (Harris, 2004a, p. 27)

Rather than submitting to and perpetuating violence, peace educators need to believe that they must take small steps. Hopefully, their passion for peace and advocacy will sustain them even at times when their transformative visions seem unattainable.

References

Bajaj, M. (2008). "Critical" peace education. In M. Bajaj (Ed.), Encyclopedia of peace education (pp. 135–146). Charlotte, NC: Information Age.

Banks, J. (2009). Human rights, diversity, and citizenship education. Educational Forum, 73(2), 100–110.

Bar-Tal, D. (2002). The elusive nature of peace education. In G. Salomon & B. Nevo (Eds.), Peace education: The concept, principles and practice around the world (pp. 27–36). Mahwah, NJ: Erlbaum.

Barash, D. P., & Webel, C. P. (2009). *Peace and conflict studies* (2nd ed.). Thousand Oaks, CA: Sage.

Battistich, V., Solomon, D., Watson, M., & Schaps, E. (1997). Caring school communities. *Educational Psychologist, 32*(3), 137–151.

Berlowitz, M. J., Long, N. A., & Jackson, E. R. (2006). The exclusion and distortion of African American perspectives in peace education. *Educational Studies, 39*(1), 5–15.

Bigelow, B. (2009). The big one: Teaching about climate change. *Rethinking Schools, 23*(4), 20–29.

Boulding, E. (1988). *Building a global civic culture: Education for an interdependent world.* New York: Teachers College Press.

Boulding, E. (1995). Feminist inventions in the art of peacemaking: A century overview. *Peace & Change, 20*(4), 408–438.

Bowers, C. A. (2004). Revitalizing the commons or an individualized approach to planetary citizenship: The choice before us. *Educational Studies, 36*(1), 45–58.

Brion-Meisels, L., Brion-Meisels, S., & Hoffman, C. (2007). Creating and sustaining peaceable school communities. *Harvard Educational Review, 77*(3), 374–379, 391–392.

Brock-Utne, B. (2000). Peace education in an era of globalization. *Peace Review, 12*(1), 131–138.

Brock-Utne, B. (2009). A gender perspective on peace education and the work for peace. *International Review of Education, 55*(2-3), 205–220.

Carter, C. C. (2004). Whither social studies? In pockets of peace at school. *Journal of Peace Education, 1*(1), 77–87).

Carter, C. C., & Clay-Robison, S. (2009, April 17). *A review of youth literature for peace education.* Paper presented at the Annual Meeting of the American Educational Research Association, San Diego, CA.

Charter of the United Nations. (1945). Preamble. Retrieved from http://www.un.org/en/documents/charter/index.shtml

Constitution of the United Nations Educational, Scientific and Cultural Organization (UNESCO). (1945). Retrieved from http://www.promotingpeace.org/2007/4/unesco.html

Cook, S. A. (2008). Give peace a chance: The diminution of peace in global education in the United States, United Kingdom, and Canada. *Canadian Journal of Education, 31*(4), 878–913.

Corcoran, P. B. (2004). What If? The educational possibilities of the Earth Charter. *Educational Studies, 36*(1), 108–117.

Crawford, P. A. (2005). Primarily peaceful: Nurturing peace in the primary grades. *Early Childhood Education Journal, 32*(5), 321–328.

Crewdson, D., & Perlmutter, D. (2003). The Environmental and Adventure School. New Horizons for Learning. Retrieved from http://www.newhorizons.org

Crum, C. E. (1953). Contributions of the American School Peace League to international education. *History of Education Journal, 4*(2), 51–57.

Curti, M. (1936). *Peace or war the American struggle 1636–1936.* New York: W. W. Norton.

Danesh, H. B. (2006). Towards an integrative theory of peace education. *Journal of Peace Education, 3*(1), 55–78.

Davies, L. (2008). UNESCO associated schools project network (ASPnet) and peace education. Retrieved from http://www.tc.edu/centers/epe/htm%20articles/DaviesASPNET_22feb08.doc

de Bie, P. (2007). Why peace education? And what is it anyway? *PeacePower* 3 (1). Retrieved from http://www.calpeacepower.org/0301/education.htm

DeBenedetti, C. (1980). *The peace reform in American history.* Bloomington: Indiana University Press.

dela Torre, L. G. (2008). *Peace education: Human rights and related fields.* Valenzuela City, Philippines: Mutya Publishing House.

Eisler, R. (2007). Building a world of partnership and peace: Four cornerstones. Retrieved from http://www.rianeeisler.com/articles/fourcornerstones.pdf

Galtung, J. (1969). Violence, peace and peace research. *Journal of Peace Research, 6*(3), 167–191.

Galtung, J. (2008). Form and content of peace education. In M. Bajaj (Ed.), *Encyclopedia of peace education* (pp. 49–58). Charlotte, NC: Information Age.

Garner, N. E. (2008). Conflict resolution programs in the schools. *American Counseling Association Professional Counseling Digest, 19.* Alexandria, VA: American Counseling Association. Retrieved from http://counselingoutfitters.com/vistas/ACAPCD/ACAPCD-19.pdf

Gervais, M. (2004). The Baha'i curriculum for peace education. *Journal of Peace Education, 1*(2), 205–224.

Goldstein, R. A. (2005). Symbolic and institutional violence and critical education spaces: In the name of education. *Journal of Peace Education, 2*(1), 33–52.

Gough, A. (2006). A long, winding (and rocky) road to environmental education for sustainability in 2006. *Australian Journal of Environmental Education 22*(1), 71–76.

Gur-Ze'ev, I. (2001). Philosophy on peace education in a postmodern era. *Educational Theory, 51*(3), 315–336.

Haavelsrud, M. (2008). Conceptual perspectives in peace education. In M. Bajaj (Ed.), *Encyclopedia of peace education* (pp. 59–66). Charlotte, NC: Information Age.

Hägglund, S. (1996). Developing concepts of peace and war: Aspects of gender and culture. *The Peabody Journal of Education, 71,* 29–41.

Harris, I. (1990). Principles of peace pedagogy. *Peace and Change, 15*(3), 254–271.

Harris, I. (1996). Peace education in an urban school district in the United States. *Peabody Journal of Education, 71*(3), 63–83.

Harris, I. (2004a). Evaluating peace education. *Journal for the Study of Peace and Conflict,* 2004–2005 annual edition, 18–32.

Harris, I. (2004b). Peace education theory. *Journal of Peace Education, 1*(1), 5–20.

Harris, I. (2008). History of peace education. In M. Bajaj (Ed.), *Encyclopedia of peace education* (pp. 15–23). Charlotte, NC: Information Age.

Harris, I., & Mische, P. (2002, October). *On the relationship between peace education and environmental education.* Paper presented at the Wisconsin Institute for Peace and Conflict Studies Annual Conference, Milwaukee, WI.

Harris, I., & Morrison, M. L. (2003). *Peace education* (2nd ed.). Jefferson, NC: McFarland and Company.

Hendrix, J. C. (1998). Globalizing the curriculum. *The Clearing House, 71*(5), 305–308.

Hermann, T. (1992). Contemporary peace movements: Between the hammer of political realism and the anvil of pacifism. *The Western Political Quarterly, 45*(4), 869–893.

Hicks, D. (2003). Thirty years of global education: A reminder of key principles and precedents. *Educational Review, 55*(3), 265–275.

Hirao, K. (1987). Peace education: A search for strategy. *Peace and Change, 12*(3–4), 59–68.

Howlett, C. F. (1982). The pragmatist as pacifist: John Dewey's views on peace education. *Teachers College Record, 83*(3), 435–451.

Howlett, C. F. (2008) The evolution of peace education in the United States from independence to the World War I era. *Encyclopedia of Peace Education.* Retrieved from http://www.tc.edu/centers/epe/PDF%20articles/Howlett_evolution_21May09.pdf

Jeffries, R. B. (2000). Examining barriers to effective peace education reform. *Contemporary Education, 71*(4), 19–22.

Jennings, T. (2009). Reclaiming standards for a progressive agenda: Human rights education standards for teachers and teacher education. In J. Andrzejewski, M. Baltodano, & L. Symcox (Eds.), *Social justice, peace, and environmental education: Transformative standards* (pp. 66–79). New York: Routlege.

Johnson, D. W., & Johnson, R. T. (2005). Essential components of peace education. *Theory into Practice, 44*(4), 280–292.

Johnson, D., & Johnson, R. (2006). Peace education for consensual peace: The essential role of conflict resolution. *Journal of Peace Education, 3*(2), 147–174.

Joseph, P. B. (2010, April 29). *Becoming peace educators: Existential, curricular, and pedagogical dilemmas.* Paper presented at the American Association for the Advancement of Curriculum Studies, Denver.

Joseph, P. B., & Duss, L. S. (2009). Teaching a pedagogy of peace: A study of peace educators in United States schools in the aftermath of September 11. *Journal of Peace Education, 6*(2), 189–207.

Joseph, P. B., & Efron, S. (2005). Seven world of moral education. *Phi Delta Kappan, 86*(7), 525–533.

Jucker, R. (2004). Have the cake and eat it: Eco-justice versus development? *Educational Studies, 36*(1), 10–26.

Kirkwood, T. (2001). Our global age requires global education: Clarifying definitional ambiguities. *Social Studies, 92*, 1–16.

Kirman, J. M. (2003). Transformative geography: Ethics and action in elementary and secondary geography education. *Journal of Geography, 102*(3), 93–98.

Langager, M. (2009). Elements of war and peace in history education in the US and Japan: A case study comparison. *Journal of Peace Education, 6*(1), 119–136.

Lederach, J. P. (2005). *The moral imagination: The art and soul of building peace.* New York: Oxford University Press.

Li, H. (2006). Rethinking terrestrial pedagogy: Nature, cultures, and ethics. *Teachers College Record, 108*(12), 2450–2473.

Lucas, A. G. (2009). Teaching about human rights in the elementary classroom using the book "A life like mine: How children live around the world." *The Social Studies, 100*(2), 79–84.

Mascari, J. (2006). U.S. conscientious objectors in World War II. *Friends Journal.* Retrieved from http://www.friendsjournal.org/

McCarthy, C. (2002). *I'd rather teach peace*. Maryknoll, NY: Orbis Books.

McClaren, P., & Houston, D. (2004). Revolutionary ecologies: Ecosocialism and critical pedagogy. *Educational Studies, 36*(1), 27–45.

McFarland, S. (1999). Nurturing the peace flower: A model for the science of peace. *Montessori Life, 11*(1), 31–35.

McFarland, S. (2004). Educating for peace: A Montessori best practice. *Montessori Life, 16*(4), 24–26.

Mikel, E. R. (2009). *Schools becoming "abundant": Enriching and expanding internal and external ecologies*. Unpublished manuscript.

Mikel, E. R. (2010, April 29). Equality for all life, really?: Ecojustice in the contemporary professional discourse of K–12 environmental curriculum. Paper presented at the American Association for the Advancement of Curriculum Studies, Denver, CO.

Miller, R. (2003). Education for a culture of peace. *Encounter, 16*(2). Retrieved from http://www.pathsoflearning.org/articles_Education_Culture_Peace.php

Mirra, C. (2008). Countering militarism through peace education. In M. Bajaj (Ed.), *Encyclopedia of peace education* (pp. 93–97). Charlotte, NC: Information Age.

Mische, P., & Harris, I. (2008). Environmental peacemaking, peacekeeping, and peacebuilding. *Encyclopedia of peace education*. Http://www.tc.edu/centers/epe/PDF%20 articles/Mische-Harris%20Environmental_22feb08.pdf

Montessori, M. (1949/1972). *Education and peace*. Chicago: Henry Regenery Company.

Morris, M. (2002). Ecological consciousness and curriculum. *Journal of Curriculum Studies, 34*(5), 571–587.

Morris, V. G., Taylor, S. I., & Wilson, J. T. (2000). Using Children's Stories to Promote Peace in Classrooms. *Early Childhood Education Journal, 28*(1), 41–50.

Morrison, M. L. (2002). Peace education in theory and practice. *The Delta Kappa Gamma Bulletin, 69*, 10–14.

Mundy, K., & Manion, C. (2008). Global education in Canadian elementary schools: An exploratory study. *Canadian Journal of Education, 31*(4), 941–974.

Ndura-Oudraogo, E. (2008). The role of education in peace-building in the African Great Lakes region: Educators' perspectives. *Journal of Peace Education, 6*(1), 37–49.

Noddings, N. (2008). Caring and peace education. In M. Bajaj (Ed.), *Encyclopedia of peace education* (pp. 87–91). Charlotte, NC: Information Age.

Orr, D. (1992). *Ecological literacy: Education and the transition to a postmodern world*. Albany: State University of New York Press.

Osborne, K. (1985). Peace education and the schools: What can we learn from history? *The History and Social Science Teacher, 20*(3/4), 33–41.

Page, J. S. (2004). Peace education: Exploring some philosophical foundations. *International Review of Education, 50*(1), 3–15.

Pelo, A. (2009). A pedagogy for ecology. *Rethinking Schools, 23*(4), 30–35.

Pike, G. (2000). Global education and national identity: In pursuit of meaning. *Theory Into Practice, 39*(2), 64–73.

Postma, D. W. (2006). *Why care for nature? In search of an ethical framework for environmental responsibility and education*. Dordrecht, The Netherlands: Springer.

Reardon, B. A. (1988). *Peace education: Educating for global responsibility.* New York: Teachers College Press.

Reardon, B. A. (1989). Toward a paradigm of peace. In L. R. Forcey (Ed.), *Peace: Meanings, politics, strategies* (pp. 15–26). New York: Praeger.

Reardon, B. A. (1997). Human rights education as education for peace. In G. Andreopoulos & R. P. Claude (Eds.), *Human rights education for the twenty-first century* (pp. 21–23). Philadelphia: University of Pennsylvania Press.

Reardon, B. A. (1999) Educating the educators: The preparation of teachers for a culture of peace. *Peace Education Miniprints No. 99.* Malmo, Sweden: School of Education. ERIC document: ED432527.

Reardon, B. A. (2001). *Education for a culture of peace in a gender perspective.* Paris: UNESCO.

Rivage-Seul, M. K. (1987). Peace education: Imagination and the pedagogy of the oppressed. *Harvard Educational Review, 57*(2), 153–169.

Roberts, S. K. (2005). Promoting a peaceful classroom through poetry. *Journal of Peace Education, 2*(1), 69– 8.

Salamon, G. (2002). The nature of peace education: Not all programs are created equal. In G. Salomon & B. Nevo (Eds.), *Peace education: The concept principles, and practices around the world* (pp. 3–14). Mahwah, NJ: Erlbaum.

Sauvé, L. (1996). Environmental education and sustainable development: A further appraisal. *Canadian Journal of Environmental Education, 1,* 7–34.

Schaps, E. (2003). Creating a school community. *Educational Leadership, 60,* 31–33.

Schimmel, N. (2009). Towards a sustainable and holistic model of peace education: a critique of conventional modes of peace education through dialogue in Israel. *Journal of Peace Education, 6*(1), 51–68.

Selby, D. (1999). Global education: Towards a quantum model of environmental education. *Canadian Journal of Environmental Education, 4,* 125–141.

Selby, D. (2000). A darker shade of green: The importance of ecological thinking in global education and school reform. *Theory into Practice, 39*(2), 88–96.

Shapiro, S. (2002a). Education against violence. *Tikkun, 17,* 44–48.

Shapiro, S. (2002b). Toward a critical pedagogy of peace education. In G. Salomon & B. Nevo (Eds.), *Peace education: The concept principles, and practices around the world* (pp. 63–72). Mahwah, NJ: Erlbaum.

Smith, G. A. (2004). Cultivating care and connection: Preparing the soil for a just and sustainable society. *Educational Studies, 36*(1), 73–92.

Snauwaert, D. (2008). The moral and spiritual foundations of peace education. In M. Bajaj (Ed.), *Encyclopedia of peace education* (pp. 67–73). Charlotte, NC: Information Age.

Sommers, M. (2003) Peace education and refugee youth. In J. Crisp, C. Talbot, & D. B. Cipollone (Eds.), *Learning for a future: Refugee education in developing countries* (pp. 163–216). Geneva: United Nations Publications.

Sommerfelt, O. H., & Vambhein, V. (2008). The dream of the good—a peace education project exploring the potential to educate for peace at an individual level. *Journal of Peace Education, 5*(1), 79–95.

Soto, L. D. (2005). How can we teach about peace when we are so outraged? *Taboo, 9*(2), 91–96.

Stanford, K. (2008). *If we must die: African American voices on war and peace.* Lanham, MD: Rowman & Littlefield.

Stomfay-Stitz, A. (1993). *Peace education in America, 1829–1990: Sourcebook for education and research.* Metuchen, NJ: Scarecrow Press.

Stomfay-Stitz, A. (2008). A history of peace education in the United States of America. *Encyclopedia of Peace Education.* Retrieved from http://www.tc.edu/centers/epe/PDF%20articles/Stomfay-StitzUnited%20States_22feb08.pdf

Suárez, D. (2007). Education professionals and the construction of human rights education. *Comparative Education Review, 51*(1), 48–70.

Synott, J. P. (2005). Peace education as an educational paradigm: Review of a changing field using an old measure. *Journal of Peace Education, 2*(1), 3–16.

Tibbitts, F. (2002). Understanding what we do: Emerging models for human rights education. *International Review of Education, 48*(3-4), 159–171.

Tudball, L. (2003). Reflections on a journey — peace education in schools. *Ethos, 11*(2), 21–26.

United Nations. (1948). *Universal declaration of human rights.* Retrieved from http://www.un.org/en/documents/udhr/

United Nations. (1959). *Declaration of the rights of the child.* Retrieved from http://www.un.org/cyberschoolbus/humanrights/resources/child.asp

Weigert, K. M. (1989). Peace studies as education for nonviolent social change. *The Annals of the American Academy of Political and Social Science, 504*(1), 37–47.

Whang, P. A., & Nash, C. P. (2005). Reclaiming compassion: Getting to the heart and soul of teacher education. *Journal of Peace Education, 2*(1), 79–92.

Wittner, L. S. (1984). Rebels against war: The American peace movement, 1933–1983. Philadelphia: Temple University Press.

Zeiger, S. (2000). Teaching peace: Lessons from a peace studies curriculum of the progressive era. *Peace and Change, 25*(1), 52–70.

Zeiger, S. (2003). The schoolhouse vs. the armory: U.S. teachers and the campaign against militarism in the schools, 1914–1918. *Journal of Women's History, 15*(2), 150–179.

About the Contributors

Stephanie Luster Bravmann
My intellectual and personal lives have always been in delicate balance, each informing the other in ways that have shaped the individual culture in which I reside. Early schooling, especially at the Francis W. Parker School in Chicago, encouraged my quest to articulate and enact my beliefs about the intellect, social justice, and being a contributing member of society. An educational foundation of rigorous exploration and individual action for the benefit of the whole prompted me to pursue undergraduate work in literature, writing, anthropology, and social psychology. It also enabled me to productively interrupt my studies—for varying periods of time—to marry, travel and teach in West Africa, raise children, and in other ways participate in the world around me.

Teaching children from preschool through the secondary grades in inner city, urban, rural, public, independent, private, and parochial schools, combined with work as a teacher in Ghana and Burkina Faso, provided me with a broad range of experiences from which to approach my doctoral studies. My academic work focused on the location of curriculum in the educational process and the constituent methods of those who mediate the curriculum for learners. A continuing interest in education in school and non-school settings, and in the teachers and learners who transact the process itself, led to a dissertation investigating the role of mentors in the lives of those considered, by dint of their accomplishments or potential, to be particularly able individuals. This undertaking enabled me to rediscover my core belief in our need to somehow facilitate each person's own search for that which is most worthy in him or herself and in society and then to live a life steeped in that worth.

Before beginning to work in higher education I was the General Studies Director and Administrator of Seattle Hebrew Academy, the Executive Director of a not-for-profit agency, and the Coordinator of School Cooperatives in northwestern Washington State. Community undertakings through the years have included work with children who are homeless and with agencies providing services for marginalized children and membership on the Seattle Coalition for Educational Equity.

I formerly was professor in the Graduate School of Education at Seattle University where I instructed both veteran teachers and those who educate children in venues outside of schools as they pursue their own masters and doctoral studies. I also have just completed several years as visiting faculty at Antioch University instructing both experienced teachers and those entering the profession. In recent years, I have been an interim school principal, a consultant, a mentor for the Small Schools Project, and as senior researcher with the Center on Reinventing Public Education at the University of Washington.

My participation in the conceptualization of this book project seems to have been a natural outgrowth of my academic and personal beliefs. The naming of things has always seemed to me to be a combination of the glib and the difficult—I truly believe that there is no single "right way" to educate because each of us, aside from our inherent equality in our humanness, is uniquely different and learns and lives in our own way. The concept of cultures of curriculum, when taken to encompass the full meanings of the word culture, best expresses for me the task that I feel we have to accomplish. I am convinced that it is through individuals that our society will be healed and writing the chapter "Developing Self and Spirit," provided me with a way to express at least some of the power that I feel an affirmatory approach can wield.

Nancy Stewart Green
My career goals have always been divided between a certain inborn inclination toward the intellectual life and my desire to oppose social injustice. After teaching high school history for two years, the first inclination led me to an academic career in history and educational foundations, including teaching for 19 years at Northeastern Illinois University in Chicago. The second was fulfilled during the 1960s when I managed a program of basic skills education for a War on Poverty agency and later my work for two decades with the Chicago Teachers Center, a part of Northeastern Illinois University that seeks to strengthen teachers and schools in the city of Chicago. In retirement, I volunteered for seven years as a reading tutor for first and second graders in an inner city Seattle elementary school.

In my research and writing, I was motivated by a desire to support the struggle of non-dominant groups. My Ph.D. dissertation reported on the effects of programs for first-generation college students in the YMCA Community College in Chicago; further research led me into women's educational history and a study of a public vocational high school (founded in 1911) for girls in Chicago. I have published in the *History of Education Quarterly, Chicago History,* the *Journal of Teacher Education,* and *Catalyst: A Journal of Chicago School Reform,* as well as in *Images of Schoolteachers in America,* and the *Historical Encyclopedia of Chicago Women.*

With this background I have found a welcome challenge in writing the chapter, "Education Through Occupations," which is related but also a departure from the chapter "Preparing for Work and Survival" in the first edition of this book. Having learned from developing the earlier chapter about the exciting recent developments in what was once called vocational education, and being persuaded of the positive impact of learning through contact with real life situations, I am pleased to present the philosophy and content of a 21st century version of John Dewey's "learning by doing."

Pamela Bolotin Joseph
This book represents a synthesis of my long-term fascination with the application of theory to life and practice. In some ways this project began geminating a long time ago because of three wonderful courses that forever changed the way I understood the world: one in American pragmatic philosophy (taken as an undergraduate) in which I began to look at the social and moral consequences of ideas and actions, another in graduate school called "Education and the Good Life" that applied philosophical conceptions to everyday life, and the first course for my doctoral professional sequence in the social studies (at Northwestern University) that introduced me to the study of culture. The concept of culture came as a bolt of lightening that eventually lead to a dissertation, an interdisciplinary analysis of the role of emotion and culture in moral development and education. The dissertation also stemmed from my teaching experiences, especially how I encountered value conflicts (my own and with others) as a social studies and language arts teacher in middle school and high school.

I have continued to study and write about moral education and the moral dimensions of teaching, but other areas that hold a strong interest are curriculum theory, the teaching profession, and the culture of schooling. The conception of this book also naturally flowed from my interests in history and the utilization of metaphor to understanding teachers' work and lives. I am the co-editor (with Gail E. Burnaford) of *Images of Schoolteachers in America* and have published in *Phi Delta Kappan, Journal of Curriculum Studies, Journal of Curriculum and Pedagogy, Journal of Moral Education, Theory and Research in Social Education, Social Education, Journal of Teacher Education, Journal of Peace Education, Asia-Pacific Journal of Teacher Education,* and have contributed to the *Encyclopedia of Curriculum Studies.*

I teach courses in professional development, history and philosophy of education, curriculum studies, and the moral dimensions of teaching. I currently am Senior Lecturer at the University of Washington Bothell. Previously I was faculty at Antioch University Seattle and National-Louis University as well as adjunct faculty at Northwestern University and Northeastern Illinois University. However my grounding experiences in education were my years as a high school history and middle school social studies and language arts teacher.

While raising my four children, I was involved in public schools as a parent and community member—including serving on a board of education and working with the PTA, community groups, and legislators for support of public education; also I was on the site council for my children's high school and a community participant in that school district's curriculum advisory board. A catalyst for writing this book was my experience on that committee. While co-writing a report to the board of education on the state reform legislation (based upon Goals 2000), I suggested that we needed to describe how this legislation represents the curricular orientation of preparing for business; another committee member responded to my comment with, "Well, what other orientations are there?" It was then I realized the importance of public discourse for imagining alternative educational visions and not just that of dominant American culture.

In writing this book, I have welcomed the opportunity to make connections between the powerful concepts of curriculum theory and classroom practice and to focus on curriculum inquiry. Also, by writing and co-authoring in the areas of liberal education curriculum, progressive work education, and the liberatory pedagogies, I expanded my understanding of progressive, critical, feminist, and multicultural pedagogies. My new chapter in this edition, "Envisioning Peace," reflects my increasing admiration for the visions of peace education, respect for the teachers who do this work, and belief that this field needs to become a serious component in all of teacher education and professional development.

Edward R. Mikel
The great themes and orientation of my professional career and civic life seemed to have been forged in the political atmosphere of my early family. We were a family of modest means and very interested in politics in the old way: as partisan party loyalists and dedicated troops marshaled for electoral-governmental politics. My family and my parents' families before us were Roosevelt Democrats—spelled with both a capital and a small-case "d." My political legacy was a deep, passionate faith in the role of government to try to make society better for those who found themselves disadvantaged, and a great deal of fractious contention among all constituencies over what that mission actually meant. For Democrats, and democrats, were constantly arguing with each other while coming together at pivotal moments to attempt to cull back the power of society's elite to have everything and to have it on their own terms.

I now understand that, in an important way, FDR merely saved American democracy for corporate capitalism. This sense grew in my experience in various modest roles in the civil rights and anti-war movements of the 1960s, the time of my own coming of age. It became increasingly clear to me that the primary constituencies of race, ethnicity, gender, and or class could take effective action together against, or for, the significant laws and policies of government and society's defining conditions. But we seldom could agree on permanent analyses or overarching goals or hold together our specific campaigns and projects for very long. Broad temporary alliances were politically necessary, but primary affiliations gave us our core identity and sustained us over the long haul.

My study of history as an undergraduate in the late 1960s, especially the past and present story of Southeast Asia, helped me gain perspective on the irreducibly multicultural nature of social life. Majoritarian oppressions are common in the history of democracy, and middling and have-not groups, divided along any of the major lines of cultural difference, have often sought to keep each weak so as to benefit themselves. In all respects, democracy is highly textured and full of possibilities as well as problems. It has not been uncommon for parties, organizations, or nations to be moved by the liberal impulse to want to "improve" the lives of those suffering and dispossessed in the social scheme of things. But the implicit arrogance of such a perspective is self-defeating. There can be no "improvement" of any life that is not autonomously determined by those who live it. And certainly there is no democracy without autonomous members.

I came rather late to the academy, having earlier in my career briefly taught junior and senior high school social studies, been a program coordinator and evaluator at a national educational laboratory, and served as a research and evaluation specialist and division administrator with the St. Louis public school district. I currently am core faculty at Antioch University Seattle and previously have been faculty at National-Louis University in St. Louis. I have presented on the topic of progressive activist teachers and activist identity, reculturing curriculum, democratic education, and ecojustice curriculum. I also am principal in the nonprofit Global Source Education and have been involved in presentations and workshops on sustainability and human rights education.

Especially since coming to higher education, teacher education more specifically, I have sought the democratic way to a fully multicultural and inclusive society through formal education. I am convinced it must begin in each locality, with democracy activated in immediate communities. Classrooms are the seedbeds of school, just as schools are a seedbed of society. Teachers and others who are in close touch with one another about progressive educational practice and policy can form broad networks for school and social change.

I have written the chapter "Deliberating Democracy" from the conviction that democracy, in its full range of workings and considerations, must spring up uniquely in every classroom. From across all these "embryonic democratic communities," however, comes a reaching out to the surrounding social world, intellectually and practically, through acts of the class group or of its members now or in their later lives. In this way, the spirit of democracy is renewed in each generation and the concrete hope of democracy re-kindled for all places in this time.

Mark A. Windschitl

The most powerful influences in my professional life have been my parents. My father has been a teacher and administrator for more than 35 years, and my mother has served on the city council and for many years has been a vital part of my hometown community of Carroll, Iowa. My parents were the early authors of the narrative of my life, and I hope that their steadfast belief in the humanistic side of education is faithfully communicated and passed on to the readers of this book.

I approached this writing task as I do all my others, drawing upon 12 years of experience in the middle school science classroom for inspiration and examples. I taught in Des Moines, Iowa, during this time, and I was constantly fascinated with how students learned, how they socialized in and out of school, and what courses their lives took after leaving the classroom.

As I moved into graduate school at Iowa State University and was exposed to a wealth of curricular, social, and cognitive models—in particular, constructivism—describing the complexities of the educational enterprise, I came to fully appreciate my former teaching life and reflected back upon it with a kind of altered vision. My interest in constructivism grew in subsequent years with more reading and reflection, eventually becoming a focus of my dissertation. I could see how constructivism could act as a logical bridge between the information-processing view of learning that supports traditional education and the more liberatory pedagogies.

Also, what permanently changed my conception of schooling was a year-long course in graduate school that emphasized critical, feminist, and multicultural theory. These powerful descriptive frameworks revealed and made clear to me what was invisible, unspoken, and suppressed in America today. I drew upon these ideas in conjunction with my classroom experiences to help me contribute to our chapter "Confronting the Dominant Order."

Since receiving my doctorate in curriculum and instruction, I have investigated learning from many different angles, but always with an eye to how learners "make sense" of their worlds, often in spite of the teachers and curriculum. My research primarily has been in the areas of cognition and instruction and science education. I am currently professor at the University of Washington in Seattle, and have written for *Phi Delta Kappan, Teachers College Record, American Education Research Journal, Educational Researcher, Review of Educational Research, Cognition and Instruction, Science Education, Middle School Journal, Journal of Research in Science Teaching,* and other publications.

I am now finishing a longitudinal study of how novice teachers develop pedagogical reasoning around sophisticated forms of inquiry for secondary students. We traced our participants' development across four contexts: their teacher education coursework, student teaching, sessions of analysis of their pupils' work, and their early years of professional work. The research group that I run is also now beginning a five-year project to develop and study a system of tools and tool-based practices for early career and pre-service secondary science teachers that support transitions from novice to expert-like pedagogical reasoning and practice. I am also the principal investigator for the University of Washington Noyce Teaching Scholars Program; this National Science Foundation project provides scholarships for math and science teachers who will specialize in working in high needs schools.

Tarajean Yazzie-Mintz (Navajo)
I am of the Salt-water clan, born for the Bitter-water clan. My maternal grandfather is of the Edgewater and Mexican clans. My paternal grandfather is of the Red-streak-into-the-water clan. In this way I am a Navajo woman.

I am a Native academic interested in working with Native teachers to understand better their instructional practice, particularly the ways in which they incorporate Native culture and language into the existing school curriculum. The historical, political, and ideological beliefs shaping schools is an ever-present undercurrent of the curricular work I seek to understand.

I became interested in curriculum studies sparked by the question: What are the ways in which culture and language shape instruction, curriculum, and learning within schools? As a preschool teacher, just outside of Seattle, Washington, I worked in a private child-learning center in a middle- to upper-middle-class neighborhood. The center provided a child-centered emergent curriculum fostering learning opportunities for young children. The children came from families with two incomes. One day our center accepted a Latino boy, Lorenzo, whose family had recently moved to the United States from Mexico City. I was proficient enough in the Spanish language to understand what Lorenzo wanted, and so he was eventually placed in my classroom. Up until this point, all the children enrolled in the center spoke English, were from the Seattle area, and were familiar with different forms of the learning institution's curriculum—i.e., learning centers, circle time, and nap time. No one else employed by the center spoke Spanish or had previously worked with a young child who spoke a language other than English. Putting early childhood educational theories and practices to work with non-White, non-English speaking young children was a challenge for us all. At the time, I am not sure any of us fully realized the impact Lorenzo had on our center, curriculum, instruction, and sense of teacher efficacy.

Two decades years later, this scenario remains very clear in my mind as I continue to wonder about how teachers conceptualize their practice, which in turn shapes the multiple curricular decisions they make in classrooms everyday. This experience continues also to fuel my desire to document the different ways in which children's cultural and linguistic backgrounds shape instruction and vice-versa. And, while Indigenous and Native education (in particular, teachers' curricular knowledge) has become the main arena of my research, I continue to learn more about how teachers in various social contexts learn to teach children who are different from them, linguistically and culturally. Naming difference in the form of social and political beliefs is a focus of investigation in this curriculum research. I have presented and written on the topics of research on American Indian education and culturally appropriate curriculum and I currently am faculty at the School of Education at Indiana University.

The chapter, "Sustaining Indigenous Traditions," is my effort to help make sense of a dynamic, ever-changing, and complex endeavor for educators: to incorporate children's cultural and linguistic knowledge in classrooms so as to sustain their Indigenous knowledge and traditions. Redefining the purposes of schooling remains a historical moment to be achieved for many, so I offer this chapter as a way to look back and, in doing so, may provide reason to move forward.

Name Index

Subject Index